IN THE LAND OF NINKASI

IN THE LAND OF NINKASI

A HISTORY OF BEER IN ANCIENT MESOPOTAMIA

TATE PAULETTE

OXFORD
UNIVERSITY PRESS

OXFORD
UNIVERSITY PRESS

Oxford University Press is a department of the University of Oxford. It furthers
the University's objective of excellence in research, scholarship, and education
by publishing worldwide. Oxford is a registered trade mark of Oxford University
Press in the UK and certain other countries.

Published in the United States of America by Oxford University Press
198 Madison Avenue, New York, NY 10016, United States of America.

Library of Congress Cataloging-in-Publication Data
Names: Paulette, Tate, author.
Title: In the land of Ninkasi : a history of beer in ancient Mesopotamia / Tate Paulette.
Description: First edition. | New York, NY : Oxford University Press, [2024] |
Includes bibliographical references and index. |
Identifiers: LCCN 2024006328 (print) | LCCN 2024006329 (ebook) |
ISBN 9780197682449 (hb) | ISBN 9780197682456 (epub) | ISBN 9780197682470
Subjects: LCSH: Beer—Iraq—History--To 634. | Brewing—Iraq—History—To
634. | Iraq—Civilization—To 634. | Mesopotamia.
Classification: LCC TP573.I73 P38 2024 (print) | LCC TP573.I73 (ebook) |
DDC 663/.420935—dc23/eng/20240326
LC record available at https://lccn.loc.gov/2024006328
LC ebook record available at https://lccn.loc.gov/2024006329

DOI: 10.1093/oso/9780197682449.001.0001

Printed by Sheridan Books, Inc., United States of America

Not to know beer is not normal.

Sumerian proverb[1]

For
Janet, Richard, and Kent Paulette
Kate Grossman

Also for
my fellow šikarologists past, present, and future[1]

Contents

Illustrations

Figures

Boxes

Prologue

Hamoukar, Syria. May 20, 2010. For the past week, archaeologist Salam Al Kuntar has been spending her days huddled over, stretched out, or balanced precariously on tiptoe at the bottom of a series of graves. Every afternoon, she emerges covered head to foot in fine dirt, exhausted from the unrelenting heat and the day's contortions. She has been slowly and meticulously excavating the contents of a 4,500-year-old cemetery.[1] Today, as Salam picks away sediment from bone, a pale, green stone surfaces. She brushes away more dirt to reveal a small cylindrical stone bead—1.5 cm in length, 1 cm in diameter—that hung from the neck of the deceased when they were laid to rest.[2] This is an exciting discovery. These little worked stones, called cylinder seals, might appear inconsequential at first glance, but they are not. Each bears an intricately carved scene, depicting humans, animals, gods, monsters, mythological figures, you name it. The scenes inscribed on the cylinders are often miniature masterpieces. But more than that, they provide a wealth of information—a glimpse at the beliefs, the rituals, the fashions, the fears, the world of ancient Mesopotamia rendered in stone. (We'll be looking at many in the pages that follow.)

It is hours before Salam can safely remove the seal from the ground. She must excavate around it, photograph it, document its precise location and orientation. Word spreads from one side of the half-mile-wide site to the other that a cylinder seal has been uncovered. Anticipation builds. By the time Salam plucks the seal from the earth, a small crowd has gathered. Everyone squints in the sun, shading their eyes, as Salam rotates the seal this way and that, trying to make out something of the scene. There seem to be pairs of figures. But what are they doing?

Cylinder seals were used as a sort of signature, akin to a medieval seal stamped in wax to authenticate a royal decree. Rolled in wet clay, they would leave behind an impression of the inscribed scene. For the scene to be legible when rolled out, it had to be carved in reverse. So it can be difficult to make these scenes out on the seals themselves. The best way to see what a seal has to show is to give it a roll in modeling clay. There's none to be found, so our house manager, Mahmoud al-Kitab, goes on a quick

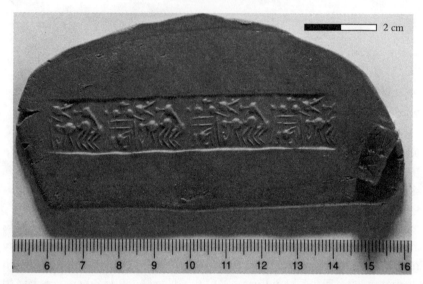

Figure P.1. Cylinder seal with *coitus a tergo* drinking scene. Hamoukar, Syria. (Courtesy of Hamoukar Expedition)

run to the nearest town—Qamishli—a two-hour drive round-trip. More squinting, guessing, and shrugging ensue. Once he's back, clay in hand, we roll out the seal and, voilà, the scene appears before our eyes (Figure P.1). Although some aspects are still hard to make out, others are perfectly clear. There is a woman, bent forward at the waist. Standing behind her is a man (one particular feature of his anatomy makes this deduction unassailable). And on the ground in front of her, a pot, from which she sips through a long straw.

This one small artifact opens up a whole series of broader questions. Who was this person laid to rest 4,500 years ago with (what we might consider) a pornographic administrative device dangling from their neck? Why was this specific seal chosen as a piece of burial adornment? Was it a long-held possession with deep personal meaning? Or was it perhaps produced or acquired specifically for the burial ceremony? Does the scene depicted on the seal tell us something about who this person was in life? Seals were often connected with specific governmental offices or professions. Could it be that the deceased was involved in sex work or, perhaps, the sexually charged domain of the tavern? Did the seal have some kind of ritual significance? And was the seal ever actually used? That is, was it regularly rolled out in wet clay to serve as a signature? If so, what might the erotic scene have signified in those contexts of use? Does it even make sense to use a term like "erotic" when discussing a culture so very different from our own?

And what exactly was the woman drinking from that jar? As we'll see, scenes that show the drinking of some beverage through long straws—whether in erotic or, more often, feasting contexts—are actually very common in the artistic repertoire of ancient Mesopotamia. We can't be 100% certain, but all signs suggest that this beverage was beer. Indeed, beer and sex, intoxication and fornication, were closely linked in Mesopotamian thought. But what about the beer itself? Would this beer have been recognizable to us as distant kin to our own beloved beverage? If we could travel back in time for a taste, would we become instant fans, or would we barely be able to choke down a straw's worth before racing back to the present?

Many of these questions are simply not answerable. But others are. In this book, we will train our focus on those that relate to beer. If you're a beer drinker—and, since you're reading this book, chances are you are—you will probably be familiar with some of the great European brewing traditions of the last millennium: Belgian, German, Czech, English, etc. But thousands of years before them all, the world's first great beer culture took root along the banks of the Tigris and Euphrates rivers in ancient Mesopotamia. That's where we're headed: the famous "land between the rivers."

I found my way into the world of Mesopotamian beer from the experimental side. A team of researchers at the University of Chicago's Institute for the Study of Ancient Cultures (ISAC) had recently launched a collaboration with Great Lakes Brewing Co. (GLBC) in Cleveland. The goal: to re-create the beers of ancient Mesopotamia using authentic ingredients, equipment, and brewing techniques. My fellow grad student Mike Fisher and I signed on to the project with gusto and, about a year later, found ourselves in Cleveland hammering out some key details with the brewing team. Let's begin there.

Pat Conway, a co-owner of GLBC, has set us up for a meeting with local artisanal bakers Kurt and Barbara Zoss. We're there to talk about bappir. This Sumerian term refers to one of the fundamental ingredients in Mesopotamian beer. But there are a couple of problems: namely, that Mesopotamian specialists can't agree on what it actually was or how it would have contributed to the brewing process. The term is often translated into English as "beer bread," but this almost certainly misses the mark. According to some interpretations, it was a dry, crumbly, barley-based, bread- or cake-like product that contained the yeast and bacteria needed to initiate fermentation. These days we add pure cultures of yeast as a fermentation starter. In ancient Mesopotamia, so the argument goes, they would have added bappir. Our plan is to test out this theory. Having already decided to forgo any effort to collect yeast on location, as it were, in Mesopotamia—that is, modern-day Iraq or Syria—we've decided to create our own sourdough culture, imbuing our bappir with some local Cleveland terroir.[3] We'll grow the sourdough culture from scratch, using yeast and bacteria that occur naturally in the local environment. Once it's ready, we'll mix it with coarsely ground barley to create a dough and then bake the dough in an oven, as we know they did in Mesopotamia. There was even a special "bappir oven" (udun.bappir in Sumerian).

We've come to the Zosses to get some guidance and perhaps borrow an oven. Our biggest question: Would it work? If we bake our bappir in a bread oven, at typical bread-baking temperatures, will any yeast survive to kick off the fermentation process? Perhaps this should have been obvious, but the answer is an emphatic no. They patiently explain that yeast can't survive temperatures above about 140°F (60°C). Fortunately, the Zosses are down to do some experimenting. One thing is clear: Our bappir won't be bread. Given the temperature restrictions, we started to envision a time-intensive, low-temperature "baking" process, really more akin to dehydration. By definition, baking involves the removal of water via dry heat in an enclosed space, but this idea of slowly drying out dough in a warm oven took some getting used to—perhaps most for the bakers, whose massive domed oven seemed wasted on such a mission.[4] But they were willing to give it a go, and we were happy to leave the bappir in their capable hands. In the end, the most successful batch that they produced was one that had been accidentally left in the oven as it cooled down gradually over a two-week period.

Is this actually how bappir was made in ancient Mesopotamia? We don't currently know, and we may never know. But we can say one thing for certain: a slowly dehydrated sourdough barley cake can, indeed, initiate and sustain sufficient fermentation to produce an alcoholic and drinkable approximation of Mesopotamian beer. We'll come back to bappir in Chapter 3 and our experimental brewing efforts in the Epilogue. For now, though, let's fast-forward again to August 14, 2013, and our first tasting event. It's 5:55 p.m., five minutes to start time. Pat Conway and I have just convened a panicked, last-minute meeting in an office adjacent to the event space. We

have just realized that we forgot to name our beers. After some frantic de-
liberation, we decide to pay homage to Enkidu and Gilgamesh, the famous
adventuring duo from the Epic of Gilgamesh.

This first event set the pattern for others to follow. To highlight our effort to be as authentic as possible in brewing methods and equipment, we
encouraged attendees to taste two beers side by side. The first, Enkibru,
was the wilder option: a milky-looking, flat, and slightly sour beer brewed
using replicas of ancient Mesopotamian ceramic vessels and bappir as a yeast
source. The second, Gilgamash, was the less intimidating option: an aromatic,
herbaceous, carbonated beer (something like a Belgian saison or farmhouse
ale[5]) brewed using the same ingredients as Enkibru but modern brewing
equipment and a commercial yeast strain. Surprisingly, when asked which
they preferred, about 50% of the attendees typically sided with Enkibru. I
wish I could offer you some Enkibru, too, but alas. If you're of age, I would
absolutely recommend that you enjoy this book with a beer in hand.

The people of ancient Mesopotamia knew how to appreciate a good
beer. They appreciated their beer often and often in large quantities. They
sang songs and wrote poetry about beer. Sometimes they got drunk and
threw caution to the wind. They even worshipped a goddess of beer,
Ninkasi. Beer was a gift from the gods, a dietary staple, a social lubricant,
and a ritual necessity. It was produced on a massive scale and was consumed
on a daily basis by people from all walks of life. The global prehistory of
beer is continually being pushed deeper and deeper into the distant past,
but Mesopotamia remains the earliest case in which we can document an
ancient beer culture in all of its complexity. This is partly due to the sources
available. Over the past century and a half, archaeologists have explored
the remains of hundreds of ancient cities and towns across the region, in
the process unearthing hundreds of thousands of cuneiform tablets (the
world's first writing) and an extensive collection of contemporary artistic
works. This abundance of source material, unparalleled elsewhere in the
ancient world, allows for a vivid depiction of the beer scene in ancient
Mesopotamia.

My aim is to guide you systematically through this source material. For
readers who wish to check my sources or dig down into a particular subject in more depth, I've provided full citations and additional explanatory
material in the endnotes. Before we hit Chapter 1, I've also included a
short crash course on the languages of ancient Mesopotamia. I'm sorry to

whack you over the head with this nitpicky linguistic info right from the get-go, but I don't want you to be surprised or confused when Sumerian and Akkadian terms start popping up in the chapters to come. You can read this section now, or you can come back to it later, if you'd prefer to head straight into Chapter 1.

Note about ancient languages

In the pages to come, you are going to encounter a lot of words in Sumerian and Akkadian, the two main languages of ancient Mesopotamia. Akkadian is a Semitic language, related to modern-day Arabic and Hebrew. Sumerian is a linguistic isolate, not related to any other known language (for guidance on pronunciation, see Box N.1). These two languages were inscribed and impressed on clay tablets and other media using a script known as *cuneiform*.[1] Each character in the cuneiform or "wedge-shaped" writing system is known as a sign, and each sign is made up of a collection of wedges oriented in different directions (vertical, horizontal, and oblique). Scholars who specialize in the study of cuneiform texts are known as Assyriologists. Those Assyriologists who focus specifically on the Sumerian language can also be called Sumerologists. Archaeologists like myself, on the other hand, work primarily with other sorts of physical remains (architecture, ceramic vessels, stone tools, botanical remains, etc.).

In this book, we will engage with cuneiform texts in four different forms: transcription, transliteration, normalization, and translation (for examples, see Box N.2). In order to study these ancient texts, modern scholars first need to reproduce an image of the text, transferring it from its original medium (e.g., a cuneiform tablet) to another (e.g., a piece of paper or a computer screen). We call this *transcription*. Because cuneiform signs were written by impressing a stylus into clay, leaving behind three-dimensional wedges, the process of transcription also means moving from three to two dimensions. This transcribing is generally accomplished using a series of agreed-upon conventions for rendering the three-dimensional wedges in two dimensions. The next step is to produce a *transliteration* that expresses the text as language using the modern Latin alphabet or some other modern script. Each cuneiform sign is converted (i.e., transliterated) into the new script. In most cases, this is done phonetically, that is, by expressing how the sign would have sounded when read or spoken. The result is a sign-by-sign rendering of the original text in a script that is legible to readers today. When transliterated into the Latin alphabet, signs that belong together as part of a single word are separated by either dashes or

Box N.1 Pronunciation guide

It has been millennia since the Sumerian and Akkadian languages were last spoken aloud by native speakers. There are, therefore, many uncertainties about exactly how these languages would have sounded. In the case of Akkadian, a Semitic language, we can make reasonable educated guesses based on comparison with related modern languages like Arabic and Hebrew. In the case of Sumerian, a linguistic isolate unrelated to any other known language, there are many more uncertainties and many ongoing debates.

Both Sumerian and Akkadian were written using the cuneiform script. In this book, you will mostly encounter them in *transliterated* form, that is, rendered using our own writing system. Many letters should be pronounced approximately as they would be in English, but others differ. For these, see the following pronunciation guide. Note the use of a variety of *diacritics*, that is, additional signs added above or below a letter to indicate some difference in pronunciation.

Short vowels:

a	as in sw*a*p
e	as in p*e*t
i	as in p*i*t
u	as in p*u*t

Long vowels:

ā, â	as in f*a*ther
ē, ê	as in r*ei*n
ī, î	as in mar*i*ne
ū, û	as in r*u*le

Consonants:

š	sh as in *sh*ot
q	like k as in *k*id
ṣ	like s but with a constricting of the throat (acceptable to pronounce as ts, as in fi*ts*)
ṭ	like t but with a constricting of the throat (acceptable to pronounce as t)
ḫ	ch as in German a*ch* or Scottish lo*ch*
ʾ	glottal stop or catch, the sound heard between n and i in "a*n i*ceman" (known as "aleph")
ĝ	debated, something like a nasalized g (acceptable to pronounce as ng)

(Much of this pronunciation guide is drawn from Huehnergard 2000: 1–3.)

periods, and words are separated by spaces. The next step is then *normalization*, when the individual signs that make up a word are joined together or otherwise transformed (i.e., normalized) to more closely approximate how the word would have actually been read or spoken. A normalized text will look like a series of words, rather than a series of signs separated by dots or dashes. The final step is to produce a *translation*, that is, to translate the text from Sumerian or Akkadian into another language, such as English, Arabic, French, or German.

You are probably already familiar with the practice of distinguishing words written in a foreign language by italicizing them. The same applies here but with a twist. Because of the close intertwining of the Sumerian and Akkadian languages throughout Mesopotamian history, modern scholars have found it necessary to add a further distinguishing factor. When shown in either transcription or normalization, Akkadian words are always rendered in italics, but Sumerian words are shown in normal type.

In both cases, there is no tradition of capitalizing the first letter of a sentence, but the first letter of proper nouns (e.g., personal or divine names) will often be capitalized. Signs that appear in all caps, on the other hand, indicate either that reference is being made to a Sumerian sign that is intended to be read in Akkadian (see Box N.2 for an example) or that the reading of the sign in question is uncertain. This uncertainty can arise from the fact that many signs could have multiple readings. That is, a single sign could represent different phonetic values or different words depending on context. For example, the sign KAŠ could be read as the Sumerian word for beer (kaš), but it could also be read as the Sumerian or Akkadian syllable bi/be$_2$ or as the Akkadian-only syllable sa$_{18}$. And, as discussed in Box N.2, it could also be read as an ideogram—i.e., a non-phonetic symbol, not intended to represent sound—indicating the Akkadian word for beer (*šikaru*).

You will also encounter signs and words written in superscript and numbers written in subscript. In neither case would these have been pronounced when reading aloud. Signs and words in superscript are what we call determinatives, cuneiform signs that were inserted to provide some kind of extra information to aid the reader. For example, the determinative "meš" in superscript indicates that the noun in question is plural, and the determinative "urudu" in superscript indicates that the noun is a thing made of copper. Numbers in subscript, on the other hand, have been added

Box N.2 Writing "Beer" in Sumerian and Akkadian

In the Sumerian language, beer was known as kaš (pronounced "kash," which rhymes with "wash"). In the Akkadian language, it was known as šikaru (pronounced "shi-ka-roo"). In each case, the word for beer could be written in a number of different ways. In Sumerian, for example, kaš could be written using either the kaš or the kaš₂ cuneiform sign.

In Akkadian, šikaru could also be written using the KAŠ sign. In other words, the word could be written in Sumerian as KAŠ but read in Akkadian as šikaru (or some version of the word šikaru, adjusted to indicate grammatical case, e.g., šikarim or šikaram). Note that I have used all capital letters here to indicate that I am referring to the cuneiform sign KAŠ but not to the phonetic reading "kaš" (because in this case the sign was intended to be read in Akkadian as šikaru). The Akkadian word šikaru could also be written syllabically, that is, broken down into its constituent syllables, either ši-ka-ru or ši-ik-ru.

Now let's look at these words for beer in context. Here is an example in Sumerian. It's a short snippet from a poem known as "The Exaltation of Inana," written by Enheduana, priestess of the moon god, daughter of Sargon, king of Agade, and the world's first named author.

Transcription				
Transliteration	er₂ – ĝa₂	kaš	du₁₀ - ga -	gen₇
Normalization	erĝa	kaš	dugagen	
Translation (literal)	tears-my	beer	sweet-like	
Translation (poetic)	My tears, which are like sweet beer ...			

Now for an example in Akkadian, taken from the Epic of Gilgamesh (Old Babylonian version), the moment when the wild man Enkidu is introduced to the delights of beer.

Transcription				
Transliteration	KAŠ	ši - ti	ši - im - ti	ma - ti
Normalization	šikaram	šiti	šimti	māti
Translation (literal)	beer	(you) drink	custom	of land
Translation (poetic)	Drink the beer (Enkidu), it is the custom of the land.			

There were also many other ways to write "beer" in ancient Mesopotamia—
for example, many different types of beer—but kaš and *šikaru* are the two
that you will encounter most often in the coming pages.

For more about "The Exaltation of Inana," see Helle 2023. I have drawn
the example here from the accompanying website developed by Sophus
Helle (https://enheduana.org/the-exaltation-of-inana, line 82). For more
about the Epic of Gilgamesh, see Foster 2019, George 1999, George 2003,
and Helle 2021. I have drawn the example here from George 2003 (pp.
176–177, Pennsylvania Tablet, line 98; Plate 2, line 98), but I have drawn the
translation from the Chicago Assyrian Dictionary (CAD Š 3 s.v. šīmtu 1a 3').

by modern scholars to distinguish different ways of writing the same thing.
Many sounds (e.g., "sa") could be written using a variety of different cuneiform signs or combinations of signs. So we add subscript numbers—e.g.,
$sa, sa_2, sa_3, sa_4, sa_{18}$—to indicate exactly which sign or sign combination was
used in a particular case (the subscript number 1 is typically omitted, i.e.,
sa rather than sa_1).

When I provide texts in transliteration, you will regularly encounter
brackets, half-brackets, and ellipses ([ ], ⌈ ⌉, . . .). Brackets indicate signs
and/or words that are not preserved for the text in question (e.g., due to
tablet breaks) but can be reasonably reconstructed based on clues in the
text or comparison with other texts or other passages in the same text. Half
brackets indicate signs and/or words that are only partially preserved for
the text in question but can be reasonably reconstructed. Ellipses indicate
breaks in the text (i.e., sections of text that have not been preserved).

When I provide texts in translation, you will encounter words in italics
and parentheses. Within an English translation, Akkadian words in italics indicate words that have been left untranslated. For example, "Drink the *šikaru*
(Enkidu), it is the custom of the land." On the other hand, English words in
italics indicate translations that are uncertain. For example, "Drink the beer
(Enkidu), it is the *custom* of the land." Parentheses in translations enclose
words that are not actually present in the original text but have been added
by the translator for clarity. For example, "Drink the beer (Enkidu), it is the
custom of the land."

Also, a few notes for specialists. First, I have chosen not to standardize the
rendering of signs across the entirety of the book. For example, I have not

sought to update obsolete sign readings that have now been superseded in the literature. Instead, in each case, I follow the rendering used in the text edition and/or commentary cited. Second, when discussing Sumerian and Akkadian words (e.g., bappir or munu), I typically do not indicate the specific sign(s) used to write the words in question (e.g., $bappir_2$ or $munu_4$), though I often provide these details parenthetically or in the footnotes. When quoting from specific ancient texts, however, I do indicate the specific sign(s) used.

Timeline

Years BCE	Mesopotamia	Southern Mesopotamia	Northern Mesopotamia
		Persian/Achaemenid (539–330)	Persian/Achaemenid (539–330)
	Iron Age (1200–330)	Neo-Babylonian (605–539)	Neo-Babylonian (605–539)
		Neo-Assyrian (950–605)	Neo-Assyrian (950–605)
1000			
	Late Bronze Age (1600–1200)	Kassite (1475–1155)	Middle Assyrian (1400–1050)
			Mitanni (1500–1250)
	Middle Bronze Age (2000–1600)	Old Babylonian (2004–1595)	Old Assyrian (2000–1775)
2000		Ur III (2112–2004)	
		Akkadian (2350–2192)	
	Early Bronze Age (3000–2000)		Early Jezireh (3100–2000)
		Early Dynastic (2900–2350)	
3000		Jemdet Nasr (3100–2900)	
	Late Chalcolithic (4200–3100)	Uruk (4200–3100)	Late Chalcolithic (4200–3100)

Chapter I

Beer in world history

He is fearful, like a man unacquainted with beer.

Sumerian proverb[1]

The ritual center at Göbekli Tepe

We begin about 12,000 years ago, in the early evening, on a gently sloping hillside in the foothills of the Taurus mountains, in a stand of wild barley.[2] Several small clusters of men, women, and children dot the slope, all diligently focused on the task at hand: the barley harvest. They gently grasp stalks of the wild grass, slicing through them with bone sickles fitted with small flint blades and collecting clusters of the precious grains in woven bags slung across backs and shoulders. A gentle breeze stirs. The light is fading, and it's time to start heading home—well, not home exactly. They gather and begin making their way toward a prominent hilltop just visible on the horizon, backlit by the setting sun. This special place, a temporary but much anticipated stop on their seasonal itinerary, would be known much later, in the twentieth century CE, as Göbekli Tepe.

Just as the sun sets, the harvesters wind their way through clusters of makeshift dwellings, grouped around campfires, toward the stone-built focal point near the crest of the hill, where they unload the day's haul of barley. There's a buzz in the air. Several new groups have just arrived from the southwest, and the evening's festivities are about to get underway. There will be music and dancing and food. And there will be beer.[3] Several teams of perhaps thirty to forty individuals each have been working hard all day, dragging into place an enormous slab of limestone, shaped like a giant T and only recently arrived from a nearby quarry.[4] It's hard work. The teams are understandably thirsty and ready to let off some steam. Luckily, there's a party in the making, as there has been every day for the past few weeks.[5] We're witnessing what anthropologists would call a work feast: in this case, one that stretches out over an extended period of time.[6] And, thanks to all those harvesters who've been venturing out into the surrounding hills each day, this work feast will include some of the world's earliest known barley beer.

The site of Göbekli Tepe was first identified by archaeologists in the 1960s, but excavations were only initiated in 1994. These ongoing excavations have produced dramatic evidence of a hilltop sanctuary where otherwise dispersed groups of mobile hunter-gatherers congregated for ritual activities and feasting.[7] The site lies on a barren hilltop in southeastern Türkiye (the newly adopted spelling for the country previously known as Turkey) about 15 km northeast of the modern-day city of Şanlıurfa. Although littered with abundant artifactual remains, the surface of the site betrayed little hint of what lay hidden beneath: a series of massive, circular stone structures, elaborately decorated with carvings of human figures, wild animals, and abstract geometric motifs. So far, the excavations have uncovered five of these structures, all dating to the tenth millennium BCE, the so-called Pre-Pottery Neolithic A (PPNA) period. Geomagnetic survey, a nondestructive means of seeing beneath the surface to detect buried archaeological remains, has revealed several more similar structures.

The main cluster of monumental, circular structures was surrounded by a bunch of smaller-scale, densely packed, structures, either rectangular or "apsidal" in shape, that show evidence for domestic occupation—that is, evidence that people were actually living in them. These were originally believed to belong to a completely separate architectural phase that dates to the ninth millennium BCE, the Pre-Pottery Neolithic B (PPNB) period. That would be a good bit later than the circular structures. But the excavators now have evidence for a period of overlap in the use of the circular and rectangular/apsidal structures. This complicates things a bit. On the one hand, it potentially undercuts their original argument—that, during the time of the circular structures, this was not a settlement proper but a special place where scattered groups of people gathered periodically for ritual events. On the other hand, it establishes a potential link between the monumental, circular structures and substantial evidence for the processing of grain-based foods in the rectangular/apsidal structures. We'll come back to this second point.

The excavators argue that we can say a few important things about the people who occupied this prominent hilltop, surmounted by monumental stone structures. First, they were hunter-gatherers.[8] None of the plant and animal remains recovered at the site show the telltale signs of domestication. Second, they were part of a broader cultural sphere that extended across the northern portion of the Fertile Crescent.[9] If you compare the iconography at the site—that is, all those vivid images chiseled into stone—with that of other sites across the region, the similarities are striking. Third, the people who assembled at Göbekli Tepe were there (at least in part) for the party.[10] When each of the circular structures went out of use, it was filled in with rubbish that included limestone rubble, chipped stone artifacts, and huge amounts of animal bone. These people were consuming unusually large quantities of meat, mostly from gazelle, aurochs, and the Asian wild ass. And there's a good chance that they were also drinking a lot of beer. Unfortunately, the evidence for beer at the site—traces of oxalate or "beer stone" recovered from several large limestone vats (up to 160 liters each)—is inconclusive.[11] It also derives from those rectangular and apsidal structures, which might have been partially—but only partially—contemporary with the circular structures. Many fragments of similar limestone vessels have, however, been recovered from the circular structures. The site has also produced lots of equipment that might have been used in grain processing (e.g., grinders, mortars, and pestles) but relatively few physical remains of cereal grains. So there are tantalizing suggestions of beer-fueled feasting at Göbekli Tepe, but we can't say for certain.

This hasn't stopped the excavators from weaving together a compelling, if speculative, interpretation.[12] In a nutshell, they argue that scattered groups of hunter-gatherers came together periodically for social gatherings at Göbekli Tepe, a place that was distinguished by its dramatic hilltop location and its monumental stone structures. We may not know exactly what happened within these structures, but their elaborate decorations suggest ritual activities that somehow linked humans with the realm of wild (that is, undomesticated) animals. Benches set around the interior edges of the structures suggest that groups of people were involved. So there was also a social or communal element to their ritual activities. And whatever was happening in these ritual spaces mattered enough to justify the investment of an enormous amount of time, labor, and resources in the construction process. Indeed, the excavators argue that the feasts held at Göbekli Tepe were a means to an end. They were work feasts, collective events designed to mobilize labor for construction projects that required large numbers of people—like a barn raising in the early United States.[13] If you want to convince a bunch of people to spend their days dragging enormous slabs of stone (up to 50 metric tons each) and raising them into place, what better motivation than the promise of food and beer—and probably some combination of music, storytelling, dancing, general cavorting, perhaps even romantic encounters—in the evenings?

The work-hard, play-hard narrative that the excavators describe breathes new life into the so-called "bread vs. beer" debate. Cooked up in the 1950s for an issue of the journal *American Anthropologist*, this virtual debate asked a group of scholars to take sides on a basic question: Did bread or beer come first in human history?[14] And, by extension, was the domestication of plants driven by a desire for bread (i.e., food) or for beer (i.e., inebriation)? Various answers were put forward, including the proposition that beer might actually be more nutritious than bread and Paul Mangelsdorf's famously dismissive query: "Are we to believe that the foundations of Western Civilization were laid by an ill-fed people living in a perpetual state of partial intoxication?"[15]

Another question: Does it really matter whether bread or beer came first? Archaeology is constantly beset by this question of "firsts," but I think it's safe to say that few archaeologists find the question particularly interesting. What is interesting, though, in the case of the bread vs. beer debate, is a broader question about how we choose to explain the domestication of plants (and animals). This is one of the big questions in the discipline of archaeology. Why in different parts of the world and at different times did humans enter into a new kind of relationship with specific plants and animals? How did these plants and animals become so dependent on us and we on them? Past explanations for domestication have tended to highlight certain kinds of causation: climate change, population pressure, economic necessity, competitive advantage. Whatever the specifics, there is often an assumption that agriculture emerged to solve a problem of subsistence, that is, to guarantee that people had enough to eat.

But what if agriculture did not emerge as a survival strategy but, rather, as a means of achieving other kinds of social, cultural, or religious goals? This is what makes Göbekli Tepe and a series of other contemporary sites so interesting. They raise the possibility that plants might have been domesticated for the sake of beer; but they also suggest that this beer was serving some kind of larger purpose. As argued by the excavators, people were gathering at Göbekli Tepe to join together in a communal construction project and to conduct communally oriented ritual activities. This effort required copious amounts of food and beer. In the effort to guarantee a steady supply of feasting provisions, they may have unwittingly (or wittingly) taken the first steps toward plant domestication. Of course, it's also possible that the feasting was the main point and the other activities just an afterthought. I like a good party. You like a good party (I assume). Why deny that our distant ancestors might have shared this same appreciation for social interaction, inebriation, and a break from the everyday?

Indeed, a predilection for mind-altering substances of one kind or another appears to be nearly universal in human societies.[16] And beer has often been the go-to option. We're increasingly learning that the roots of beer stretch back deep into the prehistoric past.[17] We've just seen one case in which beer might have played a role in the origins of agriculture. But just as agriculture emerged independently in different parts of the world at different times, so did beer. There was no single aha moment, when some brilliant (or hapless) prehistoric innovator discovered (or stumbled upon) the magic of fermenting grain into alcohol; that is, there is no single, ultimate origin point for the beers of the world. Although we are only just beginning to get a handle on this complex history, all indications suggest that beer has been discovered many times in the history of the world. In this chapter—as a prelude to our dive into ancient Mesopotamia—we're going to widen our lens to the global scale and think about beer from a world-historical perspective. I want to highlight both the deep historical roots of beer and the global diversity of brewing traditions past and present.

What is beer?

I've been using the word "beer" without actually defining it. For many readers, the word probably calls to mind a fermented beverage brewed with malted barley and flavored with hops. Yes, that certainly is beer. But beer can be, has been, and is much more than that. You'll see many different definitions in the literature: for example, definitions that reserve the term "beer" for beverages brewed with malted grains (or malted barley in particular) and others that maintain a distinction between ale and beer. Here, I'm going to follow the late, great Michael Jackson—no, not *that* Michael Jackson, I'm talking about the visionary beer historian—who keeps things simple and broad: "Beer is a drink made from fermented cereals."[18]

I was tempted to add a rider, specifying that the drink must be an alcoholic drink. As we'll see later, though, some scholars think that Mesopotamian beer might actually have contained little to no alcohol. So we'll leave this an open question for now and avoid the more restrictive definition. I would, however, like to add another rider. As suggested by Patrick McGovern in his wide-ranging survey of ancient alcohol, let's specify that the principal component of the beverage must be a cereal grain.[19] Otherwise, we would have to disqualify any beverage that also includes some other kind of fermentable sugar: for example, a maize beer livened up with a touch of honey or, as we'll see in Mesopotamia, a barley beer with a touch of date syrup. Also, while we're at it, let's add one further rider to distinguish beer from its higher-proof derivatives like whiskey; beer has not been subject to a process of distillation. So here's our basic definition: *Beer is an undistilled beverage whose principal component is fermented cereal grains.*

From a brewing perspective, there are three basic steps that unite the beers of the world and distinguish them from other fermented beverages. First, the starches in a grain must be broken down into fermentable sugars. Unlike the countless fruits that humans have learned to ferment into wine, cereal grains do not offer immediate access to the simple sugars required for fermentation. Break the skin on a grape, and the sugary pulp is ready to go; indeed, it will often start fermenting right away, since yeasts are often present on grape skins. In the case of grains, the fermentable sugars are bound up in starch molecules intended to provide food for the young plant. These starches must be broken down into their constituent parts, typically by means of enzymes, in order to gain access to the requisite simple sugars. Second, these fermentable sugars must be extracted from the grain and suspended in a liquid—the liquid that will eventually become beer. Third, this liquid must be introduced to the microbial agents of fermentation. Certain yeasts, for example, would love nothing better than to chow down on all those sugars and transform them into alcohol. In many cases, bacteria are also involved: for example, lactic acid bacteria that specialize in converting sugars into lactic acid. Ultimately, these three simple steps are all that's needed to produce beer from any number of cereals.

In reality, of course, the brewing process can be significantly more complicated, and the range of variability in beers and brewing techniques is enormous. One key distinguishing feature is how one chooses to break down the starches in the grain, a process known as saccharification. Humans have discovered three primary methods, all of which depend on enzymes.[20] First, there is malting, the method used in ancient Mesopotamia and for most of today's commercially produced barley beers. The basic idea here is to hijack the grain's natural growth cycle and make use of enzymes contained within the grain itself. You just need to soak the grain in water for a bit and then remove it from the water, at which point it will start to germinate. Enzymes within the grain, primarily amylase, will kick into gear and start breaking down starches to provide food for the growing plant. You can then halt the process (e.g., by drying or the application of heat) and do as you wish with the sugars and enzymes. This malting process has a deep history and can be achieved in a myriad of different ways, from the simple to the exceedingly complex. The second method of saccharification is often called mastication or salivation. It relies on an enzyme—amylase again—that's present in the saliva of many humans. Yes, that means someone has to either chew the individual grains or pop a wad of ground-up grain into their mouth and let their saliva get to work. For example, the maize beers known today as *chicha* were and are often brewed with the aid of human saliva.[21] The third method relies on the enzymes present in certain kinds of filamentous fungi, such as the mold *Aspergillus oryzae*. Interestingly, this form of saccharification often takes place simultaneously with, not prior to, fermentation. It is especially common in the brewing traditions of East and Southeast Asia, where mold is often introduced as part of a mixed fermentation starter that also includes yeasts and bacteria.

So not everyone brews their beer in the same way. That's hardly an earth-shattering statement. But let's run through a few other key axes of variation.

How about acidity? In recent years, there's been a sour beer revolution in the United States. Suddenly, beers that would have been considered undrinkable—or at least really, really weird—by the vast majority of American consumers have caught fire, opening up a whole new spectrum of beer flavors. The tart or sour quality that sets these beers apart has long been appreciated by beer connoisseurs in other parts of the world. And before yeasts could be isolated and inoculated into beers, most beers are likely to have been somewhat sour. So we're not just talking about the famous Belgian beers (lambics, Flemish sours, etc.) that inspired the recent craze. Many traditional African beers, for example, are prized for their acidic kick, intentionally generated by brewers via a phase of lactic fermentation that precedes the alcoholic fermentation.

Many of these African beers are also distinguished by their texture: not a thin, highly filtered, fizzy liquid but a thick, murky soup or porridge.[22] And then there's the issue of flavoring ingredients. Like the stouts and porters of British tradition or German dunkels, many beers are and have been flavored with grain products (either malted or unmalted) that have been roasted, toasted, or otherwise modified. Hops, the other backbone of the flavor profile in the Euro-American tradition, can add a broad range of flavors, not to mention preservative qualities, but in the global history of beer many other ingredients have also been used to achieve specific desired flavors: bitterness, heat, sweetness, floral and fruity notes, spicy undertones, etc. Finally, potency can range widely. Examples from the lower end of the spectrum include *kvass* from Russia and Eastern Europe, reaching a mere 1%–1.5% alcohol by volume (ABV), and the table beers of Belgium, about 1%–3.5% ABV. Toward the upper end, one could cite the wee heavies of Scotland, clocking in at around 5.5%–9% ABV; the rice "wines" of China and Japan, at 15%–20% ABV; and some punch-you-in-the-face efforts to up the ante by adventurous craft brewers in recent years that reach (without distillation, the usual means of upping the proof) as high as 67.5% ABV.[23] As a general rule, though, beers have tended to hover somewhere in the vicinity of 3%–6% ABV.

The prehistory of beer

So, one key feature that distinguishes beer from other fermented beverages is an extra processing step: the conversion of starches into fermentable sugars. Many fruits, for example, can be fermented into wine with almost no effort at all. And all it takes to ferment honey into mead is the addition of some water. Watering down the honey reduces the high sugar concentration and allows yeasts in the honey to emerge from dormancy and leap into action. Beer requires some extra effort. Given this simple fact, it's extremely unlikely that beer was the earliest alcoholic beverage enjoyed by humans. A variety of nonhuman animals—including elephants, tree shrews, and birds—have been known to indulge in drunken feasts, when the opportunity presents itself: for example, when they come across a cache of overripe, but highly nutritious, fermenting fruits or a tree trunk filled with honey that has started to ferment.[24] Sometimes they clearly enjoy these experiences and even appear to seek them out. Our early ancestors would almost certainly themselves have come across such naturally occurring alcoholic beverages—and, having given them a taste, discovered the inebriating effects so beloved in our present world.[25] Exactly when humans decided to try their hand at intentionally producing these beverages is another matter and very much an open question. Still, it's unlikely that beer would have been first on the list.

How and when might that extra processing step required to produce beer have been discovered? We'll probably never know for certain. Archaeology is not really cut out for the identification of moments in time. What are the chances that an archaeologist is going to come across traces of that fateful afternoon (or, more likely, *those* fateful afternoons scattered across time and space) when some creative, observant, or just plain lucky soul, or souls, discovered the correlation between saccharification and fermentation? The chances of uncovering that particular aha moment are extremely slim. But we can make some good, educated guesses.

Here's one simple, three-step sequence that could explain the first successful voyage from raw barley to frothy beer in SW Asia (i.e., the broader Mesopotamian region)—a hypothetical scenario set during the Epipalaeolithic period (around 10000 BCE), when the region was occupied by a cultural group that we call the Natufians.[26] First, some industrious Natufian, planning ahead for tomorrow's breakfast, decides to soak some barley in water, a trusted method of breaking the barley down and removing toxicity. After soaking, they set the barley aside and then promptly forget all about it. By the time it's rediscovered a few days later, some of the grains have sprouted. Today we would call this whole soaking-and-sprouting process malting. Having relocated the misplaced and now sprouted barley, our unwitting Natufian brewer grinds it, mixes it with water, and heats it up to make a porridge—a perfectly normal method of dinner prep, but also very similar to what we would now call mashing. Finally, surmising that the leftovers might make for a tasty breakfast, they leave the porridge out overnight. Ambient yeasts colonize the porridge and transform it into a noticeably tastier and noticeably intoxicating mush, a process that we would now call fermentation.

This scenario strikes me as eminently reasonable. It doesn't require any major leaps of faith on our part or any hypothetical lightning bolt of sudden intuition on the part of the Natufians (though they would certainly have been capable of this). Did it actually happen? We'll probably never know, so a better question might be *could* it actually have happened? In an article titled "What was brewing in the Natufian?" a trio of archaeologists set out to answer exactly this question.[27] Building on a thorough review of the plants available at the time, existing methods of food processing, and the contemporary technological repertoire, their answer was a resounding yes. Yes, all of the pieces were in place for a happenstance discovery. And there was strong motive to replicate the happy mistake. We know that the Natufians were into feasting, and—I think we can all agree—feasting is just better with beer. Some enterprising Natufian may very well have discovered beer. But the evidence was all circumstantial. There was no smoking gun.

What would this smoking gun even look like? One possibility would be the recovery of intact grains of malted barley or some other malted cereal. But the archaeological recovery of malted grains is actually a relatively rare occurrence, since the grains themselves are typically preserved only when they've been charred, and signs of malting can be difficult to detect.[28] In the absence of whole, malted grains, another promising avenue of research has emerged in recent years. Where organic residues have been preserved (e.g., inside ceramic or stone vessels), it is now possible to examine individual starch granules under a scanning electron microscope.[29] At extremely high levels of magnification, each different type of starch granule has a distinctive morphology or shape that often allows for identification to the tribe or genus level: for example, the Triticeae tribe that includes barley and wheat or the *Avena* genus that includes oats. Identification to the species level is more conjectural. It relies on educated guesswork, drawing in other kinds of evidence and knowledge about the species common in the region.

What is most interesting, though, about starch granule analysis is signs of modification. When starch granules are subjected to various forms of processing—like malting, mashing, and fermentation—their morphologies are impacted. What began as a squishy looking spheroid, for example, might end up pitted, marked with deep fissures, hollowed out, swollen, or otherwise distorted. And each type of modification can be linked to specific kinds of processing. So, our analytical tool kit now includes a means of identifying direct evidence for malting, even when the malted grains themselves are not preserved, and a means of glimpsing traces of other steps in the brewing process.

One team has recently used starch granule analysis to identify very early evidence for brewing at the site of Raqefet Cave in Israel.[30] During the Natufian period (c. 11700–9700 BCE), this cave functioned as a cemetery. Archaeologists have identified approximately thirty human burials at the site, as well as animal bones that probably derive from funerary feasts. These feasts might also have included the region's (and for now, at least, the world's) earliest known beer. In the area surrounding the burials, approximately 100 cup-, bowl-, and funnel-shaped scoops had been carved into the bedrock and into large boulders. The team argues that at least three of these stone receptacles once played a role in the brewing of beer. Two large boulder "mortars" (think, the bowl-like part of a mortar–and–pestle combo) contained starch granules that showed signs of malting: in particular, a distinctive hollowed-out structure and pitted surface. The team thinks that these mortars were used for storing malted wheat or barley, among other foods. Another mortar, this one carved into the bedrock, included starch granules with signs of the sort of gelatinization that takes place during mashing, that is, when crushed grains are infused in a heated liquid. They argue that this mortar was used for grinding up ingredients, mashing them in hot water, and fermenting them into beer.

This evidence from Raqefet Cave potentially pushes the date for the "discovery" of beer in SW Asia back into the Epipalaeolithic period, that is, potentially some 2,000 years before the evidence from Göbekli Tepe that we saw earlier. And, again, there's tantalizing evidence for a connection to feasting. So, it now appears that the Natufians, an innovative group of hunter-gatherers who made the first moves toward a more sedentary existence and probably undertook some of the earliest experiments in crop cultivation, might also have given us the earliest beer in SW Asia.

A yawning gap of more than 6,000 years separates the early evidence for beer In the region from the next solid evidence for beer (c. 3400 BCE). Was all knowledge of beer lost in some unfortunate episode of cultural forgetting, only to be rediscovered thousands of years later? My hunch: We've just missed it. The kind of scientific and technological firepower necessary to identify faint traces of beer in the archaeological record has only become widely available in recent years. And, thanks to the fascination with "firsts," energy has been poured into the search for earlier and earlier evidence. As new scientific techniques are applied more broadly in the coming years, I predict that we're going to find beer pretty much everywhere, from the early days right on through. (Indeed, malted barley recovered at the site of Kenan Tepe in southeastern Türkiye, from levels dating to the mid-fifth millennium BCE, has already offered a glimpse of what's to come.[31])

If we step back and consider the global prehistory of beer, there's a lot more to work with. This is a dynamic field. Organic residue analysis, in particular, has effected a revolution of sorts in recent years and stands poised to radically rework our understanding of the geography and chronology of prehistoric beer. In ten or twenty years, things are going to look very different. Biomolecular archaeologist Pat McGovern of the University of Pennsylvania Museum—"the Indiana Jones of Ancient Ales, Wines, and Extreme Beverages"[32]—has played a prominent role in conducting these analyses and in bringing the results to a public audience. McGovern has drawn particular attention to the early importance of mixed beverages— which he sometimes calls grogs or extreme beverages—that combine elements of beer, wine, and/or mead.[33] When it comes to sourcing fermentable sugars, our prehistoric ancestors do not appear to have been purists. They threw in whatever they could get their hands on. Or, to put it more charitably, they were avid experimentalists, perhaps willing to risk the occasional stomach-turning failure in search of the sublime. Or perhaps just in search of inebriation. The more fermentable sugars, the higher the alcohol content (up to a point).[34]

If we look at China, for example, where some of the most exciting results have emerged in recent years, early beverages incorporated a range of different fermentable sugars. In many cases, the residues preserved within early ceramic vessels could either indicate mixed beverages or reuse of the same vessel for a series of different batches, each using different ingredients. But I think it's reasonable to follow McGovern's lead and assume that mixed beverages were common. As early as 7000 BCE, for example, the inhabitants of a Neolithic site known as Jiahu in the Yellow River Valley were drinking a beverage made from honey, rice, and grapes and/or hawthorn fruit—a concoction combining elements of mead, beer, and wine.[35] Around 4000–3000 BCE, people at the site of Dingcun were brewing up beverages with millet, rice, Job's tears (a perennial, tropical plant in the Poaceae family of grasses), wild Triticeae grass seeds, and snake gourd roots (a tropical vine that produces long fruits akin to summer squash); for purposes of saccharification, they appear to have been relying on a mixture of malting and molds.[36] Around 3000 BCE, brewers at the site of Mijiaya used broomcorn millet, barley, Job's tears, and tubers of some kind.[37] And between about 2400 BCE and 2200 BCE, a beverage made from rice, honey, fruit (probably grape and/or hawthorn fruit), and possibly barley and a plant resin (or herb) is in evidence at the site of Liangchengzhen.[38] So the "extreme" beverage tradition appears to have persisted for at least 5,000 years in early China.

Creative experimentation also appears to have been the rule in prehistoric Europe.[39] People were drinking beers, wines, and meads, and they were drinking beery-wines, meady-beers, and winey-beery-meads. For example, in a cave known as Can Sadurní near Barcelona, Spain, a ceramic vessel dating to the late fifth millennium BCE preserved traces of barley beer, possibly augmented with the fruits of the strawberry tree.[40] At the site of Balfarg in southeastern Scotland, fragments of two ceramic vessels dating to 3000–2600 BCE preserved traces of barley, oats, flax, honey, and flowers and/or herbs (meadowsweet, goosefoot, cabbage/mustards).[41] Perhaps most interesting was the presence of black henbane, a poisonous plant in the hemlock family that is known to have been intentionally exploited for medicinal and hallucinogenic purposes in the past. If (and this is a big if) these ingredients were all mixed together and fermented, they could have produced a particularly extreme and almost certainly dangerous beverage. Another well-known example comes from the site of Egtved in Denmark.[42] Here, around the year 1370 BCE, a woman age 16–18 was buried in an oak coffin and placed beneath an earthen mound. When this burial was discovered and brought to light in 1921, more than 3,000 years later, the contents were incredibly well-preserved: hair, skin, nails, tooth enamel, bits of brain, woolen clothing, leather shoes, a bronze belt plate, jewelry, and a leather bag containing the cremated remains of a child. What most interests us here, though, is a birch-bark container that lay at her feet. It probably once held a beer-mead-wine hybrid made from wheat, honey, cowberries, cranberries, and bog myrtle. Since her discovery, the so-called "Egtved Girl" has inspired all manner of tribute, including a movie (*The Egtved Girl: Life of a Bronze Age Teenager*), a musical (*Egtvedspigen*), a comic book (*Egtved Pigen*), and a beer (*Egtvedpigens Bryg*).

The prehistoric world was awash in experimental alcoholic concoctions. I've just given you a small sampling from the increasingly lengthy list of mixed beverages once available in our world. As more and more of these prehistoric delights are being brought to light, we actually find ourselves in the midst of something like a revival in the craft of experimental mélange. Today, many craft brewers are more than willing to experiment with beverages that cross the boundaries between beer, wine, and mead. As palettes broaden and adventurous brewers seek to break new ground, hybrid beverages are no longer just a thing of the past. Whether they realize it or not, these experimental brewers are reaching back to the deepest roots of their art.

The retro trend belies a more crucial point: Wherever and whenever ancient brewers concocted the earliest experimental cocktails, these brews eventually evolved, through complex and twisting pathways, into the beverages that we now know and love. Much of the early history (that is, the prehistory) of beer was a history of beer-adjacent beverages, inventive hybrids that included grain as one source of fermentable sugars among others. And these hybrids almost certainly built on a much deeper history of fermenting fruits, honey, and other naturally occurring sources of sugar. But over the past 10,000 years, give or take, an extremely diverse global hodgepodge of local brewing efforts gradually crystallized into a series of distinct, regional beer-brewing traditions that are still with us today, each focused more narrowly on a specific grain or grains (barley, wheat, rice, corn, millet, sorghum, etc.).

Being a Mesopotamian archaeologist, I'm going to stay in my lane from here on out and focus on what I know best, rather than attempt to cover all of the world's great brewing traditions. But I want to reiterate two key points. First, the history of beer is not just a history of barley beer. The brewing landscape past and present is much more interesting and much more variegated than many accounts would suggest. The key is to look beyond the European barley beer tradition. Second, despite many assertions to the contrary, it makes little sense to cite Mesopotamia or Egypt or any-where else as the ultimate origin point for beer. The truth of the matter is that beer emerged independently in many different places and times and developed along distinct trajectories in different parts of the world. There was no ultimate origin point for beer, and there is no single, clearly marked historical pathway leading from there to here.

Why focus on Mesopotamian beer at all, then? For anyone interested in the deep history of alcoholic beverages, Mesopotamia offers our earliest and best chance to explore an ancient beer culture in its full complexity. The progress that has been made toward defining the very first episodes in the story of beer—the prehistory of beer—is exciting, but we're gen-erally able to catch just the faintest glimpse of those early brews and the people behind them. Our access to the world of ancient Mesopotamia is on an entirely different level. As you'll see in the coming pages, we know an exceptional amount about not only the beers of ancient Mesopotamia, but also the people who were making and drinking them, the places where these people lived and worked, the taverns and temples and tombs where they did their drinking, the stories that they told about beer, their preferred styles of drinking, their brewing equipment and drinking par-aphernalia, and the gods and goddesses who governed their lives and who were also partial to a drink. This next-level access to the world of ancient Mesopotamian beer is, ultimately, a result of the source material available—not just the types of source material but also the sheer quantity. In my experience, many people are surprised by just how much we know about the Mesopotamian past.

You may note, though, as we get into the nitty-gritty, that I tend to hem—even haw—when interrogating the evidence and our interpretations of it. *Isn't he the expert?* you might query. *Shouldn't he of all people know this stuff?* The truth of the matter is that there are many things that no one ac-tually knows for sure. For better or worse, when it comes to the study of the distant past, uncertainty is just a part of the game. And, frankly, I raise an eyebrow when anyone starts speaking too confidently about Mesopotamian beer. Pat Conway from Great Lakes Brewing Co. never tires of pointing out that my answer to any question about the field is likely to be "Hm, good question. I'm not sure" or "We just don't know." Laugh all you want, Pat, but those are answers that we can build on, that open up space for further questions and further research. So I propose that we embrace that uncertainty, get it out in the open, and run with it. When I say that we don't know this or we're unsure about that, what I'm really saying is: there are many more puzzles to be solved.

Chapter 2

The land between the rivers

The Epic of Gilgamesh

You may know the story already.[2] It's a story about the human condition, the fear of death, what it is that makes a person a civilized human being. And right at the heart of the story we find beer. The setting is Uruk, home of the legendary king Gilgamesh. Restless and worried, the king recounts a dream to his mother, the goddess Ninsun.

> The stars of the heavens appeared above me,
>   like a rock from the sky one fell down before me.
> I lifted it up, but it weighed too much for me,
>   I tried to roll it, but I could not dislodge it.[3]

The wise goddess knows the meaning of the dream. The people of Uruk, fed up with the actions of the increasingly tyrannical king Gilgamesh, have lodged a complaint with the gods. They have begged for some aid against this "savage wild bull," unequaled in strength and beauty, and his incessant harassment. And the gods have devised a plan. They will send down a

fierce warrior to confront and ultimately befriend the troublesome king.
As Ninsun explains to Gilgamesh: "[A] mighty comrade will come to you,
and be his friend's saviour."[4] This mighty comrade is the wild man Enkidu.

Fashioned out of clay by the goddess Aruru, Enkidu is thrown down
from heaven into the wild lands to live among the gazelles. But he is not,
of course, destined to remain there. A hunter sees him, drinking water with
the herds, and hightails it to Uruk to inform Gilgamesh. The king then
sends a woman named Shamhat out to lure Enkidu back to the city—
Shamhat, who heroically "took in his scent" and "did not recoil." She strips
off her clothes and offers herself to Enkidu. Suitably impressed and, let's say,
inspired by this first glimpse of a naked woman, Enkidu accepts. They make
love for seven days and nights, at which point the gazelles no longer recognize Enkidu as one of their own. It's a sort of Garden of Eden moment.
Enkidu's sexual encounter with Shamhat has closed off one world to him
and opened up another. He's no longer at one with the wild. He's on his
way to becoming a civilized human being. But he's not there yet. And this
is where beer comes into the picture.

Having effectively captured his attention—and sealing the deal with
another week's worth of sex—Shamhat sets about convincing Enkidu to
accompany her back to Uruk, where he can challenge Gilgamesh and
give the people some respite. Enkidu is into the idea, but he can hardly
make an appearance in the glamorous big city in his present state: naked,
dirty, hairy, foul-smelling, unkempt, and unacquainted with the ways
of polite society. First off, he needs clothes, which Shamhat provides.
Second, he needs to learn how to eat and drink like a fully fledged
human being—no more grazing on grass with his gazelle friends. It's
time to learn how to eat bread and drink beer. Enkidu is skeptical at first,
but he comes around.

> Bread they set before him,
>   ale they set before him.
> Enkidu ate not the bread, but looked askance.
> How to eat bread Enkidu knew not,
>   how to drink ale he had never been shown.
>
> The harlot [i.e., Shamhat] opened her mouth,
>   saying to Enkidu:
> "Eat the bread, Enkidu, essential to life,
>   drink the ale, the lot of the land!"

Enkidu ate the bread until he was sated,
   he drank the ale, a full seven goblets.
His mood became free, he started to sing,
   his heart grew merry, his face lit up.[5]

So Enkidu's first encounter with beer leaves him pleasantly tipsy and, presumably, even more fully on board with this whole "human civilization" thing. Any society capable of producing and appreciating this magical liquid can't be all bad, right?

The Epic of Gilgamesh is one of the oldest and most famous pieces of literature in the world: a rollicking tale of adventure, loss, desperation, and personal growth—not to mention a sustained reflection on death, fame, human-divine relations, and, well, the meaning of life.[6] Since its rediscovery in the nineteenth century, when the cuneiform writing system was deciphered, the epic has captured the attention of audiences worldwide. But the Epic of Gilgamesh is not just a story that we in the modern world happen to connect with, nor is it one that just happens to have been preserved by chance. It was immensely popular in the ancient Mesopotamian world. It was taught in schools, copied by generation after generation of students, translated into other contemporary languages, deposited in royal libraries. It was one of the canonical texts of ancient Mesopotamia, a cultural touchstone that would have been familiar to pretty much everyone. At the same time, the story of Gilgamesh was not static; it evolved. The "standard" version of the epic (written in the Akkadian language) appears to have come together during the late second millennium BCE, but its ancestry reaches back at least into the third millennium BCE. We have fragments of an early version, for example, that dates to the Old Babylonian period (2004–1595 BCE). And, during the reign of the Third Dynasty of Ur (2112–2004 BCE), a series of stories recounting the exploits of Gilgamesh were written down (in the Sumerian language) and probably performed at the royal court in Ur. The later epic borrowed some, but not all, of its material from these earlier stories.

The point that I want to make here is simple. The fact that beer plays a key role in Enkidu's transformation is not just a sidenote, an incidental detail in some random fairy tale that someone happened to jot down in clay. The taming of Enkidu by means of sex, bread, and beer is a pivotal moment in one of the most beloved stories of ancient Mesopotamia. And this tells us something about their perspective on beer. Enkidu has to learn how to drink beer because that's what humans do. They eat bread, and they drink beer. To be more precise, that's what the cultured, civilized urbanites of Mesopotamia do. In their world, beer was not just a form of sustenance or pleasure; it was also a means of distinguishing us from them—whether this "them" lay in the distant, primitive past (before people knew any better); the not-so-distant periphery of the Mesopotamian world (inhabited by un-couth, uncultured barbarians whose humanity was, in fact, up for debate); or the animal realm.

The Epic of Gilgamesh also introduces one other point of discussion to which we will return again and again. In ancient Mesopotamia, drinking beer could lead to inebriation or, at least, tipsiness. That may seem an ob-vious point, but it is not, in fact, a point of general agreement in the ac-ademic literature. Some scholars are convinced that the beers of ancient Mesopotamia were low or extremely low in alcohol content.[7] I am not one of those scholars, but this question deserves some sustained attention. If the beverage that Mesopotamians loved so much was only mildly (or not at all) intoxicating, this will have a significant impact on how we assess the broader role of this beverage in Mesopotamian society.

Mesopotamia

In the course of his adventures, Gilgamesh traveled the length and breadth of the known world. Before we go any further, let's talk a little bit about this world. What exactly is Mesopotamia? First, one crucial point: the people of ancient Mesopotamia never actually used the word Mesopotamia.[8] They weren't Mesopotamians, at least not in their own minds. Their sense of home, identity, and affiliation was usually more closely tied to specific cities than to any broader geographical designation. We've borrowed the term, ultimately, from Alexander the Great, who named one of the provinces within his newly acquired empire Mesopotamia, which is Greek for "be-tween the rivers." The Roman Empire subsequently adopted this same label for a province stretching between the Tigris and Euphrates rivers in what is today southeastern Türkiye. But we use the term to refer to a broader re-gion: basically, all of modern-day Iraq and parts of northeastern Syria and southeastern Türkiye (Figure 2.1).

In current usage, however, the term "Mesopotamia" is not just a ge-ographical designation. It also incorporates a chronological dimension.

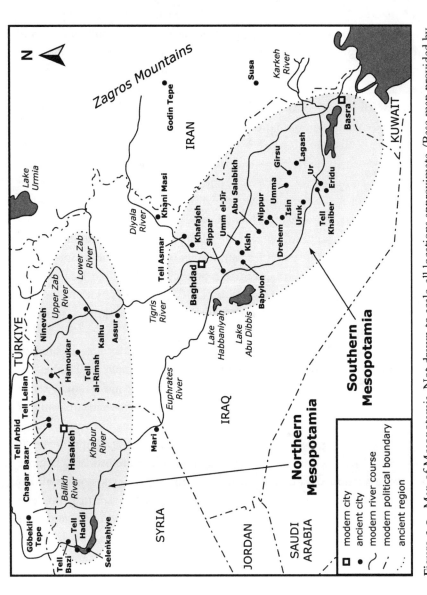

Figure 2.1. Map of Mesopotamia. Not drawn to scale, all locations approximate. (Base map provided by Institute for the Study of Ancient Cultures, University of Chicago)

We don't use the term "Mesopotamia," for example, when discussing the modern region or its recent history; we use it when discussing the region's ancient (and often, specifically, pre-Islamic) past. This usage might not seem problematic on the surface, but it is tied to a deep history of European colonial intervention, denigration of the region's modern inhabitants, and cultural expropriation. As the term "Mesopotamia" fell into disuse in the post-Roman world, other geographical designations rose to the fore. The term "Iraq," for example, was in use as early as the tenth century CE and was maintained through the long period of rule by the Ottoman Empire. The term "Mesopotamia" was only revived in the nineteenth century CE, as European colonial powers began to establish an increasingly strong presence in the region. And this terminological move was no accident. The colonial powers were heavily invested in a rapidly expanding effort to uncover the remains of the region's ancient past. And the results were spectacular. European audiences were riveted by the news of new discoveries. Especially following the decipherment of the cuneiform writing system, a whole civilization was coming into view, one previously known only through occasional references in the Bible. Boatloads of statues, relief carvings, cuneiform tablets, and other artifacts were shipped back to Europe, forming the basis for some of today's best-known museum collections.

In the process, this newly discovered ancient civilization—located in what was then considered the Orient or East—was explicitly claimed by the West and slotted in as a founding moment in the history of Western civilization. One common narrative, for example, envisioned a passing of the torch of civilization from Egypt and Mesopotamia to Greece to Rome and then onward to France, Germany, Britain, and/or the United States. If you've ever taken a course in Western Civilization, you're probably familiar with some version of this story, which persists today. It's a story built on cultural expropriation. If Europeans were going to lay claim to the venerable ancient past that was coming to light, that past had to be separated from the modern-day inhabitants of the region. One means of driving a wedge between the ancient and modern people of the region was through a simple act of naming. The ancient region would be Mesopotamia, the modern region, Iraq. This is all to say that the term "Mesopotamia" is not a neutral, value-free label. It is a useful way of referring to the ancient region bounded approximately by the Tigris and Euphrates rivers, but we need to bear in mind the problematic legacy of the term and do our best to guard against perpetuating that legacy.[9]

In any case, the region is anchored by the Tigris and Euphrates rivers. Both arise in the Taurus mountains in what is today eastern Türkiye and receive much of their annual flow from snowmelt in those mountains. Both are also joined by several tributaries during their journey down to the Gulf. The Euphrates is joined by the Balikh and Khabur rivers, and the Tigris, by the Greater Zab, Lesser Zab, Adhaim, and Diyala rivers. The Tigris and Euphrates were absolutely essential to life in Mesopotamia, especially in the drier, southern part of the region. The rivers and their associated canal systems provided water for irrigation and other purposes, and they served as crucial corridors of transportation and communication. The land between these rivers is extremely flat in the area south of modern-day Baghdad and somewhat less flat (but still pretty flat) further to the north. The region is then bounded by foothills that rise up quickly to high mountain ranges on the north and east, and by arid steppe and desert on the west and southwest.

Several further geographical terms will appear in the coming pages. First, there is the distinction between southern Mesopotamia (also known as Lower Mesopotamia or the alluvium) and northern Mesopotamia (also known as Upper Mesopotamia or the Jezireh). This distinction rests, ultimately, on rainfall. In northern Mesopotamia, rainfall was sufficient to support rain-fed agriculture, while in southern Mesopotamia agriculture would have been impossible without irrigation. The two regions were separated by a zone of arid steppe, occupied primarily by nomadic or seminomadic herders. The northern and southern regions often followed divergent historical trajectories, but, by the same token, those trajectories were often intertwined to a greater or lesser extent. Second, within southern Mesopotamia, there is the distinction between Sumer (*not*, as many people seem to think, Sumeria) and Akkad. This native or emic contrast between a southern region (Sumer) closer to the Persian/Arabian Gulf and a northern region (Akkad) closer to modern Baghdad applies primarily during the Early Bronze Age (3000–2000 BCE). Third, there is the distinction between Babylonia and Assyria, which applies primarily during the Middle/Late Bronze Age and the Iron Age (2000–331 BCE). Babylonia is basically another term for southern Mesopotamia, and Assyria, another name for northern Mesopotamia, especially the region along the Tigris river that formed the core of the Assyrian Empire.

Archaeological and historical sources

As we have seen, much of the landscape in Mesopotamia ranges from the very definition of flat to the gentlest of gently rolling. Ancient towns and cities rise up from this landscape in the guise of what look to be natural hills. Thanks to a long-lived tradition of building over and over and over again on the same spot for hundreds or thousands of years—coupled with relatively short-lived building materials, like sun-dried mudbricks—human settlements gradually rose higher and higher above the surrounding plains. Today, we use the Arabic term *tell* (meaning "mound" or "hill") to refer to these distinctive, human-made settlement mounds (Figure 2.2).

They can rise as high as 40 meters (130 ft.) above the surrounding ground surface and can reach an extent of 750 hectares (1,900 acres) or more. They can vary significantly in shape: ranging from small, steep-sided, cone-shaped hillocks to more extensive, low mounds that rise only a few meters above the ground surface and vast, irregular, multi-mounded areas cut by gullies and ancient canals. These imposing remains of ancient settlements, built up over time in layer-cake-like fashion, litter the landscape. Agatha Christie, who was married to the archaeologist Max Mallowan and spent many summers with him on excavations in Syria, wrote a wonderful memoir about her time there. Here's how she describes the landscape near the Balikh River in Syria:

Figure 2.2. Photo of a tell, Tell Qarqur, Syria, with excavation trench running from top to bottom. (Photo: Jesse Casana)

Five minutes later we see a streak of green ahead—it is the vegetation bordering the river. A vast Tell looms up. Max says ecstatically: "The Balikh— look at it! Tells everywhere!" The Tells are indeed imposing—large, formidable, and very solid-looking. "Whacking great Tells," says Max.[10]

In plenty of cases, such as the city of Erbil (ancient Arbela) in the Kurdistan region of northern Iraq, these ancient tells are still occupied today.

Archaeologists have undertaken excavations at hundreds of tells across Mesopotamia, but their investigations have only scratched the surface of what remains. I'm often asked, "Is there anything left to find?" The answer is an emphatic yes. Although early excavators did sometimes work on a truly massive and, unfortunately, truly destructive scale, most sites have only been excavated in a very piecemeal fashion. And thousands of archaeological sites across Mesopotamia have never been touched by trowel (the archaeological tool par excellence). Many of these have been identified in the course of what's known as archaeological survey, that is, the systematic, nondestructive (i.e., without excavation) examination of surviving surface remains, often across broad geographical areas. Others are known only from their appearance on satellite imagery or aerial photographs. So, there's still a lot left to find. At the same time, some of the best known and most important sites in the region have been radically decimated by looters over the past few decades to feed a thriving international trade in illicit antiquities, a trade driven by wealthy foreign collectors and exacerbated by years of turmoil, economic sanctions, and poverty. Famous ancient cities such as Umma, Isin, and Mari now resemble lunar landscapes, pockmarked by hundreds or thousands of massive looters' pits. Enormous quantities of information have been lost in the course of these ongoing, uncontrolled, and undocumented excavations, and the irreplaceable cultural heritage of the region's modern inhabitants has been systematically siphoned off into the hands of unscrupulous, often criminal, collectors across the world.

When scientifically excavated and recorded, the archaeological sites of Mesopotamia can be a gold mine—not in the literal sense (although gold does sometimes make an appearance) but in the sense of data, information, knowledge. The architecture and artifacts recovered offer a detailed and vivid glimpse into the lives of the region's ancient inhabitants. Architecturally, the remains don't always announce themselves in the same way that, say, the pyramids of ancient Egypt or the stepped temples of ancient Mexico do. Mesopotamia does have an equivalent, the famous *ziggurats* or stepped temple platforms that dominated the skylines of Mesopotamian cities. But apart from the heavily reconstructed ziggurat at Ur and some other fragmentary examples, these no longer lord it over their surroundings as they once did. The lower visibility of Mesopotamian architecture is due, in part, to the simple fact that much of this architecture today lies buried. It also comes down to a choice of building materials. Stone was difficult to come by on the floodplains of southern Mesopotamia, but clay was not. Not at all. It was literally everywhere. Most buildings were built with either sun-dried mudbricks (the cheaper option, liable to melt away over time) or oven-baked mudbricks (the more expensive but more durable option). And the sun-dried ones, in particular, simply do not survive as well as stone.

What about artifacts—the vast world of things, from the most humble of everyday items to the rarest and fanciest of luxury goods? What has managed to endure the millennia to testify, if only obliquely, to lives once lived, thoughts once thought, pursuits once pursued? First, it's important to mention that organic materials survive poorly in the region's climate and are only preserved in rare circumstances (e.g., anaerobic, extremely arid, or water-logged conditions). Wooden items, for example, occasionally survive, but for the most part the world of ancient Mesopotamian wood is left to our imaginations. But all is not lost! Cuneiform tablets and artistic works preserve a wealth of information about this and other elements of the perishable, organic world. For instance, although few traces have survived, we know that brewing vessels were sometimes kept on wooden stands; we know that brewers used wooden stirring implements; and we know that drinkers often quaffed their beer through long reed straws.

What has survived, above all else, is pottery. So. Much. Pottery. Archaeological sites in Mesopotamia are typically covered in a more-or-less continuous layer of the fragmented bits of pottery that archaeologists call sherds. (Note: We do *not* call them shards.) And ceramics, from the tiniest of fragments to completely intact vessels, are typically recovered in the tens of thousands during excavation—both a blessing (compared to, say, the British Isles, where twenty sherds can sometimes seem like a windfall) and a curse (unless you happen to be one of those special and greatly appreciated individuals who really enjoys spending your days picking slowly through mountains of heavily abraded ceramic fragments). Ceramic vessels were essential to both the brewing and consumption of beer in Mesopotamia, and we will return to them again and again in the coming pages. We will also examine some other key ceramic items, such as the wonderful molded clay plaques that provide a vivid glimpse into many aspects of daily life during the early part of the second millennium BCE. These clay plaques include some of the best exemplars of the erotic scenes that I described in the Prologue.

So, Mesopotamia—especially southern Mesopotamia—was rich in clay but poor in stone. Some stone was available locally, but the highest quality stone was imported from surrounding regions.[11] For example, the inscription on a statue of Gudea, ruler of the city of Lagash around 2150 BCE, tells us that diorite was brought from the land of Magan (today's Oman) and sculpted into his likeness.[12] And the intricately carved cylinder seals that we will return to were often made from colorful, high-value stones, such as lapis lazuli and carnelian, that made their way to Mesopotamia from as far away as Afghanistan and the Indian subcontinent.[13] On a more prosaic level, a variety of stone implements came in very handy in the agricultural and culinary realms. Chert, quartzite, and other related stones, for example, were chipped or flaked into useful shapes: projectile points, blades, scrapers, etc. Other kinds of stone were ground into usable shapes. These "groundstone" objects include, for example, a range of grinders and pounders that would have featured prominently in the tool kit of cooks and brewers.

What about the plant world, the fundamental source of brewing ingredients? Archaeologists regularly recover "archaeobotanical" remains of both the macro- and the micro- variety. Macrobotanical remains are visible to the naked eye and include, for example, individual grains of barley and wheat. These are often only preserved if they've been subject to charring. Fortunately for us and less fortunately for the original inhabitants, buildings have a tendency to burn down. The result: a field day for the archaeobotanist or (if you prefer the tongue-twister often employed in the US) paleoethnobotanist. Microbotanical remains are, as you might suspect, microscopic. The classic example is pollen, but, as we've already seen, recent advances in organic residue analysis have also brought a range of other microbotanical remains into our field of vision: lipids, starch granules, and phytoliths, for example.[14] These tiny plant remnants, found adhering to or absorbed into ceramic vessels and other containers, are upending what we once thought we knew about ancient alcohol.

And then there are cuneiform tablets. Somewhere in the vicinity of 3200 BCE, someone (or maybe someones, plural) had a bright idea: "What if I take some of this clay over here, form it into a squarish, flattish sort of shape, and then draw little pictures in the clay with this reed? Oh, yeah, that looks nice. And look how it dries out and hardens over time. Could I, perhaps, use lumps of clay like this to jot down the number of sheep in that pen over there or the number of beer jars that I just sent over to what's-his-name? That would be super useful." The answer is yes. Yes you could, and yes it would. And you would have just invented the world's first writing.

There's still a lot of uncertainty about the earliest days of the cunei-form writing system. What we know for certain is that the first "proto-cuneiform" writing was invented during a particularly dynamic period. In the first cities of southern Mesopotamia—the city of Uruk, in particular—people were living in a radically new kind of urban environment: dense, crowded, and much more populous than anything that had come before. Across the board, things were getting more complicated. Any effort to con-trol and coordinate life in these cities would have had to face an unprece-dented challenge of information management. And, as you might suspect, some people were indeed interested in taking charge of things. As a series of nascent institutions took shape—the world's earliest known experiments in state formation—people were actively experimenting with a series of different information-storage technologies: clay tokens, clay balls with tokens inside, cylinder seals, clay tablets bearing numerical notations. The first proto-cuneiform tablets emerged as part of this suite of information technologies.[15]

The cuneiform writing system began its life as a pictographic system. That is, the earliest proto-cuneiform signs were pictures. Actually, the *very* earliest cuneiform signs were numbers, impressed into the clay with a round-ended stylus. But soon after, recognizable items like pig heads, human heads, bowls, and fish (as well as other items that are not so recognizable, at least to us) were incised into the surface of the clay with a pointed reed stylus. The distinction between incising and impressing is important and would play a key role in the later development of the cuneiform system. Incising (i.e., dragging a pointed stylus through the clay) may be the way to go if your goal is to draw realistic-looking pictures. But, as the writing system increased in complexity, someone had another bright idea, perhaps some-thing like this: "What if we could stop laboriously incising the pictographs into the clay and, instead, impress them? That would make writing less like drawing and more like stamping. And maybe that would cut down on writing time and improve efficiency?" Whatever the genesis, this innovation had been adopted by about 2500 BCE, transforming the writing system and giving rise to the distinctive cuneiform or "wedge-shaped" signs that would define the script for the next three thousand years. From this point on, incised lines were replaced with impressed, triangular wedges. And this move quickly took the writing system in a more abstract direction. As naturalistic, curving lines were replaced with linear wedges, it became more and more difficult to recognize the original pictographs (Figure 2.3).

It's now generally agreed that the earliest proto-cuneiform writing was being used to record Sumerian, a language with no known relatives. About 700 years later, the script was adapted and used to record Akkadian, a Semitic language related to modern Arabic and Hebrew. Sumerian and Akkadian were the primary languages of ancient Mesopotamia, and these are the languages that you will encounter in the coming pages. The cuneiform script, however, was also used to record a range of other languages in neighboring regions: for example, Hittite, Hurrian, Elamite, and Urartian. For the first few hundred years, the script was used for only a very restricted set of purposes: basically, either for accounting or for making lists. The scribes of ancient Mesopotamia were list-makers extraordinaire. Over a period of several thousand years, for example, they maintained an evolving tradition of so-called lexical lists, that is, lists of words revolving around a common theme: things made of wood, fish, cities, deities, textiles, cheeses, birds, professions. But, during the period from about 2800 to 1800 BCE, use of the script also spread beyond the realm of administration and vocabulary to include royal inscriptions, hymns, poems, epics, king lists, letters, law codes and legal documents, omen lists, medical treatises, etc., etc.[16]

Each type of source material that I've mentioned here comes burdened with its own unique set of interpretive challenges, its own set of biases,

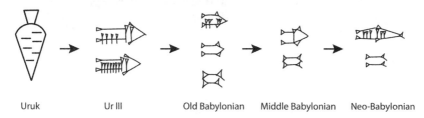

Uruk   Ur III   Old Babylonian   Middle Babylonian   Neo-Babylonian

Figure 2.3. Evolution of the cuneiform sign KAŠ ("beer") over time. (Redrawn after Labat 1976: 122–123)

blind spots, twists, and turns. The evidence does not speak for itself. Well, of course, in some sense it does. Cuneiform tablets, after all, were designed to transmit messages across space and time and have accomplished that task astonishingly well. But we can't just take what they have to say at face value. And the same applies to archaeological remains and visual depictions. Each piece of evidence that has managed to survive into the 21st century CE offers just a glimpse into a past reality that was once every bit as complicated, ambiguous, divided, and divisive as our own.[17]

In this regard, two big issues deserve attention, among many others. First, hundreds of archaeological sites have been explored by archaeologists, and hundreds of thousands of cuneiform texts are available for study, as are innumerable artistic depictions. But these are all preserved in an extremely patchy fashion. We do not have access to a comprehensive and continuous record of life in ancient Mesopotamia. What we do have is tiny points of light and occasional bursts of brilliant illumination in an otherwise dimly lit space, sometimes veering into pitch black. Particular people, places, and things may suddenly stand out in stark detail within our source material, but they are always embedded within a broader world that remains unknown and perhaps unknowable. And they never tell the whole story. Second, much of the available source material is skewed definitively toward the needs, interests, and perspectives of a powerful and wealthy subset of the population. Most ordinary people did not know how to read or write and could not afford to surround themselves with fancy artwork and other finery. Although plenty of exceptions could be cited, most scribes and artisans worked under the patronage of palaces, temples, and wealthy households. The archaeological record—which is, for the most part, composed of a bunch of trash accidentally left behind and fortuitously preserved—offers a potential means of developing a more democratic perspective on the past. But this potential has been compromised, to some extent, by a long-lived archaeological fixation on the finer things: monumental architecture, luxury goods, the wielders of power and influence.

Chronological concerns

In this book, you will encounter three basic chronological frameworks: one numerical, one archaeological, and one historical. Let's start with numerical dates. When referencing specific years or year ranges, I use numerical dates BCE (Before the Common Era) and CE (Common Era). This is just a secular version of the BC/AD system: BCE = BC, CE = AD. If a numerical date is an approximation, I insert a "c." beforehand (short for Latin *circa*). I also regularly refer to centuries and millennia rather than specific dates or date ranges. The eighth century BCE, for example, would be the period from 800 to 700 BCE. The third millennium BCE would be the period from 3000 to 2000 BCE. The third millennium CE (2000–3000 CE) is where we are right now.

Next, archaeological chronologies. Archaeologists around the world employ a bewildering variety of terminological frameworks for breaking the past up into bounded time periods. These tend to vary from region to region, but they can also vary within a region: either because specific subregions merit their own separate periodizations or because not everyone can agree on the best system to use. In this book, at the macro level, we'll be dealing with a framework derived from the venerable three-age system (Stone Age, Bronze Age, Iron Age). This tripartite breakdown is a far-from-perfect but still useful holdover from archaeology's early days as an academic discipline in the nineteenth century CE. It's based on changes in material culture and, in particular, on the introduction of new materials over time. There are many variations and subdivisions to contend with, but only a few are relevant here. When I want to make reference to big-picture chronological distinctions in Mesopotamia, I'll divide the timeline up into the following sequence of periods, beginning near the end of the Stone Age: Epipalaeolithic (meaning just immediately right after the Old Stone Age), Neolithic (meaning New Stone Age), Chalcolithic (meaning Copper Stone Age), Early Bronze Age, Middle Bronze Age, Late Bronze Age, and Iron Age.

When I want to be more specific, I will also refer to region-specific archaeological subphases of these periods. In this part of the world, the tradition has been to name such subphases after the archaeological site where the material culture distinctive to that phase was first identified. It would be kind of like naming a new species after the place in which it was first discovered, rather than, say, after the person who first discovered it. We have, for example, two subphases for the Chalcolithic period: Ubaid (pronounced "oo-bay-id," after Tell al-Ubaid) and Uruk (pronounced "oo-ruk," after Uruk).

Once you get into the Bronze Age, archaeological chronologies start to intersect and overlap with historical chronologies, that is, with chronologies based on developments documented in the written record. This can get pretty complicated, with periods defined variously by archaeological (i.e., material culture), linguistic (i.e., language), paleographic (i.e., cuneiform script), and political (i.e., ruling dynasties) criteria. There's no need to try to disentangle that mess here. The timeline provided at the beginning of the book shows the basic sequence of historical periods that you will encounter in the coming pages. You can always flip back to this timeline for reference. Also, whenever I mention either archaeological or historical periods, I provide numerical date ranges in parentheses to keep us grounded chronologically. As a general rule, I've rounded off the dates in these ranges, rather than providing you with to-the-year accuracy, which isn't really possible anyways, given our uncertainty about dates up through the end of the Bronze Age. Once we get into the Iron Age, where we can be more certain, I've opted for more precise dates.

Beer in Mesopotamian history

The history of ancient Mesopotamia is full of unsolved mysteries, long-simmering debates, and interpretive challenges that defy straightforward resolution. It is also a history of pivotal moments and transformative episodes that, for better or worse, took the human story in radical new directions. And beer was never far from the center of the action. This humble yet weighty beverage offers an illuminating vantage from which to recount and interrogate some of the big questions of Mesopotamian—and, indeed, human—history. As a roadmap for what's to come and a brief introduction to Mesopotamian history, let's consider several of these fundamental questions that will resurface repeatedly over the course of the book.[18]

Beer and the state

When it comes to pivotal moments in human history, probably none has generated more archaeological discussion than the origins of the state.[19] Even the effort to define exactly what a state is has occasioned decades of debate. For convenience, let's just say: a form of political organization in which a centralized government claims to exercise authority over a relatively substantial subject population. We live in a world of states—so much so that it's difficult to imagine anything else, difficult to imagine a world not carved up into a patchwork of more-or-less autonomous political entities, each exercising sovereignty within its own well-defined territory. The state has come to seem inevitable. It has been naturalized, made to seem a simple fact of life, a natural phenomenon, an inescapable feature of the way things are. But travel back in time five thousand years or so, and it was no such thing. There was nothing inevitable about the emergence of the first states. And they did not come into the world fully formed. The history of Mesopotamian states is a long and complicated history of experimentation, contestation, failure, and collapse, just as much as it is a history of triumphant state builders leaving their mark on the world. Opinions differ quite dramatically about these early states: about what they were, the scope of their power, their footprint on the ground, the relative success of their propaganda, the possibilities for resistance.

Most specialists, though, would agree that sometime just before 3000 BCE, during the Late Chalcolithic or Uruk period, a threshold was crossed. Mesopotamia was no longer a land of complex chiefdoms (the terminology here is hotly debated) but a land of states. There's a ruler of sorts who shows up regularly in the artistic record, a codified hierarchy of professional offices or occupations, a cadre of administrators keeping careful tabs on resources, massive buildings with elaborate decoration, images showing violence and prisoners of war, the first clear evidence for slavery. This standard account has, however, recently been called into question.[20] Is it possible that the newly emergent cities of the Uruk period might actually have been an early experiment in large-scale collective governance—ruled not by kings and their minions but by councils of concerned citizens? Perhaps. The evidence leaves plenty of room for debate, but I still see signs of a nascent centralized state.

And from this point forward, the history of the region is typically narrated as a history of states: a drama dominated by the rise and fall of dynasties, kingdoms, empires. During the ensuing Early Dynastic period, for example, cities popped up across the region like mushrooms, and around them coalesced a collection of small kingdoms or city-states, each under the rule of a divine patron with an earthly king as representative. In relatively short order, city-states transitioned into regional-scale conquest states, most famously under the expansionist Akkadian, Ur III, and

Old Babylonian dynasties. And then expansion reached a zenith under a series of empires: first, the Neo-Assyrian, then the Neo–Babylonian and Persian (or Achaemenid). These were massive, sprawling conglomerations that stretched well beyond the bounds of Mesopotamia proper.

There are plenty of problems with such a state-centered account of Mesopotamian history.[21] But, for our purposes, one thing is certain: Across nearly three thousand years of Mesopotamian history, beer was a matter of official state concern.[22] Whatever the scope of their domain—a city and its environs, the entire alluvial plain of southern Mesopotamia, or vast territories and many disparate peoples—kings built breweries and kept tabs on production. And they oversaw the distribution of beer to many different constituencies, both human and divine. Royal authority was a gift from the gods, and these sometimes fickle patrons expected offerings of beer on a daily basis. In the chapters to come, we will see that ensuring an uninterrupted supply of beer for divine consumption was not an abstract notion but the most concrete form of realpolitik, a precondition for political survival from the Early Dynastic up through the Persian period. Time and again, we will see that beer was also a necessity at high-level state ceremonies, such as the state-sponsored banquets of the Ur III period, known simply as "the pouring of beer," or intimate royal gift-giving ceremonies when Ur III kings "drank beer in the house of" various highly placed individuals. We will also witness institutional breweries dispensing beer to palace staff for daily sustenance, to laborers at work on state-sponsored construction projects, and to female prisoners of war and their children. There were different types of beer for different occasions and different people, some stronger than others, some more refined or brewed with higher-quality ingredients, some intended as little more than a means of meeting basic dietary needs.

So beer was a multifunctional resource for these early states, deployed in pursuit of a variety of different aims: ensuring divine support, courting local elites and foreign dignitaries, creating and maintaining bonds of dependency between ruler and ruled, financing infrastructure projects and temple renovations. And its role as a tool in the state-making arsenal evolved over time. For example, beer remained the dominant beverage in Mesopotamia across the millennia, but grape wine from the surrounding hill country gradually transitioned from difficult-to-acquire luxury item in the third millennium BCE to more widely available competitor by the first millennium

BCE. And date wine, only rarely attested up to this point, also entered the marketplace in force during the first millennium BCE. So the landscape of alcoholic beverages diversified over time, leading one to wonder whether beer managed to maintain its particular sort of political cachet or whether it might instead have been relegated to a more marginal role.

Beer and the city

The process of state formation in Mesopotamia was paralleled by another process of equal import: urbanization.[23] As we just saw, the first cities sprang up during the Uruk period and were then joined by a host of others during the Early Dynastic period. From this point onward, Mesopotamia was a land of cities. The rural landscape was still populated by many smaller settlements, and the region witnessed phases of marked decentralization, when substantial chunks of the population left the cities for the country-side. But cities had come to stay. These earliest cities known to world history have inspired a bevy of questions, theories, and debates. Not least is the fundamental issue of definition. What exactly is a city? At what point in its development can we say that a settlement has crossed the nebulous but (for us, at least) symbolically loaded boundary between town and city? Many answers have been offered, none completely satisfying. If we set the tricky issue of definition aside, though, many other interesting questions have been explored: how and why cities first emerged, whether they grew up organically over time or were imposed suddenly from on high, how they were organized, where their food came from, what it was like to live in them, how and why some persisted for millennia while others fell to ruin.

In the pages to come, we will stop off at many of these cities to check out their distinctive brewing traditions and beer cultures. We will visit the arche-typal city of Uruk itself, where proto-cuneiform documents from the Uruk period offer a first glimpse into the operation of an urban brewery. We will visit temple breweries in the Early Dynastic cities of Girsu and Lagash and a palace brewery in the Old Babylonian city of Šubat-Enlil. We will observe the brewing of beer within taverns in Old Babylonian Sippar-Jaḫrūrum, Late Bronze Age Tell Bazi, Neo-Babylonian Borsippa, and Persian-period Nippur. We will even catch occasional glimpses of homebrewers at work in residential areas, busily bent on meeting the daily needs of their households and ready to offer the appropriate hospitality to any thirsty visitors. We will also explore beer consumption across the cities of ancient Mesopotamia, whether at work or play, at home or in the tavern, at fancy banquets, grave-side memorials, or temple ceremonies.

These snapshots of beer in the city offer vivid illustrations of the ubiquity of the beverage and the diverse contexts in which it was produced and consumed, but they do not yet amount to a comprehensive account of beer in the urban landscape. For example, was there typically a neighborhood tavern on every corner? Or were drinking establishments sequestered in particular areas or pushed to the margins? Were breweries a conspicuous feature of city life, contributing their distinctive aromas to the urban smellscape? Would one expect to see porters carting beer and brewing ingredients here and there during a stroll through the city? What about gaggles of inebriated tavern patrons staggering through the streets, singing drinking songs at the top of their lungs? And how drastically different was the beer scene in, say, the Early Dynastic city of Khafajeh, Old Babylonian Ur, Kassite Nippur, or the sprawling Neo-Assyrian and Neo-Babylonian imperial capitals of Kalhu, Nineveh, and Babylon? These cities shared some characteristics in common, but they also differed quite dramatically in other respects. So we should expect beer to have occupied a distinctive position in each.

Beer and the economy

Beer was a staple food in Mesopotamia, a sign of abundance and prosperity, and a necessity at celebrations, ceremonies, diplomatic meetings, and other special events. There's no question that it was an enduring mainstay of the economy. But consideration of the economic position of beer intersects with a series of larger debates, in particular, a long-running dispute over the nature of the Mesopotamian economy.[24] We know that the primary organs of the state, the so-called palace and temple institutions or "great organizations," were major economic players—managing huge tracts of agricultural land, employing substantial workforces to support their needs, storing up reserves against calamity, loaning out funds to constituents on rather steep terms—but just how dominant were they? Was the institutional economy essentially the entire economy? Or was there substantial space for private economic activity beyond the institutional sphere? The evidence from certain periods, most notably the dense administrative archives of the Ur III period, has sometimes been taken to indicate extreme institutional dominance. But during other periods, especially the Old Assyrian, Old Babylonian, and Neo-Babylonian periods, we see evidence for a thriving private economy: family firms engaged in profit-maximizing trade ventures, private entrepreneurs managing institutional assets, private enterprises taxed by the state but otherwise going about their own business. This question of the structure of the Mesopotamian economy—of the balance struck between the institutional and private sectors and how this relationship evolved over time—continues to inspire substantial research and debate.

Beer sat right at the institutional-private nexus and, therefore, offers an excellent entry point into the discussion. We will examine administrative records that track the ingredients delivered to institutional breweries and the beer sent out from these breweries to dependent individuals and households. We will visit the ruins of palace and temple breweries uncovered by archaeologists. We will encounter taverns owned by private individuals, family firms, and entrepreneurial priestesses, taverns where customers could acquire beer in exchange for payment, taverns that paid taxes to the state in the form of spent grain, taverns that were frequented by sex workers plying their trade. We will even see an elaborate ritual conducted to guarantee future profit for the owner of a tavern. We will examine letters in which housewives are instructed to buy grain on the market to make beer, and we will visit houses where excavators uncovered the remains of home brewing equipment and ingredients. Beer was both an item of intense governmental concern—a crucial part of the institutional economy—and a commodity produced, purchased, and consumed by private individuals without any sort of state intervention.

Beer and inequality

From at least the Uruk period onward, Mesopotamia was a society of unequals, of haves and have-nots—or at least a society of some who had a whole lot more than many others. The question of exactly how this situation came to be and how it played out over the centuries has captured the attention of generations of scholars.[25] Some early voices suggested a straightforward case of top-down exploitation: An emerging priestly class, exercising a monopoly on access to the divine, had cunningly managed to dupe the ignorant masses into accepting a new status quo that allowed for unheard-of levels of wealth inequality.[26] According to this reading, the temples at the heart of Mesopotamian cities were not products of a sincere devotion to the gods but parasitic financial institutions designed to funnel wealth to a privileged few. This decidedly bleak view of raw economic calculation masquerading as religion should definitely be tempered, but it's undeniable that the growth of institutional power in Mesopotamia was accompanied by a shift in the distribution of wealth. And the general, cumulative trend over the centuries—though such things can be difficult to measure and many caveats could be raised—was almost certainly toward an increasing gulf between the richer and poorer segments of the population.

At the same time, inequality was not just a matter of relative wealth. From the very earliest days of state making in the region, we have evidence for warfare, prisoners of war, and the enslaving of human beings. Mesopotamia may never have been a slave society on par with Classical Greece or Rome, but enslaved persons—whether captured in battle or sold into debt slavery—were present in substantial numbers throughout the history that we will explore in this book. There is also the fundamental issue of gender inequality. This was a patriarchal society that did not, in general, afford the same opportunities to women as to men. That fact is inescapable. But we will see that women were active across many domains and occupied a wide variety of roles, some of which offered a substantial degree of economic, legal, and/or professional autonomy.

The lines of difference that cut across Mesopotamian society were far from static. Inequities rooted in wealth, slavery, gender, age, status, profession, etc., evolved over time. And beer was a key element in this dynamic landscape—aiding in the production, maintenance, papering-over, and undercutting of all these different sorts of difference. The drinking of beer, for example, could bring people together and help build bonds of camaraderie and community. But it could also foster division, exclusion, and disparity. And it could do all of this at once. The unifying force of joint beer consumption was exploited time and again in Mesopotamia history but often in contexts that also allowed space for the marking of social difference.

So, when we see the inhabitants of Early Dynastic city-states coming together for community-affirming ritual festivities, the citizenry of Late Bronze Age towns sharing food and drink in a temple courtyard, or tens of thousands of imperial subjects summoned for an enormous feast to celebrate a new Neo-Assyrian palace, the unifying potential of a shared drink will be on full display. But keep your eyes open for the flip side, for signs of special treatment for a restricted few, for the flaunting of wealth and status on a public stage, and for other indications of inequality and exclusion. When we consider the elite banquets that appear so often in the artistic record, the exclusionary element is hard to miss. But so are the support staff who made these events possible. The servers, singers, harpists, and dancers who populate banquet scenes—not to mention those who labored behind the scenes—deserve our attention just as much as the attendees.

Likewise, when we sift through the evidence for beer production, note the gendered dimensions of the brewing industry. Why is it, for example, that women were the ones doing the brewing at home and in the tavern, under the benevolent eye of the goddess of beer, while men occupied the position of brewer at the institutional level? Is this a straightforward case of gender discrimination in hiring practices or perhaps the result of a gradual usurpation of what was once considered a distinctly female art? Or is it, in fact, an illusion generated by the source material available? We will explore these questions of equity and difference and many more in the pages to come. As today, beer may have been the quintessential drink of the masses in ancient Mesopotamia, but it was also a potent means of distinguishing us from them on many different levels.

Beer can open up new perspectives on these four big questions— questions about the state, the city, the economy, and inequality—because it was a unique sort of product: an everyday foodstuff that was also an intoxicating substance and a powerful symbol of abundance, belonging, sociability, celebration, and the good life. In ancient Mesopotamia, beer was many things at once, and it occupied a complicated position within a world sometimes strikingly similar and sometimes radically different from our own. If you want to understand what life was really like in the Land Between the Rivers, there's no better place to begin than beer.

Chapter 3

Beers and brewing ingredients

I would make the beer sweet but my neighbor would not appreciate it.

Sumerian proverb[1]

The archaic texts from Uruk

The year is 3000 BCE (give or take). We're in Uruk, the largest city in the world, home to somewhere in the vicinity of 40,000 people.[2] A man named Kushim steps out of his front door onto a bustling street and begins making his way toward the city center. It's still early and still pleasant out. Here in the southernmost reaches of ancient Sumer, the summer heat can be intense. As he reaches an intersection, Kushim glances down the cross street to his right. He can vaguely make out a hint of the Euphrates in the distance, where a morning mist rises from the surface of the wide, slow-moving river. Up ahead, the city skyline is dominated by two high points, illuminated by the slanting rays of the rising sun. Kushim takes in the familiar but still inspiring vista. On the left, a single gleaming white temple sits atop an enormous platform with sloping sides, a thin plume of sacrificial smoke drifting upward toward the realm of the gods. On the right, a cluster of brilliantly decorated monumental buildings clamors for attention atop the second high point, the political, ceremonial, and administrative heart of the city. Kushim is heading in the general direction of this complex. He's on his way to work.

After about 20 minutes of navigating his way through the twisting streets and the various obstacles thrown in his way—errant pigs, a gaggle of children playing catch, porters carting heavy loads of merchandise toward the river—Kushim arrives at his destination. He glances up at the nondescript facade of pale brown mud plaster and takes a deep breath before plunging through the wooden door and into an open courtyard, where he's met with a hive of activity. Two men emerge from a storeroom carrying sacks of grain on their shoulders. Another hefts a basket filled with sprouted grain. Peering into a dimly lit room on the right, he watches two more lug a ceramic vessel brimming with a brownish liquid across the room and pour the contents deftly into another waiting vessel.

After some quick greetings, Kushim heads back across the courtyard, where he stops at a door that's shut tight and secured to the doorframe with a rope wound around a wooden peg. He has a quick look at the lump of clay affixed to the rope and peg. Yes, the image impressed in the clay matches the image on the cylinder seal hanging around his own neck. Whew. No one else has entered the room since Kushim left work yesterday. Everything should be as he left it. He breaks the clay sealing, opens the door, and enters a small room lined in wooden shelves. He heads straight over to a shelf across from the doorway and picks up a squarish piece of hardened clay, about four inches on each side and about half an inch thick. After scrutinizing some markings incised into the clay and consulting another, smaller clay tablet from a nearby shelf, he breathes a sigh of relief. He had spent half the night tossing and turning, but there was no need to worry. Everything matches up. The deliveries of malted and ground barley sent in by the city administration last week line up perfectly with the jars of beer that he sent out for delivery yesterday. All is in order at the brewery. So Kushim heads back out into the courtyard to check in with his team and make sure that everything is set for the day's docket of tasks. There's a festival coming up, and the brewery is on a tight schedule.

At least that's how I imagine it. In sketching out this brief moment in the life of Kushim and the brewery under his supervision, I've taken a few liberties.[3] We don't actually know exactly where the brewery was, what it looked like, or how many people it employed. We don't know that there was a separate, locked room where tablets were stored on shelves. In fact, we can't even say for certain that Kushim was in charge of a brewery. One team of experts has argued that he was, instead, the manager of a storehouse that stocked brewing ingredients.[4] There's even a chance that Kushim wasn't a personal name at all but rather some kind of professional title, institutional office, or administrative unit.[5] And either way, it's unlikely that the word was actually pronounced "Kushim." We don't know how the two proto-cuneiform signs that we refer to as "KU" and "SHIM" (based on parallels with better-known signs from a later time period) would have been read in this early period, if they were intended to be pronounced at all. It's possible that the signs had not yet acquired a clear phonetic reading. That is, they might not yet have been intended to signify specific sounds or words in a specific language.[6] Also, we don't know for certain that this "Kushim" was active in the city of Uruk, as opposed to some other city in southern Mesopotamia.[7]

We don't even know that the tablets Kushim examined—which do exist in real life today in a museum in Berlin—were produced in a brewery or storehouse at all. There's increasing evidence that the administrative documentation of many tasks in ancient Mesopotamia took place elsewhere and after the fact. In other words, there's a reasonable chance that Kushim's tablets were not on-the-spot records, jotted down in the heat of the moment, as each batch of beer was brewed up and sent on its way. Instead, they may have been post hoc efforts to summarize and tidy up a rather messier reality—something like I have to do each year when I put my taxes together and submit them to the government for review.[8]

What we do know is that someone was keeping careful tabs on the production, storage, and delivery of grain and grain products. And the items of interest included beer and brewing ingredients. How do we know this? In 1988 a group of major museums joined forces to purchase a collection of eighty-five proto-cuneiform tablets that had been held in a private collection known as the Erlenmeyer collection. Many of these tablets revolved around the administration of grain products, and eighteen of them specifically mentioned Kushim. As with many objects purchased on the international art market, these tablets were almost certainly illegally excavated (in this case, probably in the late 1950s) and therefore wrenched out of their original archaeological context without any form of recording. They probably came from either Uruk or another city known as Jemdet Nasr, but we may never know for certain.[9] Although a huge amount of potential

information has been lost, they still offer a fascinating glimpse into beer
and brewing at the very beginning of recorded history. As soon as people
had the ability to write things down, they were writing about beer. These
proto-cuneiform or "archaic" texts,[10] dating to about 3000 BCE, are the
earliest known written evidence for beer in the world.

   In total, about 5,820 archaic tablets and tablet fragments (with a date range
of 3200–2700 BCE) are currently known.[11] Most of these, about 5,000 in
total, come from the city of Uruk. And most of the tablets from Uruk were
found in the remains of that cluster of elaborately decorated monumental
buildings that caught the eye of our imaginary Kushim as he made his way
to work. Kushim's morning commute took him in the direction of what we
now call the Eanna precinct, a special zone that later came to be associated
with the goddess Inana, whom we'll meet again in Chapter 7 (Figure 3.1).
Excavations first kicked off at Uruk in 1912 but really got going in 1928.

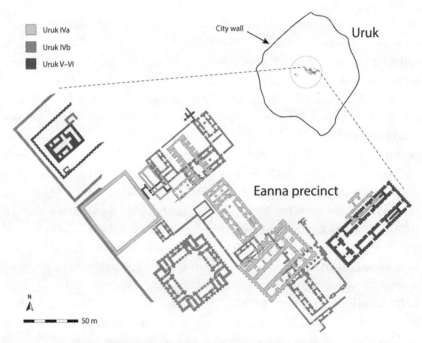

Figure 3.1. Uruk, Eanna precinct. The location of the Eanna precinct within
the site of Uruk is shown at the top right. Different colors of gray indicate
architecture dating to the Uruk V–VI, Uruk IVb, and Uruk IVa phases. (Lamassu
Design, https://creativecommons.org/licenses/by-sa/3.0/deed.en, with
adjustments to orientation, coloring, labels, and legend)

Since then, German teams have mounted annual campaigns at the site, interrupted only by war and the resulting local and regional instabilities.[12] The results of this long commitment to the site of Uruk have been impressive, to say the least.[13] Remains from many different time periods have been uncovered, but the monumental constructions of the Eanna precinct and the associated archaic texts are the most famous finds.

The Eanna precinct was the ceremonial heart of the city of Uruk—a dramatic landscape of bright colors, imposing architectural facades, spacious courtyards, and columned halls. Whatever was happening here, it was clearly something special. But what was it? What purpose did this capacious and grandiose complex serve? Who was allowed in? Who was not? And what did they do there? Many opinions have been offered, but we don't really know. Some of the buildings were almost certainly temples. To anyone familiar with the architectural traditions of earlier and later Mesopotamia, their floor plans cry out "temple!" The floor plans of other buildings are much less vocal, not nearly so transparent in asserting a function. And the frustrating thing is, we have little to go on besides floor plans.

In most cases, all that was left of the buildings in the Eanna precinct was wall foundations or wall stumps. When these buildings went out of use, they were torn down, their remains leveled off, carted away, dumped into pits, used as leveling fill, and otherwise redeposited in preparation for new constructions. If any archaeologists had been present for these demolition events, tears would have been shed. Sure, it's nice that they left behind those bits of wall foundation—something is better than nothing, after all—but did they really have to do such a thorough job, removing all traces of the building interiors? Demolition crews and cleanup crews (and just super tidy people in general) are a thorn in the side of the archaeologist. We much prefer a good rapid, unexpected abandonment—think fire, volcanic eruption, invasion—where everybody drops all of their stuff in surprise and hightails it. What we want is in situ evidence, that is, artifacts and other remains left in their original place of use or discard. In the case of the Eanna precinct, what we have instead is redeposited material: debris moved here and there, perhaps carted in from somewhere else (who knows where), and unceremoniously (we presume) dumped into pits and used as leveling fill. The upshot is that we have virtually no way of knowing what once took place in many of the buildings, except through inferences based on the preserved floor plans. And all that construction and destruction work left behind a stratigraphic mess that has proven difficult for archaeologists to untangle.[14]

Why have I gone on this little digression about archaeological uncertainty and preservation conditions in the Eanna precinct? Because this is where the 5,000 archaic texts from Uruk were recovered. In many cases, our best guess is that the tablets were originally produced and archived somewhere in the general vicinity, before being deemed no longer relevant and discarded and/or used as construction material. But we can't be certain. Archaeologists care a lot about *context*, that is, the exact location in which an artifact was recovered and all the other objects and deposits found in association with that artifact. Context is a fundamental tool of archaeological interpretation. In the case of the archaic texts from Uruk, we do know something about their context (e.g., tablet x was recovered within leveling fill used to create the foundation of building y), and this context provides us with some information (e.g., tablet x dates to a period before the construction of building y). But, given the importance of these tablets, we're talking about some pretty poor archaeological context. Fortunately, though, it is possible to recognize subphases within the development of the script itself (e.g., script phases Uruk IV and Uruk III), and that allows us to assign a relative date to many of these early tablets (e.g., Uruk IV before Uruk III).[15]

To summarize: The core of the world's first city was occupied by a complex of elaborately decorated monumental buildings. In many cases, we do not know exactly what these buildings were used for. Many of the world's earliest known written documents were found in redeposited debris and the leveling fill that was used to construct foundations for these buildings. We don't know exactly where or when these tablets were produced.

That doesn't sound very promising. But let's have a look at the tablets themselves. They're fascinating, even though they cover only a restricted range of subject matter. As we saw in Chapter 2, the earliest writing in Mesopotamia was not used to record epic literature, philosophical reflections, or royal propaganda. Writing was invented to serve more mundane purposes. Approximately 85% of the known archaic texts are administrative documents.[16] Writing was first and foremost an accounting tool, a means of wealth management for a nascent group of elite power brokers (or, in a more charitable reading, a means of increasing the efficiency of their efforts to manage a complex urban economy). The administrative documents can be broken down into two types: primary and secondary.[17] Primary documents are things like bills and receipts, small tablets that record just the basics about a specific transaction or a group of related transactions (e.g., the types and quantities of goods transferred from one administrative unit to another and the people involved). Secondary documents are more complicated accounts with larger numbers of entries and more complex formatting (e.g., summary accounts that compile information from a series of primary documents). In any case, most of the known archaic texts are administrative documents. The other 15% are lexical lists, collections of words that revolve around some common theme: city names, pigs, vessel types, wooden objects, titles/professions. But that's it: administrative documents and lexical lists.

So what does all of this have to do with beer? Let's get back to Kushim and his brewery (bearing in mind all the caveats that we've already discussed). One thing is certain: Kushim's remit included the management of brewing ingredients. And in this regard he was also concerned with the beer produced using those brewing ingredients. Across the corpus of archaic texts, a number of different pictographic signs were used to refer to beer in general and to specific types of beer (Figure 3.2).[18] There can be no doubt about the pictographic nature of these signs. Each clearly depicts a vessel (though rotated ninety degrees counterclockwise): narrow at the opening and neck, wider at the shoulder, and then ending in either a pointed or rounded base. The signs are then further distinguished with other markings, for example, a vertical line running upward from the

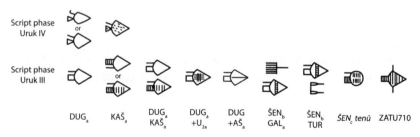

Figure 3.2. Proto-cuneiform signs for beer. Some of these appear to be general designations for beer or containers for beer. Others indicate different types or qualities of beer, but the distinctions are not well understood. We also do not know exactly how these signs would have been read (i.e., the specific words that they represented). The sign names written below are based on the later evolution of the signs in question. (Redrawn after Englund 2001: 29, Appendix)

shoulder or horizontal dashes across the body of the vessel. Unfortunately, we don't currently know how to translate these signs. We don't know, for example, whether the beers were distinguished from one another by color, taste, texture, strength, or something else entirely.

Let's imagine that we're back at the (hypothetical) brewery with Kushim. After a busy morning, rushing here and there to make sure that everything's prepped for next week's festival, he retires to the (hypothetical) archive room for some peace and quiet, a bite to eat, and maybe a short nap. Once he's ready to face the afternoon, he opens the door and steps out briefly into the sun-drenched courtyard, where the rest of his team is lounging in the slivers of shade left behind by the midday sun. He stirs them into action with a few friendly jibes and then turns his mind to his plans for the rest of the day. Perhaps he'll pay a visit to the maltster a few streets over to check up on the batch of malted barley that he's expecting in a few days' time. Or maybe he'll take care of a few household errands that he forgot yesterday. And then he remembers: that pile of paperwork that he keeps putting off. With a sigh, he steps back into the archive room and grabs several small clay tablets from the "to-do" shelf just to the right of the doorway. He spreads these out on a bench in the center of the room and considers each in turn. Each lists a series of beer deliveries sent out from his brewery. His task now is to create a summary tablet that tallies up the beer delivered to several of the destinations that appear in these tablets and then calculate the ingredients used to brew all that beer. If he can't provide a clear demonstration for exactly what he did with all those sacks of barley groats and malted barley sent in last month,[19] there will be hell to pay. He can't afford to fall short again in his monthly accounts and have to cough up the difference from his family's own stocks.[20]

Let's have a look at one of those small "primary" tablets that Kushim pulled off the shelf and then at the "secondary" account that he compiled over the course of the afternoon. These are real tablets—I promise—not figments of my imagination. The first is known as MSVO 3, 6 (Figure 3.3).[21] We're just going to look at the obverse (i.e., front side) of this tablet, which documents the delivery of beer to four different officials. The obverse of the tablet is divided up into a series of cases, that is, boxes defined by a single vertical line running down the center and a series of horizontal lines. Each case contains a unit of information. For example, the second case from the

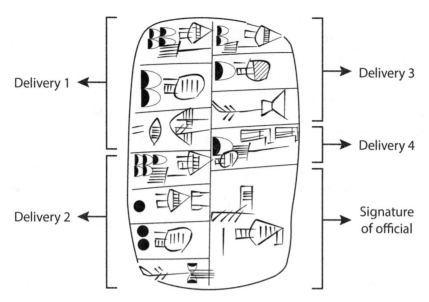

Delivery 1

Delivery 2

Delivery 3

Delivery 4

Signature
of official

Figure 3.3. Primary account documenting the delivery of beer. MSVO 3, 6. 3200–3000 BCE. Dimensions of tablet: 91 (height) x 60 (width) x 18 (thickness) cm. (Redrawn after Nissen et al. 1993: Fig. 39; for dimensions, see https://cdli. ucla.edu/P005317)

bottom on the left side includes one pictographic sign, depicting a jar of a particular type of beer, and two circular numerical signs.

As far as I'm concerned, one of the most fascinating, mind-bending, and just all-around strange aspects of the archaic texts is their treatment of numbers. During later periods, Mesopotamian scribes employed a so-called sexagesimal system. This is a numerical system that combines features of our own base-ten (or decimal) system with a base-six system. For those unaccustomed to working with non-decimal numerical notations, the sexagesimal system is strange enough. But the archaic texts take things to another level. So far, we have good evidence for the simultaneous use of thirteen different numerical systems and tentative evidence for several more.[22] One system was used to measure barley by volume, one, malted barley. Another system was used to count grain products, cheese, and fresh fish. Another was used to count humans, animals, textiles, and wooden implements. Etc., etc. And some signs were shared between systems. A circular impression like the one that appears in MSVO 3, 6, for example, can indicate ten in one system and six in another. So you have to know what is being counted (or at least which numerical system is being used) in order to know what the count is. Why would anyone in their right mind come up with such a convoluted approach to counting? We don't really know, but it's certainly an interesting question. And you can probably imagine the nightmare for anyone attempting to understand these early texts. The decipherment of the archaic numerical systems over the past century stands out as a major (and still ongoing) achievement.

But let's get back to MSVO 3, 6. Many of the cases on the obverse of the tablet provide a simple piece of quantitative information: x jars of y type of beer. But some are different. If you start reading from the top left and follow the cases downward, the third case from the top does not include any number signs. The pictographic signs in this case refer to a specific official. And the preceding two cases indicate the number of jars of two different types of beer that were delivered to this particular official. If we keep reading downward, the final four cases on the left side of the tablet read as follows: 1) five large jars of a particular type of beer, 2) ten small jars of the same type of beer, 3) twenty jars of another type of beer, 4) the name/title of an official. These four cases, documenting the delivery of beer to a specific official, are particularly interesting because they appear verbatim in Kushim's summary account.

That summary or "secondary" account is known as MSVO 3, 11 (Figure 3.4).[23] We will look at both the obverse (front) and reverse (back). The obverse looks very similar to MSVO 3, 6. It lists off the jars of beer delivered to a series of officials or, in some cases, for specific events (probably festivals). What's different is that the information on this tablet has (probably) been compiled from a series of primary documents like MSVO 3, 6. In fact, some of the information may have come directly from MSVO 3, 6. The four cases at the bottom of the central column record exactly the same number of jars of the same types of beer delivered to the same official. So, the obverse of the tablet is a summary account that compiles information about a series of beer deliveries. To understand the real purpose of the tablet, though, we need to flip it over and look at the back.

The reverse is more complicated, and it's all about brewing ingredients. It's signed at the bottom center by Kushim. Let's assume that Kushim was an actual person and that he composed this tablet. His goal on the reverse was to work out the total quantity of brewing ingredients used to brew all of those jars of beer listed on the obverse. The calculation proceeds in three

Deliveries of beer

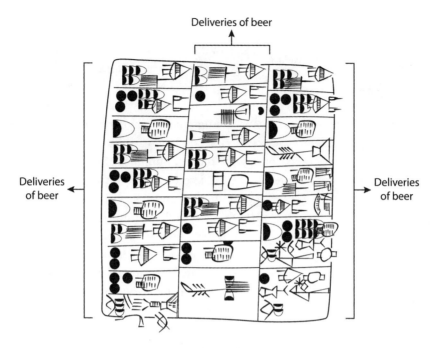

Deliveries of beer

Deliveries of beer

Total jar count for four beer types

Total groats and malt for all beer types

Total groats and malt for four beer types

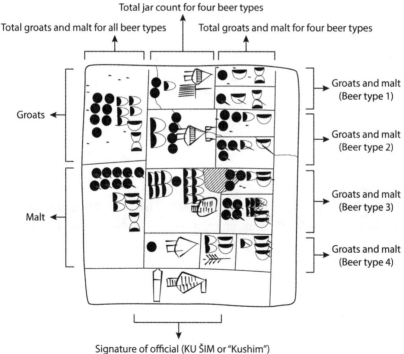

Groats and malt (Beer type 1)

Groats and malt (Beer type 2)

Groats

Groats and malt (Beer type 3)

Malt

Groats and malt (Beer type 4)

Signature of official (KU ŠIM or "Kushim")

Figure 3.4. Secondary account documenting the delivery of beer and brewing ingredients. MSVO 3, 11. 3200–3000 BCE. Obverse above, reverse below. Dimensions of tablet: 107 (height) x 98 (width) x 28 (thickness) cm. (Redrawn after Nissen et al. 1993: Fig. 39; for dimensions, see https://cdli.ucla.edu/P005322)

steps. First, he reviews the other side of the tablet and comes up with a total jar count for each of the four types of beer.[24] These totals appear (for some reason) in the central column on the reverse. The case at the top center, for example, records twenty-one large jars of a particular type of beer. (Interestingly, Kushim actually made a mistake in tallying up these jars. The total should have been twenty-six.[25]) Second, he calculates the quantity of brewing ingredients used to brew the requisite number of jars of each type of beer. These totals are listed in the right column. Two primary ingredients are listed: barley groats (i.e., cracked barley) and malt (i.e., malted barley). For example, the case at the top right records the barley groats used to produce those twenty-one large jars of beer that we've already mentioned. And the case below records the malted barley used to brew those same twenty-one jars of beer. This breakdown is repeated for each of the four types of beer, though again with what looks like an arithmetical mistake for the final beer type. (We'll discuss both groats and malt in more detail below, but I can't resist pointing out the markings that distinguish the numerical system used specifically for recording malt. Each number sign features a little slash that cuts down diagonally toward the bottom right—almost certainly a visual reference to the distinctive root sprout or "chit" that emerges from a germinating grain of barley during the malting process.) Third, Kushim adds up all of the groats and malt from the right-hand column and records a total for each in the left-hand column. He then inscribes his signature at the bottom.

What can we take away from all this? Well, for one thing, the archaic texts are a gold mine of information when it comes to early brewing activities. They tell us about the ingredients used to brew specific types of beer, about the distribution of beer to consumers, and about the organization and administration of the brewing industry. They also tell us that beer was very much an institutional product, its production and distribution carefully monitored by the authorities, and that it was, in fact, a key resource for the emerging institutions. At the same time, these documents hint at the deep roots of a practice well-attested among Mesopotamian administrators during later periods (not to mention their modern counterparts): covering one's butt. In a world of detailed administrative surveillance—one made possible or at least more effective by the invention of writing—Kushim had to provide detailed documentation for his use of brewing ingredients and for the outputs of his brewing activities. We also learn one more interesting fact about Kushim: He was a pretty sloppy administrator. Either that or he was intentionally cooking the books.[26]

The search for beers and brewing ingredients

As we've seen, the majority of the archaic texts uncovered from the city of Uruk were administrative documents. They offer a glimpse into the workings of an increasingly complex urban economy. They also offer a glimpse into the emergence of a new set of institutional organizations intent on managing and monitoring certain aspects of that urban economy. The cuneiform writing system was invented to serve the needs of these institutional organizations. Indeed, throughout Mesopotamian history, the documents available to us for study skew heavily toward the needs and interests of the institutions. Just like today, mounds and mounds of paperwork were generated in the effort to keep track of institutional assets of one kind or another. And those assets included beer and the ingredients used to brew it. Throughout Mesopotamian history, therefore, the cuneiform record includes abundant references to different types of beer and to brewing ingredients.

So what were the main brewing ingredients in Mesopotamia? Sounds like a pretty straightforward question, right? Well, let me assure you: It is not. Before we get down into the nitty-gritty of what we do and do not know about specific brewing ingredients, I would like to offer some preliminary thoughts about *how* we know what we know.

One option is to turn to archaeological remains, that is, physical traces of the ingredients once used to brew beer. Carbonized grain, for example, is regularly recovered by archaeologists. Imagine for a moment that Kushim, finished with the most urgent of his bookkeeping tasks and decidedly unenthused about tackling the rest, sets out for a midafternoon stroll around the neighborhood. He runs into an old friend over by the temple square, and the two decide to catch up over a beer at the tavern. Minutes turn into hours, as they sometimes do at the tavern. When they eventually emerge back into the light of day, there's not much light left. The sun is setting. As he hastily makes his way back to the brewery, Kushim smells smoke in the air. As he gets closer, he hears shouting. He turns a corner, and his heart stops. The brewery is completely engulfed in flames, columns of smoke billowing up into the evening sky. Some neighbors are doing their best to put out the flames, but it's clearly too late. Kushim has heard the horror stories from fellow brewers. He's always been careful to double-check all of the heat sources in the brewery before locking up for the day. But today he's arrived back well after the rest of his team has left. One of them must have forgotten to douse the flame beneath one of the mashing vessels. One little mistake, and everything is gone. Kushim is starting to feel nauseous. How is he going to break the news to his superiors? And how will he ever pay them back for all those sacks of malt and barley groats piled up to the roof beams in the brewery storeroom? He is clearly the responsible party in this scenario. It wouldn't be unheard of to demand one of his children as a debt slave. What's he going to tell his wife? Their worst nightmare has come true. And what was he doing at the crucial moment? Hanging out at the tavern.

If we were to excavate the remains of Kushim's storeroom, 5,000 years in the future, there's a decent chance that we would recover some of the stored grain that went up in flames that day. The sacks would be gone, but carbonized grain survives well in the archaeological record. Would we be able to figure out that this grain was destined for use in brewing? If some of the malted barley was preserved—with clear signs of malting intact—we might. As we'll see, malted barley is a pretty reliable indicator of brewing, but it's only occasionally identified in the archaeological record. (For example, the excavators of the Late Bronze Age site of Kuşaklı Sarissa in Türkiye have used the presence of carbonized barley with signs of malting—alongside other evidence—to argue that one room within a massive temple complex was serving as a temple-brewery.[27]) Without the telltale signs of malting, we would probably be hard-pressed to discern the function of Kushim's storeroom.

What if we excavated one of the brewing rooms instead? Could we hope to recover traces of brewing ingredients left within the vessels used for mashing or fermentation? It's less likely that we would find any macro-botanical traces remaining here, for example, carbonized cereal grains. What we might find is organic residues adhering to the insides of the vessels or preserved within their fabric. This kind of evidence is beginning to emerge in Mesopotamia, but we're still in the early days of residue analysis in the region. What about the tablet room where Kushim kept his archives? What might we recover there in the ashes? The shelves would almost certainly be gone. If the fire burned hot enough and long enough to bake the tablets, however, they would probably survive. And, as we've seen, they contain some fascinating information about brewing ingredients. But accessing and interpreting this information is no trivial matter.

Here we enter the domain of Assyriology. We often speak about the decipherment of the Sumerian and Akkadian languages in the past tense, as if the decipherment process ended with the first successful translation efforts in the mid-nineteenth century. The groundbreaking contribution of these early efforts is undeniable. In a very real sense, they cracked the code to the cuneiform writing system and, as a result, made illegible texts once again legible (for the first time in about 2,000 years). But saying that they "cracked the code" suggests a moment of sudden illumination: They just needed to find the right cipher, plug it in, and everything would fall into place. Sumerian into English. No sweat. Well, that is not how things went down, to put it mildly. Nearly two centuries into the future, the decipherment of the languages of ancient Mesopotamia is still very much an ongoing process.

Assyriology is not a field for the faint of heart (or the impatient). The obstacles standing in the way are substantial, and progress is often slow. Assyriologists are not only confronted with the task of working out the subtleties of a series of long-dead languages recorded in a complicated script that fell out of use 2,000 years ago. They also must accomplish this task armed only with an extremely fragmentary body of source material: an abundant but more-or-less random sampling of ancient documents, subject to the vagaries of preservation and recovery and now scattered across museum collections throughout the world. This is not the place for a detailed introduction to the field of Assyriology. Instead, I would just like to offer a quick thought experiment to give you a flavor for the challenges involved in teasing out information about brewing ingredients.

I've grabbed a selection of text snippets from items around my house that mention the word malt. You're a translator in the future, tasked with researching the meaning of this poorly understood English word, and all

you have to work with is these scraps of text and others like them. What do
you do? How would you approach the problem?

The Original **Malted** Milk Balls™
Naturally and artificially flavored.
Ingredients: Sugar; Whey (Milk); Partially hydrogenated palm kernel oil;
   Corn syrup; **Malted** milk (Barley **malt**; Wheat flour; Milk; Salt; Sodium
   Bicarbonate); Cocoa . . .

For a' his meal and a' his **maut**,
For a' his fresh beef and his saut,
For a' his gold and white monie,
An auld man shall never daunton me . . . [28]

Bairds	Munich	5.0
Bairds	Light Carastan	15.0
Bairds	Carastan (30°-40°L)	34.0
Bairds	Dark Crystal	75.0
Bairds	Extra Dark Crystal	135.0
Bairds	Chocolate **Malt**	475.0[29]

Dortmunder Gold Lager
Balanced & Smooth
A hometown hero, draped in a people-pleasing blend of smooth **malt** and
   crisp hop flavors.
Six 12-oz. cans

It's a pretty daunting challenge, right? Your best bet would probably be (at
the very least) a two-pronged approach, focusing on context and comparison. You might start by doing your best to specify the nature of each text
fragment, potentially a daunting task in itself. With the benefit of insider
knowledge (of the English language and of life in the twenty-first century
CE in general), you can probably make some good guesses. But here's a cheat
sheet for what was listed above: 1) some text from the back side of a box of
Whoppers candy; 2) several lines from the poem "To Daunton Me" by the
Scottish poet Robert Burns; 3) part of a chart showing commercially available malts in the United States (columns: malt company, malt name, average
color SRM, i.e., Standard Reference Method); 4) some evocative advertising
from a box containing a six-pack of Great Lakes Brewing Co. beer. Next,
you might move on to the content of the text. What kind of information
is being conveyed? And where does the word "malt" fit into this? Do the

surrounding words provide any hints about the meaning of this word? With some hypotheses in mind, you might then compare the usage of the term "malt" in the four text fragments. Do you see any similarities? Do these different examples seem to converge around a general zone of shared meaning? Or might the term incorporate several distinct meanings? What does the variant spelling (maut) in one of the texts indicate? Could it be a mistake? Or does it suggest some kind of chronological or regional variation? If the latter, can you assume a stable meaning across time and/or space? If you've had a thorough training in the field, you might also be able to draw on some broader linguistic knowledge about related words, potential etymologies, etc. But I think we can agree that it wouldn't be an easy task.

Now imagine that similar levels of uncertainty apply to many of the other terms that appear in the text fragments: not just names of companies and places but key descriptive terms like "chocolate" and "smooth." And, to throw another wrench in the works, imagine that many letters in the script used to write English can be read in a number of different ways; that is, they can indicate different sounds, either alone or in combination. We already have this in English (e.g., the letters "A," "E," "G," "W," and "T" in the preceding sentence), but crank it up to another level. What if the letter "M" had six different potential phonetic readings, giving us pronunciations ranging from malt, balt, and palt to salt, falt, and valt (each indicating a different word with a different meaning)? And what if the letter "T" had a similarly broad range of readings? And then, finally, imagine that the English word "malt" and its derivatives were regularly written in a completely different language—let's say, Scottish Gaelic. So, on that Whoppers box, imagine that both the words "malt" and "malted" were replaced with the word "braiche." But the word "braiche" was not meant to be read as the Scottish Gaelic term that it is. Instead, whenever you see that word written in an English text, you are intended to read it as "malt" or some other derivative, such as "malted," depending on the context.

Now we're starting to approach the kind of challenges that Assyriologists face in the task of reading texts from ancient Mesopotamia: an abundant but fragmentary collection of texts preserved in bits and pieces across a period of about 3,000 years, cuneiform signs that can be read in many different ways, a complicated intermixing of the Sumerian and Akkadian languages, and significant uncertainties regarding the precise meaning of specific terms. In this context, piecing together information about brewing ingredients and the beers themselves—how they might have looked, tasted, and smelled; variations in quality; their alcohol content, etc.—can be very difficult. As we'll see, many blind spots, uncertainties, and disagreements remain.

Malted barley

Let's dive down into the world of brewing ingredients with a few more text snippets, this time drawn from ancient Mesopotamia, rather than from our own world. These texts were all originally written in Sumerian or a mix of Sumerian and Akkadian. Here, they're translated into English, but I've left the term "munu" untranslated (highlighted in bold type).

When a widow has spread **munu**$_4$ on the roof, the birds did not yet eat that **munu**$_4$ up there. The pigeon then did not tuck the head under its wing.[30]

munu$_4$
watered **munu**$_4$
rinsed **munu**$_4$
sprouting **munu**$_4$
sprouted **munu**$_4$
cleaned **munu**$_4$
compressed **munu**$_4$
munu$_4$ broken apart[31]

The king who used to eat marvellous food grabbed at a mere ration. As the day grew dark, the eye of the sun was eclipsing, the people experienced hunger. There was no beer in the beer-hall, there was no more **munu**$_4$ for it. There was no food for him in his palace, it was unsuitable to live in. Grain did not fill his lofty storehouse, he could not save his life. The grain-piles and granaries of Nanna held no grain.[32]

600 liters **munu**$_3$,
according to the menials' measure,
received (by)
Mutu-ramê.
Among the barley of the threshing floor
Month I,
day 30,
limmu Zabzabu.[33]

For you, I will clear away from the **munu**₄ the droppings of the little birds. For you, I will clear away from the grain the droppings of the rodents. For you, I will clear away from the grain ears the beaks of the locusts. May the lord eat this produce . . . [34]

So what is this mystery ingredient, known as munu in Sumerian? It's malted barley or malt for short. We see mention of barley and rinsing and sprouting and spreading out on a surface. For anyone familiar with modern European-derived brewing traditions, the most obvious candidate has to be malt. And the Assyriologists concur. Indeed, here we have a point of general agreement within the Assyriological community: Mesopotamian beers were built on a backbone of malted barley, known as munu in Sumerian (written munu₄) and *buqlu* in Akkadian.[35] In at least one sense, then, they share a clear kinship with the barley beers that many of us know and love today.

As we saw in Chapter 1, cereal grains like barley, rice, and maize require some processing before they can be transformed into beer. Each kernel of grain is first and foremost a seed (or fruit). Its primary purpose in life is to produce a new plant. At a coarse scale of analysis, each kernel is made up of three key elements: an embryo, a reserve of food for the plant-to-be (held in the endosperm), and an outer husk to protect the contents. The brewer's primary goal is to purloin and repurpose the food reserves—feeding them not to the growing embryo but to the brewer's partners in crime: yeast and bacteria. These tiny, alcohol- and acid-producing machines are happy to do the brewer's dirty work, but they're a little bit picky when it comes to food. They can't metabolize the starches that have been stored up as food in the endosperm. To satisfy the yeast and bacteria, brewers need to find a way to break those starches down into "fermentable" sugars (i.e., sugars deemed acceptable by the microbes). The key to this saccharification process is enzymes: proteins that help accelerate certain chemical reactions, in this case the breaking down of starches into simple sugars. The most important one here is amylase.

As we saw, there are several different ways to access the appropriate enzymes and introduce them to the cereal grains. One can rely on saliva, for example, or molds. One can also hijack the seed's built-in mechanism for breaking down starches by convincing it that it's time to start growing. The secret? Just add water, allow time for a good steep, and then remove from the water. The seed will think that it's time to initiate germination. A set of pre-packaged enzymes will be activated and will get to work on the stored-up starches. Germination can then be abruptly halted via drying or heat—preserving a perfect little package of starches, sugars, and enzymes for the use of the brewer. This sleight of hand is called malting.

Other grains can be and regularly are malted, but malted barley performs particularly well in beer production.[36] And Mesopotamia was up to its ears in barley—especially southern Mesopotamia, where barley was by far the dominant cereal crop.[37] Put these two facts together, and you have a recipe for beer production on a large scale. We don't know exactly when malted barley first arrived on the scene in Mesopotamia, but, by the time of the earliest written documents, malt had clearly become a major focus of institutional attention. Administrators like Kushim were tasked with monitoring this valued commodity and its transformation into beer. The institutional interest in malt endured across the millennia and has left an extensive but highly selective paper trail. Accounting documents generally have very little to say about how malt was produced or how it was used in the brewing of beer. Administrators were concerned, above all else, with accountability: "Here's what I was given (e.g., malt and a team of laborers), and here's what I produced and sent onward (e.g., beer). Everything checks out." So they were primarily interested in documenting those particular moments when barley, malt, beer, and other products changed hands.

A "beer archive" from the site of Tell Leilan (an ancient city variously known as Apum, Šehna, and Šubat-Enlil) in Syria, for example, gives us a detailed glimpse into the world of an official named Mutu-ramê.[38] The 527 tablets that make up the beer archive were all found in one room (Room 12) within a building that the excavators interpret as a palace (the Northern Lower Town Palace or Qarni-Lim Palace).[39] The tablets fall into two groups: Eighty tablets document the receipt of brewing ingredients, and 447 document the delivery of beer to specific individuals and groups. In both cases the official responsible was Mutu-ramê. Although Mutu-ramê probably wasn't a brewer himself, he was clearly responsible for overseeing the production and distribution of beer. And, like other administrators, he was concerned with accountability. When brewing ingredients arrived, he documented receipt of the delivery with a tablet. When the brewery under his care distributed beer to consumers, he documented the delivery with a tablet.

The two most common brewing ingredients delivered to Mutu-ramê were malted barley and barley to be malted. I've already shown you a typical receipt from this archive (see the fourth of the munu documents above):

600 liters of malt received by Mutu-ramê on the thirtieth day of month one in the year of Zabzabu. Thanks to the inclusion of dates on the tablets, we know that the archive documents the delivery of brewing ingredients to Mutu-ramê over a period of twenty-one months. And we can compare the ingredients delivered with the beer distributed during this period of time. Mutu-ramê distributed beer pretty much every day, but he received deliveries of brewing ingredients more sporadically (three to six deliveries per month). Interestingly, there appears to be a mismatch between the quantity of ingredients received and the quantity of beer produced—presumably because we're missing the documentation for some of Mutu-ramê's beer distributions.[40] Perhaps the tablets documenting distributions to some other destination were kept in a different archive for some reason.

Malted barley is all over the place in the written record: in administrative records, lexical lists (the second munu document above), literary tales (the first and third munu documents above), divine hymns (the fifth munu document above), etc., etc. You would be well within your rights to expect a similar showing in the archaeological record. But you would be wrong. Surprisingly few traces of malted barley have been recovered by archaeologists working in Mesopotamia.[41] And there has been no major effort to compile such traces and use them as evidence for the brewing of beer. It's unfortunate. Malted barley is typically considered one of the most reliable archaeological indicators of beer brewing. Malt can certainly be put to other uses—such as malted milk shakes or malted milk balls—but it has overwhelmingly served as a base for beer. So the presence of malt is a pretty dependable sign of brewing activities.

It's just that the archaeological identification of malt can be tricky. First, the barley grains have to be preserved. They usually don't survive well unless they've been charred and carbonized (or deposited in an extremely dry or waterlogged locale). Second, the grains have to show signs of malting. When a grain has been allowed to germinate, for example, a groove-like channel will often be left behind on its dorsal side for the benefit of future archaeobotanists. But the malting process can also render a grain more fragile and, therefore, less likely to survive intact.[42] As we discussed in Chapter 1, though, it's now possible to see signs of malting even when the grains themselves are no longer present. Viewed under a scanning electron microscope, the organic residues left behind within ceramic or stone vessels can preserve traces of tiny starch granules that have been impacted by the malting process. This innovative technique has been used to demonstrate the brewing of beer in a number of recent case studies,[43] but it has not yet been applied to remains from Mesopotamia.

So, even if we can't see it very well in the archaeological record, we know that malted barley was a key brewing ingredient in Mesopotamia. And we know that it was available in significant quantities and regularly moving around the urban landscape. But malt doesn't grow on trees (or stalks). It has to be produced. So what do we know about the production of malt in Mesopotamia? How was malting accomplished? Where? With what equipment? And by whom? Unfortunately, no step-by-step description of the malting process has been preserved. Instead, we have to make do with a complicated body of Sumerian and Akkadian terminology, supplemented by occasional, brief, and not always crystal-clear literary vignettes.

In Box 3.1 I have provided a brief summary of the main stages in the malting process and the relevant Sumerian/Akkadian terms. This table is far from comprehensive. The ancient terminology is scattered across

Box 3.1 Stages in the malting process

We can only outline the malting process in a very basic sense. Here I provide a rough and very tentative outline of the main stages, with the relevant Sumerian and/or Akkadian terminology (after Stol 1989: 323–325, Sallaberger 2012: 316–317).

"Soaking" barley for malt	*ana buqli ṣapûm*
Allowing barley to "rise" or swell	*rabûm*
"Horn grows"	munu$_4$ si mu$_2$
"Horn comes out" (i.e., germinated malt)	munu$_4$ si e$_3$
"Horned" malt, "sprouted"	*qarnānum, nurbu*
Bringing malt to "roof" or "drying floor"	ur, *meštû/maštû*
"Layering" or "spreading" malt out to dry	*kamārum*/šu-du-ul, *šeṭûm*
Dry sprouted barley	še-si-UD-DU-a
Winnowing of malt germ by "blowing" or "plucking"	*našāpum, napāṣum*
Winnowed malt	*nušaptum, tappīṣum*
"Roasting" of malt	*šawûm*
Purified/kilned malt	munu$_4$-ME-a
Coarsely grinding malt	*hašālum*/gaz
Ground malt	ba-ba munu$_4$

a diverse collection of cuneiform documents spanning the full span of Mesopotamian history and, in many cases, is subject to ongoing debate among Assyriologists. In a nutshell, though, the cuneiform record includes potential references to steeping, germination, drying/heating (to halt germination), cleaning, grinding, and perhaps further modification with heat (to result in malt cakes or some other roasted/toasted product). We also learn that malting was conducted by professional "maltsters" (munu$_{3/4}$.mu$_2$, munu$_4$.e$_3$ / $b\bar{a}qilu$),[44] and there are references to "malt houses."

This does not mean, however, that malting was *only* conducted by specialist maltsters working in dedicated, special-purpose facilities. The maltsters that appear in written documents were by and large institutional employees. Perhaps they moonlighted on the side—producing malt for other customers—but we are left in the dark about that aspect of their work. I'm going to keep hammering this point home, because it's important: The written record in Mesopotamia skews heavily (but not entirely) toward the interests of the institutional organizations and elite households. Only seldom (and/or in an oblique fashion) do cuneiform documents shed light on what ordinary people did in the privacy of their own homes, places of business, etc. Take the example of the widow spreading green malt out on the roof to dry in the first munu document above. Occasional glimpses of daily life like this are just the tip of an enormous iceberg.

Archaeology offers one means of probing the depths of that submerged iceberg. But there's a catch. We don't have a clear understanding of the archaeological signature of malt production, that is, the set of physical remains that would be left behind in a space once used for malt production. As we've already seen, direct traces of malted barley are hard to come by. That places the burden of proof on other "archaeological correlates": for example, equipment used in the malting process or byproducts of the process. And here I think we run up against a two-pronged problem of inappropriate expectations and ambiguous evidence.

First, expectations. We should not expect to find what we often think of as "traditional" malting today: the European floor malting tradition, for example, where large quantities of malt are spread out in huge, cavernous spaces to germinate. We need to think much smaller in scale. A look at the ethnographic literature offers up more promising analogues—for example, malting operations where soaking and germination take place within a medium-size ceramic vessel and the malt is then spread out in the sun to

halt germination. The equipment required is often pretty minimal: a ceramic vessel or two, some kind of ladle, perhaps a sieve, and maybe a mat to
spread beneath the drying grain. And the same goes for spatial requirements.
A small courtyard or some unencumbered roof space is often sufficient for
the drying stage.

Let's take the brewery at Tell Leilan as an example. In the text discussed
above, Mutu-ramê receives 600 liters of malted barley. How much is 600
liters? It's about the volume of two standard-size bathtubs. Sometimes
Mutu-ramê received more than this and sometimes less. And sometimes he
received barley that he was meant to malt himself, as much as 1,200 liters.
If his facility needed to malt that full 1,200 liters of barley in one batch,
they still wouldn't necessarily require a huge amount of space—perhaps
just a decent-size courtyard or rooftop where they could spread out four
bathtubs' worth of barley. To spread 1,200 liters of barley out to a depth
of, say, 2 centimeters, a space of about 8x8 meters would suffice.[45] Even
allowing for the fact that that 1,200 liters of barley would have expanded
in volume during the germination process, we're still not talking about a
massive space requirement.

The second problem is ambiguous evidence. Imagine for a moment that
you're an archaeologist (. . . or, if you already are an archaeologist, imagine
that you're this particular archaeologist). You're nearing the end of a three-
month field season in southern Iraq. The last two weeks have been brutal, as
you and the rest of the team push yourselves to complete everything before
the end of the season. You've been supervising excavations in a residential
neighborhood that dates to the Old Babylonian period (2004–1595 BCE).
Previous seasons have revealed mainly private homes. This season, though,
your team has just finished excavating one corner of what seems to be a
larger, nonresidential building oriented around an open-air courtyard about
10 meters on each side.[46]

The one room that you've excavated completely includes three medium-
size ceramic vessels lined up along one wall, all smashed in place when the
roof collapsed 4,000 years ago. These have the look of storage jars. Against
the perpendicular wall lie two more, smashed, medium-size vessels. They're a
little more globular in shape but are otherwise pretty generic looking. They're
not obviously cooking vessels and do not, for example, bear any clear traces of
burning on the exterior. A small cup was recovered within one of the vessels.
In the opposite corner of the room, there's a large oven, whose domed roof

has collapsed in on itself. The project archaeobotanist has been examining bag after bag of soil samples, as you haul them in each day, but has yet to identify any well-preserved plant remains. What do you make of this room? How would you connect the dots to arrive at the correct interpretation? (Hint: In my imagination, the courtyard building that I've described was once a brewery. This room and its long-vanished roof were dedicated to malting. It had vessels for storing raw and malted barley, vessels for soaking and germination, a flat space on the rooftop for drying the germinated barley, and an oven for roasting it. But, from the perspective of the archaeologist, all of this equipment could also have served a variety of other purposes.)

The problem with malting is that it didn't necessarily require any distinctive, purpose-built equipment. Or, if it did, we don't currently know what that equipment was. A space dedicated to malting might look very similar to a space used for a variety of other tasks. And, especially if we're looking for malting activities on the household scale, malting might have been conducted within the same space as many other household activities, perhaps using exactly the same equipment. There's no guarantee—in fact, it's very unlikely—that every household had its own special malting room fitted out with a dedicated set of ceramic vessels, etc.

A number of scholars, though, have suggested that ovens might offer a way out of this impasse. If we could demonstrate that ovens of a particular type were used either for halting germination (an alternative to spreading the malt out in the sun) or for roasting the finished product, these distinctive ovens could serve as a sort of "marker" for malting activities. We could, for example, seek some guidance from the island of Cyprus, where archaeologists have interpreted an odd, oven-like feature as a malt-drying kiln.[47] They've even put their interpretation to the test by building replica ovens, malting their own barley, roasting it, and using it to brew beer. Back in Mesopotamia, a number of excavated ovens have also been tentatively linked with malting: for example, at the site of Umm el-Jīr in Iraq and at the sites of Hamoukar, Tell Arbid, and Tell Hadidi in Syria.[48] Unfortunately, the actual evidence for how each oven was used is pretty slim. What we would really like to see, in each case, is some in situ traces of malted barley to clinch the argument, but we've had no such luck so far.

So that's where things stand in regard to malted barley, one of the two fundamental brewing ingredients in Mesopotamia. Let's turn our attention now to the other: bappir.

Bappir

Beer has often been imagined as bread in liquid form. Liquid bread. To equate beer with bread is to highlight the nourishing, life-sustaining properties of the beverage. For many people past and present, beer has served as a fundamental source of daily sustenance, and beer certainly did function as a form of food in Mesopotamia. Here, though, I would like to highlight another sense in which the beers of Mesopotamia might qualify as liquid bread. It is possible that the other key brewing ingredient, alongside malted barley, was in fact a sort of bread or cake. In other words, Mesopotamian beer might have been brewed with bread. Or it might not have been. It depends whom you ask. Let's have a look at this other fundamental but enigmatic brewing ingredient, known as "bappir" in Sumerian (written bappir₃, bappir₂, bappir)⁴⁹ and "*bappiru*" in Akkadian (written either syllabically or using a logogram).⁵⁰

Bappir is sometimes translated as "beer bread," but this might be misleading. To avoid any confusion, let's just stick with the original Sumerian term bappir. This product appears in hundreds of cuneiform documents: administrative records, lexical lists, letters, literary texts, recipes, etc. And there can be little doubt that its primary use was for the brewing of beer. But what exactly was bappir, and what role did it play in the brewing process? Here we enter trickier territory. Assyriologists have been piecing together evidence and theorizing about the nature of bappir for more than a century, and still there is no solid consensus.⁵¹ And this particular puzzle is tightly bound up with a series of other points of uncertainty and contention (regarding both the translation of specific terms and the brewing process more generally).

Here, for example, you see two different translations—the first by Miguel Civil, the second by Walther Sallaberger—of the same passage from the most famous of Mesopotamian brewing documents: the Hymn to Ninkasi, goddess of beer.

> Ninkasi, you are the one who handles dough (and) . . . with a big shovel,
> Mixing, in a pit, the **bappir₂** with sweet aromatics.
> You are the one who bakes the **bappir₂** in the big oven,
> Puts in order the piles of hulled grain.⁵²

Ninkasi, your rising dough, it was formed with the stately spatula,
an aroma of mellow honey, the mixed **babir**$_2$,
your **babir**$_2$ (clumps), they were baked in the stately oven,
they are neatly arranged sheaves of gu$_2$-nida-emmer.[53]

The differences might seem relatively minor, but the two translators—
both of them highly accomplished Assyriologists—have, in fact, proposed
very different interpretations of bappir. The first, Miguel Civil, envisions
bappir as a barley bread that was flavored with aromatic herbs and employed during the mashing stage.[54] As part of an experimental brewing
effort in the late 1980s, for example, he and his collaborators chose to
re-create bappir as a twice-baked bread akin to biscotti. They added this
crunchy, granola-like bread directly to the mash, where it could contribute starches, proteins, and flavors for the beer-to-be (see Epilogue).[55]
The second, Walther Sallaberger, envisions bappir as a sourdough, that
is, an actively fermenting dough colonized by a mixed culture of yeast
and bacteria. This sourdough could be, but was not always, dried out in
an oven for purposes of storage and transportation. Its primary function within the brewing process was to permit the intentional addition of yeast in a controlled and reproducible fashion. In Sallaberger's
scenario, bappir would not have been added to the mash but, instead,
would have been added later in the process as a fermentation starter.[56]
Both are reasonable interpretations, backed up with careful reference to the cuneiform record and detailed philological arguments. But
both cannot be correct (unless, of course, bappir was a rather nebulous category that encompassed a broad range of bread-like or bread-
adjacent brewing ingredients that could be used in different ways . . .
but this seems unlikely).

So what exactly do we know about bappir? We know that it was made with
barley. Administrative documents, for example, regularly record the delivery of
barley (še in Sumerian, še'u in Akkadian) specifically earmarked for the production of bappir.[57] We also know that bappir was sometimes flavored with
"aromatics" and/or a sweet syrup (usually date syrup, sometimes honey).[58]
As we just saw in the Hymn to Ninkasi, the preparation of bappir could also
involve the mixing of a dough and the use of some kind of oven or stove.[59]
These last points find support in administrative documents from the town of
Garšana (Ur III period, 2112–2004 BCE), which reference workers who were
"employed at kneading . . . bappir" and "employed at baking bappir,"[60] and also
in a vignette from a literary text known as the "Debate Between Sheep and
Grain."

Again, Grain addressed Sheep: "When the **bappir** has been carefully prepared in the oven, and the titab tended in the oven, Ninkasi (the goddess of beer) mixes them for me . . . [61]

In lexical lists (i.e., vocabulary lists), we get some hints about the different ways in which bappir could be processed or, perhaps, different stages in the production of bappir. For example, the following list (in Sumerian with accompanying Akkadian equivalents) includes spread, crushed, soaked, dried, and cleaned bappir.

> **Bappir**
> spread **bappir**
> just right **bappir**
> crushed **bappir**
> soaked **bappir**
> dried **bappir**
> cleaned (?) **bappir**[62]

Different types and/or qualities of bappir were also recognized.[63] Several documents from Garšana (Ur III period, 2112–2004 BCE), for example, record the use of ordinary bappir and good bappir to brew ordinary beer and good beer for a series of funerary feasts honoring a man named Šu-Kabta. In the example shown here, I've translated the ancient measurements into approximate metric values. We'll return to these documents and to Šu-Kabta in Chapter 7.

> 40 kg good **babir$_2$**
> 50 kg ordinary **babir$_2$**
> 442.5 liters malted barley
> 40 liters good groats
> 300 liters ordinary groats
> 300 liters good beer and 600 liters ordinary beer[64]

At Garšana, bappir was always measured by weight, but elsewhere—for example, in the city of Girsu during the Early Dynastic and Ur III periods—it was regularly measured by volume. In other cases, it was measured by count or by the jar or sack (perhaps loaves or cakes or clumps).[65] We also have at least one reference to bappir that has gone bad. In a letter dating to the Old Assyrian period (2000–1775 BCE), a woman named Tarām-Kūbi (1895–1865 BCE) writes to her husband Innāya, a merchant who has moved abroad to conduct business. She implores him to send funds so that the stocks of barley in the family household (that she currently occupies) can be replenished.

> Send me silver before your arrival, and let it be deposited in your sealed storehouse. Concerning all the silver to be sent, do not be afraid; the silver will indeed come to your house. Now is the (harvest) season! Send silver so they can store barley for you before your arrival. The **bappiru** I made for you has become too old.[66]

It's also worth mentioning that, as far as we can tell, bappir was used primarily for brewing beer. But it does sometimes appear as a cooking ingredient: for example, in a recipe for a vegetable stew called "Unwinding," where dried bappir is crushed and scattered over the dish before serving.[67]

> Unwinding. Meat is not used. You prepare water. You add fat. (You add) kurrat, cilantro, salt as desired, leek, garlic. You pound up **bappiru**, you sift (it) and you scatter (it) over the pot before removing it.[68]

But bappir was first and foremost a brewing ingredient.[69] In fact, the word for brewer (Sumerian lunga, Akkadian *sirāšû*) was written with the logograms "lu$_2$" (meaning "man") and bappir$_2$.[70]

These scattered hints about the nature of bappir leave a lot of room for uncertainty and debate—many puzzles still to solve. *First*, what exactly was bappir? Was it a bread? Or a cake? Something closer to granola, biscotti, or crostini? Or, as some evidence suggests, a dry powder of sorts? Did it perhaps appear in a variety of different forms? And was it a fermented product akin to sourdough? *Second*, what exactly was bappir made with? Definitely barley, but was it malted or unmalted? And what else? *Third*, how did bappir fit into the brewing process? Was it added directly to the mash to contribute fermentable sugars and flavors? Or was it added later to initiate fermentation? Or did it play some other role entirely? *Fourth*, did the term bappir/ *bappiru* retain its precise meaning across the millennia of Mesopotamian history? Were the individuals writing in the Early Dynastic period referring to exactly the same product as those writing in the Old Babylonian period (seven hundred years later) or the Neo-Babylonian period (almost 2,000 years later)? *Fifth*, who made the bappir, where did they make it, and with what equipment? *Sixth* and finally, how essential was bappir to the brewing process? Was all beer brewed with bappir? Or only certain types of beer? Or only beer brewed by certain individuals or institutions? These are all open questions.

No comprehensive study of the written evidence for bappir exists, but many specialists have weighed in on the issues and have come up with creative ways of interrogating the evidence. From early on, for example, attention has been devoted to the specific cuneiform signs used to write the word bappir. The long-standing assumption that bappir was a sort of "beer bread" rests in part on such evidence. During the Early Dynastic period, the word could be written by combining two pictographic signs: a sign meaning "bread" (depicted visually as a bowl) written inside a sign that could be read "beer" (depicted visually as a jug). Hence, beer bread. There are plenty of reasons to doubt this interpretation, not least the fact that bappir could also be written in other ways that do not permit such a straightforward reading.[71] The effort to extract information about bappir from "paleography" (i.e., the study of the conventions of the cuneiform writing system) is a tricky business.

And the same goes for "metrology" (i.e., the study of measurements). Let's look at one quick example—an effort to understand the density and texture of bappir during the Ur III period—to illustrate the kind of data that's available and the kind of results that can be achieved.[72] The argument is a little complicated, but I think it's worth the effort. We need to start with one key piece of background information. Today, if we want to compare the value of two different products, we typically express that relative value in monetary terms. Product A is worth x dollars, and product B is worth y dollars. For us, money functions as a universal standard of value. In Mesopotamia, there was no exact equivalent to money as we know it today, but they did employ standards of value in a similar fashion. Relative value could be expressed in silver (by weight), for example, or barley (by volume). Here, we're particularly interested in the use of barley as a standard of value. Institutional administrators regularly applied mathematical conversion factors to translate the value of particular quantities of particular products (e.g., bappir) into equivalent volumes of barley. These barley values are the linchpin of the argument. (Note: Volume measurements here are recorded in sila, written $sila_3$, and weight measurements in mana. These ancient units of measurement can be translated into the metric system as follows: 1 $sila_3$ ≈ 1 liter, 1 mana ≈ 0.5 kg.).[73]

To calculate the density of bappir, we need to know the weight of a given volume of bappir (density = weight/volume). But the scribes of Mesopotamia recorded bappir either by weight or by volume, not both at the same time. So we need to get a little creative. How might one establish a connection between bappir measured by weight and bappir measured by volume? The answer is barley value. We have several documents that specify the barley value for specific *volumes* of ordinary bappir (measured in sila$_3$) and several other documents that specify the barley value for specific *weights* of ordinary bappir (measured in mana). If we break down the numbers in these documents, we learn that barley value was calculated as follows.

1 sila ordinary bappir = 1⅕ sila barley
1 mana ordinary bappir = 1⅕ sila barley

As luck would have it, both 1 sila and 1 mana of ordinary bappir have the same barley value: 1⅕ sila barley. In other words, 1 sila of ordinary bappir (a volume measurement) is equal to 1 mana of ordinary bappir (a weight measurement).

1 sila ordinary bappir = 1 mana ordinary bappir

We can take this one step further and argue that 1 sila of ordinary bappir weighed 1 mana. To calculate the density of this bappir, we just need to divide weight by volume. So the density of ordinary bappir would be 1 mana/sila. Translated into the metric system (see above), this gives us a density of 0.5 g/cm^3. We can then compare this density with some other grain-based products from our own world.[74]

Density of ordinary bappir = 1 mana/sila = 0.50 g/cm^3
Density of sandwich bread = 0.23 g/cm^3
Density of brioche bread = 0.27 g/cm^3
Density of proofed lean bread dough = 0.47 g/cm^3
Density of rye bread = 0.58 g/cm^3
Density of pumpernickel bread = 1.09 g/cm^3

The suggestion here is that a density of 0.5 g/cm^3 indicates that bappir was a dry and airy bread of some sort.

One further calculation, again based on barley value, lends extra support to this assessment. In this case, we can compare the barley value of "good bappir" (babir$_2$ saga$_{10}$) and "crushed good bappir" (babir$_2$ saga$_{10}$ naĝa$_3$). A given volume of crushed good bappir had twice the barley value of good bappir. In other words, crushed good bappir was twice as dense as good bappir.[75] The upshot is that good bappir lost half of its volume when crushed. This suggests that the good bappir was a light, airy, bread-like product.[76]

I think it's a solid argument. And I suspect that those scholars who envision bappir as a dried out, fermented dough that functioned as a fermentation starter are correct.[77] As we'll discuss further in the Epilogue, I have tested this version of bappir in a series of brewing experiments that demonstrated the basic viability of the idea. And there's plenty of evidence for analogous products in our world today.[78]

From my own perspective, though, one big question is what bappir production, storage, and use would look like archaeologically. Some archaeologically recovered ovens have been tentatively linked with bappir production, but the evidence is slim.[79] Beyond the possibility of special-purpose bappir ovens, it's entirely possible that bappir production would have left behind relatively few physical traces. Equipment-wise, for example, the production of a fermentation starter called *nuruk* in Korea requires little more than a stone grinder, a wooden mold, a cloth, and some straw (most of which would not typically survive well in the archaeological record).[80] With the increasing application of residue analysis, there may be some hope of following the lead of scholars working in Egypt, where residues have been used to interrogate the assumption that bread was used in the brewing of Egyptian beer.[81] But, ultimately, our broader uncertainty about the nature of bappir means that it's difficult to know exactly what it is that we should be searching for.

Other grains and grain products

From the lightest mass-market American lager to the darkest dunkel and the inkiest black stout, many of today's most beloved beers owe their distinctive colors and flavor profiles to the addition of unmalted grains ("adjuncts") and/or malted grains that have been processed in some fashion ("specialty malts"). The same was true in ancient Mesopotamia. We may be a little hazy on some of the details—surprise, surprise—but at least some beers included these additional elements. A number of grains and grain products make an appearance. In the Early Dynastic city of Girsu, for example, "golden beer" (kaš$_2$ sig)[82] was sometimes brewed with equal parts malted barley, unmalted emmer wheat, and bappir. "Dark beer" (kaš$_2$ gi$_6$) on the other hand, was brewed with one part malted barley, one part bappir, and two parts of another grain product known as titab.[83] Let's look at a few of these grain-based ingredients, beginning with the unmalted grains and then moving on to two products of uncertain or, at least, debatable character.

Two unmalted grains make a regular appearance in the beers of Mesopotamia: barley (še/še'um)[84] and emmer wheat (ziz$_2$/kiššatu).[85]

Each appears primarily in processed form. For example, the Sumerian word imĝaĝa and Akkadian word *dišiptuḫḫu* almost certainly refer to dehusked (or hulled) emmer, a key ingredient in many beers.[86] As we already saw in the Archaic Texts from Uruk, groats were also a key ingredient in the brewer's arsenal. Known as niĝara in Sumerian and *mundu* in Akkadian, groats could be produced from either barley or emmer wheat.[87] And different qualities were recognized: for example, ordinary, second-quality, and good groats.[88] But what exactly were these groats? Here I think there's some potential for confusion. The term "groats" can refer to a grain from which the husk/hull has been removed. But it can also refer to a dehusked grain that has been coarsely crushed, cracked, or cut. My sense is that Assyriologists have this second meaning in mind when they refer to groats. The term niĝara, after all, basically means a thing (niĝ) that has been milled/ground (ara).[89] But it's often difficult to tell exactly which meaning is intended. And what about archaeological evidence for these unmalted grains? Carbonized grains of both barley and emmer wheat are regularly recovered by archaeologists, as are the grinding stones and other equipment that would have been needed to process these grains. Without other corroborating evidence (e.g., malted barley, brewing vessels, beer residues), though, there's little reason to assume that any particular grains were specifically used for brewing.

Let's turn now to two other brewing ingredients of uncertain character. Both involved the use of grain in some fashion, but there's no solid consensus on exactly what that fashion was. First, a product known as titab in Sumerian (written titab$_2$, titab) and *titāpū* in Akkadian.[90]

What do we know about titab? Thanks to a series of documents that record deliveries of barley specifically destined for titab, we know that it was made from barley. And there's a good chance that the barley was malted. In cuneiform documents, the word titab is written using a combination of the signs gug$_2$ (meaning "cake") and munu$_4$ (meaning "malt").[91] Based on this orthographic argument, titab is often assumed to have been some kind of malt cake. If correct, it might explain why titab had its own special-purpose oven. The udun titab or "oven (for) titab" appears in the "Debate Between Sheep and Grain" and also in lexical lists among other oven types.[92]

Interestingly, titab was also spread out on a special-purpose reed mat at some point during the brewing process. The ⁱᵍkid titab / *ki-tu₂ ti-ta-pu* or "reed mat (for) titab" is well attested in the written record. A number of documents record the dimensions of this mat (in the range of 6.0–7.5 m²) and the materials used in its manufacture.[93] During the Ur III period (2112–2004 BCE), for example, one document from the city of Garšana mentions a "reed mat for titab coated with bitumen."[94] And another—which accounts for the work done by a mat weaver over a period of two years—specifies the size of the mat (c. 3.5 x 2m),[95] the materials employed, and the days of labor required.

> 1 reed mat for **titab**, 7 cubits in length, 4 cubits in width. (Manufacture required:) 2[+n bundles] of reeds, 5 liters of house bitumen, 1⅔ date palm spines (and) 1⅓ days labor.[96]

A literary text known as the "Debate Between Reed and Tree" gives us a glimpse into the fate that might befall a titab mat after its usefulness had worn off.

> The large reed mats, when they get old, [are thrown] to the mouth of the kiln,
> The reed mats for the **titab**, which one used to roll up (carefully) [are now used for] fences.[97]

As we saw in the "Debate Between Sheep and Grain," titab was at least sometimes mixed together with bappir during the brewing process. Indeed, we already saw that titab was used alongside bappir and malted barley to brew "dark beer" in the city of Girsu during the Early Dynastic period. And, importantly, it was *only* used to brew dark beer at Girsu, not the other known beer types. Some further tidbits of information can also be gleaned from lexical lists, where we encounter, for example:

> watered **titab**
> ready **titab**
> "open" **titab**
> spread **titab**
> warm **titab**
> cleaned (?) **titab**[98]

This list of different sorts of titab might offer us a glimpse into the production process, that is, into some of the actions that were performed during the making of titab: watering, spreading out, warming, cleaning. But it's only a very brief glimpse.

In his pioneering translation of the Hymn to Ninkasi (see Chapter 4), Miguel Civil translates titab as "cooked mash."[99]

Ninkasi, you are the one who spreads the cooked mash [titab] on large
    reed mats,
Coolness overcomes . . . [100]

In accompanying notes, he offers the following explication: " . . . once the mash had reached the right point, it was taken out of the oven and spread on reed mats to cool off." It's a little difficult to understand exactly what's going on here. But I suspect that it's a matter of trying to fit a square peg into a round hole—trying to translate an ancient term using modern brewing terminology that is not up to the task (for more on this, see Chapter 4).

We typically use the term "mash" to refer to the porridge-like mixture of malt and water that is heated up in order to activate enzymes in the malt and facilitate the process of transforming starches into fermentable sugars. The most valuable part of that mash is the liquid component. It's the liquid, after all, that will eventually be converted into alcohol to become beer. Spreading (or pouring?) the cooked mash out onto a large reed mat to cool, so that that valuable sugary liquid seeps away and you're left with just the solid matter, strikes me as counterintuitive. Civil almost certainly had something else in mind. But his use of our term "mash" has muddied the waters. Indeed, in a more recent comment on the brewing process, Civil interprets titab as "a dried ingredient made from green malt" that was added to the mash (sun_2 or $sumun_2$) alongside bappir.[101] Unfortunately, this revision has not made its way into the many reproductions of Civil's translation of the Hymn to Ninkasi that are currently out and about in the world and accessible to a general audience. For that matter, even the authoritative Akkadian dictionary—the Chicago Assyrian Dictionary—translates titāpu as "beer mash."[102]

But I think most specialists would agree in broad terms with Civil's reassessment. Most see titab as some kind of malt-based product that went into the mash, for example, to contribute the "dark" elements to dark beer. And many have in mind some kind of cake-like or crumbly product.[103] In his own translation of the Hymn to Ninkasi (see Chapter 4), Walther Sallaberger has recently proposed a different interpretation.[104] He argues that titab was not an ingredient prepared prior to brewing but an intermediate product extracted during the brewing process. Basically, he sees titab as the spent grain left behind after a first round of mashing and fermentation. Still retaining sufficient starches and sugars to fuel a second round of brewing, this solid matter could be collected and dried out to produce dida (another enigmatic product; see Chapter 4).

There's much less to say about the next ingredient, known as ninda kuma in Sumerian (written ninda kum$_4$-ma).

𒉌𒅁𒄣𒈠

The term means something like "bread [ninda] which has had kum done to it."[105] Since kum means "(to be) hot," we can perhaps envision some kind of heating in parallel to titab production.[106] Like titab, ninda kuma appears in documents from the city of Girsu during the Early Dynastic period. And, like titab, it was made from barley. The key difference is that titab was used only in the production of "dark beer" (kaš$_2$ gi$_6$), while ninda kuma was used only in the production of "sweet dark beer" (kaš$_2$ gi$_6$ dug$_3$-ga). So perhaps ninda kuma served a similar purpose to titab but with an additional element (or higher level) of sweetness. And perhaps it was a roasted malt product that would have contributed dark colors and caramelized flavors to the beer. One key metrological detail—four parts barley were used to produce three parts ninda kuma (by volume)—suggests that the malt employed in making ninda kuma had been crushed and sieved so that it was reduced to 75% of its original volume.[107]

Date syrup

The idea of adding date syrup to beer might seem a little odd at first glance, but it's not really so strange. If you're a moderately adventurous beer drinker, there's a decent chance that you've tried something comparable at some point. Honey and various sorts of syrup are regularly added to beers these days. There are basically two options. A brewer can add the syrup early in the process (e.g., during the kettle boil) to boost the concentration of fermentable sugars. Or it can be added after fermentation to contribute sweetness and flavor. The first category would include, for example, beers to which honey has been added prior to fermentation, a pretty common practice among brewers today. Option two is, I think, less common and less familiar to many drinkers. But, when done well, the addition of syrups post-fermentation can lead to delicious results. I'm thinking, for example, of the tradition of adding flavored syrups (e.g., green woodruff or raspberry syrup) to Berliner weisse, a beer style that has seen a resurgence in recent years. And then there's what might be my favorite beer of all time (so far).

The Lambic Doux served from a ceramic pitcher at The Publican restaurant in Chicago was a blend of young lambic, aged lambic, and a rotating cast of flavored candy sugar syrups. I've never been so sad to finish a beer.

I wish I could say that the many tasters who tried our re-created Mesopotamian beers blended with date syrup just before serving shared this sentiment. But they did not. I believe "cloying" was the general consensus. Perhaps we overdid it on the date syrup. Or perhaps this is how the drinkers of Mesopotamia liked their beer. But it's also possible that they would have joined our tasters in turning up their noses at a beer sweetened with date syrup after fermentation. Maybe they were purists: Add the date syrup before fermentation or never. We don't really know.

What is certain is that they did, at least sometimes, add a sweet syrup to their beers. In some cases, this sweet syrup might have been honey, but in most, it was probably date syrup. Although one could get one's hands on honey in Mesopotamia, it was relatively rare, while dates were available in abundance. What's frustrating for us is that they didn't generally distinguish between the two types of syrup in writing. Both were known as lal (written lal$_3$) in Sumerian and *dišpu* in Akkadian.[108]

Occasionally, literary texts do tell us that the syrup added to beer was specifically date syrup (lal$_3$ zu$_2$-lum-ma or "honey of dates").[109] But dates and date syrup are conspicuously absent from the administrative accounting of beer and brewing ingredients until the Neo-Babylonian period (605–539 BCE), when a new kind of "beer" entered the scene: date beer.[110] This was not a barley beer spiked with dates or date syrup. It was an alcoholic beverage made just from dates: in other words, date *wine*. But, just to throw us all for a loop, they decided that there was no need to distinguish the two drinks linguistically. The Akkadian word *šikaru* could now mean either barley beer or date "beer."[111] They did occasionally add a rider to specify either a barley or date beverage, but it was not the norm.[112] This is all to say that dates do appear alongside beer in accounting documents during the first millennium BCE. Prior to this, we just have a few references to "dates (for) drinking" and dates delivered to a brewer for beer.[113] In most cases, neither dates (zu$_2$-lum/*suluppû*) nor date syrup (lal$_3$ zu$_2$-lum-ma) show up during the enumeration of brewing ingredients.[114] So it's entirely possible that date syrup was only occasionally or selectively added to barley beer.

The argument really comes down to just a smattering of references in literary texts. In this passage from a Sumerian text known as "Enki's Journey to Nippur," for example, the god Enki has just traveled from his own city, Eridu, to the city of Nippur to visit his father, Enlil. As soon as he arrives, Enki gets to work preparing beer for a feast. (As another reminder of the wiggle room that exists in our translations, I've provided two different translations of the same passage. Question marks and ellipses indicate points of uncertainty.)

> Enki reached for (?) the beer, he reached for (?) the liquor. He had liquor poured into big bronze containers, and had emmer-wheat beer pressed out (?). In kukuru containers which make the beer good he mixed beer-mash. By adding **date-syrup** to its taste (?), he made it strong. He......its bran-mash.[115]

> Enki approached (to make) beer, he came forward (to prepare) fine beer. Into a bronze tube (?) he poured out the fine beer. At the same time, he mixed emmer-wheat beer. In the kukurru-container he mixed its bran-mash for a good beer. He poured **date syrup** into its mouth—he made it (the beer) good. (When) its bran-mash became syrup, he spread it out to cool.[116]

This text makes clear reference to the use of date syrup (lal$_3$ zu$_2$-lum-ma) as a brewing ingredient.[117] What's not so clear is when Enki added the date syrup and, therefore, how it played into the brewing process.

As we've seen, a sweet syrup could have been added either before fermentation to boost the alcohol content or after fermentation to contribute sweetness and flavor to the finished product. The first translation of "Enki's Journey to Nippur" seems to nod toward both of these options: the date syrup contributes both taste and strength. The second implies neither one nor the other: the date syrup makes the beer good. Of course, the mention of beer-mash and bran-mash could indicate that the date syrup was added before fermentation, during the mashing stage, but this argument would hinge on how one interprets the Sumerian term duh (here rendered as "beer-mash" and "bran-mash" but elsewhere usually translated as just "bran").[118]

So far, the archaeological record has had little to say about the use of date syrup for brewing. But excavations on the islands of Bahrain and Failaka in the Persian/Arabian Gulf have provided a glimpse into the world of date processing, as well as a tentative connection to brewing. There are basically two ways of making date syrup. One is heat. In modern-day Sudan, for example, dates are boiled in water for several hours to break down their flesh. The resulting "heavy, red-brown, honey-like syrup" is then strained through cheesecloth, leaving residues that can be further dissolved into syrup through boiling and straining.[119] The other option is pressure. Accounts from Iraq during the nineteenth and early twentieth centuries CE, for example, describe the heaping up of dates within mud-walled enclosures or containers. The pressure exerted by the pile itself forces the syrup from the dates. It then runs out through outlets in the base where it can be collected in waiting receptacles.[120]

At the site of Ras as Qala'a on the north coast of Bahrain, within a fortified palace dating to the Islamic period, excavations in the mid-twentieth century uncovered two rooms specially built for the extraction of date syrup by pressure.[121] The walls of the rooms were covered in clay plaster, and the gently sloping clay floors were provided with special baulks and channels that led downward toward tanks below floor level. Noting the striking similarity between these remains and the "date honey rooms" (*madbasa* in Arabic) still used in the region at the time, the excavator argued that baskets full of dates would have been piled up at the upper end of each room, the weight of the baskets gradually pressing the juice from the dates. The in-floor channels would then direct the juice downslope into the waiting tanks.

These Islamic-period *madbasa*, which fall well beyond the chronological bounds of the present book, were considered the earliest known examples until similar features were uncovered at the same site of Ras as Qala'a in a building dating to the Kassite period (c. 1600–1500 BCE).[122] Excavations on the island of Failaka in Kuwait have uncovered what may be two further examples, dating to c. 1750 BCE and 1850–1500 BCE.[123] The first of these was located within a whole complex of rooms that might have been dedicated to the extraction and storage of date syrup. In this complex, excavators also recovered a huge ceramic vessel, nearly 300 liters in volume, with a hole pierced in its base. As we will see in Chapter 4, this vessel type is generally taken as a pretty solid indicator of beer brewing. So it's possible that the facility was dedicated to both brewing and the production and storage of date syrup. Taken together, this archaeological evidence from Bahrain and Failaka—neither located within Mesopotamia proper but both closely linked with Mesopotamia for much of their history—offers a glimpse into the evolution of date-processing equipment over a period of several thousand years.

Aromatics

The Reinheitsgebot or "purity law" of 1516 CE famously laid down the law about brewing ingredients in Bavaria. Water, barley, hops. That's it. Anything else, and it's not beer. Today, we're a little more tolerant of deviation from the recipe, but those same three ingredients still take center stage. For many drinkers immersed in the European-derived brewing tradition, in partic- ular, it's difficult to imagine drinking a beer without hops. We even have a thriving subculture of self-proclaimed hopheads devoted to the diverse flavors and aromas of the *Humulus lupulus* flower. But many beers of the past (and present) did not (and do not) include any hops whatsoever. If you're curious about what this hop-free beer might taste like, just check in with your local craft beer store. They'll probably have some options for you to try. Inventive brewers have increasingly been exploring an alterna- tive terrain of aromatic ingredients. Some are explicitly drawing inspiration from the European tradition of "gruit" beers, flavored with a variable mix- ture of herbs (e.g., mugwort, yarrow, heather, sweet gale, juniper berries, ginger). Others are seeking to develop a connection with their local en- vironment and a distinctive local terroir by foraging for ingredients: herbs, fruits, nuts, seeds, mushrooms, flower petals, pine cones, tree branches, bark, leaves, roots, etc.[124]

Like these modern experimental brews, the beers of ancient Mesopotamia were not flavored with hops. How do we know that? Well, to put it bluntly, hops did not exist in ancient Mesopotamia.[125] The interpretation of ancient plant names is fraught territory, but that's the current consensus. No hops. So what additional flavorings, if any, were employed? Unfortunately, the cu- neiform record offers very little information about the specific "aromatics" (Sumerian šim, Akkadian *rīqqu*) that might have been added to beer until the Neo-Babylonian period (605–539 BCE), when a plant called *kasû* comes to the fore.[126] This plant appears to have been used in the brewing of both barley beer and date wine. Records documenting the delivery of ingredients to brewers, for example, list quantities of *kasû* alongside both dates and barley. So we have clear evidence for a specific plant that was used to flavor beer during the Neo-Babylonian period. That's pretty exciting, right? If we know what aromatics they were using, we have a real chance of learning something about the actual taste of their beer. Well, not so fast.

When it comes to translating the Akkadian term *kasû* and its Sumerian equivalent gazi, there is nothing remotely resembling a scholarly consensus.[127] Depending on which authority or which argument you choose to trust, the plant could be cassia, cuscuta/dodder, mustard, beet, carob, or wild licorice. It's also entirely possible that the *kasû* used exclusively to brew beer during the Neo-Babylonian period (605–539 BCE)[128] was an entirely different animal (well, plant) from the gazi that appears in large quantities as a "standard spice" for foods 1,500 years earlier during the Ur III period (2112–2004 BCE).[129] Meanings can evolve significantly over such long periods of time. And we cannot assume either a strict equivalency or a common trajectory of development for the Akkadian term *kasû* and the Sumerian term gazi.

Given that the scribes of ancient Mesopotamia kept detailed records of the brewing ingredients delivered to institutional brewers from the earliest written records onward, why don't we see evidence for the delivery of aromatic plants or other flavoring ingredients to brewers until the Neo-Babylonian period? Some specialists have suggested (or implied) that aromatics just weren't used until then. Otherwise, they would have shown up in the documentation.[130] Personally, I'm skeptical. They spiced their food liberally with a broad range of flavoring ingredients but were strict purists when it came to beer? Maybe. But it seems unlikely.

Perhaps archaeology has something to offer here. As our ability to collect and analyze both macro-botanical remains (e.g., seeds) and microscopic organic residues increases, our ability to identify traces of those aromatic brewing ingredients absent from the written record also increases. I'm thinking, for example, of the kind of evidence recovered from a special "kitchen" located within the royal palace at Ebla, an Early Bronze Age (2450–2300 BCE) city in Syria.[131] Along one wall of the room, a line of at least eight horseshoe-shaped fireplaces was embedded within a high bench that stretched the length of the room. Cooking pots were found still sitting in place atop some of the fireplaces. Cooking pots were also found smashed on the floor.

Most exciting, though, were the carbonized plant remains (e.g., seeds, charcoal, stems) found scattered throughout the room—in the pots, on and around the fireplaces, on the floor. The usual suspects were present: food plants like cereals, legumes, olives, and grapes. But they were present in small quantities (e.g., 376 seeds). Most of the botanical remains (e.g., 1,359 seeds) came from a diverse medley of wild plants, many with medicinal and/or psychoactive properties. Thirty-five different varieties were present, including spurge, calendula, chamomile, poppy, cleavers, hawthorn, heliotrope, and many more. And burnt, melted, glossy residues preserved within some of the pots and fireplaces provide evidence for resin extraction, boiling, and the preparation of beverages. This room, situated right at the heart of the royal palace, appears to have been a special-purpose kitchen where a broad range of wild herbs with special properties were processed for medicinal and/or other uses. There's no direct indication of a connection to beer brewing in this case, but we can cross our fingers for similar discoveries in the future that do show a connection to brewing.

Yeast

Louis Pasteur (1822–1895 CE) is one of the most famous figures in the history of beer. And for good reason. He gave us yeast, those masterful, microscopic fungi with the ability to poop out magical elixir. Of course, the yeast (alongside various bacteria) had always been there at the brewer's side, going about their appointed task, taking in sugar and giving back alcohol in return. It's what they were born to do. And they were already being called yeast at this point. It's just that there was a lot of uncertainty about exactly what they were and what role they played in the brewing process. Pasteur fixed all that. Through a series of carefully constructed lab experiments, he was able to demonstrate two key facts: 1) yeasts were not chemical byproducts of alcoholic fermentation but living beings and 2) they were, in fact, the agents (if not the only agents) behind fermentation. So Pasteur gave yeast, the humble workhorses of the brewing world, recognition as animate collaborators in the brewing process.

Thanks to his successful isolation of a particular strain of yeast that was sufficient to create beer on its own—that is, without the aid of other microbial agents—he also gave the world a new kind of beer, easier to make and less variable, and he gave brewers a new level of control over the brewing process. There can be no doubt that Pasteur's breakthrough research on yeast and its role in alcoholic fermentation was a revolutionary event, ushering in a new era in the history of brewing. But by the time Pasteur came along, humans had already been exploiting, encouraging, studying, nurturing, benefiting from, and coevolving alongside yeast for many thousands of years. They just had different names for the force behind fermentation and different ways of conceptualizing its action.

Mesopotamian brewers did not recognize the existence of those microscopic alcohol factories that we call yeast. They did, however, employ some words that might approximate more closely to our notion of leaven, culture, or starter. These words are, in Sumerian, saḫin, si, and agarin.

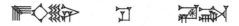

They appear together in a section of the lexical list Urra = ḫubullu, right after a section devoted to different types of beer and just before the section devoted to bappir.[132] But their meanings are far from clear. Let's have a quick look at each in turn, paying particular attention to the translations offered by three different commentators: Leo Oppenheim, Miguel Civil, and Walther Sallaberger.

First, saḫin or saḫindu (written sa-ḫi-in and sa-ḫi-in-du$_3$) and the related Akkadian terms sikkatu and saḫindu.[133] In his pioneering study of the brewing lexicon preserved in the lexical list Urra = ḫubullu, Oppenheim was not willing to go out on a limb and offer a translation, but he suggested that the etymology of the term saḫindu (perhaps borrowed into Sumerian as saḫin) might indicate "some kind of compacted or crushed dish." In a more recent study of the same text, Civil translates saḫindu and šik-ka-tu$_2$ as "yeast (?)." Sallaberger follows suit, translating saḫin, saḫindu, and sikkatu/šikkatu into German as "Sauerteig Hefe" (sourdough yeast/culture).[134] So there's some general agreement here, but very little to go on. These terms just don't appear very often in association with brewing. And their use should not be taken to imply an understanding of the microbiological roots of fermentation. Something like "leaven" would probably be a closer equivalent in English (or even "yeast" as the term was used prior to Pasteur).

In Urra = ḫubullu, the entries for saḫin and saḫindu are followed by the term si. This is a well-attested word that means "horn."[135] In the context of malted barley (in particular, in the constructions munu$_3$ si-mu$_2$ and munu$_3$ si-e$_3$), the "horn" seems to refer to the root sprout or "chit" that emerges from the barley grain during germination.[136] In Urra = ḫubullu, though, we encounter the term si on its own, and its meaning is uncertain. Oppenheim reads si as an alternate writing for the word šim, which he translates "wort" (i.e., the sugary liquid produced by infusing malt in water, prior to fermentation).[137] Civil, on the other hand, writing half a century later, chooses to leave the term untranslated.[138] Sallaberger has more recently suggested that we take si ("horn") in a metaphorical sense, as a reference to the "rising" of a fermenting sourdough.[139] Indeed, in the fourth stanza of the Hymn to Ninkasi, the word si appears in direct association with the word for dough (niĝ$_2$-sila$_{II}$). Civil had struggled to interpret this line, arguing that it might refer to the dough for a special sort of bread: "Ninkasi, you are the one who handles dough (and) . . . with a big shovel."[140] Sallaberger, though, thinks that si might refer specifically to a "rising" dough: "(Ninkasi,) your rising dough was formed with the stately spatula."[141]

The last of our three terms is agarin (Akkadian agarinnu), which can mean "mother" or "mother-creator." It can also mean "crucible." The Pennsylvania Sumerian Dictionary gives the general meaning of "matrix," that is, the environment or material in which something develops.[142] The term agarin appears twice in the section of Urra = ḫubullu that we're examining, written in two different ways.[143] In one, it's written phonetically as a-ga-ri-in. In the other, it's written $^{a-ga-ri-in}$agarin$_4$. This is interesting because the sign that we call agarin$_4$ is actually a combination of the signs ama ("mother")[144] and šim ("aromatic substance, beer malt").[145] So the writing (if not the pronunciation) of this word incorporates the concept of mother. In their discussions of the lexical list, both Oppenheim and Civil stick closely to the maternal angle. Oppenheim gives us "mother-brew," and Civil, "'mother' (of the beer)."[146] It's easy to see how the concept of mother might tie into the concept of leaven or starter. Indeed, in English today we refer to the SCOBY (symbiotic culture of bacteria and yeast) responsible for the fermentation of kombucha as the mother. But we don't really have good evidence that the people of Mesopotamia recognized such a link. Interestingly, in his translation, Sallaberger actually flips the direction of semantic influence. He renders agarin/agarinnu as "fermenting, rising sourdough" and suggests that this meaning might have given rise to a metaphorical use of the term to reference the swelling womb, hence mother.[147]

In fact, Sallaberger has proposed that the three terms saḫin, si, and agarin should be understood as different stages in the life of a sourdough starter.[148] He envisions saḫin/sikkatu as a sort of concentrated starter, si as the rising (in some cases, bubbling[149]) starter that has been activated through the addition of water and flour, and agarin/agarinnu as an actively fermenting sourdough culture. And he sees all three of these as preliminary to the production of bappir, which then serves as the main vehicle for introducing yeast and bacteria into the brewing process. I find Sallaberger's reconstruction compelling, but plenty of other (largely, speculative) scenarios for the addition of a leavening agent have been put forward. Some, for example, have suggested that yeast was transferred to the unfermented wort via the addition of grapes (or other fruits that host yeast on their skins) or the dregs from a previous batch of beer. Others have suggested that the yeast made its way onto the scene in a less intentional fashion: for example, wafting in on the wind or lurking within the cracks and crevices of previously used, but minimally cleaned, brewing vessels.[150]

As to the yeast themselves, very few physical traces have been recovered from archaeological sites in Mesopotamia. As far as I know, the only example comes from Tell Bazi, Syria. The excavators have reported the recovery of "fossil" yeast cells from brewing vessels but have not provided any further information.[151] Rather than looking for the actual physical remains of ancient Mesopotamian yeasts, let's turn our attention to their modern descendants and work our way backward. Here we enter the realm of yeast genomics and, in particular, evolutionary genomics—a rapidly developing field that's been progressing in leaps and bounds in recent years. The basic idea is that modern-day yeast genomes preserve traces of the deep evolutionary history of different species and strains of yeast. As more and more genomes are sequenced, it's increasingly possible to specify the geographical origin point of specific yeasts, their domestication history, and their movement over time. Recent analysis of wild (i.e., non-domesticated) yeasts from China and Taiwan, for example, suggests that *Saccharomyces cerevisiae*—the species from which most commercial yeast strains available today derive— was first domesticated in East Asia and then spread out across the world.[152]

It has generally been assumed that the breads and beers of ancient Mesopotamia—like most of today's breads and beers—were the work of *Saccharomyces cerevisiae*. But this assumption may need to be revised. We don't yet know exactly when and how *Saccharomyces cerevisiae* made its way out of East Asia, but it's possible that it had not yet arrived in Mesopotamia by the time of the first experiments with baking and brewing. So the early beers of Mesopotamia (and surrounding regions) might have been brewed in collaboration with other species of yeast, not to mention various bacteria. If correct, this finding could have significant implications for the taste and alcohol content of Mesopotamian beer. As any fan of traditional Belgian lambics or the new generation of "wild ales" will tell you, other microbes can lead to very "other" flavors. At the same time, alcohol production rates and alcohol tolerance can also vary significantly among different species and strains of yeast. The brewing specs of certain yeasts (including some wild yeasts) have by now been firmly established, but the broader gamut of wild yeasts remains terra incognita (or terra only partially cognita).

Suffice it to say, a lot of effort is currently being devoted to these tiny animalcules, our primary partners in the brewing process.[153] As we learn more about exactly which species of yeast and bacteria were responsible for specific ancient beers, we move closer and closer to being able to say what these beers might have actually been like to drink—their aromas, flavors, textures, and alcohol content.

The beers of ancient Mesopotamia

Depending on where you live, there's a good chance that your local watering hole offers up a decent selection of different types of beer: pilsners, pale ales, porters, and stouts; witbiers, bitters, and bocks; dubbels, tripels, saisons, lambics, goses—the list goes on. If you like variety, today is a pretty glorious time to be a beer drinker. But, if we zoom out and consider the full spectrum of beer types, most of the beers that you'll find on tap or on store shelves today fall within a pretty tight grouping. These are beers brewed with malted barley, various adjunct grains, and hops, the flowers of the *Humulus lupulus* vine, revered for their distinctive contributions of bitterness, aroma, and flavor. As we saw in Chapter 1, a full accounting of beer types past and present would need to cover much broader territory. In working to understand the beers of ancient Mesopotamia, I want to encourage you to embrace a broad conception of what counts as beer and to think outside the box (or bottle or can) of whatever beers are most familiar to you. It's certainly possible that some beers present in today's world offer reasonable analogues for the beers of the distant past, but it's also possible that nothing quite fits the bill, that we're dealing with beers that have effectively gone extinct.

Let's start in the city of Girsu (Early Dynastic III period, 2550–2350 BCE), where a unique collection of cuneiform documents sheds light on several different types of beer.[154] Some of the relevant documents are basically monthly ledgers, listing out the processed and unprocessed grains that the temple had disbursed to various destinations over the course of the month in question. In these we learn, in particular, about the specific grains and grain products that were delivered to brewers to serve as ingredients. A second set of documents tells us more about the character of the finished product. These documents record the delivery of beer by brewers and what we would now call the "grain bill" for each batch of beer. They tell us how much beer was brewed, what type of beer was brewed, and the specific quantities of grains and grain products employed.

For example, here are the first four lines on one tablet, offering us a breakdown of the grain bill for a batch of golden beer. (Note: One ban equals about 6 liters, and one gurgur equals about 9 liters.[155])

> 5 gurgur [45 liters] golden beer
> Its emmer 3 ban [18 liters]
> Its malt 5 ban [30 liters]
> Its bappir 3 ban [18 liters][156]

This might not seem like a lot to go on. But it's about as close as we get to a recipe for beer in Mesopotamia. And, indeed, these documents from Girsu are often referred to as "recipes," even if the label isn't entirely warranted. They tell us nothing, for example, about how the beer was brewed or about any non-grain ingredients. There's also plenty of room for debate about the specifics: for example, about the systems of weights and measures employed (e.g., how these relate to our own systems and to one another) and about the beer types (e.g., how to translate their names and how to reconstruct their recipes).[157] But they do offer a crucial glimpse into the relative proportions of ingredients used to brew specific types of beer.

I've put together a chart that compares the grain bills and the ratios of dry ingredients to beer for the five beer types (Box 3.2).[158] As we've seen, there was a "golden beer" (kaš$_2$ sig), brewed with malted barley, emmer wheat, and bappir (the much-debated "beer bread")—sometimes in equal parts, sometimes with a higher proportion of malt, and sometimes with no emmer at all. There was also a "dark beer" (kaš$_2$ gi$_6$), brewed with malted barley, bappir, and titab, the enigmatic grain product perhaps responsible for contributing to the "dark" character of this beer. And there was a "sweet dark beer" (kaš$_2$ gi$_6$ dug$_3$-ga), brewed with malted barley, emmer wheat, bappir, and ninda kuma, that other enigmatic ingredient that presumably contributed something to both the sweet and the dark character of this beer. A "reddish brown beer" (kaš$_2$ si$_4$), on the other hand, was brewed with exactly the same ingredients as golden beer—malted barley, emmer wheat, and bappir—but in a much higher concentration, probably resulting in

Box 3.2 Beers and brewing ingredients at Girsu

Marvin Powell (1994) has published a detailed analysis of the ingredients used to produce five different types of beer in the city of Girsu during the Early Dynastic period. In many cases, several different recipes—that is, several different accounts that document different proportions of ingredients—are preserved. Here, I have translated these beer "recipes" from the ancient system of volume measurements into the metric system using the following conversion factors (Powell 1994: 101–104).

1 sila ≈ 1 liter	1 gurgur ≈ 9 liters	1 mud ≈ 40 liters
1 ban ≈ 6 liters	1 sadug ≈ 24 liters	

Golden beer (kaš₂ sig)

Emmer wheat	12 liters	24 liters	60 liters	18 liters	36 liters	
bappir	12 liters	24 liters	60 liters	18 liters	36 liters	18 liters
Malted barley	12 liters	24 liters	60 liters	30 liters	60 liters	30 liters
Total ingredients	36 liters	72 liters	180 liters	66 liters	132 liters	48 liters
Total beer	24 liters	48 liters	120 liters	45 liters	90 liters	36 liters

Ordinary dark beer (kaš₂ gi₆)

titab	12 liters
bappir	6 liters
Malted barley	6 liters
Total ingredients	24 liters
Total beer	24 liters

Sweet dark beer (kaš₂ gi₆ dug₃-ga)

Emmer wheat	18 liters	6 liters	0 liters
ninda kuma	18 liters	6 liters	66 liters
bappir	24 liters	6 liters	66 liters
Malted barley	36 liters	12 liters	66 liters
Total ingredients	96 liters	30 liters	198 liters
Total beer	72 liters	18 liters	198 liters

Reddish-brown beer (kaš₂ si₄)

Emmer wheat	192 liters	72 liters
bappir	192 liters	96 liters
Malted barley	288 liters	120 liters
Total ingredients	672 liters	288 liters
Total beer	180 liters	90 liters

Strained beer (kaš₂ sur-ra)

Emmer wheat	72 liters
bappir	72 liters
Malted barley	96 liters
Total ingredients	240 liters
Total beer	90 liters

both a deeper color and a higher-alcohol beer. Finally, there was a "strained beer" (kaš$_2$ sur-ra), also brewed with a high concentration of malted barley, emmer wheat, and bappir but probably sieved or filtered in some fashion.

We don't know how typical such beers were for the Early Dynastic period or even for the city of Girsu. But we can certainly say that the terminology used to categorize beer varied from place to place and evolved over time. About six hundred years earlier (3000 BCE), for example, the archaic texts from the city of Uruk—recall our visit with the brewer Kushim—reference at least nine types of beer (Figure 3.2). The proto-cuneiform signs indicating these beer types are difficult to translate, but the documents do allow for some comparison of their differing composition, at least with respect to the malted barley and barley groats employed.[159]

If we jump forward into the Akkadian period (2350–2192 BCE) and head to the city of Umma, on the other hand, we encounter another system for categorizing beer types. Economic records from Umma refer to beer types using a sort of proportional notation. Beers were distinguished, not by color, but by the relative quantity of barley used to brew each type (measured in sila). There was, for example, 30-sila beer, beer brewed using 30 sila of barley. And there was 50-sila beer, 60-sila beer, and 70-sila beer. These labels might indicate the quantity of barley used in brewing a standard measurement of 30 sila (approximately 30 liters) of beer. So twice as much barley went into 60-sila beer as into 30-sila beer.[160] That's a substantial difference. Assuming that the barley in question was malted barley—the main contributor of fermentable sugars for these beers—the beer names at Umma probably indicate a scale of increasing strength/quality, with 30 at the low end and 70 at the high end.

The parallel is not exact, but this numerical system calls to mind the 70- and 80-shilling ales of Scotland that I enjoyed in my undergraduate days.[161] The shilling value was a holdover from earlier times, reflecting the relative cost of the beers. And that relative cost was, in turn, a reflection of the higher duties that brewers had to pay on beers that included a more substantial malt bill. More malt equaled higher taxes, which equaled higher cost for the consumer. More malt also equaled higher alcohol content and higher quality in the eyes of the consumer. We can probably envision something similar for Akkadian-period Umma. In this case, though, we're viewing the beers through the eyes of the institutional administrator. We don't actually know how the drinking public referred to their beers of choice. Perhaps they used the proportional notation (Hey, barkeep! Give me another jug of "60"!) or perhaps something else entirely (Hey, barkeep! Give me another jug of "super extra special"!).

In fact, during the subsequent Ur III period (2112–2004 BCE), a proportional system for naming beer appears to have existed alongside a system of qualitative grading. There was "2 beer" (kaš 2), "3 beer" (kaš 3), and "4 beer" (kaš 4), presumably reflecting a scale of increasing malt content and/ or strength. But there was also "ordinary beer" (kaš du) and "good beer" (kaš saga$_{10}$).[162] And these latter types were distinguished not (or not only) by the quantity of the ingredients employed but by their quality. As we already saw, for example, a tablet from the city of Garšana documents the food and drink produced for a feast held to honor the death of Šu-Kabta. For this feast, 300 liters of "good" beer and 600 liters of "ordinary" beer were brewed using malted barley, bappir, and groats—"good" bappir and groats for the good beer and "ordinary" bappir and groats for the ordinary beer.[163]

The ranking of beers by malt content and quality continued into the Old Babylonian period (2004–1595 BCE). For instance, a brewery archive from Chagar Bazar (ancient Ašnakkum) in Syria references a four-tier hierarchy of beer types: kaš *gur-nu* (beer of inferior quality), kaš us$_2$ (ordinary beer), kaš sig$_5$ (beer of good quality), and kaš *ša ZU-mi-šu* (beer of superior quality). Like many beer names, the precise translation of each term is subject to debate. The study that I'm relying on here opts for an interpretation that emphasizes relative quality, in part because the texts specify exactly how much barley went into each type.[164] The beers at the low end of the scale required only 0.25 liters of barley per liter of beer, while those at the upper end required 1.5 liters of barley per liter of beer. These same beer types also appear elsewhere, in other archives from other sites, where they can also be linked with a ranked scale of increasing malt content. Indeed, it may be that the same basic hierarchy of beer types—defined by relative malt content—stretches all the way back into the Early Dynastic period.[165]

As you might suspect, distinctions in the quality of beer produced were paralleled by distinctions in how and to whom that beer was distributed. During the Old Babylonian period, for example, "ordinary" beer (kaš us$_2$) appears especially in accounts documenting the bulk dispersal of food and drink to large groups of, shall we say, less important people. "Good" beer (kaš sig$_5$, sometimes translated as "rare" or "fine" beer), on the other hand, appears more often in the form of individualized disbursements, that is, distributions of beer to specific individuals, such as the palace dependents that we will see receiving beer from the brewery at Tell Leilan in Chapter 6.

A variety of other beer types also pop up in Old Babylonian documents. Tablets from the site of Tell al-Rimah (ancient Qattara), for example, reference a "sweet beer" (kaš ṭābu) that was doled out there in equal measure to the good beer. Elsewhere we find a beer known in Akkadian as *kurunnu*, in Sumerian as kurun (written kurun, kurun$_2$, kurun$_3$), a word that can also mean good, sweet, or blood. Indeed, the term might have entered the drinking lexicon, via this three-way polysemy, to indicate "a sweet red alcoholic beverage of high quality."[166] This beer makes a regular appearance in Sumerian literature: for example, multiple times in the following passage from a šir-namursaĝa ("a song of warrior quality") that celebrates the goddess Inana on behalf of Iddin-Dagan, king of Isin (ruled 1976–1956 BCE).

> Everybody hastens to holy Inana.
> For my lady in the midst of heaven the best of everything is prepared (?).
> In the pure places of the plain, at its good places,
> On the roofs, on the rooftops, the rooftops of the dwellings (?),
> In the sanctuaries (?) of mankind
> Incense offerings like a forest of aromatic cedars are transmitted to her.
> They sacrifice alum sheep, long-haired sheep, and fattened sheep for her.
> They purify the earth for the Mistress, they celebrate her in songs.
>
> With ghee, dates, cheese, and seven sorts of fruits,
> They fill the tables of the Land as first-fruit offerings for her.
> They pour dark **kurun** for her,
> They pour light **kurun** for her.
> Dark **kurun**, ulušin,
> And ulušin for my lady
> Bubble in the šagub-jar and the lamsari-vat for her.
> From pastes of honey mixed with ghee,
> They bake date-syrup cakes for her.
> They pour out early-morning **kurun**, flour, flour in honey,
> Honey, and wine of sunrise for her.
> The personal gods of the people also attend upon her with food and drink.
> They purify the earth for the Mistress, they celebrate her in songs.[167]

The precise character of kurun remains uncertain—the Chicago Assyrian Dictionary gives us the equivocal "a choice kind of beer or wine"—but this particular banquet laid out for Inana includes what might be three different varieties of kurun: dark, light, and early-morning. The same passage also mentions ulušin (Akkadian *ulušinnu*), defined variously as "emmer beer" or "date-sweetened emmer-beer."[168] The Akkadian word *dišiptuḫḫu*, meaning emmer wheat, was also used to refer to a type of emmer beer. And texts from the city of Mari reference a beer known as *alappānu*, possibly "a beer of bittersweet taste" that borrowed its name from the word for "a specific bittersweet taste" found in fruits like pomegranates and dates.[169]

Some of the terminology that we've been examining here was extremely long-lived, stretching from at least the Early Dynastic period up through the Old Babylonian period and beyond. Texts from the time of the so-called First Sealand dynasty (1732–1450 BCE), for instance, also make reference to kaš sig (fine or good beer, written kaš sig₅), alongside other types without the same deep pedigree: in particular, *marsānu* (perhaps "stirred" beer) and *našpu* (perhaps "golden" or "strained" beer).[170] This longevity in the lexicon of beer and brewing is certainly significant, but we cannot assume that continuity in terminology signifies continuity in any other regard. The kaš sig of the Early Dynastic period may have borne little resemblance whatsoever to its First Sealand namesake nearly a thousand years later. The parameters that define what qualifies as good—not to mention what qualifies as beer (or, in this case, kaš)—can hardly be expected to have remained stable across such a span of time, equivalent to the chronological distance separating us from the time of William the Conqueror.

Before wrapping up this quick tour through the beers of ancient Mesopotamia, we need to visit the first millennium BCE. As we've discussed before, things get a little complicated during this period with the rising importance of date wine, a beverage that was also considered "beer" (KAŠ/ *šikaru*) by the people of the time. The philological challenges that one must confront here are substantial—both in teasing out the distinction between barley beer and date wine and in understanding how different words for beer and specific beer types relate to one another.[171]

At this time, when Sumerian had definitively and long since died out as a spoken language, scribes would often use the Sumerian sign KAŠ when writing about beer, intending for it to be read in their own Akkadian language as *šikaru*, the generic term for barley beer and/or date wine. They also regularly used the old Sumerian writing KAŠ.SAG—this is that same kaš sig or "good beer" that we've encountered in earlier periods—in a similar fashion, as a catchall means of referring to date/barley beer. These beers could then be further qualified as new, old, sweet, or white, and often it's clear that they were primarily made from dates.[172] But some beers were specifically made from barley. These include a "brewer's beer" or "beer of the brewer" (*šikar sibî* or *šikar sabî*) that might point toward the actively fermenting and almost certainly sediment- and husk-heavy beers that were served through a straw in the tavern. One might imagine a (very) rough parallel to the draft beers of today: in other words, a beer type defined not by color or taste but by locale and manner of consumption, though perhaps with clear implications at the time regarding other

Box 3.3 Beers in the lexical list *Urra = ḫubullu*

beer for the tigi-songs
dark beer
white (?) beer
emmer beer
great emmer beer
red beer
great beer
2:1 beer (i.e., "2 grain:1 beer" beer)
3:1 beer
1:1 beer
beer "in the middle of the sea"
triple beer
foaming beer
beer without foam
cloudy beer
pressed/filtered beer
clear/clean beer
beer for libations
beer for religious rites
beer for religious meals
beer for the offering of first fruits
beer for the jar rack
beer for the throat (?)
beer pleasant to the throat (?)
diluted (?) beer

aspects of the beverage.[173] There was also still a beer called *kurunnu*, made specifically with *billatu* (Sumerian dida), a much-debated, barley-based brewing ingredient or intermediate brewing product that we'll discuss further in Chapter 4.[174]

So much of the relevant terminology for beer types was preserved over the centuries and millennia, but the precise meaning of specific terms did not necessarily remain constant. And many different systems of classifying and characterizing beer show up in the cuneiform record, often employed alongside or in parallel to one another. There's perhaps no better way to highlight the diverse landscape of beer types than to have another look at Urra = *ḫubullu*, that lengthy, bilingual linguistic compendium of the late first millennium BCE, which includes a section devoted specifically to different sorts of beer. Box 3.3 shows a selection from the beer list.[175] That's a lot of different beers—each with its own distinct rendering in Sumerian and Akkadian and each considered, for whatever reason, worth including in this carefully curated list, which moves on next to brewing ingredients. Of course, we don't actually know that the beers named here would all have been recognized at the time as distinct styles, as we think of beer styles today. And many of the terms here are subject to significant uncertainty and/or debate. But don't let anyone tell you that ancient beer was just an undifferentiated sludge or that the discerning palates of our own age have only recently injected an element of sophistication into the realm of beer tasting and typology. There must have been Mesopotamia beer nerds (or connoisseurs, if you prefer) to rival any of our own.

Chapter 4
Brewing technologies and techniques

Ninkasi, the fermenting vat, which makes a pleasant sound,
You place appropriately on (top of) a large collector vat.

Hymn to Ninkasi[1]

The Hymn to Ninkasi

We begin this chapter with a clay tablet (Figure 4.1). Known as Ni 4569, it would once have been roughly rectangular in shape (taller than it is wide) but is now a little rough around the edges.[2] More than a little. The nearly four millennia that have passed since it was created (Old Babylonian period, 2004–1595 BCE) have not been particularly kind. The faces of the tablet are heavily cracked, and most of its edges, broken away. Each side (i.e., the obverse and reverse) is divided into two vertical columns of cuneiform script. And each of these columns would originally have included approximately thirty-five horizontal lines of text. Many lines are either partially preserved or missing entirely, especially on the left-hand side of the tablet. Fortunately, though, the tablet is well enough preserved that we can make out a good chunk of its contents: a series of distinct but related texts, each relatively brief, all written in the Sumerian language.

The first four are love songs. A bunch of love songs and love poems have come down to us from ancient Mesopotamia.[3] These were not

Column 1   Column 2

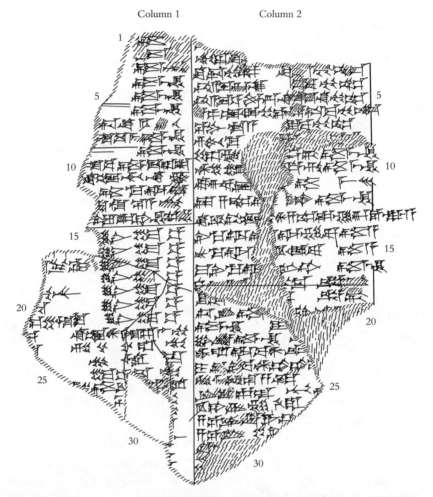

Figure 4.1. Fragmentary cuneiform tablet that includes the Hymn to Ninkasi and the Drinking Song. Ni 4569. (Redrawn after Kramer 1963: Fig. 9)

extemporaneous creations, intimate missives hastily scrawled out in the heat of the moment and delivered to (or performed for) that special someone. Some were "official" love songs, connected in one way or another with royal cult, temple ritual, and state religion. Others were probably closer to folk songs, passed down orally and perhaps performed at festivals and other, less formal occasions. These songs were liberally peppered with references to sex, both overt and more metaphorical. And many featured beer. Many also featured the archetypal divine lovers Inana and Dumuzi as protagonists (see Chapters 6 and 7 for further discussion of love songs, beer, and sex). Ni 4569 begins with four such love songs,[4] before finishing up with the two texts that really interest us here: the Hymn to Ninkasi, goddess of beer, and a so-called Drinking Song. These two texts are of fundamental importance for the history of beer and brewing in Mesopotamia.

Ni 4569 was excavated at the site of Nippur in Iraq in the late nineteenth century CE.[5] We know very little about exactly where it was found, but we do know that it was part of a cache of tablets that ignited a bitter feud between two collaborators turned rivals. As far as I know, John P. Peters and Hermann Hilprecht never came to actual blows, but they faced off in a protracted legal battle and regularly denounced one another in public during a heated back-and-forth that raged on for the better part of two decades.

In 1905, for example, Peters published a report in the *Journal of the American Oriental Society* excoriating his colleague.[6] Both were leading members of a University of Pennsylvania team that had conducted excavations at Nippur between 1888 and 1900. In a portion of the site known as Tablet Hill, the expedition had turned up some 20,0000 cuneiform tablets, which Hilprecht argued were the remains of a "Temple Library." In his lengthy, systematic, and often quite personal commentary on Hilprecht's supposed temple library, Peters alleged (among a series of charges) that "the method in which this discovery has been handled is such that it appears to be impossible to rely upon any statement made by Dr. Hilprecht, unless supported by such manifest and palpable proof that his statements can be checked and verified by others, or by the contents of the inscriptions themselves."[7]

As academic takedowns go, that's pretty savage. But I haven't brought up this spat between scholars solely for the spectacle of it. I want to draw your attention to the less-than-ideal means by which cuneiform tablets were mined from the site of Nippur, packed up in boxes, and carted away with maddeningly little attention paid to their original archaeological context. Here's how Peters summarized the situation.

> Dr. Hilprecht declares that 17,200 or 23,000 or 24,000 (his statement is different in different publications) tablets were taken out of that "library" and "hurriedly examined" by him. He had, in fact, about twenty specimen tablets to examine. . . . The other tablets were packed as they came, without labels or other marks by which their exact provenance could be determined. Tablets from quite different parts of the mound might be packed in the same box, if they were discovered at or about the same time.[8]

No labels. No information about provenance. Even Hilprecht himself concurred: " . . . our knowledge as to how and precisely where the tablets were found is extremely limited."[9]

Granted, in those days archaeology was still in its infancy as a discipline. And plenty of early excavations were little more than glorified mining expeditions: massive teams of local excavators, overseen by a handful of foreigners, moving dirt on a truly impressive scale, with the express purpose of collecting treasures to fill out museum collections and private collections in Europe and the United States. But this particular trove of tablets from Nippur opened up a whole new world of previously unknown Sumerian literature, and without any inkling of their original context, it was impossible to know what all these pieces of Sumerian literature were doing there.

Thankfully, in 1948, nearly 50 years after the first archaeological campaign at Nippur came to an end, the University of Pennsylvania and the University of Chicago teamed up to initiate new excavations at Nippur. Archaeological methods had progressed significantly in the intervening years. During the third season (1951–52), in a rather unpretentious, run-of-the-mill house referred to as House F, excavators made an exciting discovery: 1,425 cuneiform tablets and tablet fragments. Seven hundred of these preserved pieces of Sumerian literature, and hundreds more preserved school exercises for scribes-in-training.[10] Yes, this was a house. But it was also a school. Here, students were educated through the copying of texts, memorization, and, not unlike today, exposure to the great literary classics. More than 80 different works of literature were represented. Thanks to the discovery of House F, it now seems likely that the earlier excavators at Nippur had not, in fact, uncovered the remains of a temple library but rather three or four small scribal schools, each well stocked with the classics of Sumerian literature.

So Ni 4569, with its four (rather suggestive) love songs and two odes to beer, *might* have once been part of a school library. That's interesting, right? The kind of thing that might cause quite the scandal today. This tablet did not make its way, as many others did, into the collection of the University Museum at the University of Pennsylvania. The system in place at the time, known as *partage*, allowed the institution sponsoring the excavations to retain a portion of the artifactual finds, but the rest were the property of the Ottoman Empire. Along with thousands of other cuneiform tablets, Ni

4569 was shipped from Nippur to the Archaeological Museum of Istanbul, where it remains to this day.

The Hymn to Ninkasi and the Drinking Song also appear together, in the same order, on two other known tablets (AO 5385 and VAT 6705), also dating to the Old Babylonian period (2004–1595 BCE). What can these add to the story? Sadly, both are unprovenanced, that is, completely devoid of archaeological context. So we know even less about where they originally came from. All we have to go on is the tablets themselves.

The one known as AO 5385 currently resides at the Louvre Museum in Paris.[11] This tablet begins with the Hymn to Ninkasi and the Drinking Song, followed by a fragmentary line that probably reads, "This is a balbale song for Ninkasi." A short love song then follows,[12] and a summary line at the end of the tablet reads, "These are two balbale songs for Inana." AO 5385, therefore, offers us two interesting pieces of information. First, it suggests that the Hymn to Ninkasi and the Drinking Song were at least sometimes considered a single text, a balbale song written for the goddess Ninkasi. Second, it suggests that this text also fell under the broader umbrella of songs written for the goddess Inana, who makes a brief appearance at the end of the Drinking Song.[13]

The other tablet, known as VAT 6705, now resides at the Vorderasiatisches Museum in Berlin.[14] It only includes the Hymn to Ninkasi and the Drinking Song. And this time the two texts are clearly separated by a horizontal line running the width of the tablet, which suggests that they were, in this case, viewed as distinct texts.[15] This tablet also offers another unique feature: a series of "glosses" (i.e., extra explanatory info noted within the text) to indicate variant ways of writing particular lines.[16] These glosses tell us that there were some slightly different versions of the Hymn to Ninkasi floating around at the time.

Indeed, the three versions that we have do not match up perfectly with one another. This is due partly to the fragmentary nature of the texts and partly to (relatively minor) variations in content. So which version of the text is the right one? And which one should we choose to translate? Well, there's really no straightforward answer to these questions. But it's a situation that Assyriologists encounter all the time. Especially in the case of famous pieces of literature that were copied and recopied many, many times over the centuries, variations (whether intentional or unintentional) were almost inevitable. There are basically two methods for dealing with this variation:

scores and composites. To create a score, one assembles all of the different versions of a text and compares them line by line. Imagine an orchestral score. And then replace each instrument with a different version of the Sumerian text. For example, here you see lines 9–10 from the Hymn to Ninkasi (A = AO 5385; B = Ni. 4569; C =VAT 6705).[17] Brackets and half brackets indicate cuneiform signs that were not preserved or only partially preserved. In some cases, it's possible to infer the original signs; in others, it's not.

9	A	aia-zu ^{d}en-ki en ^{d}nu-dim$_2$-mud-e
	B	ama-zu [^{d}nin-til$_3$] nin abzu-a
	C	ama-zu ^{d}nin-til$_3$ nin abzu-[ ]

10	A	ama-zu ^{d}nin-til$_3$ nin abzu-a
	B	aia-[zu ^{d}en-ki en ^{d}nu]-$^\ulcorner$dim$_2$-mud$^\urcorner$-e
	C	aia-zu ^{d}en-ki en ^{d}nu-dim$_2$-mu[d-]

In this example, the main difference between the three versions (A, B, and C) is that the order of the two lines has been switched in source A. The difference really jumps out at you in the score. So hopefully you can see the value of this approach. It can be messy, though. Just imagine that you were comparing, not three, but ten or twenty different versions of this text. For practical purposes, it's often useful to create a single "composite" text that draws together elements from the different versions. Here's how the composite for lines 9 and 10 would look, along with a translation.[18]

9   ama-zu ^{d}nin-til$_3$ nin abzu-a
       Your mother is Nintil, the queen of the Abzu.

10   aia-zu ^{d}en-ki en ^{d}nu-dim$_2$-mud-e
       Your father is Enki, the lord Nudimmud.

As you can see, the composite follows the line order from sources B and C.

We'll dig down into the Hymn to Ninkasi and the Drinking Song in the coming pages. For now, though, let's start with the briefest of summaries and a translation for each. I'm giving you the classic English translation by Miguel Civil (Box 4.1).[19] We'll have a look at a more recent translation by Walther Sallaberger—and bring these two versions into conversation with one another—in due course.[20] The Hymn to Ninkasi consists of 48 lines of text that can be grouped into twelve stanzas.[21] Each four-line stanza

Box 4.1 **Hymn to Ninkasi** (a-zal-le u-tu-da, "Borne by the flowing water")

1 Borne *by* the flowing water [. . .],
2 Tenderly cared for by Ninhursag.
3 Ninkasi, borne *by* the flowing water [. . .],
4 Tenderly cared for by Ninhursag.

5 Having founded your town on "wax,"
6 She finished its great walls for you.
7 Ninkasi, having founded your town on "wax,"
8 She finished its great walls for you.

9 Your father is Enki, the lord Nudimmud,
10 Your mother is Ninti, the queen of the abzu.
11 Ninkasi, your father is Enki, the lord Nudimmud,
12 Your mother is Ninti, the queen of the abzu.

13 You are the one who handles dough (and) . . . with a big shovel,
14 Mixing, in a pit, the bappir with sweet aromatics.
15 Ninkasi, you are the one who handles dough (and) . . . with a big shovel,
16 Mixing, in a pit, the bappir with sweet aromatics.

17 You are the one who bakes the bappir in the big oven,
18 Puts in order the piles of *hulled* grain.
19 Ninkasi, you are the one who bakes the bappir in the big oven,
20 Puts in order the piles of *hulled* grain.

21 You are the one who waters the earth-covered malt,
22 The *noble* dogs guard (it even) from the potentates.
23 Ninkasi, you are the one who waters the earth-covered malt,
24 The *noble* dogs guard (it even) from the potentates.

25 You are the one who soaks the malt in a jar,
26 The waves rise, the waves fall.
27 Ninkasi, you are the one who soaks the malt in a jar,
28 The waves rise, the waves fall.

29 You are the one who spreads the cooked mash on large reed mats,
30 Coolness overcomes. . . .
31 Ninkasi, you are the one who spreads the cooked mash on large reed mats,
32 Coolness overcomes. . . .

33 You are the one who holds *with both hands* the great sweetwort,
34 Brewing (it) with honey (and) wine.
35 Ninkasi, you are the one who holds *with both hands* the great sweetwort,
36 Brewing (it) with honey (and) wine.

37 [. . .],
38 [You . . . the sweetwort to the vessel].
39 Ninkasi, [. . .],
40 [You . . . the sweetwort to the vessel].

41 The fermenting vat, which makes a pleasant sound,
42 You place appropriately on (top of) a large collector vat.
43 Ninkasi, the fermenting vat, which makes a pleasant sound,
44 You place appropriately on (top of) a large collector vat.

45 You are the one who pours out the filtered beer of the collector vat,
46 It is (like) the onrush of the Tigris and the Euphrates.
47 Ninkasi, you are the one who pours out the filtered beer of the collector vat,
48 It is (like) the onrush of the Tigris and the Euphrates.

consists of two lines that are then immediately repeated verbatim, except
for the addition of a shout-out to Ninkasi. The upshot is that the text really
consists of just twenty-four unique lines. The first three stanzas are devoted
solely to introductory info about Ninkasi: her birth, parentage, etc., leaving
a tight nine stanzas to celebrate Ninkasi as the archetypal brewer. In these
thirty-six reverent lines, we see Ninkasi in her element, brewing up a batch
of beer from start to finish.

The Drinking Song, consisting of thirty-one lines of text, can be
broken down into three sections (Box 4.2).[22] The first (lines 49–57) lists
off and celebrates the "beautiful" vessels used for brewing and serving
beer, which are described as "ready on (their) pot stands." The second
(lines 58–68), addressed to an unknown but probably female host, reads
like a sort of toast: "May the heart of your god be well disposed towards
you!... May Ninkasi live together with you!" Along the way, it extols the
pleasant effects of beer consumption and references a ritual associated
with the founding of a building. The third section (lines 69–79) seems to
be a response by the host, written in first person. The speaker promises
an "abundance of beer," highlights the euphoric effects of beer consumption, and closes with a nod to the goddess Inana. Civil suggests that this
drinking song might have been written to celebrate the inauguration of
a new tavern and that the unknown host might have been the proprietor
of said tavern.[23] Sallaberger is less committal but envisions some kind of
festival or celebration, one that was taking place outside the world of official temple ritual.[24]

To recap, then, we have two brief songs, preserved on only three known
tablets, where they always appear together as a unit. These fascinating but
cryptic texts allow us to peek behind the curtain and glimpse the brewers
and drinkers of ancient Mesopotamia at work and play.

Finding process in poetry

We don't know for sure that the Hymn to Ninkasi and the Drinking
Song were "drinking songs" in the proper sense, that is, songs meant to
be sung while drinking. But, just for the sake of argument, let's pretend
that they were. Our present world is full of drinking songs, whether spur-
of-the-moment, one-time-only, on-the-spot improvisations or venerable
old standards with a deep history of borrowing, addition, subtraction,

Box 4.2 **Drinking Song** (gakkul-e gakkul-e, "The Gakkul, the Gakkul")

49 The gakkul, the gakkul,
50 The gakkul, the lam-sa$_2$-re,
51 The gakkul, which makes the liver happy,
52 The lam-sa$_2$-re, which rejoices the heart,
53 The ugur-bal, a fitting thing in the house,
54 The ša$_3$-gub, which is filled with beer,
55 The am-am, which carries (the beer of) the lam-sa$_2$-re,
56 The . . . reed buckets and the reed pails of . . . ,
57 The beautiful vessels, are ready on (their) *pot stands!*

58 May the heart of your god be well disposed towards you!
59 Let the eye of the gakkul be our eye,
60 Let the heart of the gakkul be our heart!
61 What makes your heart feel wonderful,
62 Makes (also) our heart feel wonderful.
63 Our liver is happy, our heart is joyful.
64 You poured a libation over the brick of destiny,
65 You placed the foundations in peace (and) prosperity,
66 May Ninkasi live together with you!
67 Let her pour for you beer (and) wine,
68 Let (the pouring) of the sweet *liquor* resound pleasantly for you!

69 In the . . . reed buckets there is sweet beer,
70 I will make cupbearers, boys, (and) brewers stand by,
71 While I turn around the abundance of beer,
72 While I feel wonderful, I feel wonderful,
73 Drinking beer, in a blissful mood,
74 Drinking *liquor*, feeling exhilarated,
75 With joy in the heart (and) a happy liver —
76 While my heart full of joy,
77 (And) (my) happy liver I cover with a garment fit for a queen!
78 The heart of Inanna is happy again,
79 The heart of the queen of heaven is happy again!

adjustment, transcription, and translation. The best of the best have survived by dint of a combination of features: catchy tunes, contagious rhythms, witty or crude turns of phrase, and, perhaps more than anything else, repetition. The end of a good drinking song begs for a rallying cry of "one more time!" These songs have often enough been written down, coopted by professional musicians, and/or recorded for posterity, but they are first and foremost products of informal, oral transmission, passed down in the act of collective performance. That's really their whole point; they're there to be sung with friends (or total strangers) while drinking. And they tend to engage with one particular subject above all others: you guessed it, drinking. In that sense, our two songs from Mesopotamia fit right in. So, before we dive down into the topic of brewing technologies and techniques, let's set the mood—and perhaps temper our expectations regarding the interpretive weight that should be placed on these two texts—by comparing them with a few more recent barroom classics. (Obviously, these songs lose a little something in the transition from rambunctious barroom to words on paper. To really set the mood, I'd suggest a quick online search for an appropriate audio version.)

Let's start with the classic "In Heaven There Is No Beer," descended from the German "*Im Himmel gibt's kein Bier.*" Composed in 1956 for a film score and now a fixture at many a college football game, this little ditty entered my own consciousness via my brother Kent's love of the great bluegrass musician John Hartford, who recorded his own rendition alongside Doug and Rodney Dillard in 1980. The main chorus is pretty straightforward.

> In heaven there is no beer.
> That's why we drink it here.
> And when we are gone from here,
> All our friends will be drinking all our beer.

The sentiments expressed here would not have been entirely foreign to the people of ancient Mesopotamia. For example, we wouldn't have to look far in Mesopotamia to find comparable expressions of pessimism regarding the food and beverage program in the afterlife ("the house whose entrants are bereft of light, where dust is their sustenance and clay their food"[25]) and exhortations to live it up in the meantime. In an early version of the Epic of Gilgamesh (Old Babylonian period, 2004–1595 BCE), Shiduri, the tavern keeper at the edge of the world, famously advises Gilgamesh to forgo his search for eternal life and focus on the here and now.

> The life that you seek you never shall find:
>   when the gods created mankind,
> death they dispensed to mankind,
>   life they kept for themselves.

> But you, Gilgamesh, let your belly be full,
>   enjoy yourself always by day and by night!
> Make merry each day,
>   dance and play day and night![26]

It's even possible that this particular episode from the Epic of Gilgamesh inspired another Mesopotamian drinking song.

It has been suggested that a text known as "The Ballade of Early Rulers" was, in fact, a drinking song (Box 4.3).[27] This reflection on bygone kings, the brevity of life, and the inevitability of death appears in a number of different versions, sometimes in Sumerian only, sometimes in Sumerian with an accompanying Akkadian translation.[28] It's a complex work, full of irony, allusion, tongue-in-cheek scholarly posturing, and "deep thoughts" more generally. One specialist calls it an "amalgamation of seriousness, wit, humor, and cynicism."[29] In Box 4.3, I'm showing you one version in particular, the one that ends with an explicit invocation of Siraš, a deity closely associated with beer and with Ninkasi. (We'll come back to these two beer deities in a moment.)

Maybe this was a drinking song, maybe not. Not everyone agrees. But an intriguing comparison can be made with *Gaudeamus igitur* ("So let us rejoice"), a well-known Latin song that dates back to at least the thirteenth century CE.[30] Today a fixture at many university graduation ceremonies and other academic events, this light-hearted meditation on the pleasures of youth, the swift approach of death, and the joy of scholarly fellowship began its life as a drinking song. Though the "Ballade of Early Rulers" may be harder for us to parse, it covers very similar territory—not least in its "seize the day" message, possibly an explicit reference to the tavern keeper's speech in the Epic of Gilgamesh. (Note that Gilgamesh, Enkidu, and their foe Huwawa all make an appearance in the Ballade.) And, with that reference to Siraš, right at the end, a similarly distant origin as a drinking song doesn't seem entirely out of the question.

Box 4.3 **The Ballade of Early Rulers**

With Enki the plans are drawn.
According to the decisions of the gods lots are allotted.
Since time immemorial there has been [wi]nd!

Has there ever been a time when you did not hear this from the mouth
   of a predecessor?
Above them were those, (and above) those kings were others.
Above (are) the houses where they lived, below (are) their everlasting houses.
Like the remote heavens, no hand, indeed, has ever reached them.
Like the depth of the underworld, one knows nothing (about it/them).
All life is an illusion.
The life of mankind was not [intended to last for ever].
Where is Alulu, the king [who reigned 36,000 years?]
Where is Entena the king, the man who ascended to heaven?
Where is Gilgameš, who, like Ziusudra, sought the (eternal) life?
Where is Huwawa, who was caught in submission?
Where is Enkidu, whose strength was not defeated (?) in the country?
Where is Bazi, where is Zizi?
Where are those great kings, from former days till now?
They are no longer engendered, they are no longer born.
Life onto which no light is shed, how can it be more valuable than death?

Young man, let me truly instruct you about your god!
Chase away grief from depression! Spurn silence!
Instead of a single day's joy, let there come a long day of 36,000 years <of silence!>
Life onto which no light is shed, how can it be more valuable than death?
As for her little child, may Siraš rejoice over you!
These are the regulations of righteous mankind!

What about our other two "songs" from ancient Mesopotamia, the
Hymn to Ninkasi and the Drinking Song? Certainly, the "Drinking Song"
expresses the kind of exuberant appreciation for the delights of beer that
one expects of a drinking song proper.

> While I turn around the abundance of beer,
> While I feel wonderful, I feel wonderful,
> Drinking beer, in a blissful mood,
> Drinking *liquor*, feeling exhilarated,
> With joy in the heart (and) a happy liver . . . [31]

This text doesn't have a title as such, but let's follow the ancient Mesopotamian convention and call it by its first line: "gakkul-e gakkul-e" (written ᵍⁱgakkul-e ᵍⁱgakkul-e).[32] The gakkul was a key piece of brewing equipment, almost certainly a vessel with a small hole pierced in its base that played a role in fermentation and/or filtering. So, in English we might call this song "The Gakkul, the Gakkul" or perhaps "The Fermentation Vessel, the Fermentation Vessel."

As we've already seen, "gakkul-e gakkul-e" kicks off with a tribute to the material culture of brewing and drinking, the "beautiful vessels" that are "ready on their pot stands." This move to give due credit to the paraphernalia that made drinking possible is not all that rare within the broader corpus of drinking songs. What is, perhaps, less common is explicit mention of the brewing process, as in the Hymn to Ninkasi (whose first line is broken but would give us a title of "a-zal-le u-tu-da . . . ," something like "Borne by the flowing water . . . ").

Let's look at two well-worn examples from our own world as a point of comparison. First, "Beer, Beer, Beer," a drinking song of uncertain but distant origins that offers about as concise a description of brewing as one can imagine. Box 4.4 shows a brief selection from the version recorded by the Clancy Brothers in 1969.[33] Second, "John Barleycorn," an old song, dating back at least several hundred years, that offers a more extended reflection on the brewing process, as experienced by John Barleycorn, the personified barley corn. Over the course of the song, we follow the protagonist across the seasons, as he grows and matures in the field, before being cruelly cut down, transformed into beer, and fed to thirsty drinkers. Box 4.5 shows a selection from a sometime-before-1782 rendition by the Scottish poet Robert Burns, whom we already met in Chapter 3. Here, the unfortunate John Barleycorn is malted, kilned, crushed, and his "heart's blood" (i.e., beer or whisky) consumed.[34]

In the Hymn to Ninkasi, the narrative progresses in a similar, step-by-step fashion, but the heroine of the tale is the brewer, Ninkasi, not the put-upon, personified grain of barley. Note, however, that the people of Mesopotamia were elsewhere perfectly willing to personify their grain. A text known as "The Debate Between Sheep and Grain,"[35] for example, pits personified versions of Sheep and Grain against one another in a heated (and inebriated) debate over their relative value to human society. Unsurprisingly, one key point in favor of Grain, the eventual winner, was her contribution to the brewing of beer.

Box 4.4 **Beer, Beer, Beer**
(The Clancy Brothers, 1969 CE)

A long time ago, way back in history,
When all there was to drink was nothin but cups of tea.
Along came a man by the name of Charlie Mops,
And he invented a wonderful drink and he made it out of hops.

He must have been an admiral, a sultan, or a king,
And to his praises we shall always sing.
Look what he has done for us he's filled us up with cheer!
Lord bless Charlie Mops, the man who invented beer, beer, beer,
Tiddly beer, beer, beer. . . .

A barrel of malt, a bushel of hops, you stir it around with a stick,
The kind of lubrication to make your engine tick.

Box 4.5 **John Barleycorn**
(Robert Burns, c. 1782 CE)

They filled up a darksome pit
    With water to the brim,
They heaved in John Barleycorn,
    There let him sink or swim.

They laid him out upon the floor,
    To work him farther woe,
And still, as signs of life appear'd,
    They toss'd him to and fro.

They wasted, o'er a scorching flame,
    The marrow of his bones;
But a miller us'd him worst of all,
    For he crush'd him between two stones.

And they hae taen his very heart's blood,
    And drank it round and round;
And still the more and more they drank,
    Their joy did more abound.

In the following stanzas from the Hymn to Ninkasi (again, following Miguel Civil's edition, and without the repeated lines), grain is put to work in the production of two key ingredients: bappir and malted barley.

> Ninkasi, you are the one who bakes the bappir in the big oven,
> Puts in order the piles of *hulled* grain. . . .
> Ninkasi, you are the one who waters the earth-covered malt,
> The *noble* dogs guard (it even) from the potentates. . . .
> Ninkasi, you are the one who soaks the malt in a jar,
> The waves rise, the waves fall.[36]

Again, I do not wish to claim that the Hymn to Ninkasi—or the Drinking Song, for that matter—was necessarily a drinking song as we understand the genre today. But, however this set of verses was composed, performed, copied down, sung, chanted, solemnly intoned, bellowed, hummed, or otherwise passed down through the years, it offers a unique, step-by-step account of the brewing of beer in ancient Mesopotamia. Of course, "You are the one who soaks the malt in a jar / The waves rise, the waves fall" is no more a recipe or set of instructions than "A barrel of malt, a bushel of hops, you stir it around with a stick." But we're going to keep coming back to this "hymn," because it's the best that we've got to work with.

Before we dive more deeply into the evidence for brewing, I want to return briefly to Ninkasi and Siraš (also known as Siris).[37] To be honest, our knowledge about both Ninkasi and Siraš is pretty hazy. During earlier periods (third–second millennia BCE), they were typically depicted as female, but later on there's some ambiguity about their gender. It's even possible that these goddesses of beer eventually morphed into gods of beer. The relationship between the two is also difficult to pin down. Sometimes Siraš is cited as the equivalent of Ninkasi, sometimes as a sibling or possibly a spouse.[38]

As far as we know, neither was tied to a particular city as their main cult site, but we have occasional evidence that they were worshipped in particular places.[39] For example, during the Neo-Assyrian period (950–605 BCE), in the sanctuary of the goddess Ningal at Ur, there appears to have been a spot (ki-gub, "socle")—known as the "House of the Dragon of Heaven" (e$_2$-ušumgal–an-na)—where one could worship Ninkasi. And there are references to temples of Ninkasi in the city of Nippur and two other cities whose names are lost.[40] Siraš, on the other hand, had a temple in the city of Assur and is known to have been worshipped in various other locales. For example, in the temple of Mandānu in Babylon, a shrine called the e$_2$-kurun-na or "House of *kurunna* (a fancy type of beer)" was listed as the "seat of Siraš" (MIN ᵈ*siraš*).[41]

In contrast to Ninkasi, the brewer, Siraš seems to have been associated more with the beer itself. It has been suggested, for example, that Siraš was "the numen of beer" (i.e., the spirit or power inherent in the beer).[42] Her name could even be used in place of the word for beer.[43] But Ninkasi was first and foremost a brewer, and we're going to focus our attention now on teasing out the details of her craft.

How was beer brewed?

Among all of the topics that we'll discuss in this book, the brewing process stands out as particularly tricky terrain. To my mind, this is where the connection between evidence and interpretation becomes most tangled and least transparent to nonspecialists. It can be very difficult to judge the degree to which unwarranted assumptions are being imported into the discussion. And summaries of the brewing process are often (but certainly not always) presented in a confident, matter-of-fact tone that downplays the hypothetical and tentative nature of the exercise. The fact is that we do not currently know exactly how beer was brewed in Mesopotamia, and we have only a weak appreciation for variability in the brewing process across space and time. Enormous strides have been made, but there is still much work to be done.

Let's begin with a look at two seductive traps that have hampered previous efforts to reconstruct the brewing process. The first trap: assuming that we can adequately explain the brewing process in ancient Mesopotamia using terminology drawn from a modern-day brewing lexicon whose roots lie in European brewing traditions. The second trap: adopting a minimalist position, that is, assuming that the brewing process in ancient Mesopotamia comprised just a few basic steps. To assess the impact of each trap, we'll have another look at Miguel Civil's translation of the Hymn to Ninkasi, and we'll bring in a comparative case from modern-day West Africa. With these warnings in mind, we'll then consider two more recent attempts to understand how beer was brewed in Mesopotamia, one relying primarily on archaeological evidence, the other on written evidence.

The terminological trap

First, the terminological trap. The translator of a text like the Hymn to Ninkasi must inevitably make some tough choices. For example, what if there's just not a good match in English (or German) for a particular Sumerian term? Or what if the meaning of the term in question is hotly debated? Do you go with a rough approximation? Do you choose sides in the debate and go all in? Or do you leave the term untranslated? In his version of the Hymn to Ninkasi, Civil leaves one key term (bappir) untranslated, but he renders others using vocabulary drawn from the European brewing lexicon (e.g., mash, sweetwort, fermenting vat).[44] Obviously, one can't just leave every difficult word untranslated. An English text in which every other word is left in the original Sumerian would hardly qualify as a translation. It would only be legible to a small club of in-the-know Sumerologists. And the whole point of doing a translation is to make the text accessible to a broader readership.

But there is a risk that something crucial about the ancient brewing process will get lost in translation. Even simple terms like "mash" and "wort" come prepackaged with a set of underlying assumptions and baggage that might distort past reality. And every translation will inevitably incorporate an element of interpretation: for example, traces of the translator's own, personal understanding of how brewing worked in the past and/or how it works in the present. There's no simple solution to such dilemmas, but we need to do our best to allow space for difference, for the possibility that the past was not like the present.

So, let's begin with one place where the present has crept unnoticed into our accounts of the past: the written evidence for brewing in Mesopotamia. What exactly do we have to work with here? We have a few rare literary sources—chief among them the Hymn to Ninkasi—that offer glimpses into the brewing process. But above all we have a rich lexicon of brewing terminology: terms for the substances involved, terms for the equipment employed, and terms for the actions performed. Certain actions, for example, were considered particularly emblematic. In English, to make beer is to "brew" beer. In the languages of ancient Mesopotamia, to make beer was to "mix" (*balālu* in Akkadian), "stir" (lu₃ in Sumerian), "squeeze" (*mazû* in Akkadian), "prepare" (*epēšu* in Akkadian), or "throw into water" (i.e., immerse or steep, *nadû* in Akkadian). But we generally still speak of the "brewing" of beer in Mesopotamia, thus losing the specific senses of action implied by the native terminology.[45]

This flattening of the past into the present also impacts our treatment of the substances involved. Again, you ask? Haven't we already beaten that particular topic into the ground? Yes, perhaps, but bear with me for a moment. For better or worse, the question of brewing process is inextricably intertwined with the question of brewing ingredients. It's not difficult to see why: If you and I disagree about what a particular brewing ingredient (say, bappir or titab) *was*, there's a pretty good chance that we'll disagree about how that ingredient *functioned* in the brewing process. In his translation of the Hymn to Ninkasi, Civil draws heavily on the English-language brewing lexicon. He translates the Sumerian šim lal$_3$ as "sweet aromatics," munu as "greenmalt," sun$_2$ as "mash," titab as "cooked mash," dida as "sweetwort." So it's not surprising that his step-by-step account of the process recounted in the Hymn to Ninkasi (see Box 4.6) also sounds a lot like what you might expect: malting, mashing, cooling, filtering, and fermentation. But there are

---

Box 4.6 Brewing process in the Hymn to Ninkasi
(as reconstructed by Miguel Civil)

1. *Preparing barley bread* (Stanzas 4–5): A dough made from unmalted barley (še) or, perhaps, malted barley (munu) is mixed in a pit with sweet aromatics (šim-lal$_3$) and then baked in an oven (udun bappir$_2$) to produce a barley bread (bappir$_2$).

2. *Preparing malt* (Stanza 6): Barley is soaked in water, spread out on a surface, and allowed to germinate under a thin layer of earth to produce greenmalt (munu$_{3/4}$).

3. *Preparing mash* (Stanza 7): Greenmalt (munu$_{3/4}$) is crushed and mixed with water to create a mash (sun$_2$).

4. *Heating mash*: The mash (sun$_2$) is heated in an oven (udun titab) to produce cooked mash (titab).

5. *Cooling cooked mash* (Stanza 8): The cooked mash (titab) is spread out on reed mats (^{gi}kid-titab) to cool.

6. *Preparing wort* (Stanza 9): The cooked mash (titab) is mixed with lukewarm water, sweet syrup (lal$_3$), and wine or grapes (geštin) to produce sweetwort (dida).

7. *Fermentation* (Stanza 10): The sweetwort (dida) is placed in a fermenting vessel (nig$_2$-dur$_2$-bur$_3$) and allowed to ferment into beer (kaš).

8. *Filtering beer* (Stanza 11): The beer (kaš) is filtered by draining it through the hole in the base of the fermenting vessel (nig$_2$-dur$_2$-bur$_3$) and into an underlying collecting vessel (laḫtan) to produce filtered beer (kaš si-im).

9. *Pouring beer* (Stanza 12): The filtered beer (kaš si-im) is poured out of the collecting vessel (laḫtan).

also some additional elements: the baking of bappir, the spreading out of the mash on reed mats to cool, the addition of wine or grapes. And there is one glaring omission. What happens to the bappir produced in step one? Where does it enter into the brewing process?[46]

In fact, if you're familiar with the modern, Euro-derived brewing process, I suspect that Civil's account might raise some further questions. If you're finding it a little difficult to understand exactly what's going on—why, for example, as we saw in Chapter 3, would they want to spread the cooked mash out on a reed mat?—remember that we may be dealing with a "square pegs and round holes" situation. Rather than helping establish a smooth channel of communication between past and present, the use of familiar, English-language brewing terminology (e.g., mash, wort) might actually be introducing additional confusion into the mix. More than that, I suspect that the use of this terminology is actually impacting Civil's reconstruction of the ancient brewing process and importing unwarranted assumptions about the substances involved and the steps followed.

To gain some perspective on the matter, let's take a quick detour to the modern-day village of Yantenga in Burkina Faso, West Africa. François Belliard has provided a concise but illuminating description of the brewing of sorghum beer in this village inhabited by members of the *gyóôhé* ethnic group.[47] I emphatically do not wish to imply that brewing practices in this village are in any sense primitive, relics of the past, or direct analogues for the distant past. This is a mindset that anthropologists have been working to expunge for the better part of the past century. Instead, we are here in Burkina Faso to reflect on a venerable, complex, and beloved brewing tradition that differs significantly from what many of us are used to. And I particularly appreciate Belliard's attention to the linguistic element, that is, the terminology that brewers use to articulate the step-by-step progression from raw grain to finished product.

The beer itself is known as *ráã*, and to make beer is to "prepare" (*kừgbɔ́*), "stir" (*rắmmr̀ɛ*), or "cook" (*dừgbɔ̀*) beer. The brewing process lasts a full two days and nights (Box 4.7; see also Figure 4.2).[48] Liquids, semi-liquids, and solids are transferred back and forth among nine different brewing vessels in a complex dance of heating, cooling, mixing, separation, filtering, and fermentation. Instead of attempting to express this intricate choreography using the poorly suited English-language brewing lexicon, Belliard gives us

Box 4.7 Brewing process in Yantenga, Burkina Faso
(as reconstructed by François Belliard)

DAY 1

1. **Milling** *(yárbɔ̀)*: Malt *(kǎmá)* must be milled. It then becomes "malt flour" *(kǎm zwá)*.

2. **Immersion** *(síìbù)*: The malt flour is immersed in jars (A/B) of water.

3. **Mixing** *(síanbɔ̀)*: The flour and water in jars A/B are mixed with the arm.

4. **Fishing out** *(yàabɔ̂)*: Once the malt flour has settled to the base of jars A/B, this "soaked malt flour" *(kǎm cágrè)* is fished out with a calabash and transferred to jars C/D, where it is combined with water. Some of this water is transferred to the "beer water" *(rǎ kʊ́ʔǎ)* left in jars A/B. Any "floating residues" *(kǎm-súgdú)* are removed from jars A/B and C/D.

5. **Adding mucilage** *(sálbɔ̀)*: A "mucilagenous vegetal ingredient" *(sánnɔ̀)*, such as certain leaves or barks, is added to the beer water in jars A/B.

6. **Cooking** *(rɔ́gbɔ̀)*: The soaked malt flour in jars C/D will now have settled to the bottom. The overlying beer water is removed and placed in basin I. The soaked malt flour is transferred to cooking pot E and is cooked with water for 2–3 hours.

7. **Recuperation of sediment** *(zóobɔ̂)*: While the soaked malt flour is cooking, the beer water in jars A/B is transferred to jars C/D. The "sediment settled by mucilage" *(pèennó)* at the base of jars A/B is removed with a calabash, strained, and dried. The beer water in jars C/D is then shared equally among jars A, B, C, and D.

8. **Cooling** *(yéeb'o)*: When the soaked malt flour is cooked in cooking pot E, white "foam" *(púh púuri)* appears. This indicates that the soaked malt flour has transformed into "brown paste" *(kɔ́grɛ̂)*. The brown paste is removed from cooking pot E and put in the jars (A/B/C/D) containing beer water in order to cool it until the second day.

DAY 2

9. ***Separation of the layers*** (*z*ʷ*àlgbɔ́*): The second day of brewing begins when the liquid in jars A, B, C, and D is clear and tastes sour. Overnight, the contents of these jars will have settled out into three distinct layers. Each layer is removed separately with a calabash. The first layer (beer water) is clear, liquid, and orange. The second ("muddy sediment," *k*ʷ*ǽŋ k*ʷ*áré*) is beige and thick. These two layers are cooked for several hours in separate pots (E/F). The third layer ("thick sediment," *bíhì*) is brown and very thick. It is filtered in the "filter" (*t*ʷ*ákká*, made up of jar G, which is pierced by tiny holes and sits above jar H), resulting in a red and creamy "sweet filtrate" (*b*ʷ*álgá*). After thirty minutes of cooking, the muddy sediment is also filtered in the filter (G/H), resulting in a very clear "insipid filtrate" ((*t*ʷ*ákk kv̄ʔǽ sàbhgá*)). The insipid filtrate is then cooked in cooking pot F for five hours, resulting in "cooked filtrate" (*sídgà*).

10. ***Cooling*** (*yéeb'o*): After cooking in cooking pot E, the beer water has become "sweet beer" (*rǽ nv̄ʔdɔ̀*), which is red and sweet. The sweet beer is removed from cooking pot E and poured into jars A and B for cooling. After cooking in cooking pot F, the cooked filtrate is poured into jars C and D for cooling.

11. ***Recuperation of sediment*** (*zóobɔ́*): Once cooled in jars A/B, the sweet beer is transferred to basin I. At the bottom of jars A/B is "sweet beer's sediment" (*kv̄v̄dɔ̀*), which is removed. The sweet beer and cooked filtrate are then mixed together in jars A/B/C/D.

12. ***Fermentation*** (*kv̀lgbɔ́*): When the liquid in jars A/B/C/D is cooled, "yeast" (*rá béllè*) is added to start fermentation. After four to six hours, the beer is ready to drink.

a more literal translation of the key terminology. The relevant substances include, for example, beer water, sediment settled by mucilage, brown paste, muddy sediment, thick sediment, sweet filtrate, cooked filtrate, and sweet beer. The sequence of steps includes soaking, draining, resting, crumbling, milling, immersion, mixing, fishing out, mucilage adding, cooking, recuperation of sediment, separation of the layers, and cooling.

Yes, the brewing process in Yantenga involves (versions of) familiar steps like malting, mashing, filtering, and fermentation. But it also involves an array of other steps and intermediate products that cannot easily be expressed in the terminology of the European brewing tradition. And any effort to do so would run the risk of glossing over much of what distinguishes the process and much of what matters most to brewers and consumers. I think there would be a value in attempting something similar for ancient Mesopotamian brewing—an account that cleaves more closely to the original sense of the Sumerian and Akkadian terminology and that avoids reliance on terms steeped in a very different brewing tradition. This is one way out of the terminological trap, a means of allowing more space for differences to emerge but also for the recognition of points of genuine similarity between brewing processes past and present.

The minimalist trap

Now for the minimalist trap. Because there are so many gaps and uncertainties in our knowledge of Mesopotamian brewing, there has been a tendency to adopt a minimalist position. Indeed, when it comes down to it, brewing is a pretty simple process. Only a few, fundamental steps are necessary to transform barley into beer. But there is no reason to assume that the brewers of ancient Mesopotamia performed only these basic steps. We are not in the territory of Occam's razor here. The simplest or most parsimonious interpretation is not necessarily the correct one.

If the roots of Mesopotamian beer lie deep in prehistory, as seems increasingly likely, then we are dealing with a brewing tradition that stretches back thousands of years into the past. We should expect the brewing traditions of the Bronze and Iron Ages to rest on a complex and tangled historical pedigree: diverse local trajectories of development, path dependencies established early in the process, borrowings and crossovers from other regions or other culinary and craft traditions, sophisticated bodies of knowledge and technical skill, entrenched patterns of training or apprenticeship, distinctive preferences, logics, tastes, and habitual ways of doing things. History is messy. There is simply no reason to assume that brewing technologies and techniques would have evolved over time toward what we might consider the most logical or most efficient option. And there's also no reason to assume that the people of the distant past were only capable of achieving the bare minimum, that is, the simplest approach to brewing, stripped down to just the basics. Even if we can't currently see all of this in the available evidence, we should approach the question of brewing technologies and techniques expecting sophistication, creativity, complexity, and diversity.

It would be unfair to suggest that Civil's account of the brewing process is somehow simplistic or unsophisticated. That's not what I mean. It isn't. But his account is, I think, emblematic of a broader tendency toward assuming that the brewing process in Mesopotamia was pretty straightforward, that the Hymn to Ninkasi's depiction of Ninkasi at work in the brewery more or less hits the key steps in the brewing process, that this is how they brewed beer in Mesopotamia. As our sojourn into the world of drinking songs has already demonstrated, I think that's asking a little too much of this particular text.

In a broader sense, though, we need to confront the possibility that all the other bits and pieces that have come down to us in the written record—all those brewing terms that we've been discussing—derive from a more complicated process. Rather than a simple set of steps that takes us from ingredients to mash to wort to beer, we might need to envision something more like we saw in Burkina Faso. Figure 4.2 shows a visual representation of that same brewing process (Day 2 only) highlighting not just the complex movement and manipulation of liquid, semi-liquid, and solid substances but also the suite of vessels that was required and the diverse functions that these vessels performed during the process. When we discuss brewing equipment later in this chapter, remember this example from Burkina Faso. A more complicated process might also entail a more complicated set of brewing equipment or at least a more complicated range of functions performed by brewing vessels.

It's also crucial to point out that there is absolutely no reason to assume that beer was brewed in just one way across the millennia of Mesopotamian history. Again, we should expect and seek out evidence for difference—for brewing techniques that varied geographically and evolved over time, for distinctions between how beer was brewed on the household, tavern, or institutional scale, and perhaps even for practices and preferences that differed from brewer to brewer.

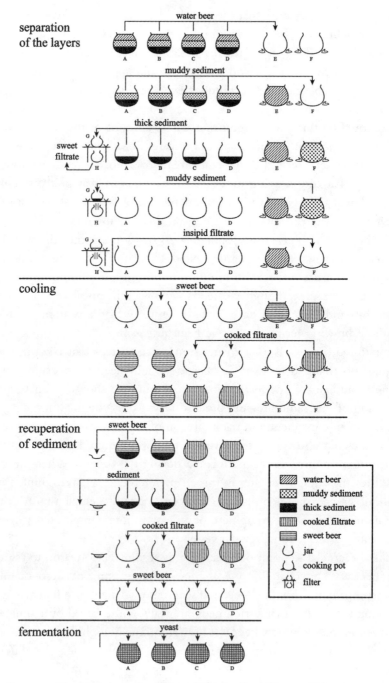

Figure 4.2. The brewing of sorghum beer in the village of Yantenga, Burkina Faso, Day 2 (Redrawn after Belliard 2011: Fig. 16.3)

The brewing process

Now, for two more recent efforts to reconstruct the brewing process in Mesopotamia. Neither of these entirely avoids the two traps— terminological and minimalist—but they both allow more space for the possibility that there was a distinctly Mesopotamian way of brewing beer. The first takes us to the site of Tell Bazi in north-central Syria. Here we have an attempt to let the archaeological record speak for itself, to set aside written materials like the Hymn to Ninkasi and, instead, tease out evidence for brewing techniques from just the material remains excavated at the site.

Between 1993 and 2011, excavations at Tell Bazi uncovered an extensive area of occupation dating to the Late Bronze Age (1400–1200 BCE).[49] Among the structures excavated were approximately fifty houses, many of which appear to have been brewing their own beer. A program of or-ganic residue analysis indicated that they were brewing this beer using a standardized set of ceramic vessels. The same basic, three-vessel brew kit was replicated from house to house. For present purposes, what's inter-esting about this is that standardized equipment suggests the existence of a standardized or, at least, broadly shared brewing process. And the excavators, in collaboration with brewing scientist Martin Zarnkow, have introduced a somewhat radical proposal about the brewing process: They argue that the beers of Tell Bazi were brewed using a "cold-mashing" technique.[50] They suggest that the conversion of starches into fermentable sugars during the mashing phase was accomplished without the addition of heat. (Ask your local craft brewer or home brewer what they think about this idea, and you're likely to get a dubious or at least quizzical look in response. But, again, just because we wouldn't do it that way now doesn't mean they wouldn't have done it that way then.) So, the Tell Bazi team has used archaeological evidence to develop a new theory about the brewing process, and they've put this theory to the test in a series of brewing experiments. The resulting low-alcohol, beer-ish beverage has garnered a good bit of attention among Mesopotamian specialists and in the popular media.

The case for cold-mashing can be boiled (or not boiled, as the case may be) down into two sub-arguments. First, the excavators point out that the cooking vessels recovered at the site are much smaller than the brewing vessels. The cooking vessels average about 15 liters, and the two key brewing vessels (one with a hole pierced in its base and one without a hole that was partially embedded in the floor) average about 90–100 liters and up to 200 liters, respectively. So the only vessels suitable for direct heating of liquid over a flame seem poorly matched to the scale of the brewing vessels. Second, the excavators argue that there just wouldn't have been enough wood around. A brewing process that required heating of the mash would have quickly exhausted the relatively meager fuel resources available in the local environment. According to their argument, then, cold-mashing was simply the only option.

But would this actually work? Can one produce a drinkable beer without heating the mash? In light of the brewing experiments conducted by the Tell Bazi team, the answer seems to be yes. Their proposed brewing process (see Box 4.8) is pretty simple: Malt some barley, grind it up, mix it with

---

Box 4.8 Brewing process at Tell Bazi
(as reconstructed by the Tell Bazi team)

1. *Preparing malt*: Barley is mixed with water in a vessel with a hole pierced in its base (presumably, with the hole plugged) and allowed to steep. The water is then removed via the hole, and the barley is allowed to germinate, either within the same vessel or on a mat. After approximately four days, this greenmalt is spread out on the roof to dry in the sun, resulting in dried malt.

2. *Cold-mashing*: The dried malt is ground using a grinding stone and then mixed with water at a temperature of 34 degrees C (93 degrees F) and a ratio of 1 part ground malt to 8.3 parts water. This "cold" mash takes place within a vessel partially buried in the ground and is stirred vigorously for 15 minutes.

3. *Fermentation*: A mixture of yeasts (*Saccharomyces* and *Schizosaccharomyces*) and bacteria (*Lactobacillus*) is added to the mash, which is then allowed to ferment for 36 hours at a temperature of 24 degrees C. The result is a highly fermented, low-alcohol (1.6% ABV) beer.

water, stir it around, add some yeast.[51] Simple certainly doesn't mean incorrect, but bear in mind our discussion of the minimalist trap.

So, is this exactly how beer was actually brewed at Tell Bazi? Maybe. But I'm a little skeptical. For one, I'm not entirely convinced by the cold-mashing argument. The small size of the cooking vessels is certainly intriguing, but it doesn't seem to rule out a heating of the mash. Could they not, for example, have employed some version of traditional decoction mashing in which part of the mash is removed, heated up, and then returned to the mash to raise the temperature? The argument for insufficient fuel resources is also intriguing but, I think, not totally convincing. What about dung fuel, for example? The team mentions this eminently renewable form of fuel—one that still plays an important role in the region today—but to my knowledge does not explain why it would not have played a role in brewing.

It is certainly useful to know that a potable and mildly alcoholic beverage could have been brewed using the technologies available at Tell Bazi and the hypothesized brewing process. What frustrates me, though, is that many people have fixated on the "mildly alcoholic" element. We'll come back to the tricky question of alcohol content in Chapter 7. But let's be clear. In no sense did the Tell Bazi experiments demonstrate that the beers of ancient Mesopotamia would have been, across the board, low in alcohol content. Pointing to evidence for the drinking of beer by children in the cuneiform record, the team *assumed* that the beers consumed at the site would have been low in alcohol content.[52] So they explicitly set out to brew a low-alcohol beer and deliberately employed a malt-to-water ratio that would achieve this end. It is entirely possible, perhaps likely, that a cold-mashing process will inevitably produce a low-alcohol beer. But, as far as I can tell, the brewing experiments at Tell Bazi have not demonstrated this fact.

For our second example, we return to the written record for a rather different interpretation of the Hymn to Ninkasi offered by Assyriologist Walther Sallaberger (see Box 4.9). It is definitely the case that Sallaberger has continued to employ some terms borrowed from the modern-day (in this case, German-language) brewing lexicon. For example, he translates Sumerian titab as "spent grain" (*Treberkuchen* in German) and sumun$_2$ as "mash" (*Maische* in German). But he also builds on more than fifty years of further scholarship since Civil's initial translation to offer a more complicated interpretation that strikes me as less beholden to familiar brewing traditions (i.e., less taken in by the terminological trap). Among other

Box 4.9 Brewing process in the Hymn to Ninkasi
(as reconstructed by Walther Sallaberger)

1. *Preparing sourdough* (Stanzas 4–5): Barley (še) is coarsely ground and mixed with reserved sourdough (babir$_2$ sah$_7$-ḫi-in) to produce fermenting and rising sourdough (agarin/*agarinnu*). Some or all (usually, one tenth) of this fermenting and rising sourdough may be reserved in a large vessel (babir$_2$ ša$_3$ laḫtan-bi) for future use. For purposes of storage and transport, the fermenting and rising sourdough may also be baked or dried briefly in an oven to produce large lumps or balls of baked or dried sourdough (babir$_2$ du$_8$) in which sufficient yeast and bacteria survive to initiate further fermentation.

2. *Soaking sourdough*: The sourdough (babir$_2$/*bappiru*) is crumbled and mixed with water to activate the sourdough and begin fermentation.

3. *Soaking malt* (Stanza 6): Malt (munu$_4$) is ground to produce malt grist (ba-ba munu$_4$), which is then mixed into water (a si-g).

4. *Mash* (Stanza 7): The soaked sourdough and soaked malt are mixed together in a mash vessel (dug sumun$_2$, *karpat muraṭṭibi*). This mash (sumun$_2$/*narṭabu*) undergoes a simultaneous but incomplete process of saccharification and fermentation that results in beer (kaš) and spent grain (titab/*titāpū*).

5. *Drying spent grain* (Stanzas 8–10): The spent grain (titab/*titāpū*) is spread out on a reed mat (^{ge}ge$_2$ titab$_2$) or cooked in an oven (udun titab) to dry. The result is dry beer or beer extract (dida/*billatu*).

6. *Mixing dry beer with water*: The dry beer (dida/*billatu*) is mixed with water in a vessel with a hole pierced in its base to initiate fermentation into beer (kaš).

7. *Filtering beer* (Stanzas 11–12): The resulting beer is filtered to produce filtered beer (kaš si-im) and decanted into an underlying collecting vessel (laḫtan).

adjustments, Sallaberger's version includes three separate phases of fermentation, multiple steeping steps, and two intermediate, partially fermented products that could be dried out and stored for later use. It also excludes the production of malt, a process that, according to this interpretation, took place within the separate domain of the maltster and does not, therefore, appear among the tasks accomplished by Ninkasi.

If your German is up to the task, I'd encourage you to have a more detailed look at Sallaberger's new take on the Hymn to Ninkasi. You'll find a compelling account of the brewing process, backed up with careful philological argumentation. But you'll also find a very personal account. Sallaberger has revisited this well-known but challenging text with new eyes, hoping to shake things up and dislodge some assumptions that emerged from Civil's initial attempt at translation. But there remains a substantial, if unavoidable, element of informed speculation and inference. In conversation with the Tell Bazi excavators and their collaborator Martin Zarnkow, Sallaberger has assembled his own distinctive vision of the brewing process, but it can be difficult to judge the extent to which this broader vision has driven his interpretation of specific elements of the Hymn to Ninkasi (rather than vice versa). Just remember: The puzzle that we're working here (the "brewing process" puzzle) is missing an unknown number of pieces. In fact, we're almost certainly working a whole bunch of different puzzles all at once, their pieces jumbled together in complex ways.

Brewing equipment

Let's move now from the brewing process to brewing equipment. This is where an archaeologist like myself feels most comfortable: in the realm of things or, as we often say, material culture. Things are the bread and butter of the discipline of archaeology. Indeed, archaeology has been called the "discipline of things."[53] And when archaeologists start talking about things, one key concept is almost certain to come up. Assemblages. We talk a lot about assemblages, and, if you listen closely, you'll notice that the term is used in a very flexible fashion. The collection of artifacts recovered from a particular site, excavation unit, building, and/or room in a building? An assemblage. The distinctive set of artifacts in use during a particular time period within a particular region? An assemblage. The functionally related group of artifacts used to fulfill some particular purpose? An assemblage. You get the picture. Pretty much anything can be an assemblage. For archaeologists, the term is a practical and flexible means of referring to groups of things. In recent years, the term has also been drafted into service across the humanities and social sciences (on a more rarified theoretical plane) as a means of talking about all kinds of dynamic, heterogeneous collectivities.[54] Although engagement with this wave of theorizing about the assemblage (aka "assemblage theory") has been extremely productive for archaeologists, here we're going to stick with the more traditional archaeological usage.[55] An assemblage is a group of things. And I want to talk specifically about the *brewing assemblage*.

These days you can walk into your local home brew shop or navigate to their website and purchase your very own home brewing kit. Neatly packaged up in a cardboard box, you'll find everything you'll need to brew up your first batch of beer. Well, not everything. But at least the key pieces of equipment that you're least likely to already own: a big plastic bucket or two, a glass carboy, an oversized funnel and colander, lengths of plastic tubing, a hydrometer, an airlock, a bottle capper, etc. On its own, any one of these objects might serve a wide variety of potential purposes. As a set, though, their joint purpose is pretty clear: the brewing of beer. When I refer to a brewing assemblage, this is what I have in mind—a distinctive set of equipment used to brew beer at some particular time in some particular place.

For all of you home brewers out there, if an intrepid archaeologist were to happen upon the buried remains of your humble abode several hundred years from now, would the artifactual inventory betray clear signs of your craft? Would the archaeologist be able to recognize and piece together the elements of a brewing assemblage? If you're a relative beginner, who only brews occasionally, there's probably a good chance that many pieces of the brewing assemblage would be recovered all packed together in the back corner or upper shelf of some closet or pantry (or wherever they've been consigned by your supportive but, perhaps, less enthusiastic significant other). Some other multipurpose and/or less mobile, but still essential, elements of the brewing assemblage might be recovered some distance away. I'm thinking, for example, of your kitchen sink, stove, and counter or that brew kettle (i.e., large stockpot) that does double-duty for the annual neighborhood chili cook-off. If you're a more dedicated practitioner, the archaeologist might have the good fortune to come across a full in situ brewing assemblage, neatly arranged in its primary context of use: say, a basement or repurposed car garage. If our archaeologist of the future were to happen instead upon your local brewpub or craft brewery, the brewing assemblage might bear some similarities but would probably look quite different (excepting, of course, the more mechanically inclined of you who have managed to install a mini craft brewery in the comfort of your own garage).

So, what can we say about the brewing assemblage in ancient Mesopotamia? What kind of equipment did brewers use to brew their beer? How did the homebrewer's tool kit compare with that of the tavern keeper and the institutional brewer? Would the same equipment make do, whether one was tasked with meeting the daily needs of one's own family, churning out beer for broad distribution, or catering to the tastes of the rich and famous? And how might the brewing assemblage(s) have evolved over the millennia of Mesopotamian history? These are big questions that can only be answered in a partial fashion. But they're absolutely crucial, especially for us archaeologists, dependent as we are on the world of material culture. Archaeologists have had a tough time identifying clear-cut, unambiguous evidence for the brewing of beer in Mesopotamia, despite more than a century of excavation. And this predicament ultimately comes down to uncertainties about the brewing assemblage. If we want to know who was brewing, where they were doing it, and how, we have to get a better grip on the question of brewing equipment. So let's take stock of where things stand at present.

We'll look first at what we know about the individual pieces of equipment needed for brewing, before turning to the evidence for sets of equipment. As we will see, one perennial challenge is establishing a connection between the cuneiform record and archaeological remains. Archaeologists have uncovered gigantic numbers of ceramic vessels, many of which must have once played a role in brewing. As organic residue analysis gains steam, we will increasingly be able to say exactly which ones. But matching these archaeologically recovered vessels up with the specific brewing vessels that appear in the cuneiform record is no easy task. The Drinking Song very helpfully lets us know that the ^{dug}ugur-bal was "a fitting thing in the house" and that the ^{dug}ša$_3$-gub was "filled with beer," and the Hymn to Ninkasi tells us that the ^{dug}nig$_2$-dur$_2$-bur$_3$ "makes a pleasant sound."[56] But what did these vessels actually look like? Were they short and squat or tall and narrow? Were their mouths open or closed? Were their bases rounded or pointy? Could they stand up vertically on their own, or did they need help? Did they come with handles? Spouts? Decoration?

What we wouldn't do for a nice, illustrated diagram with clear labels telling us exactly which vessels were which and explaining their various uses. If our focus here were ancient Egyptian brewing, we would actually have something approximately comparable. The artisans of ancient Egypt regularly produced two- and three-dimensional depictions of brewers at work, and sometimes they even provided captions to let the viewer know exactly what was going on: "pouring the mash," "straining," "filling the jars," "closing the jars," etc.[57] But we have nothing comparable from Mesopotamia. The art of beer was squarely focused on the drinking, not the brewing, side of the equation.

Brewing vessels

In Box 4.10 I have compiled a far-from-comprehensive list of Sumerian and Akkadian terms for specific pieces of brewing equipment.[58] The list is dominated by vessels. Some of these are well attested in the cuneiform record, allowing for some pretty firm inferences about their nature and function. For others, we can do little more than speculate based on subtle etymological and contextual clues. Let's consider a few examples, beginning with our old friend the gakkul.

If (and this is a big "if") the Sumerian drinking song that we met earlier in the chapter was indeed a bona fide drinking song, perhaps we can envision a particularly enthusiastic tavern patron urging their compatriots into song with an exuberant shout of "gakkul-e gakkul-e!" The assembled crew of motley characters then launches into a spirited but probably less-than-perfect rendition of the old classic, paying homage first of all to the most iconic of brewing vessels. The gakkul (a term borrowed into Akkadian as *kakkullum*) was the quintessential brewing vessel.[59] In a Sumerian tale known as Lugalbanda and the Anzud Bird,[60] for example, the hero Lugalbanda is lost in the mountains. His only hope is to convince the mythical Anzud bird, who lives thereabouts, to show him the way home. What to do, what to do? Cunning hero that he is, Lugalbanda comes up with a foolproof scheme: He'll ply Anzud and his family with beer and sweets. Then how could the well-fed and well-lubricated bird refuse to help? And to put this plan into practice, Lugalbanda will rely, in particular, on the aid of Ninkasi.

> . . . Ninkasi the expert who redounds to her mother's credit. Her ^{na4}gakkul [vessel] is of green lapis lazuli, her ^{gi}lam-sa$_2$ [vessel] is of refined silver and of gold. If she stands by the beer, there is joy, if she sits by the beer, there is gladness; as cupbearer she mixes the beer, never wearying as she walks back and forth, Ninkasi, the ^{giš}buniĝ [bucket] at her side, on her hips; may she make my beer-serving perfect.[61]

Box 4.10 Sumerian and Akkadian terms for brewing equipment

The cuneiform record includes many references to pieces of brewing equipment. Here I have a provided a list of some of the relevant Sumerian and Akkadian terms, as well as approximate translations drawn from the scholarly literature. Translations that appear in quotation marks are based on etymological clues (e.g., nouns whose verbal roots suggest a particular function). Translations that do not appear in quotation marks are based on the context in which the words are used and other clues. Given our significant uncertainties regarding the brewing process, many of these translations should be considered extremely provisional. For citations, see endnote 58.

^{dug}am-am / ^{dug}am-ma-am	Small beer vessel; beer jar
^{gi}ba-an-du$_8$	Bucket
^{geš}buniĝ / ^{gi}buniĝ$_x$ / buniĝ / ^{gi}buniĝ / ^{geš}buniĝ$_2$ / ^{geš}buniĝ$_3$	Trough, bowl, or bucket
dag-dug	Vessel stands
dug titab	Vessel for titab
^{dug}dur$_2$-bur$_3$ / ^{dug}nig$_2$-dur$_2$-bur$_3$	"(Whose) bottom (is) a hole"; fermentation vessel
^{dug}dur$_2$-PU$_2$	Fermentation vessel
^{dug}ellaĝ-si-sa$_2$ / ^{dug}lam-di-re / ^{dug}lam-sa$_2$-re / ^{dug}lam-re / ^{dug}lam-si-sa$_2$ / ^{giš}lam-re / lam-di / ^{gi}lam-di	Beer vessel (collecting vessel?); brewing vat
^{geš}gan-nu-um kaš	Vessel stand for beer
^{gi}kid-titab	Reed mat for titab
^{dug}kir$_2$ / kir / gir$_3$ / gir$_{16}$ / gir$_{13}$	Vessel for liquids, especially beer
^{dug}gakkul / ^{gi}gakkul	Fermentation vessel; mash tub
^{dug}laḫtan	Beer mixing vessel; beer vat
^{dug}ma-an-ḫara$_4$ / ^{dug}nam-ḫara$_4$ / ^{dug}ma-ḫara$_4$	"Collecting vessel"
^{giš}mar niĝ$_2$-sur-ra	Shovel for beer
^{dug}nig$_2$-dur$_2$-bur$_3$-tur-ra	"Small" fermentation vessel
^{dug}ša$_3$-gub	Beer vessel
udun-bappir	Oven/kiln for bappir
udun-titab	Oven/kiln for titab
^{dug}u-gur-bala / ^{dug}ugur$_2$-bala	Beer production vessel
ammammu	Large beer jar
dannu	Storage vessel (for beer, wine, etc.)
gangannu / *kankannu*	Wooden rack for storing vessels
ḫubūru	Large beer vessel

kakkullu / kakkultu	Fermentation vessel; vessel for making beer, for storing liquids
kannu	Wooden rack for storing vessels
kirru	Standardized container for beer
kītu titāpu	Reed mat for *titāpu*
laḫtānu	Large mixing and collecting vessel for beer
marru	Spade, shovel (for baking and preparing *bappiru*)
muraṭṭibu / muraṭṭibtu	"Moistening"; vessel for keeping beer mash moist
nablalu	Mixing instrument (for beer)
namḫāru	"Receiving vessel"
namzītu	"Squeezing vessel"; fermentation vessel
napraḫtu / naparaḫtu	"Fermentation vessel"
narṭabu	Beer wort vessel
naspû	"Soaking vessel"
pīḫu	Standard-capacity jug of beer
šagubbu	Vessel used in brewing
šiddatu	Wooden rack for storing vessels
tēbibtu	Vat used in brewing beer
terḫu	Vessel

A gakkul made from lapis lazuli (the nearest source of which would have been the region of modern-day Afghanistan), a lam-sa$_2$ vessel made from silver and gold. Sounds a little extravagant. But we're talking about primo, divine-grade brewing equipment here.

On the earthly plane, the vast majority of these vessels would have been made of fired clay (i.e., ceramic).[62] The gakkul, though, could also be fashioned from metal, and it appears in a lexical list dedicated to objects made from reed. We have only meager hints regarding the overall shape of this vessel. A Neo-Assyrian-period tablet from the city of Assur, for example, compares the shape of a certain *ḫuḫāru* bird trap to the (presumably, more familiar) shape of a *kakkullum* vessel: "The *ḫuḫāru*-trap looks like a *kakkullu*-vat, its . . . , its base is wide, its opening narrow."[63] A ceramic sherd excavated on the island of Failaka in Kuwait, though, offers what may be contradictory testimony. The rim of this wide-mouthed vessel very helpfully preserved a self-referential cuneiform inscription: "1 *kakkullum* vat (belonging to?) Jatara[ ], son of Gurd[a?]."[64] In the Drinking Song, we also learn that the gakkul had an "eye." Could this metaphorical eye have been the opening at the mouth of the vessel? Perhaps. But my money is on a different opening: a hole pierced in the base of the vessel.

Indeed, the gakkul belongs to a broader family of so-called *Lochbodengefässe*, German for "vessels-with-a-hole-in-the-bottom."[65] One of these, the $^{dug}nig_2$-dur_2-bur_3 (also written $^{dug}dur_2$-bur_3), takes us from the realm of the eye into an entirely different zone of bodily metaphor.[66] Sure, when translating this term, one could go for the less colorful option of "vessel with a hole in its base," but it can also mean "vessel with a butthole" ($^{dug}nig_2$ = vessel, dur_2 = buttocks, bur_3 = hole).[67] Personally, I'm not sure how I'd feel about drinking the liquid that emerged from this vessel's butthole, but to each their own, I guess. The $^{dug}nig_2$-dur_2-bur_3 is rare in the written record, but it does make a prominent appearance near the end of the Hymn to Ninkasi, where it sits above an underlying laḫtan vessel. (We'll get back to vessel pairs like this in a moment.) More common in the written record is the vessel known in Akkadian as *namzītum*, a term that's derived from the verb *mazû*, meaning "to squeeze, to produce a liquid."[68]

In one sense, all of these terms for vessels with a hole pierced in the base can basically be considered synonyms: gakkul = *kakkullum* = $^{dug}nig_2$-dur_2-bur_3 = $^{dug}dur_2$-bur_3 = *namzītum*. Indeed, lexical texts sometimes explicitly equate them with one another.[69] And they could even stand in for one another. In Akkadian texts the word *namzītum* could be written either phonetically (using a series of syllabic signs, e.g., na-am-zi_2-tum) or using its Sumerian equivalent (e.g., dug-nig_2-dur_2-bur_3), which would have been read in Akkadian as *namzītum*. At the same time, though, it's entirely possible that these terms incorporate subtle morphological (i.e., shape) or functional (i.e., use) distinctions that elude us at the moment. The use of these terms certainly varied across space and time. And we can hardly expect either their precise "meanings" or their referents in the material world (i.e., the vessels themselves) to have remained static.

We don't even really know what these vessels-with-a-hole-in-the-base were doing in the brewing process. Were they fermentation vessels, as has often been argued? Filtering vessels? Something else entirely? The jury is still out and may be for some time. What we do know is that they were considered a fundamental piece of brewing equipment in Mesopotamia.

And that single hole in the base makes them eminently identifiable in the archaeological record. As a general rule, when it comes to vessels meant to hold liquids, one tries to avoid poking a hole in the base. Perhaps you're familiar with that old classic, "There's a Hole in the Bucket"? I know I am. My parents have been gradually perfecting their own rendition over the years (performed live, in costume, for their children's school talent shows, for example). But the point is: A vessel with a single hole in the base stands out in the archaeological record.

And this fact has not gone unnoticed.[70] Many archaeologists have embraced the vessel-with-a-butthole as a potential "archaeological correlate" for brewing activities. Although not a one, as far as I know, has embraced the rather graphic reference to human anatomy possibly implied by the Sumerian phrasing. Who knows. Maybe it will catch on. And I guess I'll be the one to blame. (Apologies, in advance, to all my colleagues out there.) In any case, if the presence of these distinctive vessels does indeed offer a more-or-less definitive means of identifying spaces where brewing once took place—and I don't think there's currently any significant evidence to the contrary—that's a huge win for archaeologists. An easy-to-identify vessel (Is there a hole in its base? Yep, there's a hole in its base.) with a well-defined function that was in use for a long period of time? Jackpot! Of course, nothing is ever really that simple, and we're always much safer relying on multiple lines of evidence. That is, after all, the whole point of our current foray into the brewing *assemblage*.

Residue analysis at the sites of Tell Bazi in Syria and Khani Masi in Iraq has now produced definitive proof that these vessels were, at least sometimes, used to brew beer.[71] That's not to say that they were always and only used to brew beer. (Recall that brew kettle that moonlights as a high-capacity chili pot.) But the recovery of actual traces of beer inside them suggests that these distinctive vessels-with-a-hole-in-the-base might indeed serve as a reasonable means of identifying brewing activities in the archaeological record. If so, the authors of a number of previous studies can breathe a sigh of relief. And we can feel confident including their efforts to specify the places where beer was brewed in our look at brewing spaces in Chapter 5.

Thanks to an analysis conducted by Alexander Sollee, we can also get some sense for the range of variation in this one element of the brewing assemblage.[72] Sollee pulled together 126 examples of *Lochbodengefässe* excavated at sites across the region and compared them along three main axes: form, volume, and findspot. During his period of focus (late third and second millennium BCE), when it comes to form (i.e., shape), the vessels fall into two main types: open and closed. But the distinction can be pretty subtle—the difference between a vessel that reaches its greatest diameter at the rim (open) and a vessel that reaches its greatest diameter somewhere below the rim, before curving back inward (closed). None of the examples illustrated by Sollee shows a very pronounced closing, that is, a significant difference between the maximum diameter of the vessel and the rim diameter. If you are not an archaeologist or a potter, you might be forgiven for thinking that they all look broadly similar (Figure 4.3).

But the open/closed distinction may very well have meant something to people at the time. During the Middle and Late Bronze Age, for example, Sollee sees a geographical pattern in the distribution of these vessels. The open version appears primarily in southern Mesopotamia, and the closed version, primarily in northern Mesopotamia (with a zone of overlap and shifting usage around the Khabur, Balikh, and Middle Euphrates rivers).[73] What might this pattern indicate? Just different traditions of ceramic manufacture, a noticeable but not particularly meaningful regional preference for open vs. closed vessels? Or was this subtle distinction in vessel form a more deliberate aesthetic choice by producers and consumers, perhaps even an intentional marker of cultural identity? Could it possibly signal differences in how the vessels were used, that is, different brewing traditions? And what about the corresponding preference for different types of vessel base: reinforced bases in the south and simple round or flat bases in the north?

I don't have an answer for these questions. But it is interesting that the distinction in vessel form is not matched by a distinction in either vessel size or "butthole" size. When it comes to volume, both the open and closed versions cover a broad range: 9–280 liters and 2–230 liters, respectively. The variation in hole diameter is similarly broad: 6–48 millimeters for both types. And hole diameter does not appear to vary in proportion to vessel volume. A big vessel might have either a large or a small hole, and a small vessel, the same.[74] So, size-wise, the open and closed versions of the vessel-with-a-hole-in-the-base cover similar territory. But it's a pretty expansive territory. The difference between 2 liters and 280 liters is approximately the difference between a large soda bottle and a 4-foot-wide fish tank. A 6 millimeter hole is smaller than a pea, while a golf ball would pass easily through a 4.8 centimeter hole.

This brings us to another important question. Can we assume that all of these pierced-bottom vessels were used for the same purpose? Sollee thinks

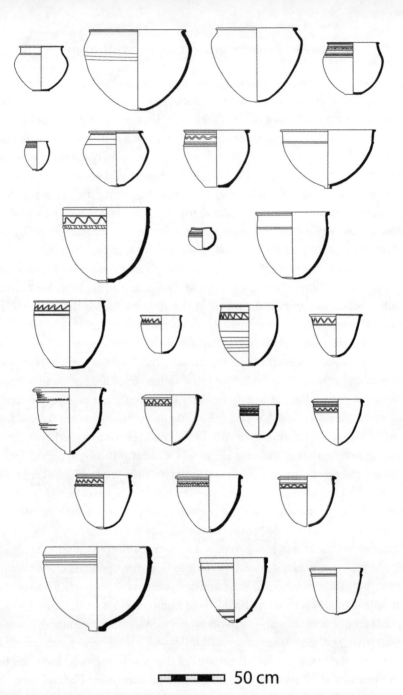

50 cm

Figure 4.3. A selection of *Lochbodengefässe* ("vessels with a hole in the base") from archaeological sites in southern and northern Mesopotamia. Vessel findspots and volumes, listed top to bottom, left to right. Row 1: Lidar Höyük (9 l), Tell Bazi (175 l), Tell Hadidi (113 l), Umm el-Marra (36 l); Row 2: Tell Shuiyukh Tahtani (3 l), Tell Munbāqa (43 l), Tell Halawa A (77 l), Tell Bi'a (93 l); Row 3: Tell Sabi Abyad (102 l), Tell Arbid (3 l), Tell Brak (84 l); Row 4: Tell al-Rimah (78 l), Tell Taya (12 l), Tell Fisna (42 l), Yorgan Tepe (16 l); Row 5: Khirbet ed-Diniye (53 l), Tall Halawa, Hamrin (37 l), Tell Genj (10 l), Tell Yelkhi (21 l); Row 6: Tell Oweissat (33 l), Tell Asmar (40 l), Tell edh-Dhibai (uncertain); Row 7: Tell el-Lahm (207 l), Susa (47 l), Choga Zanbil (24 l). (Redrawn after Sollee 2012: Abb. 3. Vessel volumes drawn from Sollee 2012: Tabelle 1.)

not, based in part on the size issue—a soup can and an oil barrel might look broadly similar in form, and both might feature a drainage hole, after all—but also on their archaeological context. Some of the vessels in his study were found alongside other potential brewing equipment. Others were found in burials, where they served as receptacles for human remains, both inhumations and cremations. Others had been tipped upside down (or, if they were created for this purpose, I suppose right-side up) and used to cap sewer drains.

There is a sense, then, in which these vessels with a pierced base were multifunctional. Or perhaps we just haven't yet adequately recognized the finer distinctions within the broader vessel type. That is, perhaps certain versions of this vessel type were used for one purpose and certain versions for another. Indeed, Sollee points to possible evidence for a correlation between vessel size and vessel function. But there's also another possibility: reuse. Objects can and very often do have complex biographies or social lives.[75] A ceramic vessel might be made and used for one purpose, but it might also then be creatively repurposed, reworked, or reinterpreted multiple times along the trajectory of its life. It might also, of course, change hands along the way. And its recognized function, value, and meaning—not to mention its name—might very well evolve over time.

Based on overall shape and the distinctive perforated base, for example, Sollee argues that the *Lochbodengefässe* seem particularly well suited to food processing, especially the separation of liquid from solid substances, as is required at various stages of the brewing process. Perhaps most of these vessels were purpose-built for brewing, but then some gradually found their way into other uses. I mean, who among you brewers out there wouldn't at least give some thought to the idea of being buried in (or alongside) your trusty brew kettle or fermenter? It doesn't sound so crazy to me. But, at the moment, we don't know whether every single vessel-with-a-hole-in-the-base recovered by archaeologists started its life as a brewing vessel. Perhaps dedicated ceramic workshops were busily churning out gakkul-like vessels that both started and ended their lives as burial urns or sewer-drain covers.

For those lucky *Lochbodengefässe* that were destined for the world of brewing, though, exactly what function were they intended to perform? They're often interpreted as fermentation vessels or filtering vessels, but both options are really just educated guesses. We don't know exactly what the hole was for, and we don't know exactly how the vessel-with-a-hole-in-the-base contributed to the brewing of beer. So, even when it comes to

IN THE LAND OF NINKASI

this most iconic of Mesopotamian brewing vessels, the fundamental question of function (which we'll return to below) remains unresolved. And it's tightly bound up with our broader uncertainties about the brewing process and the brewing assemblage.

Vessel pairs

Let's crawl out of this *hole* hole that I've dug us into and have a look at some groups or sets of brewing equipment. In the written record, what really jumps out is vessel pairs.[76] Certain brewing vessels are regularly mentioned in the same breath, so to speak, as certain other vessels, and these vessel pairs appear to have functioned together as a unit. In the closing lines of the Hymn to Ninkasi, for example, we meet one pair: nigdurbur + laḫtan.

> Ninkasi, the ^{dug}nig$_2$-dur$_2$-bur$_3$, which makes a pleasant sound,
> You place appropriately on (top of) a large laḫtan.
> You are the one who pours out the filtered beer of the laḫtan.
> It is (like) the onrush of the Tigris and the Euphrates.[77]

We learn that the nigdurbur sat above the laḫtan. We learn that the laḫtan contained filtered beer. And we learn that the nigdurbur, made a "pleasant" (or, alternatively, "loud"[78]) sound.

We've already met another piece of Sumerian literature—a šir-namursaĝa song written for the king Iddin-Dagan (Chapter 3)—that offers a particularly vivid description of the sound produced by a second vessel pair: šagub + lamsari (here written ^{dug}šag$_4$-gub and ^{dug}lam-sa$_2$-ri). The translation that we read earlier tells us that the vessels made a bubbling sound: "Dark beer [kurun], emmer beer [ulušin], and emmer beer [ulušin] for my lady bubble in the šagub-jar and the lamsari-vat for her."[79] Indeed, depending on whose interpretation you wish to follow, the phrasing in the text might indicate either a bubbling, gurgling, or splashing sound.[80] But these are all just efforts to make sense of a wonderful example of onomatopoeia that I think works just as well on its own, in the original Sumerian. What the text really says is something like this: "The ^{dug}šag$_4$-gub and the ^{dug}lam-sa$_2$-ri make a dubul-dabal sound." If you're having trouble imagining this sound, try saying it out loud a few times in a row—dubul-dabal, dubul-dabal, dubul-dabal—and I think you'll get the picture. If that doesn't work for you, one scholar has suggested "blop blop" as the equivalent in French.[81] Was it the sound of water being drained off to allow barley grains to germinate after soaking, the sound of a vigorous fermentation bubbling away, the sound of a filter hard at work, or the sound of finished beer being decanted for serving? It's hard to say. Whatever it was, though, it was the sound of beer, and it promised good things to come.

We can also add a few more vessel pairs to the list. During the Ur III period, for example, ugubala + lamre (written ugu$_4$-bala, lam-re$_6$) and (nig)durbur + manhara (written nig$_2$-dur$_2$-bur$_3$ / dur$_2$-bur$_3$ / dur$_2$-PU2, ma-an-hara$_4$). And, from the Old Babylonian period onward, *namzītu* + *namhāru* and *namzītu* + *lahtanu*.[82] Teasing apart the subtle distinctions among these different vessels and vessel pairs (e.g., distinctions in size, form, function, context of use, etc.) is no simple matter.[83] Perhaps they were all basically equivalent or, at least, variations on a common theme: a vessel with a hole in its base that sat above a collecting vessel, so that liquid of some sort could run from one down into the other. It's not out of the question. But it's also far from certain.

Brewing assemblages

These two-vessel sets are interesting, but they hardly comprise a full brewing assemblage. We know that the cuneiform record includes references to all kinds of other brewing equipment. But can we say anything about the actual set of equipment used in any particular brewery? Or in a particular tavern or household? Didn't those compulsive list makers of ancient Mesopotamia ever think to channel their cataloging urge toward producing some inventories of brewing equipment? Why yes, of course they did. The first verse of the Drinking Song ("gakkul-e gakkul-e"), for example, might include such an inventory. Civil has suggested that the song was composed to celebrate the inauguration of a new tavern. And what better way to begin than with a list of the "beautiful vessels" ready to deliver up beer to the tavern's thirsty customers?

> The gakkul, the gakkul,
> The gakkul, the lam-sa$_2$-re,
> The gakkul, which makes the liver happy,
> The lam-sa$_2$-re, which rejoices the heart,
> The ugur-bal, a fitting thing in the house,
> The ša$_3$-gub, which is filled with beer,
> The am-am, which carries (the beer of) the lam-sa$_2$-re,
> The ... reed buckets and the reed pails of ... ,
> The beautiful vessels, are ready on (their) *pot stands!*[84]

Of course, this poetic roll call of brewing vessels hardly constitutes an inventory in the proper sense. The cuneiform record only includes a smattering of genuine inventory texts that enumerate the specific pieces of brewing equipment actually present in particular locales.

For example, two inventories from the city of Girsu offer us a glimpse of brewing vessels in the home during the Early Dynastic period.[85] One of these lets us peek into a vessel storeroom in the house of a man named Kēnum.[86] Each entry in the inventory includes a number (i.e., a vessel count) followed by the name of the vessel in question, sometimes qualified with further info (e.g., clean, broken, etc.). Here, in parentheses/italics, I've also included Walther Sallaberger's comments about each vessel type, but these interpretations are not set in stone.

5 ^{dug}kur *(storage vessels, for oil?)*
5 ^{dug}kur-KU.DU$_3$ *(pithoi)*
6 ma-ḫara$_4$ *(receiving vessels)*
x + 2 laḫtan$_2$ *(beer-pithoi)*, beer is poured in
x + 1 laḫtan$_2$ *(beer-pithoi)*, they are cleaned, broken
3 gar$_3$-bala *(brewing vessels)*, they are cleaned
1 gakkul$_2$ *(fermentation vessel)*
2 lam-re *(beer vessels)*
1 filter for a beer drinking tube:
with Kēnum, the one of the jar warehouse,
are present.
Uru-inimgina, ruler of Lagaš.
Eniggal,
the captain, counted it. 1 year.[87]

Why have the contents of Kēnum's vessel storeroom been carefully counted, catalogued, and committed to writing? We may never know for certain, but it feels a little invasive, doesn't it? Like we've snuck into Kēnum's house and made a beeline for his stash of brewing equipment to conduct our own private inspection and, perhaps, look down our noses a bit at those broken laḫtan vessels. I can envision a similar list compiled at my own house, one that ends instead, "with Tate, the one of archaeology, are present (in the laundry room, up on the highest shelf . . . where his wife made him stash everything)." My inventory would, I believe, include several broken hydrometers, all dropped on the floor and shattered, of no further use now, but kept nonetheless. And the word "dusty" would almost certainly appear repeatedly.

But back to Kēnum. That's a pretty substantial assemblage of brewing vessels for a single household. The number and variety of vessels present in this household storeroom suggests, perhaps, that we should not focus too much attention on the iconic vessel pairs and their distinctive "dubul-dabal" sound. The paired vessels might have been just one element within a more extensive brewing assemblage. Cast your mind back for a moment to our brief ethnographic visit to Burkina Faso. The brewing process described there by Belliard included at least nine different vessels, two of which were organized into a filter system: one vessel (with holes pierced in the base) sitting on a stand above the other. What if the paired vessels in Mesopotamia served a similar and, all things considered, relatively minor role in the brewing process? The fact that these paired vessels were essential for brewing and were recognized as the quintessential tools of the brewer does not mean that they were the only vessels needed during the brewing process.

But neither should we allow ethnographic comparisons to color our expectations too heavily. After all, many of the vessels in Kēnum's vessel storeroom appear elsewhere (i.e., in other texts) as part of vessel pairs. And we don't know which of the vessels in the storeroom might have been used together during the brewing of beer. Perhaps the storeroom included several different vessel pairs, each of which could be used independently. Or perhaps it was just filled with a mishmash of old and/or backup brewing equipment. It's important to remember what kind of text we're dealing with here: an inventory listing the vessels present in a storeroom. Let's say that calamity struck just after the writing of this text and Kēnum's house went up in flames and was immediately abandoned. Future archaeologists might very well come across that exact storeroom complete with its collection of brewing vessels. But they might also come across—perhaps in a neighboring room or courtyard—the household's primary set of brewing equipment, hastily dropped or left sitting in place (with malt soaking or beer fermenting merrily along) as the flames swept across the structure. This archaeological snapshot might offer a more complete look at the household brewing assemblage than what was kept hidden away in the storeroom. This is all just conjecture, of course. In fact, it's also possible that the text we're looking at might have been a different sort of inventory, not related to Kēnum's house but to his workplace, the jar warehouse.

Let's jump now from the Early Dynastic period (2900–2350 BCE) into the Neo-Babylonian and Persian periods (605–330 BCE). During the first millennium BCE, a broader range of texts offer up brewing equipment inventories. There's just one little problem. At this point, date "beer" (i.e., wine) has arrived on the scene. And the terminology employed—whether for the beverage itself, the place where the beverage was produced, or the equipment, actions, and processes involved—is often borrowed directly from the domain of barley beer. In some cases, it's clear that a particular "brewery" was engaged in the production of either barley beer or date wine. In other cases, the situation is murkier.

For example, one brewing contract from the city of Borsippa revolves around the production of *billatu* for presentation to the god Nabû.[88] We already met *billatu* briefly in Chapter 3 and earlier in the current chapter in Sallaberger's account of the brewing process. Was it a brewing ingredient? An intermediate brewing product? A dried-out beer that could be reconstituted with water? A distinct type of beer? All of the above? Opinions differ, but the mention of *billatu* places us firmly in the realm of barley beer. And this contract helpfully lists off the equipment involved in its production. Here's the relevant part of the contract, which specifies that Rīmūt-Bēl (one party to the contract) has given Nabû-ušallim (the other party) use of the brewing equipment for the purpose of producing the *billatu* in question.

> 8 *namḫari* (vessels), 18 *dannu* (vessels) which . . . , 1 *esittu* (stone mortar),
> 2 *bukannu* (wooden pestles), 1 *nablalu* (reed mixing tool), 1 . . . ,
> 1 *nappû* (sieve), belonging to Rīmūt-Bēl, are at the disposal of Nabû-ušallim.[89]

It is noteworthy that this list includes *namḫaru* vessels but not the *namzītu* vessels that are typically paired with them—perhaps an indication that *billatu* production did not require the otherwise obligatory vessel with a hole in its base.[90]

For comparison, here's another contract, probably also related to the brewing of barley beer. This one is all about brewing equipment. There are three individuals involved. We'll call them Person 1, Person 2, and Person 3.

> Equipment for the work
> of the brewer on [x] day
> of the month Arahsamnu, by Person 1 (*Ba-la-ṭu*),
> was checked and

given to Person 2 (D.AG.*it-tan-ni*).
1 *nablalu* (reed mixing tool), 15 *namḥari* (vessels)
5 *namzīti* (vessels)... (?)
1 vessel with *silqu*
5 tools... (?)
the *paqqāju*-worker... (?)
In the presence of Person 3 (D.[x] ...]
One each ...
... (?)
... (?)[91]

Hopefully, it's clear what's going on here (despite the poorly preserved lines toward the end). Person 1 has checked over a collection of brewing equipment and then handed that equipment over to Person 2, with Person 3 acting as a witness to the transaction. Among the pieces of equipment listed, we see both *namḥaru* and *namzītu* vessels and also, as in the previous contract, a reed tool for mixing.

Contemporary contracts for the brewing of date wine suggest a significant degree of overlap in the equipment required. If we visit the city of Nippur, for example, the wealthy and well-connected Murašu family had its fingers in many different pies, one of which was the business of date farming. Indeed, investment was poured into date production during this period. Dates had become a key commodity—to the point that they were functioning as a sort of currency unto themselves.[92] Yes, money did grow on trees. So, it's hardly surprising that the Murašu family archive includes many documents that revolve around dates and their various uses. In one contract, for example, a brewer is given the following items and is expected (that is, contractually obligated) to "brew and deliver 100 *dannu*-vessels of sweet beer."[93]

100 gur (18,000 liters) of dates
100 *dannu*-vessels packed in leather
  6 *namzītu*-vessels
  2 *namhari*-vessels
  2 workers
10 gur (1800 liters) *kasû*-plant[94]

Given the explicit mention of a large quantity of dates and no mention of barley, the "sweet beer" under contract here is almost certainly date wine. Also, note the inclusion of a large quantity of *kasû*, that enigmatic "aromatic" that we encountered in Chapter 3. The *kasû*-plant may have been used to flavor barley beer, but it is particularly associated with the production of date wine.

If we head northwest from Nippur to the city of Babylon, we encounter another influential merchant family, the Egibi. Their extensive investment portfolio included not just date wine production, but also the tavern business. And their tavern-related interests extended beyond the city of Babylon. For example, two contracts written up on the eleventh day of the ninth month of the sixth year of the Persian king Cambyses (who ruled 529–522 BCE) revolve around the setting up of a tavern in the city of Kish (about 12 km east of Babylon).[95] The proprietor of this tavern is to be Ishunnatu, a woman enslaved to Itti-Marduk-balâṭu, a well-known member of the Egibi family.

One of the two contracts enumerates the pieces of furniture and other equipment entrusted to Ishunnatu by a man named Marduk-iqîšanni for the purpose of setting up the tavern—a sort of starter package that can be reclaimed by Marduk-iqîšanni after a period of two and a half months. The list includes:

5 ᵍⁱˢna₂ (beds)
10 ᵍⁱˢgu-za (chairs)
3 ᵍⁱˢbanšur (tables)
1 *ingurinu* (?)
3 *sirpu* (shears)
1 *marri* anbar (iron spade)
1 *qulmû* (axe)
1 *namzîtu* (beer vessel)
1 *kankannu* (vessel stand)
1 *mušahhinu* (cooking pot)
1 *šiddatu* (vat)
1 *maššanu* (?)
1 *arannu* (chest)
1 ᵍⁱ*ušukullatu* (? of reed)[96]

The second contract specifies that Itti-Marduk-balâṭu (of the Egibi family) has himself provided some further equipment and ingredients, as well as a substantial supply of "good quality beer" to get things going. His contribution includes:

50 *tannu* kaš du₁₀-ga	50 jars of good quality beer
60 gur zu₂-lum-ma	10,800 liters of dates
2 *mušahhinu* zabar	2 bronze cooking pots
7 gu₂-zi zabar	7 bronze cups
3 *baṭu*	3 bronze bowls
4 gur gazi^sar	720 liters gazi/*kasû*[97]

The second contract also explicitly excludes the set of equipment in the first contract from its own purview. The list of items "not included" closely matches the other contract, with a few deviations. For our purposes, most noticeable is the addition of a second *namzîtu* vessel and a *namhâru* vessel (a conspicuous absence in the first contract).

Given the enormous quantity of dates entrusted to Ishunnatu, there can be little doubt that we're dealing here with a tavern that was in the business of producing and selling date wine (rather than barley beer). And, apparently, one could operate such a tavern—or at least get such a tavern up and running—with a pretty minimal assemblage of brewing vessels: a couple of *namzîtu* vessels, a *namhâru* vessel, a vessel stand, and a smattering of other vats, bowls, and cups that may or may not have been used for brewing. That's an interesting point about the scale of the brewing assemblage, and we'll come back to it later.

But let's take a moment to reflect on some of the other pieces of equipment mentioned. A small collection of tables and chairs. Sure, that makes sense. Customers are going to want somewhere to hang out while sipping their date wine. But what about those five beds? Perhaps this tavern doubled as an inn, a cozy spot where out-of-towners could find both a reasonably priced jug of wine and a bed for the night. Perhaps. But there's also another possibility. As we'll discuss in Chapter 7, taverns were regularly associated with prostitution. That's not too surprising, I suppose. Taverns past and present have very often been known to facilitate romantic rendezvous of one sort or another. But is it possible that the Mesopotamian tavern was more explicitly and intentionally linked with prostitution? Those five beds allotted to Ishunnatu are, at the least, suggestive.[98] Maybe her tavern doubled as an inn. Maybe it doubled as a brothel. Maybe both. Given the need for at least three cooking pots (*mušahhinu*), customers could also probably expect to find a bite to eat there. Perhaps they were served up dishes that featured homegrown vegetables cultivated in an attached garden plot with the iron spade (*marri* anbar) that shows up in the contract.[99]

While the Egibi and those in their employ may have catered to the needs of everyday folks—locals and visitors in search of beer, rest, and/ or hanky-panky—around the same time, in the city of Uruk to the south, some in the service industry were serving a more rarified clientele. At this point, as during the city's first heyday, Uruk still belonged to the goddess Inana/Ishtar, and her temple complex, the Eanna, was still the religious heart of the city. This would all change quite dramatically a few years down the road, during a cultic reorientation orchestrated under the Achaemenid Persian ruler Darius I.[100] But for now all eyes were focused on Ishtar. And Ishtar had needs. In particular, she needed her food and drink. One of the most essential tasks performed by the Eanna temple personnel was the provision of daily sustenance for the goddess. There's nothing particularly novel about that. Just as human as the rest of us (in some ways . . . in others, of course, not at all), the gods of ancient Mesopotamia had to be fed. And the cuneiform record has a lot to say about this crucial task foisted off onto humanity.

What's unique about the Neo-Babylonian Eanna temple is that we have a series of inventory tablets that tell us about the equipment employed in the task. As you might suspect, the equipment was on the fancy side. I mean, you wouldn't dare prepare a meal for Ishtar using plain old ceramic vessels, would you? No, you wouldn't. You would use only the finest silver and gold. And you would want to keep a close eye on this super posh set of pots and pans. Indeed, you would store them in a special building known as the *bît urinni*, a sort of temple treasury for cultic paraphernalia. You would take them out periodically for a good once-over to make sure they were all still there and in tip-top shape. And you would definitely write everything down. If something were to disappear, a paper trail would be essential.

We have five such inventory texts from the Eanna temple, spanning a period of 27 years.[101] One even specifies that the equipment was taken out so that it could be polished. The five inventories—which don't match up perfectly, but pretty darn close for a stretch of three decades—list off a total of between 71 and 100 pieces of equipment. There are silver pots, pedestals, vats, and braziers. There are golden torches and golden harps. There are vases made of alabaster. But what interests us here is the brewing equipment. All five lists start off with the following items (with a few variations):

1 silver *adaru* vessel
16 silver *dannu* vessels
15 silver *kankannu* pedestals
3 silver *namḫaru* vessels
2 silver *šiddatu* pot stands
4 silver *namzītu* vessels[102]

By now, you should be more than familiar with several of these. The presence of *namzītu* and *namḫaru* vessels, in particular, is a pretty clear signal that we're in the realm of brewing.

Can we say for sure that any of these fancy silver vessels were used for brewing actual beer? The texts themselves offer a few hints, but nothing decisive. The *namzītu* entry in each list, for example, is followed by the qualification "for the altar" (*ša birit šiddi*). And several of the texts specify that the whole assemblage of inventoried objects was taken out of storage for performance of the *šalam bīti* ceremony, a ritual that took place within some kind of cubicle surrounded by a curtain.[103] Does the fact that the brewing vessels in these inventories functioned primarily in a ritual capacity imply that they were not actually used for brewing on the earthly plane? I don't think we can make that leap. So let's just say hypothetically that they were used for brewing (or at least serving or displaying) beer in the flesh. Do we know whether anybody actually drank that beer? And do we know whether that "beer" would have been beer, as opposed to date wine? Nope.

But this brings up an interesting point about technological crossover. When the Mesopotamian palate took a turn toward date wine and brewers started producing date wine on a significant scale, did they borrow heavily from the world of beer brewing? Were the same people brewing both beverages? Was there significant crossover in technologies, techniques, and skill sets? I mean, we know that the beverages themselves were considered similar enough, at some level, that they could both be considered "beer." And we know that some key vessel types were employed in the brewing of both beverages.

Today, we tend to think of beer and wine as entirely different beverages, the result of two distinct production processes, each requiring its own specialized repertoire of equipment. But I wonder if this strict dichotomy might break down in the case of ancient Mesopotamia. As we've already seen, some of the world's earliest alcoholic beverages appear to have been beer-wine or beer-wine-mead hybrids, and such hybrids have reemerged in recent years. So the line between beer and wine has, in fact, often been quite hazy. And the evidence for the addition of date syrup to barley beer in Mesopotamia might indicate that they enjoyed a beer-wine hybrid. But I suspect that there might also have been a closer kinship—closer than we're accustomed to—between beer and wine at the level of production technologies and techniques. (At least when it comes to date wine. Grape wine is another matter.)

I find this potential technological crossover interesting because of an article by Bill Sillar that I read years ago while working on my doctoral dissertation.[104] According to Sillar's argument, when searching for a solution to some kind of technical problem, we humans tend to poach from what we already know. More often than not, our solution will involve borrowing technologies and/or techniques from one domain of our experience and applying them to another. How we perceive of the problem as a problem and how we go about trying to solve it are heavily dependent on our specific cultural and historical context. The upshot is that different societies will tend to favor particular ways of representing and manipulating the material world—for example, specific technical actions or processes that crosscut a variety of different domains.

More than that, these culturally specific orientations toward technical problems often occupy such a central position that they take on a special metaphorical power, seeping out of the technical domain and into the broader cultural lexicon. For example, I've just done my best to *boil down* the key points of Sillar's article for you, *distilling* the main thesis, *reducing* the argument down to its essence, *condensing* a complex line of reasoning into a few bullet points. See what I'm doing there? The English language is full of such metaphorical references to techniques and processes. When trying to conceptualize the domain of ideas and argumentation, we often resort specifically to a suite of terms that revolve around particular ways of processing liquids.

Perhaps it's not all that radical to suggest that brewing technologies and techniques were transferred from the domain of barley beer to the domain of date wine in Mesopotamia. But, for those of us seeking to identify traces of brewing in the archaeological record, it's an important question to tackle.

If they were basically using the same brewing assemblage to produce both barley beer and date wine, how might we hope to distinguish these archaeologically? (I suppose the obvious answer is a lot more organic residue analysis.) And what might this kinship in production processes tell us about the character of the beverages themselves?

At the same time, I like how Sillar encourages us to think about the bigger picture: the possibility that these specific methods of food processing might have been bound up with a set of deeply ingrained, culturally specific orientations toward the material world. For example, how does the evidence for brewing in Mesopotamia jibe with proposals for a big-picture, deep-time distinction between the "boiling" cultures of Southwest Asia and the "roasting" cultures of Africa?[105] Can we see traces of a distinctively Mesopotamian way of thinking about and manipulating the material world—a suite of concepts, actions, processes, and tools that crosscut different technical domains and perhaps also *infused* (or *permeated* or *saturated*) their broader repertoire of symbolic associations, metaphors, and turns of phrase? I don't know, but I think it's an angle that's worth exploring.

If our focus here were ancient Egypt, we would definitely want to take a detour now into the artistic record. Intent as they were on guaranteeing a steady supply of beer for the afterlife, the Egyptian elite often insisted that their tombs be decked out with artistic renderings of beer production. Whether in the form of wall paintings, raised reliefs, or three-dimensional wooden models, these detailed vignettes show brewers and their underlings busily (or not so busily, in some cases) at work among the tools of their trade: vessels, vats, sieves, stands, stirring implements, etc. Alas, Mesopotamia offers us very little in the way of brewing scenes. I don't believe that anyone has done an exhaustive search for such scenes, but I'm only aware of a few depictions on cylinder seals that might fit the bill.[106]

The most convincing of these appears on an Akkadian-period (2350–2192 BCE) seal that currently resides at the Louvre in Paris (Figure 4.4).[107] The main scene shows a seated deity receiving offerings from two standing figures. The first of these figures carries a goat, and the second, a bucket of some sort. Behind the offering bearers—and also, as it happens, behind the seated deity, since everything comes full circle when you roll a cylinder across wet clay—a smaller scene is squeezed in beneath the seal's cuneiform inscription. Here we a see a figure, bent at the waist, reaching out with both arms to manipulate a pair of vessels. One vessel is suspended above

Figure 4.4. Cylinder seal with a possible brewing scene and an inscription reading "Ur-Zu, the brewer." AOD 21, CCO D 21. (Courtesy of Louvre Museum)

the other on a stand. And then behind these is another vessel standing on the ground. If you view the scene with the eye of faith (and squint really hard), there's even perhaps a hint of something passing between the two paired vessels. Could this be our iconic set of paired brewing vessels? And perhaps even a glimpse of the beer itself, dripping down from the upper to the lower vessel? I'm inclined toward a (cautious) yes, due in large part to the inscription directly above, which reads: "Ur-Zu, the brewer."

If this is indeed a brewing scene, what can it tell us about brewing equipment? Let's look at the vessel on the stand. It has what looks to be a rounded bottom, a restricted neck, a flaring rim, and a high shoulder—a profile that matches up very nicely with many of the vessels-with-a-hole-in-the-base that have been recovered archaeologically (and, therefore, perhaps with the *namzîtu* and related terms). The stand itself seems pretty minimal, perhaps just a simple wooden tripod or something of the sort. Underneath the stand, we see a squat, straight-sided tray or vat: not, I think, what many have in mind when they envision a *namhâru* or collecting vessel. And then, off to the left, we have a much larger jar (assuming that it is depicted to scale) with a pedestal base, restricted neck, flaring rim, and three horizontal decorative bands (two at the shoulder and one near the base). These three vessels may not represent a full brewing assemblage, but it's a rare treat to see them depicted together in their context of use.

Unfortunately, the archaeological evidence for brewing assemblages in Mesopotamia is also pretty scarce for the time being. Recent work at the sites of Khani Masi and Tell Khaiber in Iraq has brought the repertoire of brewing equipment at these sites into closer focus, but neither has yet shown us a more-or-less coherent brewing assemblage recovered all together as a set in situ.[108] For this, there are really just two good case studies to explore: 1) the brewing sets uncovered at Late Bronze Age (1400–1200 BCE) Tell Bazi in Syria and 2) the so-called four-part sets recovered within burials at a series of sites dating to the Early Dynastic and Akkadian periods (2900–2192 BCE).

At Tell Bazi, pretty much every household appears to have been brewing its own beer. And they were using a standardized set of brewing vessels. Like on the Ur-Zu seal that we just examined (in number, if not form/function), this set included three basic vessels: a large, open-mouthed vat with a thickened rim and flat or rounded base (up to 200 liters in volume), a smaller, open-mouthed vessel with a more pronounced shoulder, a flat or rounded base, and a hole pierced in the base (90–110 liters in volume), and large storage jars (Figure 4.5). Organic residue analysis identified traces of oxalate and occasional starch grains within the vats and pierced-bottom vessels, and carbonized barley was regularly recovered from the large storage jars.[109] For the excavators, this all adds up to the very reasonable conclusion that the three-vessel set was used in the preparation of beer. Exactly how it was used is up for debate. As we saw earlier in this chapter, the excavators have proposed that the pierced-bottom vessel was used for

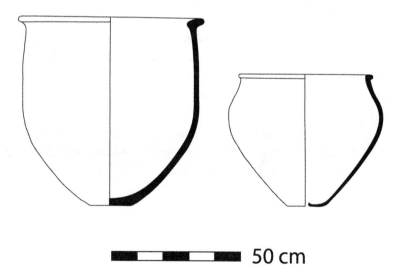

50 cm

Figure 4.5. Household brewing assemblage featuring large, open-mouthed vat and smaller, open-mouthed vessel with a hole pierced in the base. Tell Bazi, Syria. (Redrawn after Zarnkow et al. 2011: Fig. 4.1)

malting, while the large, open vat was used for mashing and fermentation (via their hypothesized "cold mashing" technique). Maybe, maybe not. But the excavators have at least demonstrated the viability of this interpretation in a series of brewing experiments.

Our second archaeological example takes us from the land of the living to the realm of the dead. If there's one near-universal in this realm, it's that the dead appreciate being sent off to the afterlife accompanied by a liberal supply of alcohol. (Obviously, this is not actually a cultural universal, but it has certainly been very, very common among human groups past and present.) In many cases, the alcohol that features so prominently in funerary rituals is meant to be consumed by those left behind to memorialize, cope with, or capitalize on the death in question. But the deceased are often left with plenty for their own uses in the great beyond. And sometimes they're left with all of the necessary accoutrements for brewing more once supplies run low. A case can be made for such afterlife-oriented brewing assemblages in Mesopotamia during the Early Dynastic and Akkadian periods.

At a series of different sites, excavators have uncovered burials that included a distinctive grouping of ceramic vessels, a so-called four-part set that looks remarkably similar from site to site.[110] The set typically includes 1) a large, open bowl or vat, 2) a cylindrical stand or "colander" with a number of largish holes pierced in its sides, 3) a bowl or "strainer" with smaller holes pierced in its base, and 4) a small cup or "tumbler" (Figure 4.6). These vessels were often recovered stacked one inside the other, so there can be little doubt that they functioned as a set of some kind. But what kind of set? What were they used for? None have been subject to organic residue analysis, so we don't have any physical traces of the substances they once contained.

I think it's safe to say, though, that all indications point toward an activity that involved a liquid. Given the context, a number of archaeologists have tentatively suggested that that liquid was beer. Most have bypassed the question of whether we're talking about beer production or beer consumption, and few have specified exactly how they envision the vessels functioning together as a set. One recent exception is Melania Zingarello, who has considered both the function of the individual vessels and their interrelations with one another, concluding that the four-part set (and the occasionally occurring five-part set) probably played a role in both the production and consumption of beer for funerary rituals.[111] Another recent

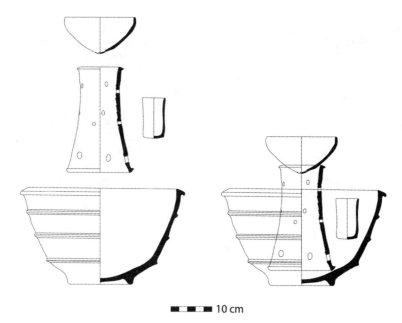

10 cm

Figure 4.6. Four-part set featuring large, open vat, cylindrical colander, strainer bowl, and tumbler. Grave 1, Abu Salabikh, Iraq. The reconstruction on the right shows how these vessels may have fit together during use. (Redrawn after Zingarello 2020: Fig. 6.1)

exception is Nicholas Postgate, who has offered an altogether different in-terpretation. He argues that these were, in fact, handwashing sets for the hereafter: the liquid involved was not beer but soapy water.[112]

These radically opposed interpretations of a well-attested but still difficult-to-pin-down set of ceramic vessels strike me as a fitting way to close out a chapter packed full of archaeological and written evidence but perhaps frustratingly short on firm conclusions. As you've seen, we know a lot about brewing technologies and techniques in Mesopotamia, but many questions remain. For now, let's wash our hands of the *how* and the *with what* of brewing and move on to the *where*.

Chapter 5

Brewers and brewing spaces

Its wine-cellar is a mountain oozing wine, from its brewery as much beer comes as the Tigris at high water.

The building of Ningirsu's temple[1]

Breweries at Girsu and Lagash

The sun god Utu peeks his head above the adjacent buildings and casts his slanting rays across a solemn gathering.[2] Near one end of a broad, flat clearing—perhaps 20 meters (65 feet) on a side—a small collection of priests and diviners, outfitted in their finest ceremonial garb, stand in a tight semicircle, all eyes directed toward a figure kneeling on the ground, bent over a small pit. From a vantage point near the center of the clearing, the king himself oversees the proceedings, flanked by a handful of his closest advisors. All attention is focused on the kneeling priest, as he gingerly lowers a gleaming white object into the pit, flashes of a metallic glint catching the rays of the rising sun.

As he pauses for a moment to offer a brief invocation, let's zoom in to examine the object in his hands. The striking white object is a pillow-shaped alabaster tablet (15 x 22 x 4.5 cm) with cuneiform signs chiseled carefully onto its upper surface (Figure 5.1).[3] If we peek underneath, more cuneiform signs are visible on its underside. And the tablet appears to be perfectly balanced atop the head of a copper statuette, human(oid) from

Figure 5.1. Alabaster tablet and copper statuette. Esplanade of Enmetena, Tello, Iraq. AO 2353. (Courtesy of Louvre Museum)

head to torso, with the horns of a deity and arms crossed on the chest, but then morphing into a pointed spike from the waist down. (On second glance, is the tablet really balancing on the figure's head? Or is it meant to give the impression that the spike has been driven through the tablet, anchoring it to the ground? Hard to say.) If we squint, we can make out another cuneiform inscription etched into the surface of the anthropomorphic spike.

What exactly are we looking at here? What is this odd combination of stone tablet and copper spike? Why are all these people here to watch as it is solemnly deposited within a hole in the ground? And what might those inscriptions have to tell us?

Let's start with the last of these: the inscriptions. The text on the alabaster tablet is on the wordy side.[4] Basically, it lists off a series of construction projects undertaken by a man named Enmetena, all for the glory of the god Ningirsu. The text on the copper spike is similar but much shorter. It gets right to the point—the specific construction project at issue here.

> [For] the god Ningirsu, warrior of the god Enlil,
> [En]-metena, ruler of Lagaš,
> son of En-anatum, [ru]ler of Lagaš,
> who built the brewery of the god Ningirsu,
> his personal god is the god Šul-MUŠ×PA.[5]

The alabaster tablet, with its lengthy list of previously completed construction projects, also eventually makes its way to the same destination: a brewery built by Enmetena for the god Ningirsu. So who is this Enmetena? Why all the fuss about his new brewery?

We're in the city of Girsu, capital of the city-state of Lagash, domain of the god Ningirsu ("Lord of Girsu").[6] The year is (approximately) 2420 BCE. And Enmetena is king—more specifically, the fifth king of the First Dynasty of Lagash (Early Dynastic IIIb period). So this is not just any brewery. It's a brewery built by the king for the city's patron deity. And the ceremony unfolding before us is taking place within the Eninnu ("House of Fifty"), the temple complex that houses the city's main shrine to Ningirsu.[7] These solemn proceedings are intended to provide the new brewery with a firm foundation, anchoring it to the ground with special copper pegs and hammering home the credentials of its royal patron. What we're witnessing is the ritual placement of a "foundation deposit" in preparation for the start of construction.

During their excavations at the site of Tello (ancient Girsu) in southern Iraq in the late nineteenth century AD, a French team under the direction of Ernest de Sarzec uncovered ten of these foundation deposits buried beneath the baked-brick pavement of a building that they called the "esplanade" of Enmetena—all with inscriptions offering testimony to Enmetena's construction of a brewery for Ningirsu.[8] One of the foundation deposits had been placed directly beneath the building's main entrance, and the others, at other strategic locations. A further set of inscriptions on four stone door sockets probably documents the restoration of this same brewery—the brewery of Ninĝirsu—by Enmetena's son and successor Enanatum II. One of the door sockets was found nearby (on the slope of Tell J); the others were found, well, elsewhere.[9] (In those days, findspots were not always recorded with the utmost precision.)

Incredibly, this set of inscribed foundation deposits excavated more than a century ago at the site Tello still offers our *only* solid confirmation for a brewery in the archaeological record of ancient Mesopotamia. Yes, you read that correctly: our only confirmed brewery. There are some other good candidates. And the evidence from Tello is far from perfect. Those were the early days of archaeology, when excavation techniques and recording procedures were often less than ideal (to put it mildly). But it seems virtually certain that the "esplanade" uncovered by de Sarzec was, indeed, the very brewery mentioned in the inscriptions of Enmetena, bearing in mind that the preserved remains might conceivably belong to a later iteration of the building (e.g., as restored by Enanatum II).

Unfortunately, we know relatively little about the building itself. The description and illustration provided by the excavators highlight a scattered collection of built installations.[10] There was a wide doorway, whose threshold was paved in baked bricks set in bitumen, and then a step down onto a baked-brick pavement. Sitting on the pavement, about 7 meters straight ahead of the doorway, was a 1.7-meter high, vaguely oval-shaped platform on which sat an "oval basin" (5.1 x 4.6 m) that had an opening on the opposite side. The excavators argued that this basin, with its sloping base paved in baked bricks with bitumen mortar, would have once held liquids. Other commentators, however, have suggested that it may have been an oven. Several meters to the right of the oval basin was the first in a line of four rectangular, baked-brick basins, each lined in bitumen and subdivided into either two or three sub-basins. To the left of the oval basin, a drainage channel cut diagonally across the space of the building. And that's basically all that we can say. What about the overall size, shape, and layout of the building (you may be asking)? Nope. The excavations did not recover traces of any exterior or interior walls—not because they didn't exist but because the French team had not yet mastered the art of identifying walls made of unbaked mudbricks. So they probably dug right through those walls.

Thankfully, we can head just down the road to the site of Tell al-Hiba (ancient Lagash) for a more meticulously excavated and recently re-analyzed

comparative example.[11] Between 1968 and 1976, an American team from
the Metropolitan Museum of Art and the Institute of Fine Arts at New York
University uncovered portions of two temple complexes at Tell al-Hiba:
the Ibgal of Inana and the Bagara of Ninĝirsu. The remains were discussed
in a series of preliminary reports,[12] but only now (more than four decades
later) are we on the brink of seeing a full, detailed, final publication of
the results.[13] In the meantime, as part of this ongoing Al-Hiba Publication
Project, Darren Ashby has recently gone back to the original excavation
records and offered a re-analysis of the Ibgal and the Bagara. So we can
turn to his 2017 doctoral dissertation for the most up-to-date look at these
temple complexes.[14]

The Ibgal ("Temple Oval"), dedicated to the goddess Inana, fits into the
"temple oval" tradition known elsewhere in Mesopotamia.[15] The Bagara,
however, offers us something different.[16] Dedicated to the god Ninĝirsu—
yes, the same Ninĝirsu that we met at the Eninnu in Girsu—the Bagara
complex comprised a collection of at least three free-standing structures,
built right up next to one another, probably atop a substantial, raised platform. Two of these structures are of particular interest (Figure 5.2). The
larger of the two, once thought to have functioned as a so-called "kitchen
temple," Ashby has reinterpreted as the main shrine of the Bagara and,
therefore, the focal point of the complex. Immediately to the east and
separated from the shrine by a narrow alley was the brewery. At least, that
has long been the assumption, and nothing in Ashby's analysis suggests
otherwise—even if he does very reasonably inject an element of uncertainty regarding exactly what sort of foodstuff might have been produced
in this building.[17] About half the size of the shrine, this probable brewery
was rebuilt a number of times, but it appears to have maintained the same
basic function from the Early Dynastic IIIb period up into the Ur III period (2450–2004 BCE).

Let's go on a little tour through one iteration of this building: the one
that Ashby calls 4HB IVB. This version of the building dates to the end of
the Early Dynastic IIIb period (2450–2350 BCE). So it would have been approximately contemporary with the brewery that we just examined down
the road at Girsu. The 4HB IVB building and its neighbor immediately to
the west (the probable shrine, known as 3HB III) were both destroyed in
a fire—perhaps one of the fires set by the rampaging army of Lugalzagesi,
king of the rival city-state of Umma. An inscription of Uru'inimgina, the

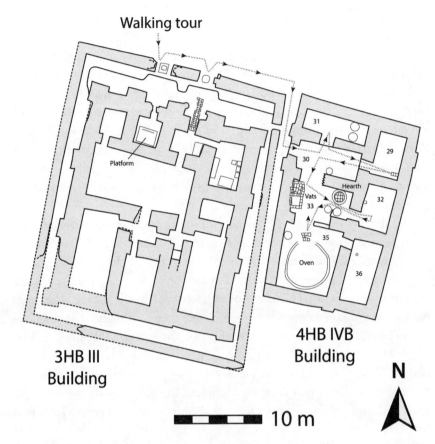

Figure 5.2. Plan of the 3HB III and 4HB IVB buildings, Tell al-Hiba, Iraq. The dotted line indicates the route of the walking tour narrated in the text. (Redrawn after Ashby 2017: Plate 26)

ninth and final king of the First Dynasty of Lagash, records an attack against Lagash by Lugalzagesi.

> The leader of Ĝiša (Umma) set fire to the Ekirbira.
> He set fire to the Antasur
> and bundled off its precious metals and lapis lazuli . . .
> he plundered the E-babbar
> and bundled off its precious metals and lapis lazuli;
> he plundered the giguna of Ninmaḫ of the sacred grove
> and bundled off its precious metals and lapis lazuli;
> he plundered the Bagara
> and bundled off its precious metals and lapis lazuli
> he set fire to the Dugru
> and bundled off its precious metals and lapis lazuli . . ..[18]

That's just a little sampling. The list goes on. During this campaign by Lugalzagesi, a whole series of important shrines in the domain of Lagash were plundered and/or set aflame, including the Bagara of Ninĝirsu and, we might suppose, the adjacent brewery.

But let's rewind the tape and wander through the brewery before that fateful day when it went up in flames.[19] Our tour begins inside the Bagara complex, just outside the entrance to the main shrine, the 3HB III building (see Figure 5.2, "Walking Tour").[20] So we're already in a restricted area. The whole Bagara complex was almost certainly once surrounded by an enclosure wall, marking it off as a special zone and restricting access to the interior. One couldn't normally expect to just walk in here off the street unmolested. But we've managed to sneak past the guards and make our way to the shrine of Ninĝirsu, which is surrounded by its own enclosure wall, built of mudbricks and rising to a height of perhaps 3 meters (9–10 feet). If we crane our necks skyward, we can see the niched and buttressed facade of the Bagara shrine rising up behind.

Two doorways lead through the enclosure wall. Peeking through the opening on the right, we can see that it lines up with a much narrower doorway leading into the Bagara shrine about five meters from where we stand. Through this inner doorway we can just catch glimpses of a small room dominated by a platform. The platform is covered with an assortment of special, ritual objects—maceheads, statues, stone vessels, weapons—that have been dedicated to the deity by the crème de la crème of Lagash society.[21] The reality is that we don't know exactly what took place in this small, isolated room and others like it elsewhere, outfitted with a large platform and its own separate access to the outside.[22] If we turn to our left, though, walk a few meters along the enclosure wall and peer through the next doorway, we're greeted with a view of the main entrance to the Bagara shrine. Wouldn't it be fun to see if we can sneak in there and check out the inner sanctum of Ninĝirsu? Yes, I'm sure it would, but our destination today is the brewery. So let's keep going.

Turning left again, we continue along the enclosure wall. After nine or ten meters, the wall makes a sharp right-hand turn, and a narrow alleyway opens up on our right. A draft of air from the alley carries the unmistakable scent of malted barley. This is the route to the brewery. We head down the alley, which constricts quickly from about two meters in width to one. On our right is the Bagara shrine enclosure wall, and on our left, another nondescript mudbrick wall. Almost immediately, a narrow door on the right leads again into the shrine enclosure, but this is nothing like the ornate entryways that we just passed. It looks more like a service entrance. A few steps further down the alley, a wider door opens in the wall on the left, and we're hit with an intense blast of malty aroma. Someone has left the wooden door propped open, so we follow our noses and slip unnoticed into Ningirsu's brewery (the 4HB IV building).[23]

We find ourselves in a small, low-ceilinged room (30 on Figure 5.2), nothing like the cavernous spaces that we associate with breweries today.[24] A steady stream of smoke drifts in from a doorway on the right, and further doors lead off to the left and straight ahead. Three ceramic vessels rest against the right-hand wall: one of uncertain size and shape lying in shadow in the corner to our right and two large vats (each a little under a meter in diameter) just beyond the doorway. Small fragments of clay are scattered here and there on the floor, the remnants of clay sealings, once attached to door pegs or containers but now broken apart and discarded.

We peek our heads into the left-hand doorway (31) and find three more large ceramic vats, each about 90 centimeters in diameter.[25] The two on our right are partially embedded in the floor. So they've been fixed in place and aren't intended to be moved around. Unfortunately, I can't tell you about all the other items that we would encounter in this room: baskets, boxes, spoons, sacks, stools, shelves, you name it. Throughout the building, everything perishable—for example, everything made out of wood—was already long gone when archaeologists arrived on the scene.

Let's try another door (29), the one situated straight across the from the main entrance.[26] We push open the door (which swings in to the right) and step into almost total darkness. Moving toward the back right corner, you stub your toe on something and bend down to check it out. Feeling around with your hands, all you can make out is some kind of small brick feature, just two courses high. What is this thing, and what exactly is going on in this room? We'll probably never know. All that the archaeologists came across in this room was this enigmatic brick feature, an emplacement for a door pivot, a clay sealing bearing a seal impression, and a bit of inlay in the shape of a feather or leaf. That's not a lot to go on. Let's head back into the entry room and try our luck elsewhere.

Turning on our heels, we exit the darkness and make our way back toward the entrance from the street. On our left, smoke still wafts gently through a crack in another doorway, the only one that we haven't yet tried. We ease the door open and find ourselves in a room (33) similar in size to the one we've just left and illuminated by flickering light.[27] There's a lot going on in here. A large rectangular tank (3 x 1.5 meters) made of baked brick stretches down the wall to our right. Peering over the edge, we suspect that the tanks hold some kind of liquid, but it's difficult to tell. To our left, we find the source of the flickering light and at least some of the smoke. A fire burns within a circular hearth that's been built into the floor of the room. And just a little bit further along, two large ceramic vessels are partially embedded within the floor.

It's not a particularly tidy space. Near the firepit, we find a piece of worked limestone and a flint blade, and, closer to the center of the room, a fragment from the rim of an alabaster bowl. Scattered here and there, we also find a stone pounder and various bits of metal. What's most surprising, though, is an intact cylinder seal, pushed right up against the side of the baked-brick tank. It's small and squat in shape; it's made of some kind of black stone; and it appears to depict a "master of animals" motif. Someone must be missing this well-crafted object. It's not the kind of thing one would casually cast aside.

Squeezing through the tight space between the fireplace and the sunken ceramic vessels, we enter a side room (32).[28] On the floor we find twelve fragments of clay sealings, each bearing a seal impression. The impressed scenes are all partial, but we can clearly see traces of animals and humans engaged in various activities. There's also a fragment of a cuneiform tablet.[29] One side seems to list off deliveries of beer to various individuals and perhaps other destinations. The other side mentions both a brewery (e_2-bappir$_3$) and a specific brewer (^{lu2}lunga$_3$) named Lugal-teš-mu. Several thousand years in the future, it's this tablet fragment that will alert archaeologists to the fact that they might be uncovering the remains of a brewery—perhaps the very brewery managed at one point by the brewer Lugal-teš-mu.

Turning around, we exit the door and squeeze back between the fireplace and the large vessels embedded in the floor. With the large, rectangular vat visible straight ahead of us, we decide to check out another room (35) to the left.[30] Passing through the doorway, we're immediately confronted by an enormous domed oven (5 m in diameter). It dominates the space, leaving little room for anything else, and belches out a substantial quantity of smoke. The only other notable feature is a large ceramic vessel placed up against the wall to the right. The thin wisps of smoke that periodically escape the mouth of the vessel suggest that something inside is smoldering.

Beating a hasty retreat back to the building's entrance, we emerge in the alleyway and enjoy a few deep gulps of fresh air. Why have I taken us on this lengthy brewery tour? Let's retire to the tavern—there must be one somewhere nearby—and discuss it over a drink.[31]

Where beer was brewed

Having located an appropriate watering hole and ordered up a few brews— perhaps a kaš sig (golden beer) for me and a kaš gi (dark beer) for you?— let's reflect a little on what we've just seen. Our foray into the Bagara gave us an up-close look at the interior space of a building that was very likely a brewery. And this was not just any brewery. It was (probably) set apart from the rest of the city behind an enclosure wall and was directly ac- cessible, across a narrow alleyway, from a (probable) shrine dedicated to the god Ninĝirsu. It was a brewery with divine connections. As we have seen, another brewery was built just down the road at Girsu by the king Enmetena at around the same time, broadly speaking. And this brewery was also located within a special ritual complex, the Eninnu of Ninĝirsu.

We know that the gods and goddesses of ancient Mesopotamia loved their beer. More than that, they expected ample supplies of beer to show up on their altars on schedule, day in, day out. The regular provision of beer and other foodstuffs for the gods was a fundamental human duty. So the beer produced in these two breweries at Lagash and Girsu was certainly beer for the gods. But it was not *only* beer for the gods. Who else might have had access to the output of Ninĝirsu's breweries? Were these breweries akin to public works projects, built by the state to provide adequate lubri- cation for the population at large? Or were they more exclusive enterprises, serving the needs of a more restricted clientele? And how typical were these breweries for their time? Was most (or all) brewing done for the glory of the gods, under the benevolent eye of the king? Did the state have a mo- nopoly on the production and distribution of beer? Or should we envision a more diverse brewing landscape that included, say, private entrepreneurs selling beer for their own profit? And how might all of this have changed over the centuries?

With these questions, we're dipping our toes into difficult and con- tentious waters. The effort to understand how people got their food and drink in Mesopotamia is tightly bound up with a series of long-running debates—debates about the economic role of the state, about the centralized redistribution of goods, about the predatory (or benevolent) nature of the palace and temple institutions, about the relative importance of private economic activity. We're not going to resolve any of these old chestnuts here. But, in a world where beer was a daily staple, the brewing of beer was a substantial sector of the economy. And one of the best ways to track changes in the scale and structure of the brewing economy is to pay attention to the spaces where beer was brewed.

Just think about recent history. Over the past half century, the United States has witnessed at least two radical shifts in who brews our beer and where they brew it. One lingering effect of the years of Prohibition (1920–1933 CE) was a mid-twentieth-century consolidation in the brewing industry that left us with just a handful of industrial-scale breweries churning out a decidedly uninspired product. Thankfully, those days of extreme centralization are now well behind us. Since the 1980s, the small-scale craft-brewing sector has been on the rise, and it now occupies a significant position within the market. Across the country, consumers can now choose among a variety of beers brewed within their own community or region, alongside brews imported from further afield. For instance, my home state of North Carolina—just one among fifty states—now boasts more than 410 breweries and brewpubs.[32] This thriving craft-beer scene, full of local variety and inventiveness, contrasts sharply with the dark days of the mid-twentieth century. Over the same period—largely thanks to a bill signed into law by President Jimmy Carter in 1978 that removed legal and financial barriers to small-scale beer production—there has been a massive uptick in home brewing, a practice with deep roots in American history. The American Homebrewers Association estimates that more than a million people in the United States now brew their own beer at home.[33]

Imagine two maps: one showing the distribution of breweries in the United States around 1970 and another showing the distribution of breweries in 2020. Each brewery is marked with a circular dot, and the dots vary in size according to the productive capacities of the breweries. These two maps would differ dramatically, documenting a rapid shift from what archaeologists call a nucleated pattern (1970) to a dispersed pattern (2020)—from a few enormous, isolated dots to an array of differently sized dots spread broadly across the landscape. Archaeologists love maps like this, maps that are able to capture and encapsulate complex historical transformations in visual form. Mapping and explaining the shift from nucleation to dispersal in the brewing industry would require engagement with a whole range of complicated issues, from economic policy and legal regulations to local food movements and cultures of connoisseurship.

I would love to see a similar set of maps covering successive periods in the history of ancient Mesopotamia. That's just a dream for the moment, but it's the kind of thing that we should be shooting for. A focus on brewing spaces offers an important means of identifying historically significant shifts in the scale and organization of beer production, whether on the local or regional scale. But there are plenty of other reasons to pay attention to brewing spaces—where these spaces were located within the community, how they were laid out inside, what they were like for the people who worked in them or lived nearby, who had access and who did not, their evolution over time.

The cuneiform record includes many references to brewing spaces, especially breweries and taverns. The problem is that cuneiform documents typically tell us very little about these breweries *as spaces*; they tell us little about location, layout, use of space, access, atmosphere, temperature, sounds, smells, etc. This missing spatial dimension ought to be right in archaeology's wheelhouse. Archaeology is fundamentally spatial in orientation. Unfortunately, when it comes to brewing spaces, we have faced a persistent problem of archaeological invisibility. Those breweries that appear with such frequency in the cuneiform record have proven frustratingly elusive for archaeologists. It could be that we've just been digging in the wrong place all this time, just barely missing those breweries by a hair's breadth. But I suspect that we're actually dealing with a failure of identification and perhaps also a failure of imagination. It can be very difficult to distinguish brewing spaces from other spaces of food production. And we don't have a clear set of templates or models in mind, that is, a clear sense for what the brewing spaces of ancient Mesopotamia should look like in the archaeological record. Recent applications of organic residue analysis have begun to chip away at this problem of archaeological invisibility, but we're still in the early days of the search for brewing spaces.

Breweries

Let's dig down a little further into the evidence for breweries by returning briefly to the question of consumers. If that building that we toured in the

Bagara complex at Lagash was indeed a brewery, who was drinking the beer produced inside? One possibility can be extracted from the cuneiform tablet that we encountered in a side room. Only part of the tablet was recovered by archaeologists. So it's difficult to interpret. But it appears to document the distribution of beer rations to specific, named individuals: people like E_2-ud-sar, Ab, Lu_2-šu-u_2-da-laḫ, and others whose names are only partially preserved.[34] Unfortunately, there's no way to prove that the building in which the tablet was found was itself the brewery mentioned in the tablet (i.e., the source of the beer rations). So we can't be certain that these three guys and their illegible compatriots received beer that was brewed by the brewer Lugal-teš-mu in that very building.

If, however, we assume that the excavated building was indeed the main brewery for the Bagara complex—another reasonable but, alas, unproven assumption—we can turn to a different set of documents. These date to the reign of Uru'inimgina, the final king of the First Dynasty of Lagash. We've already met him. It was during his reign that the Bagara was plundered and, perhaps, set on fire by the enemy king Lugalzagesi. Uru'inimgina's wife, Sasa, was in charge of an organization known as the Emunus or "Female Quarter,"[35] the domain of the goddess Bau, wife of Ninĝirsu. We happen to know a lot about the Emunus under Sasa and her predecessor Baranamtara (wife of Uru'inimgina's predecessor Lugalanda), thanks to an archive of about 1700 cuneiform tablets that provides a detailed glimpse into the management of the organization.[36]

Let's focus our attention on one particular event that's illuminated by this documentation. Each year the goddess Bau was honored with a festival in the city of Girsu. In preparation for the four-day event, high officials from across the city-state contributed foodstuffs from their domains, almost certainly delivered in person and with great ceremony.[37] I want to highlight one of these so-called mašdaria deliveries in particular. In the second year of Uru'inimgina's reign, the temple-lord (saĝĝa) of the Bagara delivered one sheep, thirty pieces of bread, and about 120 liters (5 sadu) of beer to Girsu for the Festival of Bau.[38] It's likely that that beer was produced within the Bagara's own brewery—in other words, within the building we had a clandestine wander through during our visit to Lagash. In the grand scheme of things, 120 liters isn't all that much beer. That's well within the capacity of a single, large gakkul vessel. But this particular 120 liters of beer packed a symbolic punch. The high-profile, ritualized collection of festival provisions from all corners of the city-state was a conspicuous sign of something bigger: the bonds of interdependence that held the political community together.[39] So at least some of the beer produced within the Bagara was serving a pretty exalted purpose.

But much of the beer was almost certainly destined for ordinary, everyday consumption. For a glimpse into the clientele who relied on institutional breweries like this to quench their thirst on a daily basis, let's take leave of Early Dynastic Lagash and head north about 500 miles and 600 years into the future. Excavations at the site of Tell Leilan (ancient Šubat-Enlil) in northeastern Syria have uncovered a brewery archive dating to the eighteenth century BCE.[40] Found on the floor of a room within the so-called Northern Lower Town Palace (or Qarni-Lim Palace), this archive includes 447 tablets that document the daily disbursal of beer to specific individuals and groups over a period of twenty months.[41] Each tablet includes a list of beer disbursements for the day in question, the total beer disbursed, the issuing authority (a man named Mutu-ramê), and the day's date. Here's a typical example (though with a shorter list of individualized disbursements than in some others):

> 28.8 liters good beer,
> food allotment for the royal harem;
> 1.2 liters for Kileš-ewri;
> 28.8 liters for the sedan carriers;
> 48 liters for the messengers;
> 3.6 liters for the embassy of Sumi-etar;
> 4.8 liters for Alminna;
> 1.2 liters for Ibbi-Amurru;
> 1.2 liters for the ombudsman.
> Total: 117.6 liters good beer,
> according to the menials' measure,
> issued by Mutu-ramê.
> Month I,
> Day 11,
> *limmu* Zabzabu.[42]

A further 80 tablets found in the same room document the receipt of brewing ingredients by Mutu-ramê.[43] So the same official was responsible for keeping track of newly arrived brewing ingredients and the outflow of beer to consumers.

Two other contemporary archives, excavated at the sites of Chagar Bazar (ancient Ašnakkum) in Syria[44] and Tell al-Rimah (ancient Qattara) in Iraq,[45] offer a similar perspective on the administrative oversight of brewery inventory. We'll return to these breweries of the Old Babylonian period in a moment. For now, I'd just like to highlight one key point. When breweries show up in the written record, what we're most likely to learn about is inputs and outputs: brewing ingredients coming in, finished beer going out. From the perspective of the institutions and their scribes, the balance sheet is what mattered most and what deserved to be committed to writing.

Written evidence for breweries and brewers

Don't get me wrong. This single-minded focus on accounting offers a wonderful resource for scholars, one that is unparalleled elsewhere in the ancient world. But one does sometimes wish that the scribes would have added a little more color to their regular reports. Bearing in mind the strong slant in the available documentation, what else can we learn about breweries (Sum. e_2-lunga$_3$) from the written record? As we saw in Chapter 4, we can often glean some information about brewing equipment, even the specific sets of vessels employed in specific locations. And we can learn something about the kind of activities that took place in the brewery: mixing, stirring, squeezing, straining, soaking, preparing, throwing, handling, forming, baking. Where administrative records are relatively continuous across the span of one or more years, there's also the possibility of using data about brewery inputs and outputs to track seasonal patterns in production and distribution.[46]

In many cases, it's also possible to glean some information about affiliation, that is, about the institutional body or elite patron behind a particular brewery—based either on criteria internal to the documents (e.g., direct mention of a palace, temple, or other institutional body) or on tablet findspots (e.g., found in association with an architectural space identified as a palace or temple). The brewery archive from Tell Leilan, for example, was recovered within a structure that the excavators interpret as a palace and almost certainly documents activities that took place within this very structure.[47] A group of about 150 tablets documenting beer production during the time of the First Sealand Dynasty (1732–1450 BCE), on the other hand, is unprovenanced.[48] Held in a private collection since the 1980s–90s, the tablets can no longer be linked with their original findspots. Frequent mentions of the palace, however, make it clear that the tablets must have derived from a palatial archive—exactly which palace remains a matter of conjecture.[49]

But, you might ask, who was actually doing the brewing? Who was doing all that stirring and squeezing and soaking and straining? This is a more difficult question but one that is at least partially illuminated by the written record. As a general rule, the individuals who appear in brewing archives are the responsible parties, that is, the people responsible for either sending or receiving brewing ingredients or beer. lu2 individuals include especially the brewer (Sumerian ^{lu_2}lunga, LU_2.ŠIM; Akkadian sirāšu, LU_2.ŠIM) and the maltster (Sumerian munu$_4$.mu$_2$; Akkadian bāqilum, LU_2.MUNU$_3$).[50] Both professions appear in the Sealand tablets. And several individuals—Qišti-Marduk, Ḥuzālu, Ṣābī-(E)-Ulmaš—appear as both brewer and maltster, their professional titles shifting according to their role in a particular transaction. For example, if receiving barley or delivering malt, they appear as a maltster; if receiving malt or delivering beer, as a brewer.[51] It may not be obvious, but these three individuals are all men, as are the other maltsters and brewers in the Sealand documents. Female brewers (sirāšītu) do occasionally appear, but, as we'll see in a bit, women were more closely associated with the profession of tavern keeper and, though the evidence is sparse, home brewing.[52]

This gendered split in the brewing profession has prompted some intriguing but, I think, so far unsubstantiated speculation about a gradual usurpation of the brewing profession by men. Is it possible that a domain once dominated by women—Ninkasi was, after all, the goddess of beer—was co-opted and transformed into a professionalized, institutionally managed, male-dominated pursuit during, say, the fourth and third millennia BCE? Can we envision a process loosely similar to the one that transpired in England several thousand years later, as the alewives or brewsters of the medieval and early modern period were sidelined and their world of small-scale brewing for local ale houses gradually overturned in favor of an industrialized brewing industry dominated by men?[53]

I don't think we can currently say for certain, but it's an angle worth exploring. A case has already been made for a parallel, but certainly not equivalent, development in the realm of textile production.[54] The argument is that institutional expansion (aka state formation) in Mesopotamia during the fourth and third millennia BCE was accompanied by a shift from linen to woolen textiles and a shift in the gendered division of labor—one that left women with less and less stake in the textile economy and increasingly alienated from the products of their own labor. Whether one buys this particular argument or not—and not everyone does—there's plenty of reason to suspect a complex and evolving relationship between gender and brewing in Mesopotamia.

Did the "brewers" that appear in palace and temple records, though, actually brew any beer themselves, with their own bare hands? Were they skilled practitioners of the brewing arts, or did their talents (or at least their job descriptions) lie elsewhere, say in the supervisory realm? Unfortunately, we don't really know. But they certainly did engage in supervisory tasks, including one particularly iconic one: the stamp (or, in this case, roll) of approval. As you know, the cylinder seal, when rolled into wet clay, functioned as a kind of official signature in Mesopotamia. In many cases, the inscription carved into the seal even recorded the name and profession of its owner. And in plenty of cases that profession was brewer.[55] We've already seen one example, the Akkadian-period seal of "Ur-Zu, the brewer" (see Chapter 4). So brewers were pencil-pushing, stamp-wielding bureaucrats in at least this one sense. They also certainly did supervise a cast of underlings. Male and female workers "assigned (to the task) of beer" (Sumerian guruš kaš-a gub-a, geme$_2$ kaš-a gub-a), for example, make a regular appearance in ration lists.[56] Occasional reference is also made to a sort of fuel and fire specialist, a "fireman" (u$_2$ gibil-la) charged with managing all things heat-related.[57] In a fascinating collection of work inspection texts and worker assignment texts from the town of Garšana (Ur III period, 2112–2004 BCE), we also catch a glimpse of workers (mostly men, but also some women) engaged in specific tasks for the brewery: pounding malt, kneading bappir, and baking bappir.[58]

As we touched on earlier, cuneiform documents have very little to say about the brewery as a physical space. It's a shame, but not a surprise. Put yourself in the shoes of the middle management, the supervisors and scribes responsible for producing and curating the administrative paper trail that dominates the written record available to us. What the higher-ups cared about was the bottom line, inputs and outputs. They didn't need to know how or where the sausage was made. So that kind of info only rarely creeps into the documentation. One exception comes again from Garšana. A substantial number of Garšana tablets document construction work, including the building of a new brewery (contrasted with the "old brewery," e$_2$ lumgi$_3$

sumun).[59] In fact, it was not just a brewery but a brewery, kitchen, and flour mill all in one (e$_2$ lumgi$_3$ e$_2$ muḫaldim u$_3$ e$_2$ kikkin$_2$), the so-called Triple Complex.[60]

This was a major construction project that could employ in the vicinity of a hundred workers, depending on the task at hand. The complex was built atop a raised platform. So the first order of business was the construction of this foundation terrace. Retaining walls were built, and then the spaces between the walls were filled in with earth carried in from elsewhere by teams of workers. But they clearly had their priorities in order. Before the foundation terrace was fully complete, they got right to work on the walls of the brewery. Once the mudbrick walls of the entire complex were finished, they tied roof beams into place, tightened the tied roof beams, plastered the gate leading into the complex, plastered interior wall faces, built stairs and an oven, and then finally waterproofed the roof and installed gutters.

Wouldn't it be amazing if we could compare this account of the construction process with the actual, physical remains of the complex? Unfortunately, no such comparison is possible. The town of Garšana has not been subject to controlled, scientific excavation by archaeologists. We don't even know exactly where the town was located. The Garšana tablets were purchased on the art market in the 1990s and then later donated to Cornell University. Significant controversy surrounded the decision to accept the donation and publish the tablets, which were illegally excavated by looters in the wake of the Gulf War (1991). The collection has now been returned to the Iraqi government, but, as with all looted objects, the tablets are devoid of archaeological context.[61] We don't know where they were found, and we can't compare the info in the tablets with any physical remains of the brewery-kitchen-mill complex, which, like so many archaeological sites across the region, may very well have been destroyed by looters.

Archaeological evidence for breweries

We can, however, take a look at the physical remains of a number of other possible breweries. Emphasis on *possible*. As we've already seen, the archaeological identification of breweries in Mesopotamia has proven challenging. Here, I'd just like to run through some of the best contenders, in each case offering a brief summary of the evidence available.

Tello, Iraq (ancient Girsu): We've already visited the "Esplanade of Enmetena," a frustratingly fragmentary structure uncovered at the site of Tello, ancient Girsu, in a location that suggests a connection with the Eninnu, a complex dedicated to the city's main god Ninĝirsu (Figure 5.3).[62] Thanks to the recovery of a series of foundation deposits, inserted beneath the floor prior to construction,[63] we can date this structure to the reign of Enmetena (c. 2420 BCE), and we can be pretty certain that it was a brewery. The foundation deposits included two different kinds of objects: pillow-shaped, alabaster tablets inscribed with a lengthy account of construction activities undertaken by Enmetena (culminating with the brewery of Ninĝirsu) and nail-shaped, bronze figurines inscribed with a shorter inscription that focuses specifically on the construction of the brewery.

The mudbrick walls of the structure, if they still existed at the time of excavation, went unrecognized by the excavators. But their records do

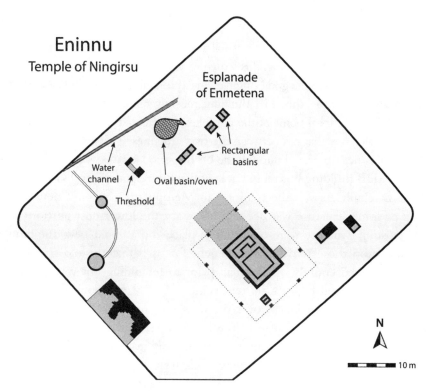

Figure 5.3. Plan of the Eninnu complex, including the Esplanade of Enmetena. Tello, Iraq. (Redrawn after de Sarzec and Heuzy 1884–1912: Plate D)

provide information about a scattered collection of features, built of more durable materials and probably all once belonging to the brewery structure. These included: 1) a 1.7-meter-wide entrance threshold made of baked bricks set in bitumen, 2) stepping down from the threshold, fragments of a baked-brick paving, 3) seven meters away from the threshold and sitting on the baked-brick paving, a large oval basin (possibly an oven) set on a 1.7-meter-high, irregularly shaped oval pedestal, 4) a row of four, internally subdivided, rectangular, baked-brick basins coated in bitumen, and 5) a water channel running across the space at an oblique angle. So we've got some waterproof basins and a channel, implying that liquids were once present, and maybe a large oven. Without the foundation deposits telling us exactly what this building was, one would be hard-pressed to make the case that it was a brewery. And even with those inscriptions, the archaeologically preserved features offer scant information about how the brewery might have actually functioned. It was in use from the Early Dynastic IIIb period through the Ur III period (2450–2004 BCE).

Tell al-Hiba, Iraq (ancient Lagash): We've also already spent some time in a probable brewery excavated at the site of Tell al-Hiba, ancient Lagash (Figure 5.2).[64] Known as the 4HB Building, this structure was located within the Bagara, a complex dedicated to the god Ninĝirsu. The 4HB Building was built right next to another structure—the 3HB Building, recently reinterpreted as Ninĝirsu's main shrine, the focal point of the complex—and could only be entered via a narrow alleyway that ran between the two structures. It was in use from the Early Dynastic IIIb period through the Ur III period (2450–2004 BCE).

The 4HB Building was rebuilt at least five times. And, when I say rebuilt, I mean rebuilt. As was the tradition in Mesopotamia, when a new version of some structure was deemed necessary, the lowermost portions of the existing structure were often left in place and a brand-new one built directly atop those remains. The benefit for us is that the old structure was not wiped entirely off the map prior to rebuilding but was, instead, partially preserved beneath its replacement. So we can track the evolution of the 4HB "brewery" over the course of multiple building phases (V–I). The basic ground plan of the building remained remarkably constant over this span of time (though we can only really see the full ground plan for phases IVB and III). New walls were typically rebuilt directly above earlier walls, effectively reconstituting the same layout of rooms in each phase. And many internal features like bins, hearths, and ovens were rebuilt (sometimes with modifications) in nearly the same spot with each rebuilding, suggesting that many rooms retained their basic function across building phases.

As we saw in our earlier tour through building phase IVB—the one that ended in a fiery destruction event—the 4HB Building included one entry point from the outside and seven rooms in total. The building was approximately rectangular in outline, about twice as long (N–S) as it was wide (E–W). The southwestern part of the building was dominated by a linear sequence of three main rooms (Rooms 30, 33, and 35). Each of these rooms gave access to one or two side rooms (Rooms 29, 31, 32, and 36), which occupied the northern and eastern sides of the building. In each building phase, the excavators uncovered a range of built features or installations, none of which would necessarily be out of place in a brewery. Large ceramic vessels had been built into many floors. There were brick pavements, drains, brick-built boxes, baked-brick tanks, hearths, and ovens, including an enormous domed oven that nearly filled one entire room. The excavators recovered a diverse collection of artifacts from the 4HB Building, though only a few offer particular insight into the brewing activities that might have taken place within. Most conspicuous was a fragmentary tablet that mentions both a brewery (e_2-bappir$_3$) and a specific brewer (^{lu_2}lunga$_3$) named Lugal-teš-mu.[65] In terms of ceramics, just one single fragment of a vessel with a pierced base was recovered,[66] hardly a convincing demonstration that this most distinctive type of brewing vessel—recall our discussion of the gakkul/namzītum in Chapter 4—was playing a major role in the building.

We can say something about the activities that took place in each room, but the picture is pretty hazy.[67] There's really not enough to piece together even a speculative account of how beer might have been produced in the building. We have evidence for storage. We have evidence for administrative practices. We have evidence for the containment or manipulation of liquids. We have evidence for heat-related activities. This all makes sense in a brewery. But where exactly might some key brewing steps like malting, mashing, or fermentation have taken place? Could some of those large "storage" vessels sunk into the floors of various rooms be mashing vessels in disguise? What about the large, baked-brick tank, partially lined in bitumen? What was happening in there? And what exactly were the various fire installations used for? Perhaps the giant oven played a role in bappir production. Or in the roasting of raw or malted grains. Perhaps the large, circular, brick-built fireplace in the adjacent room was used for heating large quantities of water for mashing. Or perhaps for the toasting of grains. Or for something else entirely. The 4HB Building may very well have been a brewery, but we can't currently say for certain. And we certainly can't say exactly how beer was brewed there.

Tell Leilan, Syria (ancient Šubat-Enlil): The beer archive from Tell Leilan, ancient Šubat-Enlil, was excavated within a building known as the Northern Lower Town Palace (Figure 5.4).[68] It's also sometimes called the Qarni-Lim Palace. Qarni-Lim was king of the city of Andarig (ruled c. 1770–1766 BCE) in northern Iraq and appears to have built and used the palace at Tell Leilan as a sort of temporary residence when he was in town. We know this, in part, because many of the tablets in the beer archive had

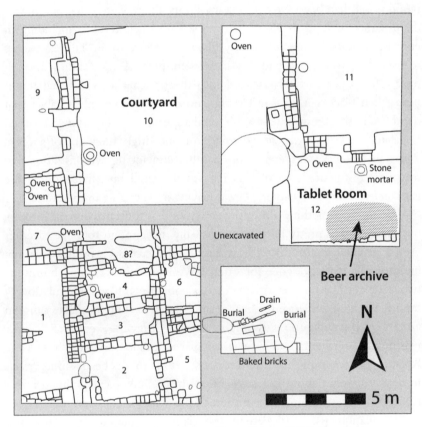

Figure 5.4. Plan of the Northern Lower Town Palace, Tell Leilan, Syria. (Redrawn after Pulhan 2000: Fig. 3)

been impressed with a cylinder seal belonging to Šamaš-dajjān, an official employed by Qarni-Lim. The inscription on the seal reads: "Šamaš-dajjān, servant of Qarni-Lim." The other seal that makes a regular appearance on the tablets did not include an inscription specifying its owner, but it probably belonged to Mutu-ramê, the man who managed the "beer office."[69]

Only a portion of the Qarni-Lim Palace was uncovered during excavation.[70] The incomplete ground plan that we have consists of a large, open-air courtyard (approx. 10 m x 10 m) surrounded on three sides by rooms of varying size, many of them only partially explored. A few tablets were recovered from the courtyard itself, but most came from the so-called "tablet room" (Room 12) immediately to the east. They were found along the southern side of the room in several dense clusters, intermingled with the remains of four ceramic vessels, all high-shouldered jars of the same type. The 647 tablets documenting the receipt of brewing ingredients and the distribution of beer clearly belonged together as part of a single archive. And this "beer archive" had been stored in the four jars.[71]

Surely, you might suppose, all that beer was being brewed somewhere nearby. Perhaps in some of the other rooms surrounding the courtyard? A reasonable hypothesis, yes, but alas unconfirmed. The excavated portion of the palace included plenty of built features and other equipment that would make sense in a brewery. But many would be equally at home in, say, a kitchen or bakery. The tablet room itself included a large stone mortar built into the floor and other flat grinding stones ("saddle querns"), as well as a large ceramic storage jar that was found flipped upside down.[72] So it's entirely possible that some phase of the beer production process—one that involved the storing and grinding of grain—was taking place in the very room where the archive was stored. But there's no way to prove that. The other ceramics recovered from the room fit the overall pattern for the palace in general: an assemblage dominated by bowls and cups, many of them decorated. So nothing particularly diagnostic for beer production.

Among the other rooms, several features stand out.[73] There were lots of ovens, lots of grinding stones, and lots of ceramics related to the serving of food. The ovens, of varying shapes and sizes, were clustered in particular rooms, sometimes in association with large quantities of animal bones. The same goes for grinding stones and serving vessels. So what we seem to have is particular rooms dedicated to particular purposes: perhaps rooms for grain processing, rooms for cooking/baking, rooms for preparing food for service, rooms for serving/eating food, and others of uncertain function. One can also speculate about potential brewing activities. Barley could have been crushed in the stone mortars; malt could have been spread out in the courtyard for drying; bappir could have been baked in any of the numerous ovens. But there's no clinching evidence here. What these rooms really look like is a sort of multi-purpose suite dedicated to various aspects of food production and service. Perhaps that food included beer. The excavators of the site have suggested as much,[74] but it's also possible that the brewery was located somewhere nearby within the unexcavated portions of the palace.[75]

In this regard, it is perhaps telling that not a single example of a vessel-with-a-hole-in-its-base was uncovered during excavation of the Qarni-Lim Palace.[76] The excavators did, however, uncover several distinctive "beer jars," possibly used for measuring out beer for distribution to consumers. Each jar could have held approximately 2.4 liters of beer, which dovetails nicely with one of the most common measurements in the beer-distribution texts: here, 2 sila equals approximately 2.4 liters. So perhaps it was in these very jars (or jars like them) that the beer tallied up in the texts was doled out on a daily basis to people like Gumushi, Awil-Adad, Memen-atal, and Japlah-El.[77]

Tell Hadidi, Syria (ancient Azu): During the 1970s, archaeologists from across the world converged on a segment of the Euphrates valley in Syria to conduct "salvage" operations. The imminent completion of the new Tabqa Dam was set to flood large parts of the valley, including a whole series of archaeological sites. In response to a call from the Syrian Directorate General of Antiquities and Museums, teams from a variety of different countries launched excavation campaigns, all working on a tight schedule in anticipation of rapidly rising waters. One of the sites excavated during this campaign, Tell Hadidi, has produced compelling (if still inconclusive) evidence for a dedicated brewing facility.[78]

Dating to the early fifteenth century BCE (Late Bronze Age), the so-called Tablet House suffered a fiery destruction that left a rich artifactual assemblage preserved in place (Figure 5.5). You can probably guess where the building got its moniker. A small collection of cuneiform tablets was recovered in the debris. These seventeen letters, administrative accounts, and legal documents don't offer much insight into the building's function, but they do suggest that it belonged to the family of a man named Huziru—perhaps to his son Yaya, who appears in one text. What we're interested in here, though, is the pottery. The excavations have not yet been

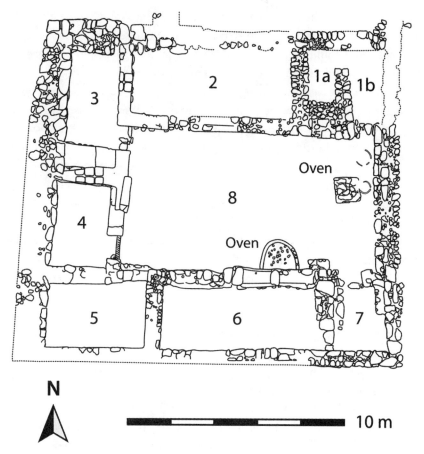

Figure 5.5. Plan of the Tablet House, Tell Hadidi, Syria. (Redrawn after Dornemann 1981: Fig. 2)

published in full, but a series of preliminary reports offer a detailed look at the ceramic inventory of the Tablet House.

Drawing on this ceramic data, one subsequent study has interpreted the building as a brewery, a special-purpose facility that was producing beer on a scale well beyond the needs of an individual household.[79] The argument rests especially on one particular feature of the ceramic assemblage: the striking number of large vessels with a hole pierced in the base. Though the excavators interpreted these as storage vessels, it seems very reasonable to equate them with the nigdurbur or *namzītu* vessels that we have already discussed at length. But there were actually two different types of pierced vessel: wide-mouthed vats with capacities in the realm of 23–175 liters and much larger versions (300–350 liters) with more constricted mouths. Perhaps there could be a functional distinction here, between, say, fermentation vessels and malting vessels, but it's difficult to say.[80]

I find the case for interpreting the Tablet House as a brewery to be pretty strong. The overall character of the ceramic assemblage does seem to fit well with the needs of a brewery, and the substantial quantities of carbonized grain recovered in the building lend further support. What I would like to see, though, is a more detailed consideration of the specific activities taking place in different parts of the building. Box 5.1 offers a brief summary of what we currently know about the contents of each room.[81] There's a lot going on in these rooms. For example, in the northwest corner of the building, Room 3 produced no fewer than thirty-nine ceramic vessels: three large "storage" jars (at least two of them pierced in the base), two large "vats" (at least one pierced), five "kraters" (i.e., large, open, footed vessels), one platter, two small bowls, eight mugs, four cups, five cooking pots, one pot stand, two medium jars, one small jar, two flasks, and three lids. (Figure 5.6 shows a selection of these). A number of grinding stones were also recovered near two of the large storage jars, with carbonized grain scattered nearby. There may even have been traces of a wooden pot stand, like those known to have been used with brewing vessels.

Did all of these items function together in the performance of some particular brewing task? If so, what task? Or is it possible that a number of different activities were taking place concurrently (or sequentially) in the room? For example, does the spatial distribution of artifacts within the room suggest distinct zones of activity? And what about the other rooms in the building? Did each have its own well-defined role in the brewing process? Or should we envision a more flexible use of space and a more diverse mix of activities in each room? The preliminary reports have already given us a tantalizing (and, in fact, detailed) glimpse of the Tablet House, but hopefully more detail about the vessels, their exact findspots, and the full spectrum of artifactual remains will eventually be provided—allowing for a more complete functional analysis of this possible brewery.

A number of other excavated structures have also been interpreted as breweries. In no case is the suggestion completely unreasonable. But in no case is the argument completely watertight either. For example, at the site of Selenkahiye in Syria—also part of the Tabqa Dam salvage

Box 5.1 Tell Hadidi, Tablet House, room contents

	Room 1a	Room 1b	Room 2	Room 3	Room 4	Room 5	Room 6	Room 8	Totals
Storage jars		4	4	3	4			5	20
Vats			1	2		2		4	9
Kraters			2	5		3	2	2	14
Platters				1	1			1	3
Strainer bowls								1	1
Small bowls			3	2	1			3	9
Mugs				8				2	10
Cups			1	4	1			2	8
Cooking pots			3	5	1	1		3	13
Pot stands				1	2				3
Globular jars	3						1	2	6
Medium jars	2		1	2	1	4		2	12
Pitchers					1			1	2
Small jars	1			1		2		1	5
Flasks				2					2
Lids			1	3		1		3	8
Miscellaneous					1			1	2
Totals	6	4	16	39	13	13	3	33	127

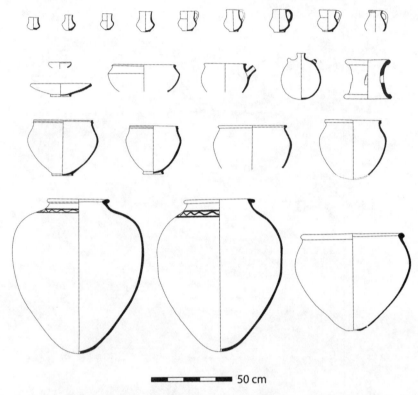

50 cm

Figure 5.6. Ceramic assemblage from Room 3, Tablet House, Tell Hadidi, Syria. (Redrawn after Dornemann 1981: Figs. 3–5)

project—excavators partially uncovered a building (c. 2400 BCE) with a few features that might suggest a brewery.[82] In an exterior courtyard, there was a large, domed oven. And then, just inside the building, they found two sherd-lined basins that emptied into two square tubs. They tentatively suggested a connection with "malting, drying, and fermenting," but it's really not much to go on.

At the site of Hamoukar in northeastern Syria, the argument for a brewery hinges especially on the interpretation of three large, semicircular (possibly domed) ovens found within several of the rooms that surrounded a central courtyard (late Ninevite 5 period, 2650–2550 BCE).[83] The excavator suggests that the ovens were used for either the drying/roasting of grain or the baking of bappir and points to several other pieces of potential evidence for brewing activities: two large storage jars, two smaller, cylindrical ovens, and fragments of several tall ceramic strainers. So, perhaps a brewery? Perhaps.

A large, fortified building (c. 1600–1475 BCE) recently excavated at the site of Tell Khaiber in Iraq has also produced some intriguing evidence for brewing.[84] In this case, the evidence comes primarily from ceramics. Two small rooms at the northeastern corner of the building produced a ceramic assemblage with many forms that suggest brewing, including what has been interpreted as an in situ "beer-brewing installation": a cup next to a closed pot stand with another cup inside and an upside-down vat for soaking/germination. Given the substantial evidence for liquid consumption elsewhere in the building—and the mention of a specific brewer named Mannu-balu-ilišu in a tablet found there—the interpretation of these rooms as a small-scale brewing operation under institutional control is probably a reasonable one, if difficult to prove once and for all. I think you get the drift. We've got lots of tentative, tantalizing, archaeological evidence for breweries but nothing that's truly definitive.

Taverns and tavern keepers

I only know of three excavated structures that have been interpreted as taverns. (Make that four. As I was finishing up this book, excavators at the site of Tell al-Hiba, ancient Lagash, where we've already seen potential evidence for a brewery, uncovered a building that they interpret as a restaurant or tavern. But few details are available at this point.) Each basically looks like a modified house, tweaked to make space for public beer consumption.

The first of these, excavated at the site of Susa in southwestern Iran and dating to the middle of the second millennium BCE, might also have included space for some other activities.[85] In a square in front of the building, about 200 clay plaques were found, many depicting erotic scenes: naked women, naked women embracing naked men, beds (both empty and occupied by couples). Inside the building, the most distinctive feature was seven large ceramic jars that had been buried beneath the baked-brick floors of a number of different rooms. They could be accessed via circular holes cut through the floors. The excavator of the site interpreted these jars as a system for storing fresh water and keeping it cool.

Another scholar, though, has suggested a different use: beer consumption. Citing the abundant evidence for the drinking of beer through long reed straws in Mesopotamia, this argument proposes that beer held in the subfloor vessels could have been consumed through straws.[86] And this connects back up with the erotic angle. As we already saw in the prologue, one common beer-drinking scene preserved in the artistic record shows a man and woman having sex, while the woman bends over and drinks beer through a straw. Perhaps such activities were taking place in this very tavern at Susa? Interestingly, this tavern—if it was indeed a tavern—was located just outside the city wall, so in some sense beyond the bounds of the city. This might support an argument for taverns as peripheral or liminal spaces, an issue that we'll come back to later.

The other two archaeologically recovered taverns come from Tell Bazi, a site that we already encountered in our discussion of brewing equipment (Chapter 4).[87] The excavations at Tell Bazi were initiated as part of another rescue project along the Euphrates River in Syria, this time in advance of floodwaters behind the Tishrin Dam (built during the 1990s to the north of the Tabqa Dam). In the end, only a part of the site was flooded, but this so-called *Weststadt* or "West Town" is the part that interests us. Here excavators uncovered fifty individual houses, laid out along curving and intersecting streets. According to their interpretation, this bustling neighborhood of the Late Bronze Age (1400–1200 BCE) also featured three inns, a bakery, a brewery, and two taverns. Again, the taverns basically look like other houses at the site but with a twist.

At Tell Bazi, there was a sort of template for house design, an idealized house layout that was replicated over and over again, though not always to the letter. The ideal house consisted of a large, rectangular room, with four smaller, square rooms arranged in a linear sequence along one of its long walls. In the case of our first tavern, known as H.38 (i.e., House 38), a partition wall cut across the rectangular room, dividing the structure into a public zone that could be accessed from the street and a poorly preserved private zone beyond (Figure 5.7).[88] A thirsty customer entering from the street would have encountered first a mudbrick table and cylindrical (i.e., *tannur*-style) oven immediately to the right and straight ahead a mudbrick bench. Turning sharply to the left, the customer could then enter the main space of the tavern, where a food preparation area, a large brewing vessel, and another *tannur*-style oven would be visible straight ahead. The placement of the brewing vessel, right out in plain view, is one thing that distinguishes H.38 from other houses, where similar brewing vessels were

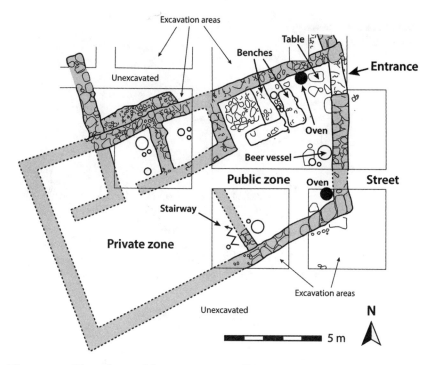

Figure 5.7. Plan of a possible tavern, H.38, Tell Bazi, Syria. (Redrawn after Otto 2006: Abb. 137)

typically tucked away beneath a stairwell. Off to the right, about five meters away, was the partition wall, pierced by a doorway leading into the building's private zone, presumably the home of the proprietor.

We may not be able to see them archaeologically, but a customer would also, of course, have encountered other people—perhaps packed densely into what was a relatively modest (approx. 5 m x 6 m or 30 m²) but probably lively space, animated by the sounds and smells of tavern life. Indeed, located at an intersection, directly across from an inn, and around the corner from another, this little tavern may have been a busy meeting spot, where locals and visitors passing through town came together over a drink and some food.

Another possible tavern was located just up the street and around a bend.[89] This structure, known as H.6 (i.e., House 6), may also have included both a private zone—a sort of truncated version of the ideal house type—and a public zone for beer consumption (Figure 5.8). The focus of the public zone

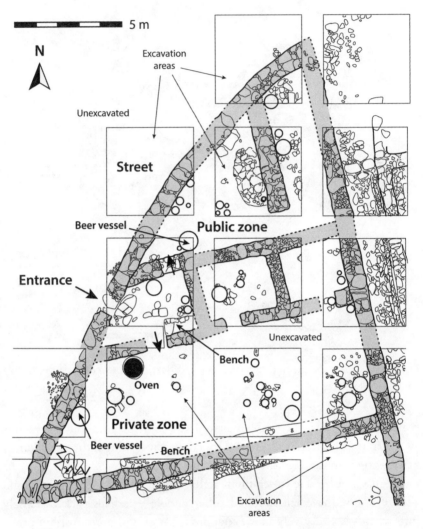

Figure 5.8. Plan of a possible tavern, H.6, Tell Bazi, Syria. (Redrawn after Otto 2006: Abb. 84)

was a courtyard, where the excavators found lots of containers related to the transport or pouring of liquids, though interestingly, no ovens. So perhaps this tavern really specialized in liquid, as opposed to solid, nourishment. A customer arriving from the street would have first entered a small vestibule, containing ceramic vessels and a mudbrick bench. To the right was a door leading into the private residence and to the left, a door leading into the public space. This (possible) tavern to the left was approximately triangular in shape, smaller than the tavern down the street, and paved in baked bricks. A large brewing vessel had been positioned just inside the doorway on the right-hand side. Perhaps we can imagine the proprietor doling out beer to a thirsty clientele right as they passed through the doorway.

And who exactly was this proprietor? What station did tavern keepers occupy in society? Were they seen as skilled craftspeople, savvy entrepreneurs, and welcoming hosts, or did they perhaps register somewhere lower on the social scale? Were they valued as providers of social lubrication, atmosphere creators, facilitators of the kind of social leveling that only a good pub can provide? Or were they merely tolerated, their houses of ill repute accepted as a necessary evil but one to be watched with a wary eye? Let's return to the Epic of Gilgamesh, for one of the most indelible characters in Mesopotamian literature, who dispenses beer and wisdom from behind a bar.

Near the end of the epic, our hero finds himself utterly consumed by a newfound fear of death. His soulmate Enkidu has died and left him alone. Seized by an intense desire to learn the secret of eternal life, Gilgamesh has embarked on a desperate effort to locate and interrogate Uta-napishti the Distant, the man who survived the great flood and was granted eternal life by the gods. He has just completed yet another in a long line of heroic feats: a race against the rising sun, through the impenetrable darkness beneath the eastern mountains. But he's dirty, unkempt, exhausted, and, to be honest, looking a little unhinged overall.

Emerging from the tunnel that took him beneath the mountains, Gilgamesh finds himself at the ends of the earth. He blinks his eyes, adjusting to the light, and takes in the strangest of gardens, overflowing not with flowers and fruit but an array of precious stones. One tree bears carnelian; another, lapis lazuli; another, hematite and agate. As he wanders through the garden, Gilgamesh is being watched. The wise Shiduri, tavern keeper at the edge of the world, is monitoring his movements. Uncertain about the intentions of this mysterious visitor from afar, she decides to bar the gates of her establishment and retreat to the roof. From there she converses with Gilgamesh, who recounts the story of his suffering and demands that she aid him in his quest. Shiduri does her best to dissuade him from attempting the perilous journey across the Waters of Death, the way to Uta-napishti's realm, but eventually she relents and offers some crucial advice.

In the standard version of the epic (first millennium BCE), her advice is practical. He must find the boatman Ur-shanabi and enlist his help.[90] In an earlier version of this episode (Old Babylonian period, 2004–1595 BCE), though, Shiduri first takes a detour into metaphysical territory. As we saw in Chapter 4, her eloquent, pithy advice sums up the ultimate futility of Gilgamesh's search for eternal life. In a nutshell: Humans are destined to die. It's inevitable. In the meantime, do your duty; take pride in the tasks that have been assigned to you. Enjoy the life that you've been given. Eat, drink, and be merry, for tomorrow we die. Does Gilgamesh heed this wise counsel? No, at least not immediately. Instead, he bemoans her philosophizing—"O, tavern-keeper, why do you talk [*this way?*]"—and presses her for the route to Uta-naishtim (the Old Babylonian antecedent of Uta-napishti). In this early, fragmented version of the epic, Shiduri's response is unfortunately truncated.[91] In the standard version, though, she grudgingly obliges and sets Gilgamesh on his way toward the boatman and an eventual meeting with Uta-napishti.[92] So, a tavern keeper occupies a pivotal role in the most famous tale of ancient Mesopotamia. What else do we know about this occupation?

The Gilgamesh episode that we've just discussed—the earlier, more metaphysical version—is preserved on a fragmentary tablet dating to the eighteenth or seventeenth century BCE. The tablet was purchased from a dealer in Baghdad in 1902 and reportedly came from Sippar, a city located on the Euphrates to the north of Babylon.[93] At that point, both Sippar proper (known as Sippar-Jaḥrūrum, modern Tell Abu Habbah) and its sister city Sippar-Amnānum (modern Tell ed-Der) had already received significant archaeological attention. Substantial quantities of cuneiform tablets, for example, had been excavated by a team from the British Museum and transported back to London, where they still reside today. But illegal excavations were also common, and many tablets—like our Epic of Gilgamesh fragment—found their way onto the local antiquities market and then eventually into museum collections.

I want to focus on a small group of tablets, six of them excavated at Tell Abu Habbah (now held in the Istanbul Museum) and one acquired on the antiquities market (now held in the University of Pennsylvania museum).[94] These seven tablets offer us a time-lapse glimpse of one specific tavern, located on Main Street in Sippar-Jaḥrūrum, as it passed from owner to owner over the years. The tavern is described as "located in Main Street in Sippar-Jaḥrūrum, adjacent to the house of Ibbi-Sîn and adjacent to the house of Šešduga."[95] We don't learn anything else about the location or the character of the tavern, but even this brief description tells us something important: the tavern was situated on a main thoroughfare and next to residential structures.

The focus of the tablets, though, is ownership—ownership of the tavern and several other pieces of real estate. During the reign of Sabium of Babylon (1844–1831 BCE), the tavern and three adjacent shops were owned by three brothers, Ilšu-bani, Adad-iddinam, and Nabi-ilīšu, the sons of a man named Awilumma. The tavern and shops must have then somehow ended up in the hands of just one of those sons, Ilšu-bani, who bequeathed them in turn to his own daughter Šāt-Aja, alongside a substantial set of further assets: five fields (45.36 hectares), uncultivated land (1140 m²), an orchard or field containing a tower, a large house, 5 kg of silver, 10 kg of copper, some wooden items, livestock (oxen, cows, sheep), and twenty enslaved people. One thing that stands out about this transaction is the occupation of the daughter Šāt-Aja. She was a nadītu priestess of the god Shamash and lived in the gagûm.

Now is not the time for a detailed discussion of the terms nadītu and gagûm, which have inspired significant debate over the years.[96] Suffice it to say that we're talking about a fascinating social institution that emerged during the Old Babylonian period (2004–1595 BCE) and then disappeared after. In a very loose sense, a nadītu was perhaps something like a medieval nun, but we shouldn't push that comparison too far. The institution clearly varied from city to city, and there's still a lot that we don't know. These women were devoted to a specific deity, were sometimes (but not always) expected to remain chaste, and sometimes (but not always) lived together within a city quarter called the gagûm. They were often well-born and well-connected and often led prosperous lives engaged not only in religious service but also in a variety of profitable business ventures.

They often entered divine service with the equivalent of a dowry, provided by their families. In many cases, this was composed at least in part of agricultural land, whose use was entrusted to the nadītu but then reverted to her family upon her death. Indeed, the institution itself probably emerged, at least in part, as a means of preventing the breakup of family landholdings over time, a means of preserving the integrity of the patrimonial estate. In a world where descent is reckoned primarily through the male line, if your daughter

gets married and takes a chunk of land with her as dowry, that land has effectively left the family estate and been transferred to another family (the family
of her husband). If, on the other hand, you install her in religious service and
give her only temporary use of that land, then it stays with the family.

The upshot is that a *nadītu* was typically not free to dispose of the land
provided by her family. She could, however, do what she wished with any
profits derived from that land or her other economic pursuits. Often, such
additional assets were eventually transferred over to another (younger)
nadītu, who would pledge to support the donor in her old age. This agreement, made while the older *nadītu* was still alive, was almost certainly
designed to forestall any efforts by the family of the *nadītu* to stake claim to
her assets upon her death—though legal documents testify to battles fought
over exactly such claims.

It is clear that Šāt-Aja, the *nadītu* of Shamash who received that tavern on
Main Street in Sippar-Jahrūrum from her father Ilšu-bani, had the freedom
to do with her inherited property as she saw fit. Indeed, Šāt-Aja was able in
her turn to pass half of the tavern (i.e., a half-share in the tavern) on to her
niece and adopted daughter Tabni-Ningal, probably also a *nadītu* or some
other kind of priestess. The transfer probably took place during the reign of
Hammurabi of Babylon (1792–1750 BCE). So we've been able to track the
ownership of a particular tavern over a half century or more.

What makes this set of real estate transactions particularly interesting,
though, is a long-running debate about whether or not a *nadītu* was even
allowed to enter a tavern, let alone own or manage one. The debate revolves
around one of the clauses in Hammurabi's famous law code. (Note: Whatever
this lengthy compilation of legal decisions was exactly, it almost certainly
was not a "law code" as we understand that term today.) This one clause,
known as CH 110, has generated more than its fair share of scholarly commentary.[97] I don't want to dig down into the philological puzzles involved.
Let's just say that opinions differ on how the clause should be rendered in
English and what it has to tell us about the relationship between the *nadītu*
and the tavern. Here's one recent translation.

> Should a *nadītu* and/or *ugbabtu* woman who does not reside in the *gagûm* open
> a tavern or enter a tavern for beer, this woman shall be burnt.[98]

One is immediately struck by the harshness of the penalty: death by burning,
just for opening or entering a tavern.

So what's going on here? Why exactly would a *nadītu* or *ugbabtu* (another kind of priestess) be punished so harshly for such an infraction? Well, first off, it's not entirely clear who it is that was subject to punishment. The Akkadian grammar allows for a few possibilities. It could be a *nadītu* who "is" an *ugbabtu*. It could be a *nadītu* "or" an *ugbabtu*. It could be a *nadītu*, an *ugbabtu*, "or any other woman" who does not reside in the *gagûm*. And there is disagreement regarding this "residing" in the *gagûm*. Should we envision women who were cloistered, that is, set apart from the outside world, secluded within the physical space of the *gagûm*? Or just women who lived within this particular part of the city? Or perhaps a more abstract kind of residing, women who were "members" of the *gagûm*? And the law, of course, is not referencing those who reside in the *gagûm* but rather those who do not. The precise nature of the crime(s) that might be committed by these women is also up for debate: Just what does it mean to "open a tavern" or "enter a tavern for beer"? Is it a crime for them to open the door and enter a tavern? Or is it a crime to open a tavern for business? Or to open the door and let customers in? And how should we understand the phrase "for beer"? Is it a crime for these women to enter a tavern in order to buy beer or drink beer? Or could it be a matter of selling beer?

And then, crucially, why would any of these actions be considered a crime punishable by death? Many answers have been offered. Some, for example, place the blame firmly on sex.[99] If all *nadītu*s were required to abide by a vow of chastity—a questionable assumption—then perhaps it would make sense to keep them well clear of the tavern, a space regularly associated with sex and prostitution. Others, though, point to the matter of ritual purity.[100] If taverns were considered ritually problematic or impure—and some much later exorcism rituals did ascribe supernatural significance to the tavern threshold—then perhaps there was a legitimate threat of ritual contamination. Or, alternatively, the infringement may have been economic in nature, perhaps the crossing of a boundary set up to protect other business people (tavern keepers, innkeepers, money lenders, merchants) from having to compete with an economically advantaged *nadītu*.[101]

It has even been proposed that this clause from the Code of Hammurabi was a different kind of protectionist measure, one designed to shore up the privileges associated with membership in the *gagûm*. According to this argument, it's not that *nadītu*s were prevented from engaging in the tavern business; it's that they were only allowed to do so within the institutional framework of the *gagûm*. In fact, in the city of Sippar at least, they may have been particularly associated with tavern ownership and certainly not barred from entry: one document seems to indicate that the initiation ceremony for a *nadītu* took place within a tavern.[102]

So, those documents testifying to a *nadītu*, Šāt-Aja, who inherited a tavern in the city of Sippar from her father, are bound up in a much broader debate about who these women were, the restrictions placed on them, and the particular privileges that they enjoyed. There's one thing, though, that I can think we can be pretty certain about: The complicated relationship between the *nadītu* and the tavern cannot be boiled down to a question of gender. Both women and men were most definitely allowed to enter taverns. And women, in particular, feature prominently in the role of tavern keeper. In the Code of Hammurabi, for example, right before that tricky clause about the *nadītu* and the tavern, we find two clauses dedicated to the female tavern keeper (Akkadian *sābītu*; Sumerian munus. kurun.na, munus.kaš.tin.na).[103]

> If a female tavern keeper should refuse to accept grain for the price of beer but accepts (only) silver measured by the large weight, thereby reducing the value of beer in relation to the value of grain, they shall charge and convict that female tavern keeper and they shall cast her into the water.

> If there should be a female tavern keeper in whose house criminals congregate, and she does not seize those criminals and lead them off to the palace authorities, that female tavern keeper shall be killed.[104]

The *sābītu* and her counterpart the male tavern keeper (Akkadian *sābû*; Sumerian lu$_2$.kaš.tin.na, lu$_2$.kurun.na) were the proprietors of small-scale drinking establishments that we generally call taverns or inns (Sumerian e$_2$. eš$_3$.dam, eš$_3$.dam; Akkadian *aštammu, bīt sābī, bīt sībī*).[105]

These figures only appear sporadically in the cuneiform record and, interestingly, in different sorts of documents. As we've already seen, female tavern keepers are referenced in the Code of Hammurabi and several other law collections, where we see them selling jars of beer on credit (with accounts to be settled up at harvest time), exchanging beer for grain, silver, oil, and/or wool (though, it appears, sometimes in a fraudulent manner), selling beer on behalf of other people (foreigners, visitors, acquaintances), and managing a space where troublemakers might gather (and, ideally, be duly reported to the palace). They also make an appearance in several royal proclamations, so-called *mīšaru* edicts that included debt relief measures.

Female tavern keepers are singled out as both debtors, whose taxes to the palace have been forgiven, and creditors, forbidden (in these particular instances) from collecting on their loans of beer and barley.[106]

Male tavern keepers also occur in the cuneiform record but often in a different context: tax records. We regularly encounter them, for example, paying (or not, as an oath taken by a certain group of village elders implies) the so-called *nēmettum*-tax. This assessment by the state could at least sometimes be paid in kind, with goods rather than hard cash (i.e., silver). We read, in particular, about payment in the form of spent grain (Sumerian duh, Akkadian *tuhhū*), that is, wet (duh-duru$_s$) or dry (duh-ud-du) brewing byproducts that were valued as a feed for livestock—as in this tax record from Sippar-Jaḫrūrum, dating to the Old Babylonian period (2004–1595 BCE), which mentions both male and female tavern keepers:

> Damp spent grain, *nēmettum*-tax of the male and female tavern keepers of Sippar-Jaḫrūrum, which (goes) from the first of the first month to the 30th of the last—(thus) one year—which was to be collected by Ibni-Marduk, which was given by order of the king for the nourishment of the cattle and the sheep of the *nakamtum* temple of Sippar-Jaḫrūrum.[107]

Spent grain actually shows up more often than you might think and not just as a means of paying taxes. As this Old Babylonian-period (2004–1595 BCE) letter, also from Sippar-Jaḫrūrum, shows, tavern keepers sometimes sold it to other parties as feed for cattle.

> Speak to the male tavern-keepers you know and get dried spent grain for 10 shekels of silver. Make it available to me! I'll send the money along after this letter. Do not neglect to keep the dried spent grain. Send me quickly the news from the tavern keepers.[108]

There's also plenty of evidence that tavern keepers fed spent grain to their own pigs, which were almost certainly raised on premises.[109]

Perhaps it's not all that obvious, but this regular association between tavern keepers and spent grain in the written record suggests one pretty clear—and not necessarily trivial—conclusion: tavern keepers were brewing their own beer. Of course, we've already seen (Chapter 4) several inventory texts from the first millennium BCE that include brewing equipment among the paraphernalia of tavern management, but in that case we were pretty clearly in the realm of date wine, rather than barley beer. Here, in the Old Babylonian period, a thousand years prior, we have numerous references to the actual physical byproducts left behind by the brewing of barley beer—byproducts that still retained some value and were funneled back into the food system by feeding them to domestic animals. Unfortunately, the written record has little else to say about the tavern as a brewing space.

As we'll see in Chapters 6 and 7, we can glean some further hints about tavern life—for example, about drinking and activities of a sexual nature—from the written and artistic records. But neither offers the kind of data that would be necessary to answer some of the bigger questions that one might wish to ask. For example, how common were taverns? Where were they typically located? How much beer were they actually producing? Is it true, as some have argued, that the tavern was a distinctly liminal kind of space, located conceptually, morally, and physically at the boundaries of decent human society? Were taverns dubious places where deviant practices were tolerated but, in a sense, sequestered away? Or were they perhaps both more accepted and more integral to the fabric of Mesopotamian society? We may not have the data yet, but the archaeological record really offers our best hope of addressing some of these bigger questions about the place of taverns—and their keepers—in the Mesopotamian world.

Home brewing

The archaeological remains uncovered at Tell Bazi have also provided another key insight about beer production: Taverns and breweries were not the sole source of beer for the community. Many, perhaps most, households were also brewing their own beer.[110] Before looking in more detail at this archaeological evidence for home brewing, I'd like to reflect briefly on what the cuneiform record has to tell us about small-scale, household-level brewing activities. To be perfectly honest, not much. The primary producers of cuneiform documents—the palace and temple institutions—were not particularly interested in what people got up to in their own kitchens. But occasional hints in letters, literary works, and other texts do testify to a thriving tradition of brewing within the home.

To illustrate, let's have a look at some letters from the site of Kültepe in modern-day Türkiye.[111] During the early part of the second millennium BCE, this central Anatolian city was known as Kanesh. It was a substantial city, ruled over by a king and queen, their palace located on a high point at the center of the city, with a broad lower town spreading out below. The site has been under excavation for many decades and has much to tell us about the people of Middle Bronze Age Anatolia. But its particular claim to fame is actually a group of foreigners who had set up shop in the lower town: merchants from Assur, a city located 600 miles to the southeast in northern Mesopotamia. These merchants lived in houses interspersed among those of local residents, but they belonged to a special entity known as the *kārum*. In a literal sense, the Akkadian word *kārum* means harbor, but the term had also come to refer to diasporic merchant communities as legally recognized, corporate bodies with well-defined rights and responsibilities vis-à-vis their host communities.

We know an exceptional amount about this particular *kārum* because the merchants left behind an extensive body of written material. Starting in the late nineteenth century CE, a distinctive type of "Old Assyrian" cuneiform tablet had been appearing on the antiquities market in increasing quantities. It was clear that the tablets were coming from the mound known as Kültepe, but a number of excavation attempts came up empty-handed. Thanks to a conversation overheard among local excavators—or, as legend has it, getting the local cook so drunk that he gave up the secret—it was eventually discovered that the tablets were not, in fact, coming from the mound itself but from some agricultural fields to the northeast. Excavations in 1925 provided immediate confirmation. But sustained archaeological work at the site only got going in 1948 and has continued to the present day.[112]

This work has brought to light not only the quarter of well-appointed houses where the merchants had established themselves but also (if you include the finds from illicit excavations) more than 23,000 cuneiform tablets stored in archives within the houses. The tablets bear witness to a carefully constructed long-distance trading system that linked the city of Assur in northern Mesopotamia with Kanesh and a series of other cities and towns across central Anatolia to the northwest. The Assyrian traders carried tin and textiles from Mesopotamia to Anatolia and returned with silver. Their business records, recovered from the houses, included a range of different types of document. But many were letters, written back and forth between family members and business associates—often these were one and the same, since the trade was organized around family firms—some living permanently in either Assur or Kanesh, others moving regularly between the two.

We have plenty of letters, for example, exchanged between husbands and wives. These can be pretty dry reading, focused squarely on matters of business and finance, but they sometimes include traces of a certain degree of marital strife. We have eight letters, for example, written to the merchant Innaya by his wife Taram-Kubi. In a particularly vivid letter, she chastises him for leaving the family in Assur without sufficient resources and vehemently contests his accusation that she has been living extravagantly:

> When you departed, you did not leave me a single shekel of silver. You cleaned out the house and have taken everything. Since you left a terrible famine has hit Assur, and you did not leave me any grain, not even a liter. I have to buy grain constantly to eat. . . .

> What is then this extravagance about which you keep on writing to me? We don't even have anything to eat. Do you think we can do foolish things? I have gathered everything I have and have sent it to you. These days I live in an empty house! The (business) season has arrived. Send me the equivalent of my textiles in silver, whatever is my share, so that I can buy ten measures of grain.[113]

Letters like this offer occasional insight into the brewing of beer within the home, a task that appears to have been accomplished primarily by women. In another letter, for example, Taram-Kubi writes to Innaya about some *bappiru* (the Akkadian word for bappir) that she has had prepared, presumably for the purpose of brewing: "(Regarding) the *bappiru* that I had prepared for you, it has become rancid!"[114] The bappir and malt needed for brewing also appear in other letters written between spouses. A woman named Lamassī, for example, assures her husband that the bappir is ready: "As for the *bappiru* about which you wrote to me, the *bappiru* has certainly been made, and it is quite ready."[115] Another merchant inquires into the quantities of brewing ingredients needed by his wife: "The *bappiru* and the malt that I left you, isn't that enough for both of you?"[116]

In some cases, the wives of the Assyrian merchants went to live with them in Kanesh; in other cases, the merchants married local Anatolian women, either as a primary wife or a secondary wife of inferior status. The merchant Aššur-nādā, for example, married an Anatolian woman named Šišahšušar as a secondary wife and shared a house with her in Kanesh. Their correspondence sheds light on her role in managing the household, a role that included looking after livestock, purchasing foodstuffs, and brewing beer. One letter from Aššur-nādā instructs her to brew some beer using malt and bappir: "Soak 10 sacks of malt and 10 sacks of *bappiru* to make (beer). If you want cereal, buy it!"[117] Both bappir and malted barley appear regularly in transactions conducted by both the merchants and their wives.[118] In other words, the procurement of brewing ingredients for home brewing was a regular domestic concern, a necessity in meeting the everyday needs of the household.

Extraordinary circumstances also sometimes demanded larger quantities of beer. One lengthy text from Kanesh, for example, tabulates the rather extensive collection of supplies purchased in advance of a visit by the writer's father-in-law and his friends. Alongside all manner of foodstuffs, furniture, firewood, clothing, etc., he purchased both beer (dispensed in the standard *kirrum* jars) and the ingredients needed to brew more, as well as the requisite drinking straws. We'll come back to drinking straws in Chapter 6. But here's a brief sample from the text, which offers a precise specification of exactly how much silver (measured in shekels and grains) was spent for each item on the list.

> When we brought our father-in-law, I paid ⅔ shekel 15 grains for a belt instead of a sash; ¼ shekel for a pair of shoes; I paid ⅔ shekel 15 grains for 3 *kirrum*-jars (of beer). I furthermore paid ¼ shekel for meat when I invited our father-in-law and his retinue. 1½ shekels of silver was also spent when I invited our father-in-law and his retinue.

> When he came from (the town of) Wahšušana, I paid ¼ shekel for a pair of shoes; I paid ½ shekel for 2 *kirrum*-jars (of beer). I paid ¼ shekel for meat when I invited our father-in-law and his retinue. I paid 4 ½ shekels for 2 sacks and 1 jar of malt. I paid 4 shekels for 2 sacks of *bappiru*. I paid 7 shekels less 15 grains for 6 sacks of barley. I paid 6 ⅔ shekels for 4 sacks of wheat. I paid 2 ⅙ shekels for *butter*. I paid 1 ⅓ shekels for honey. . . . ⅙ shekel for drinking straws for the *kirrum*-jars. . . .[119]

The feasts offered to the visitors, who were traveling from the Anatolian city of Wahšušana, were part of the preparations for the upcoming marriage of the writer's sister.

The upshot of all this should be clear: during the early second millennium BCE, individual households at Kanesh and Assur were brewing their own beer for both everyday consumption and more elaborate feasting events. We have already encountered some other traces of home brewing in the written record, in particular household inventory texts that included brewing equipment. To my knowledge, though, no one has conducted a thorough review of the cuneiform corpus searching for such evidence of home brewing.[120]

And the same applies to the archaeological record—with the glaring exception of Tell Bazi. Let's return briefly to this site in north-central Syria. Among the fifty houses excavated in the *Weststadt* (i.e., the neighborhood with the two taverns), nearly every one appears to have been brewing its own beer and/or wine.[121] And, as we've already seen in Chapter 4, they were doing this with a standardized set of ceramic vessels: a large, open-mouthed vat that was embedded in the floor, a smaller, open-mouthed vessel with a hole pierced in the base, and large storage jars. We can quibble about exactly how these vessels might have functioned together in the brewing of beer, but their general function as a brewing assemblage seems pretty unassailable, backed up as it is by organic residue analysis. Currently, no other site in Mesopotamia can offer such a detailed look at brewing spaces on the household level.[122]

As we've already seen, the houses themselves were not exactly standardized, but they did tend to follow a common template: a basic idea of what a house should be.[123] And that template included a preferred spot for brewing. The large brewing vat—larger than any other vessel in the house—was typically placed beneath the stairway that led up to the roof. It was immobile, dug down into the floor, and was often found in association with the smaller vessel with a pierced base. Activities related to brewing (e.g., the processing of brewing ingredients) certainly could have taken place in other parts of the house, but the brewing vat probably acted as a focal point for the home-brewing assemblage.

As an example, let's have a quick look at House 1 (H.1), the first house excavated in the *Weststadt* at Tell Bazi.[124] This structure is a good example of the basic house template, although it is also missing some key features. The house backs up to a street, but it can't be entered directly from the street. Let's begin there. We're walking eastward down the broad street, about eight meters wide. On our left, we see a narrow doorway (less than a meter wide) and decide to see what lies beyond. After passing through the doorway, we find ourselves in a long, narrow passageway. Continuing for about twelve meters, we then take a right and see a wooden door standing ajar ahead of us on the right, about five meters further along. We give it a few quick, polite knocks and are greeted by a teenage boy, who invites us in. We've clearly disturbed him in the middle of some task—his hands and clothes are covered in a fine dust—but we explain our interests, and he lets us have a look around.

We've entered along one of the short sides of a long, rectangular room (c. 4 m x 12 m). Ahead of us and slightly to the left, at the center of the room, a fire smolders within an oval-shaped hearth. The space around the hearth has been left open, but beyond it, along the back wall of the room, we can see several individuals busily working away and an array of objects scattered around them. Before checking out what's going on back here, we turn to the left and see a stairway against the long wall, leading upward toward the corner of the room. Between us and the stairway, there's a sort of stone emplacement, surrounding a huge, open-mouthed ceramic vat that's partially buried in the floor. Noticing a pleasant, malty aroma coming from that general direction, we peek over the rim and see a brownish liquid bubbling away. Our generous host offers us a taste. It's definitely somewhere in the vicinity of beer but a little bit different than what we're used to: lightly effervescent, with a mild tartness and, if I'm not mistaken, a hint of alcohol at the end. So this is where the home brewing happens.

Let's continue, though, with our tour of the rest of the house. To the right of the entrance, a door leads into the first of four small, square side rooms, arranged in a linear sequence along the long wall of the main room. These seem to be functioning primarily for the storage of various household goods. The last two, for example, are packed full of ceramic vessels of all shapes and sizes. In the back right corner of the main room, there's a cluster of ceramic vessels and, along the right-hand wall, a seating area, where two young children are sitting cross-legged on cushions enjoying a midafternoon snack. In the back left corner, several older children and two adult men are arranged in clusters, working with stone weights, stone beads, pierced shells, and terracotta figurines. It's this craft production area that really sets House 1 apart from other houses at the site. Normally, one would expect to find an altar for household rituals along the back wall and a bench running from the back left corner part of the way down the long wall. In House 1, where that bench would normally be, we find instead a food preparation area, where an adult woman and teenage girl are busy getting ready for the evening meal. On that note, we realize that it's probably time to take our leave and let the family go about its business. We thank them and head back toward the main door, sneaking another peek at their brewing setup— tucked up against the corner stairway—on our way out.

Chapter 6

Drinkers and drinking practices

Beer is a bull. The mouth is its stairway.

Sumerian proverb[1]

Cylinder seals with banquet scenes

On Sunday, February 26, 1928, readers of the *New York Times* would have come across the following headline, displayed in the top left corner of page eight of section three ("Times Week-end Correspondence").

ROYAL TOMBS OF UR RICH IN TREASURE

Crowns and Cloak of Queen Shub-ad Marvels of Artistic Work

———

KING'S GRAVE A SHAMBLES

———

Fifty Persons Sacrificed to His Spirit—Wife's Piety Led to Tomb's Desecration[2]

The story, delivered via special cable from London, recounted a series of dramatic discoveries by archaeologist C. Leonard Woolley. Since late 1922, the soon-to-be-dubbed *Sir* Leonard Woolley had been conducting excavations in the fabled ancient city of Ur (modern Tell al-Muqayyar, Iraq), a city whose name would have resonated for many readers, birthplace of the biblical Abraham.[3] The same readers might also have been familiar with another name, Nebuchadnezzar II, the notorious king of Babylon (604–562 BCE) who had besieged and destroyed the city of Jerusalem and deported large numbers of Jews to Babylonia. Nebuchadnezzar was a prolific builder. His infamous capital at Babylon was a sprawling, glittering metropolis, the skyline dominated by the great *ziggurat* of Marduk (also known as the Tower of Babel). Under his patronage, the city was reshaped on a monumental scale and transformed into an imperial center truly worthy of the name.[4]

Nebuchadnezzar also commissioned numerous construction projects in the city of Ur. It was these structures, especially within the so-called *temenos* enclosure, that occupied Woolley's excavation team for the better part of the first five seasons of work at the site.[5] The *temenos* was an enormous walled compound that contained many of the city's most important buildings. Its roots stretched back millennia into the past. Woolley's team managed to uncover a whole series of monumental structures within the *temenos* enclosure, many dating to the time of Nebuchadnezzar. They were also probing down into earlier levels in various places. Midway through the fifth season (1926–27), Woolley decided to return to an area near the southeastern corner of Nebuchadnezzar's *temenos* wall, where his very first trial trench (Trench A) during season one had revealed a collection of earlier burials. This proved to be a wise choice. In less than three months, the team uncovered another six hundred burials. And they kept at it for three further excavation seasons (1927–28, 1928–29, 1929–30). All told, Woolley and his team excavated 1,850 intact burials in what would come to be known as the Royal Cemetery of Ur.[6]

Most of the burials were relatively simple: a body carefully arranged in a rectangular pit, surrounded by a modest assortment of personal belongings.[7] But a small subset stood out from the rest. In Woolley's estimation, sixteen graves, all dating to the Early Dynastic IIIa period (2600–2450 BCE), were royal in character. There's plenty of room to dispute his claim—and many have—but there's no doubt that these particular burials belonged to members of the upper crust. Like the other burials in the cemetery, they had been dug down into a trash dump, piles of debris cast out by the inhabitants of an earlier settlement on the site. This debris actually proved to be extremely rich in artifactual material, especially cylinder seal impressions, so much so that Woolley called the debris layers the "Seal Impression Strata."

The "royal" burials comprised elaborately constructed tomb chambers that had been set down within deep shafts and provided with an astounding assortment of opulent grave goods. And an astounding assortment of human beings. The Royal Cemetery offers our only real evidence for human sacrifice in ancient Mesopotamia.

The most famous tomb is PG 800, built for a queen once known as Shub-ad (thanks to a mistaken reading of the cuneiform signs) but now known as Puabi (Figure 6.1).[8] Puabi was just under five feet tall and about forty years old at the time of her death. She was laid to rest alongside three other individuals—almost certainly attendants—and dressed in finery fit for a queen: a headdress of gold, lapis lazuli, and carnelian; a cape, belt, and accessories composed of thousands of beads of gold, lapis lazuli, and carnelian; a golden ring for each finger; and three cylinder seals.[9]

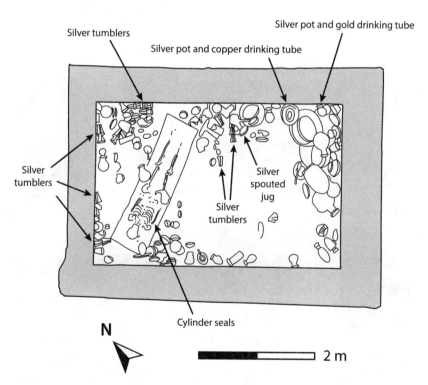

Figure 6.1. Plan of the Tomb of Puabi, indicating location of cylinder seals and drinking equipment. Royal Cemetery of Ur, Tell al-Muqayyar, Iraq. (Redrawn after Woolley 1934: Plate 36)

Let's train our attention on these three cylinders of lapis lazuli, a rare imported material that signified wealth and status in Mesopotamia (Figure 6.2). One cylinder was inscribed with the name of the queen, a crucial piece of identifying information. But all three also featured intricately carved pictorial scenes. Though not identical, the scenes followed one another closely in organization and theme. Each was divided into two horizontal registers, stacked one atop the other. And each showed a version of the classic

Figure 6.2. Cylinder seals found by the right upper arm of Puabi. Tomb of Puabi, Royal Cemetery of Ur, Tell al-Muqayyar, Iraq. Top: B16728 (Courtesy of Penn Museum), Middle: 121544 (Courtesy of British Museum), Bottom: 121545 (Courtesy of British Museum)

"banquet scene," playing out across both registers. One seal shows only female participants, all dressed in the same type of skirt and all wearing their
hair in a bun gathered at the nape of the neck (Figure 6.2, top).[10] Some of
the women sit on stools and raise conical cups toward their mouths. Others
stand in attendance. Off to the side, there is a group of three musicians, one
playing a four-stringed lyre and two clapping cymbals or singing. The scene
also includes a table piled with food. A second seal, bearing the inscription "Puabi, queen," shows a variation on the theme (Figure 6.2, middle).[11]
Drinkers sit on stools and raise cups to their mouths, attended by standing
figures and a table with food, but this time both men and women are
depicted. The third seal introduces a further variation (Figure 6.2, bottom).[12]
Alongside participants who sit on stools and drink from cups, waited on by
attendants, a woman and man sit on stools and grasp long straws that emerge
from a large vessel sitting between them on a stand.

So Puabi's three cylinder seals all show versions of a banquet scene. Her
burial chamber (4.35m x 2.80 m) was also well set up for such a banquet,
presumably to be held in the afterlife.[13] The chamber was found packed full
of objects, including an assemblage of extra-fancy drinking equipment: a
spouted jug made of silver; an array of gold and silver "tumblers" (not unlike the conical cups that appear in the banquet scenes), and two drinking
tubes (also directly recalling the banquet scenes). One tube, made of gold
leaf attached to long-disintegrated reed, was found emerging from the
mouth of a silver jar. The other, made of copper encased in lapis lazuli, was
found right next to another silver jar. Those jars almost certainly once held
beer, and only the best of the best.

Puabi's tomb chamber was once thought to have its own associated
"death pit"—a chamber filled with dead bodies, both human and nonhuman, decked out in their finest outfits and carefully arranged in a sort
of funerary tableau.[14] It basically looks like a funerary procession that has
come to a halt in a deep shaft alongside the tomb chamber and then just
crumpled to the ground in place. Indeed, it has long been assumed that the
participants, either willingly or not, were standing there in position, drank
a cup of poison, and died on the spot. But it's now clear that at least some
of the individuals in the death pits were killed elsewhere with a blow to
the head. Their bodies were then treated with heat and/or preservatives,
dressed, and transferred to the appropriate spot in the death pit.[15] It's also
now clear that the death pit once associated with Puabi's tomb actually
belongs with some other unknown and unexcavated tomb chamber.[16]

Right next door to Puabi's tomb, about seven meters to the southeast,
lay another death pit. This so-called Great Death Pit (PG 1237) offers us

another glimpse into the world of Early Dynastic banqueting.[17] The pit contained a whopping seventy-three sacrificial victims, most of them lined up neatly in rows. Only five were men; the other sixty-eight appear to have been women.[18] Much ink has been spilled in the effort to tease out exactly what was going on in this particular death pit, whose associated tomb chamber has not been recovered.[19] For example, a recent reconstruction by the Penn Museum envisions a lavish banquet with attendees seated on stools and drinking from cups, while being entertained with music and dancing.[20] Here, though, let's just focus on two of the people interred in the pit and their lapis lazuli cylinder seals.

Near the eastern corner of the death pit, alongside many other bodies, lay the best-dressed of its occupants (Body no. 61), a woman decked out in luxurious jewelry and accessories.[21] Her single cylinder seal included a banquet scene, showing three females, each seated on a stool and holding a cup, all facing left (Figure 6.3, top).[22] Another individual stands in front of them by a table bearing food. In the opposite corner of the death pit, two individuals lie somewhat isolated from the throng. One of these two (Body no. 7) was found with a cylinder seal bearing another banquet scene, divided into two horizontal registers (Figure 6.3, bottom).[23] An inscription on the seal reads "Dumu-kisal," perhaps the name of the seal's owner or possibly a phrase meaning "child of the gipar." If the latter, these individuals interred in the Great Death Pit may have borne some connection to the gipar, home of the entu-priestess, high priestess of the moon god in Ur. The banquet scene on the seal shows seated participants drinking from cups and straws, as well as a collection of standing figures engaged in a musical performance. There is a man holding a staff and five women playing cymbals. All six face toward center, where a woman is playing a bull-headed lyre, while two smaller figures dance beneath. When the Great Death Pit was excavated, what do you think was found lying just inches away from the head of Body no. 7? If you guessed an ornate bull-headed lyre, as well as another lyre made of gold and one of silver, you would be correct.

How drinkers drank

The seven cylinder seals that we've just examined—from the tomb of Puabi and the Great Death Pit at Ur—offer a fascinating glimpse into the graphic representation of drinking practices during the Early Dynastic period. But these are just a tiny fraction of an exceptionally rich artistic corpus. The

Figure 6.3. Cylinder seals found with Body 61 (top) and Body 7 (bottom) in the Great Death Pit, Royal Cemetery of Ur, Tell al-Muqayyar, Iraq. Top: 30-12-3, Bottom: 30-12-2 (Courtesy of Penn Museum)

Royal Cemetery of Ur alone has produced at least thirty-four cylinder seals that show some variation on the banquet scene.[24] And one groundbreaking study of banquet scenes from the Early Dynastic and Akkadian periods listed 615 examples, not all of them (but most of them) inscribed on cylinder seals.[25] A more recent study, considering only those that come from good archaeological contexts (i.e., that do not derive from the antiquities market, deprived of information about their original context), lists 300 examples.[26] In either case, we're talking about a substantial body of artistic material, dedicated specifically to a distinctive kind of drinking occasion.

Do we know exactly what it was that people were meant to be drinking in these banquet scenes? No, at least not in the case of beverages sipped from cups or goblets. Maybe it was meant to be beer? Maybe wine? Maybe both? At the least, I'd say it's very likely that some sort of alcohol was intended. (Unfortunately, the artists of ancient Mesopotamia did not feel the same urge to caption their works as contemporaries in ancient Egypt, where we might expect some kind of short explanatory remark or bit of dialogue wedged in alongside—something like "Drinking beer in the palace" or "Hey, you, servant! Bring me more beer!") In the case of beverages consumed through long straws, though, we can be a little more confident. These were almost certainly beer.

Drinking through straws

Perhaps there was some particular significance to the use of a straw. Maybe straws were employed only for specific types of beer, such as those that required filtering at the moment of consumption. Maybe there were certain contexts in which straws were appropriate and certain contexts in which they were not. Maybe only specific sorts of people used straws. Maybe straws were considered an old-fashioned style of drinking. Maybe a little bit avant-garde. Or maybe they just offered a more sociable means of sharing a drink among friends, family, colleagues, or sexual partners. And you can bet that there was some sort of etiquette involved, some set of unwritten rules governing appropriate behavior around the communal beer pot. We don't currently understand the finer points of drinking straw culture in Mesopotamia, but let's look at the evidence that we have to work with.

The earliest depictions of the practice (some debatable) date back to the fourth or fifth millennium BCE. But the real heyday is the Early Dynastic period (2900–2350 BCE), when banquet scenes regularly show one or more seated individuals grasping long straws that emerge from the mouths of large vessels (Figure 6.4). And sometimes no drinkers appear, just vessels with straws, ready and waiting. A single vessel might feature as many as five or six straws (even nine in one case), or as few as one. The straws themselves are not depicted in the greatest of detail. They're basically just lines, either straight or curving. But the vessels are a different story. There are vessels with pointed bases and sharp carinations at the shoulder, round-bottomed vessels with sloping shoulders, vessels with narrow necks that flare out suddenly to wide lips, oval-bodied vessels with funnel-shaped necks, vessels encircled by a single decorative band, vessels entirely covered in decorative bands, vessels depicted as three circles one atop the other, vessels with feet (allowing them

Figure 6.4. Cylinder seal with banquet scene showing drinking straws. A11464, D.27514. (Courtesy of the Institute for the Study of Ancient Cultures of the University of Chicago)

to sit flat on the floor), vessels without feet, sitting on a range of different pot stands (Figure 6.5).[27] The list goes on. And there's often enough detail that one can legitimately go on a search for the counterparts of these vessels in the archaeological record.[28]

But let's return to the straws. Most would have been made from reed, which was available in great abundance in Mesopotamia. Archaeologically, reed does not survive well in the region, but in some fortunate cases the remains of reed drinking tubes have survived. One example comes from a Late Chalcolithic (4000–3800 BCE) wine-pressing installation at the site of Areni-1 in Armenia.[29] Near the winepress, reed stems were found inside an earthenware wine pot, suggesting that the reeds may have been used for consuming wine. Areni is situated well beyond the bounds of Mesopotamia proper, up in the Caucasus, the heart of wine country, so an association between reed straws and wine consumption seems perfectly reasonable.

But it's an interesting case to consider, because the linkage between drinking tubes and beer in Mesopotamia remains largely conjectural.[30] Arguments tend to revolve around the issue of filtering. Many of the beers would have included a significant component of grain husks and other chunky bits, so the argument goes, and the use of straws would have helped to filter these out. I don't see any particular problem with this conclusion, but we don't really know that the beers were in need of filtering. Our best evidence for that comes from the straws themselves and from the fact that

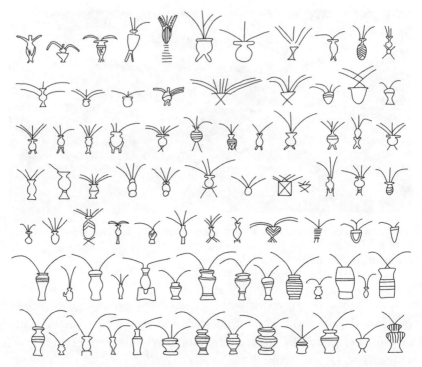

Figure 6.5. Vessel types shown with drinking straws in banquet scenes. Dating as published by Selz: top two rows (Early Dynastic II/IIIa), middle three rows (Early Dynastic IIIa), bottom two rows (Akkadian). (Redrawn after Selz 1989: Abb. 9, 12, 18)

some beers were explicitly called out as "filtered" or "strained" beers. So the argument can get a little circular here. The beers must have needed filtering. Why else would they have used straws? Therefore, the straws must have been used for filtering. And they must have been used for filtering beer, rather than something else, because the beers needed filtering. (Or something like that.)

Yes, if the beers were full of detritus that one didn't necessarily want to drink, a reed straw probably would have functioned pretty well as a filtering mechanism. Perhaps more important, it would have drawn off beer from well below the surface of the liquid, where husks and the like tend to float around. But we also have examples of special filter tips that had once been attached to the end of drinking straws, the end that would have been submerged in the beer. At Tell Bazi, for example, bronze filter tips were recovered from a number of different houses and from a ritual feasting context in a temple (Figure 6.6).[31] These filters were 5.35–6.2 centimeters in length and 0.85–1.5 centimeters in diameter. Made of sheet bronze, they were open at one end. That's where the reed would have been attached. They then tapered toward the tip, where the bronze had been folded over. Small perforations would have allowed beer into the tube, while filtering out unwanted materials.

Similar items in bronze and other materials (e.g., bone) have been found at a number of sites in Mesopotamia and beyond.[32] And they have often been recovered inside or in close association with vessels that could have once held beer or some other beverage. At the site of Chagar Bazar in Syria, for example, Max Mallowan excavated at least nine of these "wine strainers."[33] Made of folded sheet copper, they were "cornet-shaped" and perforated in their lower halves. Crucially, most of them also preserved traces of reed adhering to their interiors, that is, traces of the reed straws to which they had been attached. They were all found within graves (Level 1, Middle Bronze Age, 1900–1600 BCE), most sitting at the

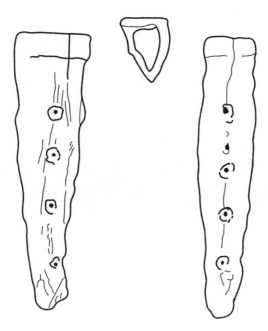

Figure 6.6. Bronze filter tip, Tell Bazi. (Redrawn after Zarnkow et al. 2006: Abb. 12)

bottom of large, flat-bottomed vases—right where you'd expect them to be if the straw-filter combo had been left in position for drinking at the time of burial.[34]

More recent excavations at Chagar Bazar have also uncovered further examples.[35] Four of the filter tips came from graves, and two, from non-grave contexts. Three of the examples from graves still had traces of the reed straw preserved inside, and all four were, once again, found sitting within medium-to-large ceramic vessels with either a flat or footed base. Figure 6.7 shows the four filters and the vessels in which they were found. (Note that the filters and vessels are not shown at the same scale.)

Let's zoom in on one of these filters, the one from Tomb 4, for a bit of context (Figure 6.8).[36] Tomb 4, a vaguely bell-shaped burial pit, had been

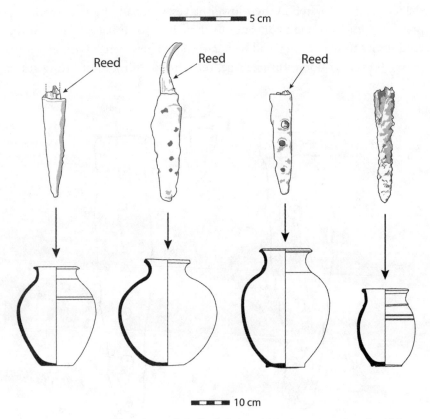

Figure 6.7. Bronze filter tips and the vessels in which they were found within a series of burials, Chagar Bazar, Syria. (Redrawn after McMahon 2009: Plates 1, 6, 7, 8, 85)

dug down below the floor of a one-room structure called Building 1, which was itself part of a larger, multiuse building complex. The tomb held a single individual, probably a female and probably of advanced age, given the wear on her teeth. She had been laid on her left side, with her limbs tightly flexed and her hands in front of her face. Two bone weaving needles, a bone spindle whorl (also for weaving), and a silver pin had been placed near her head. At her feet were two medium-size, narrow-mouthed ceramic jars: one with a ring base and four reddish-brown painted bands at the shoulder and

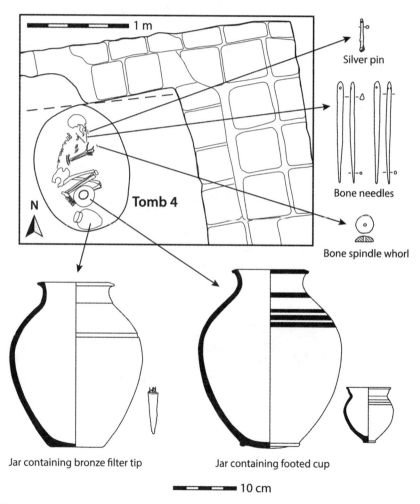

Figure 6.8. Plan of Tomb 4 and assemblage of artifacts, Chagar Bazar, Syria. (Redrawn after McMahon 2009: Plate 1).

one with a flat base and a single excised band at the shoulder.[37] A footed cup or "fine ware beaker" was found inside the first jar and a bronze filter tip inside the second.[38] The choice to include a beer (or wine) jar and a drinking straw with bronze filter tip in this burial was apparently a pretty common one at this point in time. Most of the bronze filter tips that have been excavated in Mesopotamia date to the second millennium BCE, and many derive from grave assemblages.

Excavations at the site of Nippur in Iraq, however, have also uncovered a bronze filter tip in a burial that dates to the late Akkadian period (2250–2150 BCE), several centuries prior (Figure 6.9).[39] This burial was the last in a series of burials—collectively known as Burial 14—that had been dug down into the courtyard of a building. The individual interred here (Burial 14, Skeleton 1) was almost certainly a male scribe named

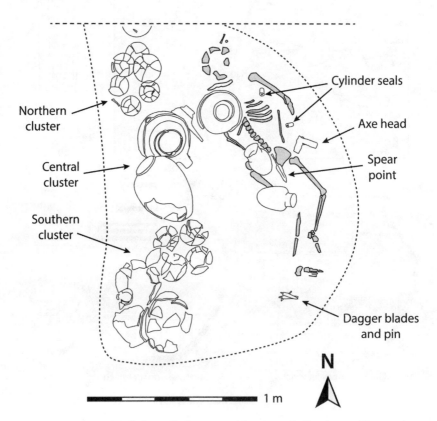

Figure 6.9. Plan of Burial 14, Skeleton 1, with arrows indicating artifacts and artifact clusters. Nippur, Iraq. (Redrawn after McMahon 2006: Plate 65)

Lugal-DUR₂. How do we know that? Two expertly crafted cylinder seals, probably the products of a palace workshop, were found by the body, one by the upper left arm, and one by the lower right.[40] The first was carved with an elaborate presentation scene, in which two gods—one of whom stands on a lion-griffin spitting fire—lead a human figure into the presence of another, seated god. The second shows a contest scene in which two nude heroes battle water buffalo and a bull-man thrusts a dagger into a lion. These are fancy seals. And both include the same inscription: "Lugal-DUR₂, scribe."

Lugal-DUR₂ was laid to rest with a rich assortment of grave goods (Figure 6.10). Among these were various items of personal adornment (a gold foil fillet, copper/bronze pins, lapis lazuli and bone beads, a gold ring), a collection of weapons (an axe head, spear point, and blades made of copper/bronze), and an impressive assemblage of ceramic and copper/bronze vessels, several placed directly on the body, the rest grouped into three distinct clusters to the west. Each of these three clusters has potential connections with beer.

The central cluster included two tall ceramic jars, but the rest of the vessels were made of copper/bronze. There was a deep pan and spouted cauldron of uncertain function and then a four-vessel set—two hemispherical bowls, a bucket, and a ladle—that bears a striking resemblance to similar sets uncovered in Early Dynastic and Akkadian period graves at several other sites (sometimes with the ladle replaced by a similarly shaped strainer). We don't really know what these four-vessel sets might have been used for, but one interpretation suggests that they were drinking sets.[41] We'll return to these in a moment. To the north of the first cluster was another one made up solely of ceramic vessels: five conical bowls, a long-necked jar, and "three nearly identical large storage jars with holes near the convex bases." Perhaps those last ones were, indeed, storage jars, but they certainly sound (and look) a lot like the *Lochbodengefässe* or "vessels with a hole in the base" that we discussed in our look at brewing equipment (Chapter 4). Finally, on the southern side of the central cluster, a third cluster of ceramic vessels included another six conical bowls and a shattered jar containing a copper/bronze filter tip with traces of reed preserved inside. As far as I know, this is currently the earliest known filter tip excavated in Mesopotamia.

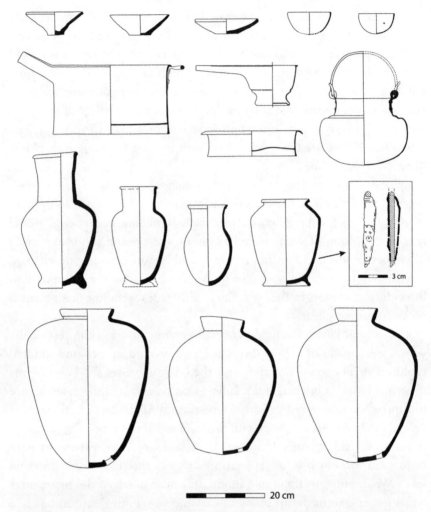

Figure 6.10. Artifacts found with Burial 14, Skeleton 1, Nippur, Iraq. Artifacts, listed top to bottom, left to right. Row 1: three conical ceramic bowls, two copper/bronze bowls; Row 2: copper/bronze pan, footed bowl, pan, bucket; Row 3: four ceramic jars, copper/bronze filter tip found within the jar to its left; Row 4: three large ceramic vessels with pierced bases. (Redrawn after McMahon 2006: Plates 152–156)

So the upshot of all this? Yes, reed straws were definitely used to filter some kind of liquid during consumption. The straws don't survive well in the archaeological record, but the metal filter tips attached to them do. As far as I know, however, the only solid evidence that these straws were used specifically for filtering beer is that one document from Kanesh—the one describing preparations for a series of pre-wedding feasts—that mentions drinking straws (*qanû*) for *kirrum*-jars, vessels that were closely associated with beer (see Chapter 5).[42] As we saw in our discussion of brewing equipment inventories (Chapter 4), there's also a potential reference to a drinking straw in an Early Dynastic text from the city of Girsu. In this inventory text, alongside a collection of different brewing vessels, we find one sim ge kaš₂ sur, that is, one filter for a beer-drinking straw.[43]

We also do have some complete straws. It's just that they weren't made of reed. They were made of metal. If you recall, two drinking tubes were recovered from Puabi's burial chamber (Early Dynastic IIIa period, 2600–2450 BCE) in the Royal Cemetery of Ur: one of gold leaf (that had apparently once been attached to a reed straw) and one of copper encased in lapis lazuli.[44] The first was found sitting in a silver jar, and the other, right next to one. But these are certainly not your everyday drinking straws. And I only know of a few other examples.[45] One comes from a grave at the site of Khafajeh (ancient Tutub) in Iraq, dating to the Early Dynastic IIIa period (2600–2450 BCE). Although already disturbed when uncovered by archaeologists—meaning that the artifactual assemblage might be incomplete—the grave produced a substantial collection of grave goods, including two cylinder seals, an animal figurine, beads, and a lot of copper objects. Among these was a copper tube. No perforations are mentioned, but it was probably used for drinking.[46]

Another example comes from a hoard of copper objects found in the Northern Palace at the site of Tell Asmar in Iraq, the ancient city of Eshnunna.[47] Two different versions of the Northern Palace were uncovered, an "earlier" version and then, built directly on top of it, the "main level." We're interested in the earlier Northern Palace, which dates to the Akkadian period (2350–2192 BCE).[48] The building—a monumental construction but probably not actually a palace—was organized around a series of courtyards, each providing access to a series of rooms arranged around its perimeter. Our copper hoard was found in one of these side rooms (E 16:35), stashed behind a wall that had then been carefully plastered over, leaving no trace of what lay behind. When archaeologists accidentally broke through this plastered wall face, they discovered a large ceramic vessel, packed full of copper objects, its opening covered over with a large ceramic bowl (c. 50 cm in diameter). The objects had not been thrown in haphazardly but were carefully nested, one within the other. The assemblage included drinking cups, lamps, daggers, flat strainers with handles, circular and boat-shaped bowls, cooking pots, and a drinking tube, 28 inches long, 0.5 inches in diameter, and perforated at one end.[49]

Two of the bowls also included cuneiform inscriptions, indicating that they had been dedicated to the god Abu, whose temple was right next door. One reads, "To Abu, has Lugal-kisala(k)-si, son of HAR.TU, presented (this)."[50] For the excavator, these inscriptions provided a clue regarding the ultimate origins of the entire hoard: This collection of items stashed carefully behind a wall in the Northern Palace was "a complete service for a banquet of ritual significance held in the temple" next door.[51] According to this argument, then, a ritual banquet of some kind was held in the Abu Temple. Afterward, the entire set of dining and drinking equipment was gathered up, packed into a ceramic vessel, and hidden behind a wall in the Northern Palace.[52] We don't know whether this exact scenario actually transpired, but it's an interesting possibility.

So, there's a lot of evidence for the use of drinking straws in Mesopotamia. If we can trust the artistic record, this was often a communal form of drinking that brought two or more people together to drink from a shared vessel. It may seem odd to many people today, accustomed to imbibing their beer from cups, glasses, bottles, and cans, but the choice to drink beer through a straw is not really all that unusual. Many people today and in the past have preferred this more communal option for consuming their alcoholic beverages. As we've seen, in Mesopotamia such drinkers are typically depicted either sitting upright or standing next to a vessel from which straws protrude. Everything looks pretty prim and proper. If you recall the Prologue, though, and our discovery of an "erotic" cylinder seal at the site of Hamoukar, you'll recall that the people of Mesopotamia also engaged in, or at least liked to depict, another, more acrobatic kind of communal beer consumption that featured a straw. I don't know of good comparative examples for this practice, but surely some other adventurous straw users out there have given it a try (or at least are going to now, now that I've put the idea in their heads).

I'm talking, of course, about sex scenes. Sex scenes with beer. And straws. The best-known examples appear on small, mold-made clay plaques (Figure 6.11).[53] These "coitus a tergo drinking scenes"[54] (i.e., intercourse-from-behind drinking scenes) were produced during a period of about 300 years,

Figure 6.11. Clay plaque with *coitus a tergo* drinking scene. AO 16681, T 1496. (Courtesy of Louvre Museum)

starting in the late Ur III period and running up into the middle of the Old Babylonian period (c. 2010–1700 BCE). Among all of the different motifs that show up on clay plaques during this period, sex scenes rank high in popularity, coming in at third place, just behind the naked woman (not having sex) and bull-eared god motifs. And the most popular sex scene appears to have been the *coitus a tergo* drinking scene—comprising, for example, eighteen of the fifty-two erotic plaques examined in the most detailed study to date.[55] This motif features a standing man penetrating a woman from behind, while the woman leans over (either just a bit or bent almost horizontal at the waist) to drink beer through a straw from a vessel that sits on the floor in front of her.

In one sense, it's very clear what's going on here. In another, not so much. Do these plaques—which would not have been prohibitively expensive to procure—offer us snapshots from daily life, a glimpse of what people were getting up to behind closed doors in the bedroom or the tavern? Could they, instead, be depicting some kind of ritual context, perhaps the much-debated "sacred marriage" ceremony?[56] Or are they operating in a different register altogether, a "magico-liminal" realm, where the plaques are a means of soliciting aid from the divine, where beer and sex are combined to evoke, attract, and draw power from the goddess Inana/Ishtar and her erotically charged domain, the tavern?[57] For whatever reason, over a pretty lengthy period of time, people of relatively modest means were choosing to display erotic drinking scenes in their homes. And the drinking in those scenes, which happen to be contemporary with many of the filter tips recovered by archaeologists, took place via straw.

Drinking from cups

But we know that not all beer was sucked through a straw. In the artistic record, for example, individuals are regularly depicted brandishing cups (Figure 6.12).[58] We don't know exactly what liquid such cups were intended to contain, but the people of the time probably had a pretty good idea. Given the ubiquity of beer and the relative scarcity of wine, beer is probably the most likely candidate. But, of course, where the goal was to represent elite actors engaged in sumptuous dining practices, beyond the reach of the riffraff, the patrons behind the art might also have wished to highlight their access to wine. So it's possible that the depiction of certain vessel shapes or gestures or styles of consumption would have signaled the presence of wine in a way that is currently illegible to us. Regardless, we know that people drank beer from cups, and the artistic record provides many depictions of people holding or drinking from cups, as well as attendants bearing pitchers, jars, buckets, and other implements for the serving of liquids.

What might these cups have looked like in real life? The archaeological record is overflowing with potential comparanda: vessels that either seem a perfect match in terms of shape, size, etc., or that seem ideally suited to

Figure 6.12. Stone plaque with banquet scene showing two seated individuals drinking from cups, two individuals carrying a large vessel suspended from a pole, other offering bearers, and musicians. (Courtesy of the Institute for the Study of Ancient Cultures of the University of Chicago)

fulfilling the same purposes. One study, for example, has drawn attention to a long-lived tradition of undecorated, mass-produced bowls/cups that were produced from the Uruk period up through the later Early Dynastic period.[59] Known respectively as beveled rim bowls (Uruk period), *Blumentöpfe* (Jemdet Nasr period), solid-footed goblets (Early Dynastic I period), and conical bowls (Early Dynastic II–III period), these expediently made vessels were often discarded whole, that is, while still in perfectly good working order. The implication is that they were intended to function as single-use, disposable containers for some foodstuff, potentially beer. And the need for such containers did not cease with the Early Dynastic period. Vessels occupying a similar niche continued to be produced well into the future:

for example, an evolving tradition of conical cups and goblets that show up in large numbers within ceramic assemblages from the Ur III period up through the Kassite period and beyond.

Some of these were more obviously dedicated to drinking than others, but each would have offered a perfectly serviceable means of delivering an individual-size portion of beer to the consumer. And, that purpose fulfilled, they could apparently have been cast aside without much fanfare. Of course, these cheap, throwaway bowls and cups might have been too lowbrow for the sort of elite banquets depicted in the artistic record. And the archaeological record includes plenty of more finely made options, whether in ceramic or various metals. The most famous examples come from the Royal Cemetery of Ur (Early Dynastic IIIa period, 2600–2450 BCE), where a rich assemblage of bronze, silver, and gold vessels was recovered in both the "royal" tomb chambers and the death pits.[60] But we also just considered some other contexts—a tomb at Nippur (late Akkadian period, 2250–2150 BCE) and a hoard at Khafajeh (Akkadian period, 2350–2192 BCE)—that included a substantial assemblage of metal vessels for serving and drinking liquids.[61]

Indeed, we saw that the tomb at Nippur included what might be a four-piece drinking set fashioned from copper/bronze. Examples of this recurring assemblage of metal vessels have been identified in graves at a series of different sites dating to the Early Dynastic and Akkadian periods.[62] Exactly how the two hemispherical bowls, bucket, and ladle (or, alternatively, strainer) functioned together as a set is a matter of educated guesswork. We can often infer basic functions from vessel form alone—i.e., this one must have been some sort of ladle, this one a bucket—but the finer points of vessel use often elude us. Especially given their recovery from funerary contexts, we can probably assume that these four-piece vessel sets were bound up with a distinctive suite of movements, gestures, routines, and/or rituals.

And then how might these vessel sets have related to the broadly contemporary "four-part sets" that we discussed in Chapter 4? If you recall, these sets of ceramic vessels featured a large, open vat, a cylindrical colander (with relatively large holes), a strainer bowl (with smaller holes), and a small tumbler. They are typically found in graves, often stacked one inside the other, giving us some sense for how they would have been arranged during use: the colander standing upright in the large vat, the strainer sitting atop the colander, and the tumbler within the vat but on the outside of the colander. It is generally assumed that they served some function related to the production or consumption of beer.[63] But what function exactly? Here, unfortunately, we're still in the realm of educated guesswork.

This is the real kicker. We have so, so many vessels to work with in Mesopotamia, an embarrassment of riches compared to some other world regions. And I think that few archaeologists working on this material would doubt that many of the vessels we encounter were used for serving or drinking beer. But we can only get so far. What's generally missing is the smoking gun, direct evidence that this particular cup found in this particular tomb, say, was actually used for drinking beer. As you might expect, our best chance of identifying that smoking gun is going to come from organic residue analysis. So far, only the Late Bronze Age site of Khani Masi (1550–1150 BCE) in Iraq has produced such confirmation. There, recent analyses have conclusively demonstrated traces of beer within, not just brewing vessels, but also serving and drinking vessels: juglets, small footed cups (c. 100–200 ml), and "Kassite" goblets (c. 300–600 ml).[64]

As we've already seen, though, there are also some other means of exploiting the diverse lines of evidence available to triangulate our way toward credible interpretations. One option is to build links between the artistic record and the archaeological record. Another option is to mine the written record for information about the form and function of particular vessel types: for example, a recent study that compares the ceramic vessels recovered from the site of Tell Khaiber in Iraq with vessels mentioned in contemporary cuneiform documents.[65] So when it comes to drinking practices—how beer drinkers drank their beer—progress is, in fact, being made on multiple fronts.

Who drank beer?

But who exactly were these beer drinkers? And what might they have to tell us about the social, political, or economic world? For example, was access to beer controlled or restricted? Was beer widely available or only to some subset of the population? Were certain types of beer harder to get one's hands on? Did one's age or gender or social status impact whether or how one could drink? In recent times, beer has often been considered a drink of the masses, a humble source of alcohol and refreshment, unlike its snootier cousin, grape wine. This distinction has begun to break down—thanks especially to the craft beer movement, which has inspired both new forms of connoisseurship and higher price tags—but it's certainly still with us. And a similar distinction can be seen in ancient Mesopotamia, where grape wine was (especially during earlier periods) a costly import, only available to those with the necessary resources or connections.[66] Beer, on the other hand, was certainly a drink of the masses. But it was also subject to variations—for example, in quality, container, or context of consumption—that allowed for the playing out of various forms of social distinction. In other words, it was enjoyed widely by people across the social spectrum but not necessarily in a uniform fashion. So we need to seek out evidence for exactly who the drinkers of beer were and how the drinking of beer might have served to identify, unite, distinguish, and/or divide them.

Mesopotamia was a "stratified" society, marked by many different ways of identifying oneself socially and inequities on a scale unheard of up to this point in history. The tomb of Puabi, queen of Ur, offers an excellent entry point into this complicated world of cross-cutting identities and newly emergent forms of social distinction. I would like to highlight three angles that impinge directly on our efforts to better define the beer-drinking population.

First, gender. If you recall, Puabi was sent to the afterlife adorned with an elaborate assemblage of accessories, including three cylinder seals, each affixed to a pin holding her cloak in place. All three seals featured banquet scenes. One depicted a total of twelve women—no men at all—engaged in various activities: drinking, serving, dancing, playing music. The other two depicted a mixture of women and men, similarly engaged. Already, just these three seals offer a tantalizing glimpse into the gendered dimensions of elite drinking practices in early Mesopotamia. And there's plenty to suggest that the funerary rituals conducted at Ur would have featured actual (not just artistically rendered) eating and drinking. Who exactly would have taken part in such funerary feasts? We may never know. But recall all those retainers, sent to their deaths and carefully arranged in ceremonial tableaux within the "death pits" in the Royal Cemetery. The vast majority appear to have been women, some found with drinking vessels, others alongside musical instruments. So there are hints here of drinking occasions during which gender was both on display (e.g., explicitly indicated via dress, hairstyle, etc.) and serving as a means of distinguishing certain people and certain roles from others.

This brings us to our second angle, status. The big thing distinguishing Puabi and the other "royal" inhabitants of the Royal Cemetery at Ur from everyone else was status. For one reason or another—wealth, family connections, divine backing, personal ambition, luck—these people had risen to positions of relative prestige and power within the society of Early Dynastic Ur. And those positions came with perks: for example, not being violently put to death for the sake of joining your social betters in the after-life. Perhaps the three retainers buried alongside Puabi in her tomb and the occupants of all those death pits ended up there by choice. Perhaps it was a high honor, and they all jumped at the chance. But I suspect not. Either way, status was playing a key role. And status was also tightly bound up with the drinking of beer in Mesopotamia. In those banquet scenes that we've been discussing, for example, the people doing the drinking are clearly dis-tinguished from the people doing the serving and entertaining.

The third angle that I would like to highlight is age. Puabi lived to about forty years old. And, if her tomb assemblage is anything to go on, she was a beer drinker. But when did she start drinking beer? Did her relationship with beer evolve over the course of her life? We have no idea. In fact, we ac-tually know very little about age and the drinking of beer in Mesopotamia. For many people today, the two are intimately connected. And many people have very strong feelings about the issue—feelings that can easily work their way into discussions of beer in the ancient past.

Drinking and gender

So let's see what the ancient evidence has to tell us about gender, status, age, and the drinking of beer. We'll begin with a fascinating piece of Sumerian literature known as Enki and Ninmah.[67] This etiological tale (i.e., one that offers a historical/mythological explanation for certain features of the world as it exists) delves into the ultimate origins and fate of humanity. A worthy subject, no question. But our primary interest here is the setting in which most of the action transpires: a divine banquet.

When the tale opens, we find ourselves in the primordial days of cre-ation. The gods have already come into existence, but humans have not yet entered the scene. The minor gods are struggling mightily under the watchful eyes of the major gods. They have been tasked with dredging up clay from the base of canals and piling it up along the sides—the quintessential form of labor in southern Mesopotamia, where irrigation was essential to life—and they are not happy. Their incessant complaining is irritating the other gods beyond belief. But Enki, the responsible party (as creator) and the one most capable of resolving the situation, is sleeping away peacefully. Angry at Enki's apathy, his mother Namma wakes him and demands action, at which point he pronounces a solution. Namma, with the aid of Ninmah and a series of other goddesses, is to pinch off a piece of clay and from it create humans, who will labor in place of the gods. Disaster averted. Unless you're the humans, whose lot in life has thus been clearly laid out from the get-go. Humans are here to work.

Passing quickly over this rather bleak view of human origins and the ultimate meaning of human life, let's get to the festivities that followed. To celebrate their collective triumph—or perhaps mostly his own triumph— Enki throws a feast. He brings out bread and roasted goat kids to eat, beer to drink. We're told that "all the senior gods" were present. But the text also names some names. The feast was attended by the goddesses Namma and Ninmah, as well as "all the princely birth-goddesses," presumably at the least those who had recently taken part in the creation of humanity: Ninimma, Šu-zi-ana, Ninmada, Ninbarag, Ninmug, and Ninguna.[68] The gods An, Enlil, and Enki were also present. So this was very much a mixed-gender affair, as was the intense, beer-stoked competition that ensued between Enki and Ninmah, testing their relative skill as creator-deities.

Can we take this literary depiction of a divine banquet as somehow exemplary of feasting practices in Mesopotamia more broadly? Probably not. Things may have worked very differently in the human and divine realms. But this and other literary descriptions of divine banquets at least suggest that the idea of men and women eating and drinking together outside of the household was not an entirely foreign concept.

In the artistic record, men and women regularly appear together in banquet scenes. As we already saw, the most thorough study compared 615 different banquet scenes.[69] A later study went back to those scenes and compiled some basic statistics about gender in the banquet scenes, focusing specifically on the scenes that date to the Early Dynastic period.[70] We should, of course, be wary of importing our own assumptions about gender presentation and gender binaries into the ancient past. Indeed, many of the banquet participants cannot clearly be assigned to a particular gender. But the artists do appear to have followed some basic conventions for distinguishing men and women, especially via the rendering of hairstyle and dress. According to this particular study, 901 individuals in the Early Dynastic banquet scenes can be assigned a definite gender. This total includes both seated banquet attendees—i.e., drinkers, since drinking is the real focus of these scenes—and standing attendants. Among 557 attendees, 229 (41%) are women, and 328 (59%) are men. Among 344 attendants, on the other hand, 82 (24%) are women, and 262 (76%) are men. So, men outnumber women in both cases but especially among the attendants. That's interesting, but how often were banquets depicted as single- vs. mixed-gender affairs? Here we have to restrict ourselves to the 202 Early Dynastic banquet scenes in which the gender of more than one seated drinker is clearly indicated. In 26 (13%) of these scenes, only women appear as drinkers; in 58 (29%), only men. But in 118 (58%)—that is, in more than half of the scenes—both women and men appear.

It's also possible to zoom in and consider the evidence in a more localized fashion. Thirty-four cylinder seals featuring a banquet scene, for example, were recovered from the Royal Cemetery of Ur. Of the twenty-nine seals that include sufficient information to judge, four (14%) show women only, two (7%) show men only, and a whopping twenty-three (79%) show both men and women.[71] We certainly can't take these numbers as an accurate reflection of reality. But I think it's significant that, when depicting elite feasting practices, artists very often chose to show men and women drinking together.

We can also turn to a more mundane and less exclusive sort of occasion: the distribution of beer rations. As a general rule, beer was not among the items doled out in standardized quantities to institutional dependents on a daily or monthly basis.[72] The more typical ration consisted of unprocessed barley that could then be transformed further into beer on one's own time and one's own dime. But there are plenty of exceptions. We've already had a look at the Old Babylonian period (2004–1595 BCE) brewery archive from Tell Leilan, for example, which documents the daily delivery of beer to specific individuals and groups.[73] The named individuals include both men and women, as do the groups. In neither case is gender always clearly specified, but beer earmarked for the royal harem (which appears in every list, typically as the first entry), wet nurses, and female carriers was certainly destined for women.[74] Beer also appears occasionally among the foods distributed to groups engaged in construction work in the town of Garšana during the Ur III period (2112–2004 BCE).[75] One tablet documents the issuing of beer, bread, and soup to a mixed-gender group that included ten builders, twenty-three crew members, two foremen, seventeen male hired workers, thirty-nine female hired workers, three overseers of hired workers, four scribes, one smith, one blind person, and one female courtyard-sweeper.[76] We don't know whether the assembled group consumed all of this food together right there on the spot, but, again, we see the distribution of beer to both women and men.

So, there's really no doubt that the drinking of beer cut across the gender divide in ancient Mesopotamia. But it's also worth mentioning one partic- ular realm where gender and beer share the spotlight, the realm of sex and seduction. In some rather graphic Sumerian poems, a male speaker compares the female object of his desire—actually, her sexual organs—to sweet beer and praises the beer of her grain.[77] In a classic piece of literature known as "Enki and Ninhursag," the god Enki (yes, him again) plies his great-great- granddaughter Uttu with beer in order to seduce and impregnate her (see Chapter 7).[78] In the artistic record, as we've seen, men and women are reg- ularly depicted having sex, while the woman but not the man drinks beer through a straw.[79] And these images may (or may not) bear some relation to the much-debated occupation of *harīmtu*. Whether or not this term should be translated as "prostitute" in English—and there has been a lot of debate about this issue—it refers to women who were particularly associated with sex and with tavern life.[80] So there's certainly something going on here at the nexus of gender, sex, and beer. At the same time, depending on how one chooses to interpret Hammurabi's law code (see Chapter 5), it's at least pos- sible that certain categories of women (such as the *nadītu*) were explicitly prohibited from drinking beer or even setting foot in a tavern.[81]

Drinking and status

Let's talk now about status. There's no question that "who you were" mattered in Mesopotamia. Again, by at least the Uruk period, this was a stratified society. Everyone was not on equal footing. Instead, the social landscape can be envisaged as a sort of layer cake, composed of a series of distinct social strata (i.e., layers) stacked one atop the other. Such a model certainly oversimplifies what was a much messier reality, and the same goes for a number of convenient but imprecise dichotomies such as elite vs. commoner and rich vs. poor. At the same time, we know that such distinctions in wealth or status were crosscut by a range of other affiliations and associations (e.g., based on kinship, residence, occupation, or religion) that further complicate the picture. But this was no egalitarian paradise. It was a world of inequality and social distinction, where one's social position could impact not only abstract qualities like relative prestige but also fundamentals such as diet, access to goods and services, and overall quality of life.

That being said, pretty much everyone was drinking beer: kings, queens, merchants, scribes, sedan carriers, governors, enslaved people, builders, messengers, carpenters, prisoners of war, generals, musicians, foreigners, soldiers, the list goes on.[82] Was that beer all the same? And was the act of drinking beer somehow innocent of social connotations, implications, and ramifications? No and no. The quest to achieve, maintain, and/or flaunt status was very often fueled by beer. Take feasting. Who do you think had the means and motive to produce all of those expensively crafted Early Dynastic banquet scenes? Hint: not your everyday farmhand, goatherd, textile worker, or courtyard sweeper. These items—cylinder seals of lapis lazuli, stone wall plaques, inlaid musical instruments—were for the well-to-do.

Indeed, it has been suggested that the banquet imagery functioned as a form of "self-indoctrination" for a small coterie of privileged movers and shakers.[83] In other words, the scenes were not really intended to be seen by the population at large. The people who sponsored the production of these images were also the primary audience for the images and the primary subject matter. They had adorned their bodies and their homes and (presumably) their feasting venues with scenes that depicted an idealized image of themselves and their own drinking practices. The situation might be roughly analogous to the drinking vessels of the Athenian symposium in ancient Greece, vessels from which attendees could both consume wine and consume idealized depictions of the drinking of wine by symposium attendees just like themselves.[84] If this interpretation is correct, the banquet scenes were serving as a marker of status and exclusivity, a means of drawing social boundaries, of setting some people and their drinking practices apart from others.

So, perhaps the banquets depicted so often in the artistic record—assuming that such banquets were actual events and not just imagined ideals—were primarily about the fostering of camaraderie among an exclusive in-group. Regardless, we should almost certainly also envisage an element of internal jockeying for position. The feast is, after all, the classic setting for "gastro-politics," all those subtle (and not-so-subtle) forms of competition, comparison, scheming, strategizing, manipulation, and coded communication that regularly play out in the domain of food and drink.[85]

If the king, his family, and retinue, say, show up one evening at your house bearing gifts in order to "drink beer" with you—yes, that's a thing that happened during the Ur III period (2112–2004 BCE), but not to just anyone[86]—you can bet that there's going to be some elaborate protocol to observe and probably some careers and reputations hanging in the balance. One slip of the tongue, one missed cue, one beer carelessly spilled in the lap of the queen, let's imagine, and there goes that marriage arrangement for your daughter, all those months of negotiation and flattery down the drain, or that cushy posting for your son in the local temple. Gastro-politics at work. And, if one recent study is correct, archaeological evidence indicates a broader tradition of small-scale, household-level "entrepreneurial" feasts in Mesopotamia during the Early Dynastic period (2900–2350 BCE).[87] The suggestion is that this beer-centered hospitality helped enterprising community members build up informal political power as a means of climbing the social ladder.

Alongside all of this striving for status, though, some feasting events may actually have helped to paper over or make more palatable the otherwise undeniable inequities in wealth and status. Several other scholars, for example, have argued that certain large-scale religious festivals, which also featured beer, were really much more about the promotion of group cohesion and communal identity.[88] We'll return to these diverse beer-drinking occasions in Chapter 7.

Drinking and age

The last angle that I would like to consider is age. As far as we know, there was no drinking age in Mesopotamia, no point before (or after) which a person was not allowed to consume alcohol. Nowhere in the Code of Hammurabi or any other law code, for example, does one encounter an explicit prohibition:

"Thou shalt not serve beer unto a child" or, to put it in proper Mesopotamian parlance, "If a woman should serve beer to a child, they shall cast her into the river." (Just to be clear. I made these laws up. They do not exist.)

Indeed, we have plenty of evidence, primarily in the form of ration lists, that beer was served to children. Again, beer was not a normal ration but rather something given out in special circumstances. And at least two of those special circumstances appear to have involved women and their children: 1) when they were working for the palace or temple, not as part of some long-term arrangement, but just for a few days here and there and 2) when they were deportees or prisoners of war, severed from their usual household ties and the associated support system. In the first case, we see women receiving about 2 liters of beer per day and their children, 1 liter per day. In the second case, we see women receiving about 20 liters of beer per month and their children, 10 liters per month.[89] One Ur III (2112–2004 BCE) document from the city of Umma, for example, lists out thirty-nine deported women and ten children by name and documents the ration of flour and beer that each received. Ganana, Kurnitum, Nuban, Ana, Bizu, Igi-ban-amzi, Ili-asu, and Annetum, for example, each received 40 liters of flour and 20 liters of beer. Andurre, Ebina, Ili-ešdar, Baran-kagal, Bilzum, Il-zima, and Ergu-kaka, on the other hand, each received 20 liters of flour and 10 liters of beer.[90]

So, children could definitely get their hands on beer in Mesopotamia. Indeed, the authorities were giving it out to them and carefully documenting the fact. I guess the question now is, what do we do with this information? Do we follow the lead of the excavators of Tell Bazi (see Chapter 4) and conclude that, if children were drinking the beer, then the beer must have been low in alcohol content? Or do we conclude, perhaps, that the people of Mesopotamia just didn't see any particular problem with children drinking alcohol (if in smaller quantities than adults)? By now, you'll probably suspect which way I lean. I'm certainly open to the possibility that some beers were low in alcohol content, but I don't think that the drinking of beer by children really offers any evidence one way or the other. This would not be the first case in world history, not by a long shot, of a society in which children were regularly allowed to consume alcoholic beverages of normal strength. But, hey, equally compelling examples to the contrary could also be cited. The Aztecs famously (in theory, at least) prohibited the drinking of *pulque*, their own preferred alcoholic beverage, by anyone under the age of seventy, except on special, ritual occasions.[91] When it comes to the question of who drank what, where, why, and when, it's best to leave our assumptions at the door and come ready to be surprised.

Chapter 7

The beer-drinking experience

You should not boast in beer halls like a deceitful man: then your words will be trusted.

The instructions of Šuruppag[1]

Inana and Enki

We've discussed who drank beer and how they drank it. Now I'd like to talk about the experience of beer consumption. Let's begin with the tale of Inana and Enki.[2] We've met these two before: Inana, goddess of love and war, Enki, god of water, wisdom, crafts, and creation. But their encounter in this classic piece of Sumerian literature offers a particularly vivid illustration of the power and the transformative potential of beer. Actually, to be more precise, it offers a particularly vivid illustration of how *the people of ancient Mesopotamia* understood the power and the transformative potential of beer. Although the text is preserved on a number of different tablets, some significant chunks of the narrative are still missing. So the tale is incomplete. But we have enough to get a pretty clear sense for what's going on.

The tale begins with a fragmentary account of Inana prepping herself and hatching a plot to travel to Enki's home and there seduce him with her charms. When we enter the plot, about six lines in, we see her donning a special crown and proceeding to assess her appearance. The verdict? Her genitals are absolutely amazing, and her plan is bound to succeed.

> She put the šu-gura, the desert crown, on her head . . . her genitals were re-
> markable. She praised herself, full of delight at her genitals, she praised herself,
> full of delight at her genitals. . . .
>
> . . . I shall direct my steps to the abzu, to Eridug, I shall direct my steps to Enki,
> to the abzu, to Eridug, and I myself shall speak coaxingly to him . . . [3]

Confident in her mission, Inana sets out for the abzu, Enki's domain deep
down in the underground freshwaters—also a name for his temple in the
city of Eridu (rendered here as Eridug).

Enki, in his great wisdom, already knows what she is up to and so begins
his own preparations. He instructs his minister Isimud to welcome her in
style, with cake and water and beer.

> Enki, the king of the abzu, who, even before holy Inana had approached
> within six miles of [the abzu] in Eridug, knew all about her enterprise—Enki
> spoke to his man, gave him instructions: "Come here, my man, listen to my
> words."
>
> . . . When the maiden Inana has entered the abzu and Eridug, when Inana has
> entered the abzu and Eridug, offer her butter cake to eat. Let her be served
> cool refreshing water. Pour beer for her, in front of the Lions' Gate, make her
> feel as if she is in her girlfriend's house . . . [4]

The minister does as he is told, and the scene is set for a high-stakes contest, pitting clever god against fearsome and beguiling goddess. The two sit
down to drink, and the game is on.

> So it came about that Enki and Inana were drinking beer together in the abzu,
> and enjoying the taste of sweet wine. The bronze aga vessels were filled to the
> brim, and the two of them started a competition, drinking from the bronze
> vessels of [the goddess] Uraš. [5]

At this point, unfortunately, things get a little cloudy in the text.
Approximately 35 lines are missing.

When the story picks up again, the action is in full swing. Enki is busy
ceremoniously handing over his precious, divine powers, one after the
other, to Inana. Enki was in possession of a whole series of special powers,
known in Sumerian as ME. The concept is difficult to translate, but these
ME are often rendered as the "arts of civilization"—all of the things that
made Mesopotamian civilization what it was. And now he's giving these all
up to Inana, apparently without a fight.

Holy Inana received heroism, power, wickedness, righteousness, the plundering of cities, making lamentations, rejoicing. In the name of my power, in the name of my *abzu*, I will give them to holy Inana. . . .

Holy Inana received the craft of the carpenter, the craft of the coppersmith, the craft of the scribe, the craft of the smith, the craft of the leather-worker, the craft of the fuller, the craft of the builder, the craft of the reed-worker. . . .

Holy Inana received wisdom, attentiveness, holy purification rites, the shepherd's hut, piling up glowing charcoals, the sheepfold, respect, awe, reverent silence. . . .[6]

And many more. Almost certainly, this was Inana's plan all along, the endgame behind her scheming, to wrest control of the ME from Enki. And having achieved this, what does she do? She gathers up the powers, boards the Boat of Heaven, and skedaddles back to her home in Uruk. Wisely, it turns out.

After another break in the text, we find Enki in a panicked state, desperately questioning his minister about the whereabouts of Inana. And we begin to get an inkling of what has happened here, of what it is that might have induced Enki to so willingly give up his divine powers.

As the effects of the beer cleared from him who had drunk beer, from him who had drunk beer, as the effects of the beer cleared from Father Enki who had drunk beer. . . . The lord looked up at the abzu. King Enki turned his attention to Eridug.[7]

Here we see the wise god Enki emerging from a drunken fog, trying to reorient himself and piece back together the events of an evening spent deep in his cups. Where am I? Where did she go? Where's all my stuff?!?!

Fortunately, his trusty minister Isimud was there to watch it all and can offer a simple explanation. Sir, you got drunk and gave it all to Inana. Enki lists off his prized powers in turn, and the answer is always the same.

Enki spoke to Isimud the minister: "Isimud, my minister, my Sweet Name of Heaven!" "Enki, my master, I am at your service! What is your wish?" "Where are the office of en priest, the office of lagar priest, divinity, the great and good crown, the royal throne?" "My master has given them to his daughter."

"Where are the noble sceptre, the staff and crook, the noble dress, shepherdship, kingship?" "My master has given them to his daughter."[8]

You get the picture. I'm not going to take you through the rest of the story, which goes on at some length to describe Enki's unsuccessful efforts to recover his lost powers from Inana.

Clearly, there's a lesson to be learned here. And perhaps the story of Inana and Enki was intended to be read as a cautionary tale of sorts. But I've started with this dramatic episode from Sumerian literature because it highlights two fundamental points about how the people of Mesopotamia understood the effects of beer consumption. First, the drinking of beer could lead to inebriation. That is, it was recognized to produce effects that are broadly similar to those that we associate with the drinking of beer today. Second, the drinking of beer could have consequences that went beyond the individual imbiber, consequences for groups of people and society at large.

In this chapter, we're going to do our best to "put ourselves in their shoes" and access the insider's perspective on the beer-drinking experience. We know a lot about the places where people drank beer, the many different sorts of occasion that featured beer, and what beer did to people, that is, the effects of beer consumption. In the pages that follow, I've drawn from written records and archaeological remains to sketch out some drinking scenes as they might have played out. Consider these vignettes historical fiction. In some cases, I've taken empirical outlines and colored them in with imaginative flourish. In others, I'm extrapolating from the minutest of details.

Often it is the broadest, simplest questions that prove most difficult to answer. For instance, given the ubiquity of the beverage, you may be wondering: Exactly how much beer did these people drink? About the same as us, give or take? Much more? Much less? Another crucial question: Why? Why did the people of ancient Mesopotamia choose to drink (or not to drink) beer? You'll hardly be surprised to learn that many people appear to have appreciated both the taste and the inebriating effects of beer. But that's just scratching the surface. Like today, beer inspired a certain degree of ambivalence. The drinking of beer was valued, indeed celebrated, but it was also recognized to be a risky proposition, a flirtation with powers beyond human control. And the motivations for drinking this potent and complicated beverage were just as varied and conflicted as today.

The pouring of beer

It's midday. The house is abuzz with activity. Servants are rushing this way and that. The lady of the house calls out orders from somewhere in a back room. All morning, porters have been arriving from the palace, loaded down with packages of all shapes and sizes, piling everything up in a central courtyard. Through a door on one side of the courtyard, some musicians can be seen setting up their gear in what seems to be the main reception room. Preparations are clearly in full swing. But preparations for what? And where exactly are we? It's clearly no ordinary residence. The house is substantial in size and filled with expensive-looking furniture and items that one surely can't just walk out and purchase in the local market. The elaborate dishes emerging from the bustling kitchen, carried on platters to be laid out in the large reception room near the building's main entrance, also imply a certain degree of wealth.

Indeed, we're in the house of Šarrum-bani, brother of Abi-simti, wife of Šulgi, king of Ur. And it seems the king is coming to dinner. Actually, looking back from our perch some four thousand years into the future, we don't really know that. What we do know is that the king is coming to "drink beer" in the house of Šarrum-bani. And he's bringing presents. Lots of presents: tables, beds, clothing, you name it—for himself, for his queen (not Abi-simti but another wife, Shulgi-simti), for his consorts (including Ninkala and Ea-nisha), for their children and entourage, for the high priestesses of Nanna and Inana. But what really establishes a connection between this particular event and a series of other similar occasions documented in the historical record is the gifting of precious metals. And the beer.

We don't know any specifics about the beer, but it's fair to assume that it was not the everyday stuff the homeowners typically brewed up for themselves. Let's imagine that several large ceramic beer vessels, actively fermenting away, were brought over from the palace earlier in the morning—perhaps suspended from a pole and carried by two men, as sometimes shown in the artistic record (see Figure 6.12). And now those vessels have been installed at the center of the reception room, a bunch of reed drinking straws stacked just off to the side, at the ready.

The bits and pieces that we know about this event at the house of Šarrum-bani come from a unique cuneiform tablet.[9] Unfortunately, the tablet has not been fully published, so I can't provide you with a translation. But a series of other texts from the ancient city of Puzrish-Dagan (modern Drehem, Iraq) almost certainly refer to similar events. And the focus of these texts is not the event itself but, rather, the fact that silver rings were distributed during the event. Here's an example.

Two silver rings of eight shekels each;
When his majesty drank beer in the brewery of Šulgi.[10]
Uta-mišaram (acted as) the maškim official.
Disbursed from Puzur-Erra.
In Uru-sagrig.
Month XI, Amar-Suen 1.
(In total:) 2 (rings).[11]

The Ur III state (2112–2004 BCE) appears to have been in the habit of giving out silver rings (weighing 5–10 shekels each, that's 42–84 grams) to various important personages: foreign rulers, ambassadors, messengers, priests and priestesses, scribes, merchants, royal wet nurses, and others with high-level connections.[12] In the example that I've quoted, we don't actually learn who received the silver rings, but we do learn that the transaction took place in a brewery in the city of Uru-sagrig. Bear in mind that the text itself, like all the others, comes from the city of Puzrish-Dagan. The appearance, in these texts, of several other locales, including Puzrish-Dagan itself, Nippur, Uruk, and Ur, suggests that the king may have presented the silver rings and other gifts during greeting ceremonies of a sort, while out traveling around his kingdom.[13]

We don't really understand the precise motivation behind the gifts, their timing, or their significance. But in a subset of cases the gifts happened when the king was "drinking beer in the house of" some particular individual. These lucky individuals included the cantor Dada, the general Nir-idagal, Lugal-kuzu, and Lu-Nanna, son of Namhani, the governor of Hamazi.[14] The written documentation testifying to such events is minimal in the extreme. What we have, after all, is basically just a fragmentary paper trail focused on the distribution of silver rings. From the perspective of the state, these occasions of beer drinking and gift giving were part of a broader political strategy. The Ur III state regularly used gifts like this—precious metals but also, for example, sheep and goats—as a means of cementing diplomatic connections and building up a network of elite supporters.[15] But I think we can assume that, for those hosting the events, the day when the king stopped by for drinks would have been a memorable (and probably stressful) occasion.

The drinking of beer within the home is only rarely illuminated by the written record, but there is plenty of pertinent archaeological evidence. The best comes from Tell Bazi (Late Bronze Age, 1400–1200 BCE), where, as we've seen, many households appear to have been brewing their own beer.[16] I think we can safely assume that much of that beer was being consumed on the premises. The ceramic inventories recovered from the houses include many small- and medium-size vessels that could have been used for serving and drinking beer. In several houses, excavators also found those bronze filter tips that would have once been attached to the reed straws used for drinking beer. Most houses also included an appropriate seating area, defined especially by a plastered bench that ran along one wall of the main room.[17]

But who was actually drinking the beer? Was it just household members? That's a more difficult question. In at least some cases, the benches might have served as a staging ground for commensality (i.e., the sharing of food/drink) on a somewhat larger scale.[18] Contemporary cuneiform documents refer to extended kinship groups known as "the brothers" that would meet periodically in the home of one member to address private legal issues, such as property sales. The benches (and the beer) may have helped facilitate these meetings or other similar occasions. So households might have been hosting events where beer was consumed by people from beyond the immediate family circle: not a feast for the king and his entourage but something beyond your ordinary, everyday meal.

Can this model be generalized at all? That is, might the drinking practices visible in the archaeological record at Tell Bazi have been part of a broader phenomenon? To think about this issue and how one might approach it, let's retreat back into the Early Dynastic I period (2900–2750 BCE), a distance of about a millennium and a half. One recent study has attacked the question of regional-scale drinking practices by focusing on one particular type of ceramic vessel: the so-called "solid-footed goblet."[19] The suggestion is that this particular ceramic type can serve as a pretty secure archaeological correlate for the drinking of beer.

So what are these solid-footed goblets? The name sounds pretty fancy. I know I, at least, feel special every time someone hands me a Belgian Trappist ale served in one of those heavy glass goblets. But these Early Dynastic goblets don't quite live up to the name. They're basically conical in shape, with a stubby little foot (Figure 7.1). They're wheel-made and were clearly mass-produced. Not to disrespect the potters responsible, but nothing about these goblets really says that anyone lavished a lot of time and attention on them—though they're certainly a step up, aesthetically,

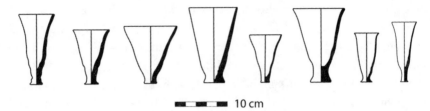

10 cm

Figure 7.1. A selection of solid-footed goblets. Early Dynastic period. (Redrawn after Benati 2019: Figs. 2–3)

from their earlier cousin, the renowned but distinctly unappealing beveled-rim bowl. In terms of capacity, they're pretty small: on average, about 0.17 liters. So, more like a champagne flute than a pint glass.

The idea behind this particular study was to look at a series of archaeological sites spread broadly across Mesopotamia, paying particular attention to where exactly these solid-footed goblets were found. Plenty were found in funerary contexts (we'll come back to this in a moment), and others, in cultic contexts. But the majority were found in household contexts and often in substantial quantities, suggesting that they were serving some purpose beyond basic household needs. This pattern, so the argument goes, would indicate a widespread tradition of small-scale, "entrepreneurial" feasts. The hosting of such events within the home would have offered a means of climbing the social ladder, of transforming hospitality into prestige, political power, and/or economic advantage. There's lots of cross-cultural, comparative evidence to draw on here, but what this sort of feast makes me think about, more than anything, is the classic mid-twentieth-century CE cocktail party. Yeah, sure, you may genuinely want your boss and coworkers (and maybe some carefully selected friends and neighbors) to come over, hang out, and have a good time, but is that really what this is about? No, it's about networking, schmoozing, showing off, demonstrating that you have what it takes to swim with the big fish.

What might the remains of one of these entrepreneurial feasts actually look like? Unless things got out of control and someone accidentally set the house on fire during the event, causing everyone to abandon ship and drop their goblets in place, we're not likely to find an archaeological snapshot of the feast in progress. What we might expect, instead, is for all of the vessels to have been collected, cleaned, and returned to their place in some storeroom, well before the archaeologist's arrival on the scene. Or, in the case of disposable vessels, we might expect them all to have been gathered up and dumped in the trash. The inhabitants of some wealthy houses in the Early Dynastic city of Isin appear to have faced this very dilemma: "Hey, that was a great feast last night—now what to do with all these empty goblets? These things were pretty cheap, right? Do we really need to save them?" The answer in this case was a definite "no." Archaeologists found large numbers of expendable, mass-produced goblets that had been dumped en masse into pits dug for the purpose.[20]

If we take leave of the Early Dynastic period and head back into the Late Bronze Age—this time, to the reign of the First Sealand Dynasty (1732–1450 BCE)—we encounter another solution and another sort of feasting. At the site of Tell Khaiber in Iraq, excavators have uncovered a large, fortified administrative building (1600–1450 BCE) containing evidence for feasting events, in addition to the brewing evidence that we briefly considered in Chapter 5. Once again, this evidence comes especially from the ceramics. A recent study has grouped these ceramics into functional categories, that is, vessel types that would have been used for specific activities: food processing, cooking, brewing, measuring, storage, transport, serving, eating, drinking.[21] Interestingly, many of the vessels for serving and drinking liquids (several different types of cup and jug) were recovered from the defensive towers that protrude outward from the building's exterior wall. Why? Possibly because the towers were serving as trash dumps. The suggestion is that the remains of commensal events held elsewhere in the building were being gathered up and stashed in the nearest convenient location, which just happened to be these towers.[22] Of course, we don't really know exactly what kind of liquid once filled all those cups and jugs. What would really clinch the case for beer drinking here—and also with the Early Dynastic goblets—is some residue preserved inside those vessels.

Exactly this kind of evidence is now available from the site of Khani Masi in Iraq.[23] In the remains of a monumental building dating to the Late Bronze Age (Kassite period, 1550–1150 BCE), excavators have recovered a collection of ceramic vessels dedicated to the serving and drinking of liquids (Figure 7.2). But not just any liquids. Residue analysis has shown clear traces of beer in many of the vessels: in juglets, in small footed cups (c. 100–200 ml), and in the period's own version of the solid-footed goblet, known as Kassite goblets (c. 300–600 ml). This beer-drinking assemblage was found smashed on the floor of a room just off the side of a large courtyard, perhaps some kind of storeroom where the vessels had once been kept on shelves.[24] So here we might have an example of the other option for post-party cleanup. The drinking probably took place in some other part of the building, perhaps in the big courtyard right next door. If the shelf hypothesis is correct, the vessels were then cleaned up and returned to their home in a storeroom—but not before traces of the beer had had time to seep down into the pores of the vessels to await recovery by archaeologists three and a half thousand years in the future.

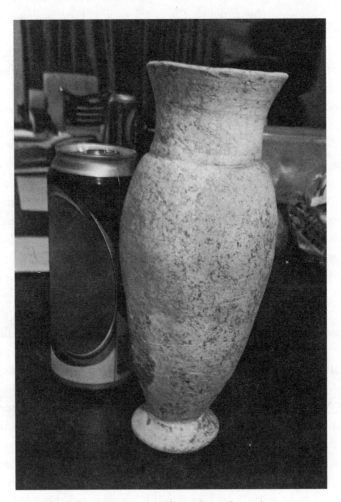

Figure 7.2. Goblet, Khani Masi, Iraq. (Photo: Jesse Casana)

The other case where we have good residue evidence for feasting and beer drinking within a monumental building comes, once again, from Tell Bazi.[25] At the center of the so-called citadel that rises up above the rest of the site, excavators uncovered a large, two-room temple (38 m x 16 m) dating back to the Middle Bronze Age (nineteenth century BCE). By the Late Bronze Age (1400–1200 BCE), when the building was destroyed in a fire, only one of the rooms was still serving a ritual purpose. In this room, beneath the remains of the collapsed roof, excavators found an assemblage of smashed ceramic vessels scattered across the floor. Residue analysis showed that several large jars and small bowls, as well as many small beakers (c. 0.08–0.16 liters), had once contained beer. Five bronze filter tips for drinking straws also suggest the drinking of beer. Unlike the other cases that we've considered here, this assemblage appears to have been recovered in its original use context, that is, in the spot where the drinking actually took place. This was a special room. There was an altar, for example. On top of it lay the remains of a bull's head and some barley; in front of it, a dense concentration of animal bones. Traces of barley, sesame, olives, peas, grapes, and pomegranate were also recovered from the room.

It's likely that these remains derive from rituals that included both the consumption and the offering of food and drink.[26] A contemporary document from the not-too-distant city of Emar, for example, describes a ceremony for the installation of a new high priestess of the god Baal.

> They will offer the one ox and the six sheep before Ba'al. They will place before the gods a beef ritual portion [?] and a mutton ritual portion [?]. They will place before the gods seven dinner-loaves, seven dried cakes, [and] two cakes [with] fruit. They will fill goblets with wine. The officials, who give the qidašu, the ḫussu-men, [and] seven [and seven ḫamša'u-men (?)] will eat and drink at the temple of Ba'al], and the men of the qidašu will get one dinner-loaf each [and] one ḫizzibu of barley-beer each.[27]

Only a select group of people would have taken part in the ceremony within the altar room at Tell Bazi. But, as suggested by other documents, a larger group would probably have been on hand in the area immediately outside.[28] Indeed, the excavators suggest that a large proportion of the community at Tell Bazi would have been present for certain religious festivals, probably gathering in the open space near the temple to present offerings and to share food and drink.

So, when it comes to feasting, we've seen royal gift-giving occasions in intimate household settings, kin-groups sharing a drink while they discuss legal matters, upwardly mobile households putting hospitality to work in their favor, discarded drinking equipment stashed in out-of-the-way corners within administrative buildings, beer-drinking paraphernalia kept in storage for later use, and ritual occasions that featured beer consumption. Many more examples could be cited. The people of ancient Mesopotamia— like most people in most places—loved a good feast. And feasts were closely tied to beer. One variety of feast in Mesopotamia, after all, was simply called kaš-de$_2$-a or "the pouring of beer."[29]

Drinking with the dead

Dusk is quickly falling into night. We find ourselves in an open space that stretches off a good way in each direction. The vague outlines of some buildings in the middle distance, just barely visible in the growing dark, suggest that we're near a town. Are we perhaps just on the outskirts of town? Or maybe even within the town but in some kind of outdoor space set aside for communal gatherings? It's difficult to say. But between us and those buildings some kind of gathering is definitely in progress. Maybe a procession? A collection of torches, bobbing and flickering like fireflies in the night, seems to be making its way slowly toward us. I think I can just make out some faces in the crowd, which must be at least several-hundred strong. And is that a slow, deep drumbeat that I hear in the background, lending the whole affair a somber, ceremonial feel? As they get closer, we notice that no one is speaking.

Just off to our left, a cluster of ceramic vessels holds some kind of stew. Next to these and in front of us are tables piled high with several different kinds of bread. And then more tables bearing some sort of sweet. Another group of ceramic vessels is filled with fresh beer, bubbling away behind us. It is not your ordinary kaš but something special.

The feast laid out before us is documented on a tablet from the town of Garšana, a place that we've already encountered a number of times.[30] I have imagined the setting as an open, outdoor space of some kind. The timing of the feast in the evening hours is also a product of my imagination. We do know, however, that the feast took place during the sixth month of the second year of the king Ibbi-Suen (Ur III period, ruled 2026–2003 BCE). That was approximately two and a half

years after the death of a high-ranking general and physician named
Šu-Kabta, son-in-law of the earlier king Amar-Suen (ruled 2044–2036
BCE) and head of the estate that features prominently in the Garšana
texts.[31] This feast was the third in a series of funerary banquets held in
honor of Šu-Kabta, the others held two months and eleven months after
his passing. Pretty much everything else that we know about the feast in
question concerns the menu or, to be more precise, the ingredients that
went into the menu.[32]

The tablet starts by listing out the ingredients for making bread: a whole
lot of bread. Four different types of flour are listed, coming to a total 554
liters. We don't know exactly what kind of bread they were making with
these flours, but other texts from Garšana mention several types. Here are
the bread-making ingredients.

> 180 liters of a particularly fine barley flour, best quality,
> 260 liters of standard barley flour,
> 54 liters of a special type of emmer flour,
> 60 liters of another special type of emmer flour, best quality:
> For bread.[33]

The next section tabulates the ingredients for making a special kind of sweet,
perhaps a date paste that was spread onto cookies made from emmer flour.

> 6 liters of flour made out of a special sort of emmer,
> 1 liter of sesame oil,
> 2 liters of dates:
> For sweets.[34]

The text then moves on to a vegetarian soup flavored with coriander, salt,
and other "good spices."

> 10 liters of good-quality groats,[35]
> 10 liters of ar-za-na [uncertain processed grain product],[36]
> 10 liters of milled beans,
> 10 liters of mashed peas,
> 5 liters of ground good spices,
> 6 liters of ground coriander,
> 5 liters of ground good salt,
> 10⅓ liters of ground gazi-plant [a common spice],
> 30 bundles of an unknown spice plant:
> For the cooking pot [i.e., for soup].[37]

Brunke argues that these ingredients would have produced enough soup to feed about 400 people. This lines up well the with volume of beer brewed for the feast, but it's nowhere near what one would expect based on the bread produced. Brunke thinks attendees would have left the feast loaded down with extra bread. Maybe? I don't know.

But what about the beer? This feast featured 300 liters of "good beer" (kaš saga). If we can assume about 400 attendees—based on the amount of soup provided—each would have received about 0.75 liters of beer. That might have been enough to lighten the mood a tad but probably not enough to send the event over the edge from solemn tribute into drunken revel. The beer was brewed with bappir, malt, and groats.

> 41.5 kg good bappir,[38]
> 240 liters (at least)[39] malt from sprouted grain,
> 210 liters of good-quality groats,[40]
> 300 liters of good beer.[41]

Interestingly, the two previous funerary feasts held in memory of Šu-Kabta each featured a lot more beer: 300 liters of "good beer," plus an additional 600 liters of "ordinary beer" (kaš DU).[42] The soup at these events was probably enough for about 600 people. If the beer was distributed equally, that would mean 1 liter of ordinary beer and a half liter of good beer per person. But probably the good beer was reserved for some subset of the guests. And perhaps the feast that we witnessed, the one with only good beer on offer, was itself for some select body of mourners—making their way out into the darkness by torchlight to raise a toast of sorts, still intent on paying due homage to Šu-Kabta two and half years after his passing.

The holding of regular meals in honor of the departed was a well-established tradition in ancient Mesopotamia. But these meals held among the living were not just about preserving the memory of the dead. They also served a distinctly practical purpose: making sure that the deceased had a regular supply of food in the afterlife. These individuals, though no longer physically present, were invited to take part in the meals and were given a share of the bounty. They were also sustained by regular offerings of food during a well-attested ritual known as *kispum*.[43]

Where did these meals and rituals take place? In many cases, they were a family affair, intimate rituals conducted within the space of the home or at least nearby. Though it takes us somewhat beyond the bounds of Mesopotamia proper, a particularly vivid illustration can be found at the site of Zincirli (ancient Sam'al) in southeastern Türkiye. In 2008, excavations in a residential neighborhood dating to the Iron Age (900–600 BCE) uncovered a well-preserved stone stele bearing both an image and an inscription.[44] The carved image depicts a man named Katumuwa, seated at a table covered in food and holding a drinking bowl in one hand. The inscription, written in a local dialect of Aramaic, begins as follows.

> I am Katumuwa, servant of Panamuwa, who commissioned for myself (this) stele while still living. I placed it in my eternal chamber and established a feast (at) this chamber . . . [45]

The inscription then goes on to let his sons—or anyone else who happens to come into possession of the chamber where the stele stands—know exactly what should be served up at this feast: one bull, five rams, and the best wine.[46] The feast is to take place once a year, and one haunch is to be saved for the "soul" of Katumuwa himself. The stele was found in a small room within a building that had once been a house but that appears to have been transformed into a small neighborhood shrine.

So, basically, while still alive, Katumuwa wanted to make absolutely certain that his relatives (or someone's relatives, at least) would provide him with adequate sustenance in the afterlife. He established a shrine, probably near his own home, and set up a stele that mandated an annual feast be held in his honor. The feast that he outlines would have been a substantial one, able to feed many more people than could have squeezed themselves into the small room where the stele stood.[47] Such a feast would have to have been held elsewhere. But certainly, if his descendants kept up their end of the deal, this would have been quite the annual event. Even if they toned it down to something more modest in scale, it would have presumably still accomplished the basic goal of keeping his soul well fed in the afterlife, while giving his relatives a reason to come together and celebrate his memory. And, yes, it's true that the stele has nothing to say about beer. But that's not surprising. The site of Zincirli is situated firmly within wine country. Plus, by the Iron Age, grape wine had more fully infiltrated southern Mesopotamia, once the very heart of beer country. A man of similar means to Katumuwa, living in Iron Age Babylonia, could almost certainly have demanded an annual offering of wine instead of beer, if he preferred.

Not content to wait for a memorial anniversary, many people apparently felt very strongly about going to the grave surrounded by food and drink or, at least, by the associated material culture. Drinking equipment features prominently in many burial assemblages. This could mean one or two vessels placed discreetly by the body, or it could mean stacks upon stacks of vessels of many different shapes and sizes densely packed into a burial chamber.

We've already seen, for example, that some of the richest graves in the Royal Cemetery of Ur (Early Dynastic and Akkadian period, 2900–2192 BCE) included drinking equipment (Chapter 6). Most of the graves in the cemetery, however, were simpler and more modestly appointed: just a single individual, lying on their side, accompanied by some personal effects (e.g., jewelry, seals, weapons, tools) and, often, some jars and bowls holding provisions. Also, as a general rule, a cup had been placed in the individual's hand, with a jar and bowl nearby.[48] So the act of drinking was given particular attention in the arranging of the burial.

At the roughly contemporary site of Abu Salabikh in Iraq, we encounter a similar situation.[49] Most of the graves dating to the Early Dynastic II period (2750–2600 BCE)[50] include both spouted jars and conical bowls for serving and drinking some kind of liquid, but often just a few of each. Some, such as Grave 1, were outfitted on a totally different scale (Figure 7.3). The individual in this grave was sent off with at least 109 conical bowls, 27 spouted jars, and one of those "four-part sets" (large bowl, perforated stand, strainer, and small mug) that we discussed in Chapters 5 and 6.

The inclusion of drinking equipment within the space of the tomb is not just a fad of the Early Dynastic period. Examples could be cited from many other periods. The big question is: Who was all this drinking (and, in many cases, eating) equipment for? Are we seeing the remains of graveside feasts, where food and drink were consumed by the living? Or are we, perhaps, seeing the prepping of supplies for feasts to be held in the great beyond? Or maybe both at once? Underworld feasts, where the recently deceased was expected to come prepared to fête his new companions in the realm of the dead, were certainly part of the Mesopotamian vision of the afterlife.

One particularly vivid account appears in a text that recounts the death of Ur-Namma, first king of the Ur III dynasty (ruled 2112–2095 BCE), and his arrival in the Underworld.

> As they announced Ur-Namma's coming to the people, a tumult arose
> in the Underworld. The king slaughtered numerous bulls and sheep,

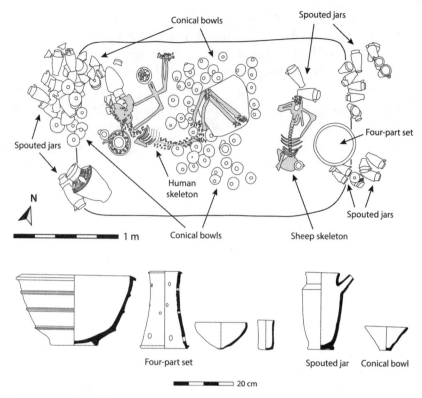

Figure 7.3. Plan of Grave 1, with arrows indicating findspots for drinking equipment. Below, illustration of four-part set, conical bowl, and spouted jar. Abu Salabikh, Iraq. (Redrawn after Martin et al. 1985: Figs. 8, 9c and Zingarello 2020: Fig. 6.1)

Ur-Namma seated the people at a huge banquet. The food of the Underworld is bitter, the water of the Underworld is brackish. The trustworthy shepherd knew well the rites of the Underworld, so the king presented the offerings of the Underworld, Ur-Namma presented the offerings of the Underworld: as many faultless bulls, faultless kids, and fattened sheep as could be brought.[51]

He then proceeds to offer a series of very specific gifts to certain key figures in the realm of the dead. So an important person like Ur-Namma had to come well prepared for his transition into the afterlife. He needed both substantial quantities of food (no beer or wine is mentioned here) and a collection of the highest quality objects targeting the predilections of specific Underworld deities.

One of those deities was the legendary hero Gilgamesh, who had—after his adventuring days were through—taken up a post as king of the Underworld. His death is not described in the Epic of Gilgamesh itself, but an earlier Sumerian poem known as the Death of Bilgames offers a fascinating account of the lead-up to his death, including a series of divinatory dreams and the preparation of his tomb. Knowing that his own death is imminent, Bilgames (the Sumerian name for Gilgamesh) dams up the Euphrates river and has a tomb built in its dry bed. In the tomb, his family, retinue, and possessions are laid out "as if [attending] a palace-review in the midst of Uruk."

> His beloved wife, his beloved child,
> his beloved senior wife and junior wife,
> his beloved minstrel, steward and . . . ,
> his beloved barber, [his beloved] . . . ,
> [his beloved] attendants and servants,
> [his] beloved goods . . . ,
> were laid down in their places,
> as if [attending] a palace-review in the midst of Uruk.[52]

As many have pointed out, this image bears an eerie resemblance to the funerary tableaux preserved in the death pits in the Royal Cemetery of Ur. Once his entourage is in place, Bilgames then proceeds to set out a series of gifts for a checklist of important Underworld deities and deceased priests and priestesses. So here, just before his death, we see the king carefully arranging both people and goods within the space of his tomb. No banquet is mentioned, but he does pour out an offering of water, before being taken into the tomb, which is then sealed and covered over by the waters of the Euphrates.

So, yes, it's likely that food, drink, and the requisite equipment were often interred with the deceased in order to facilitate their transition into the afterlife and/or ease their time there. But it's also very likely that the eating and drinking assemblages uncovered by archaeologists in burial contexts derive, at least in part, from actual meals held among the living during funerary ceremonies. If this is the case, we might learn something, not just about the dead, but also about the living by scrutinizing the feasting equipment recovered in burials. Funerals are often, after all, just as much about the (re)negotiation of relationships and identities in the world of the living as about mourning the death of a particular individual.

In this regard, two aspects of the feasting assemblages in tombs stand out: the materials employed and the quantity of vessels included. Such assemblages often comprise a mixture of ceramic vessels and vessels made from more costly materials, in particular stone (e.g., limestone, calcite, lapis lazuli, even obsidian) and metal (e.g., copper, silver, gold). Perhaps the fancy vessels were destined specifically for use in the after-life, serving either as personal tableware fit for eternity or as gifts for the denizens of the netherworld, like those proffered by Ur-Namma and Bilgames. Alternatively, differences in the quality of feasting equip-ment might offer some insight into status differences among the living participants in a funerary feast. Or the simple presence of certain types of luxury items might serve to index the wealth, status, and connections of those hosting the event (e.g., the family of the deceased). The quantity of vessels entombed with a particular individual might perform a similar function: Large numbers of vessels equals a well-attended feast equals largesse on a grand scale equals a sign of affluence, generosity, popularity, and/or an extended network of friends, family, acquaintances, supporters, or dependents.[53]

Beer on the job

The sun is beating down relentlessly. Several small clusters of men huddle together in the few bits of midday shade available. Behind them looms some kind of low, raised platform and, off to the side, the skeleton of a structure that's just beginning to take shape. The platform itself is still under construction. Stacks of sun-dried mudbricks lie nearby, waiting to be set in place. The men, doing their best to relax in the slivers of shade, are cov-ered in dust and sweat. One group briefly breaks into song, before quickly collapsing into a fit of shared laughter. Others chat in hushed whispers. All raise bowls to their lips to take frequent sips of some kind of thick, yel-lowish liquid.

Off some distance to the side, two other men lounge under a cluster of date palms, whose canopy offers the best piece of real estate at the height of the day. These two, dressed in clean, white tunics, are clearly operating in some kind of supervisory role. Near them, a small tablet has been left out in the sun to dry. We sneak a peek.

> 15 liters of ordinary beer
> the builders
> drank
> during construction of the foundation terrace of the brewery and [...][54]

The tablet is written in Sumerian, using a script that clearly belongs in the later part of the third millennium BCE. But where are we exactly?

We're back in the town of Garšana, where we recently witnessed the funerary feast for Šukabta. But Ibbi-Suen (ruled 2026–2003 BCE) is not yet king. The Ur III state is still under the rule of his father Šu-Suen (ruled 2035–2027 BCE). We're at a construction site. And, yes, those workers are drinking beer—a hearty beer, thick as porridge. Since we actually know quite a lot about this particular construction project,[55] we can say that the fourth line of that tablet—which was, in fact, damaged at some point, leaving the last word illegible—would once have read: "during construction of the foundation terrace of the brewery and [mill]." As we discussed in Chapter 5, these two structures were part of a brewery-kitchen-mill complex, the so-called Triple Complex. And since the new brewery is still under construction, the beer must have come from some other brewery in the vicinity.

Many different types of workers were engaged in this construction project: scribes, foremen, builders, enslaved persons, ox-drivers, boatmen, brick carriers, foresters, as well as various support staff (millers, cooks, bakers, brewers) and others pressed into occasional service on construction-related tasks (fullers, felters, leather workers, weavers).[56] In return for their work, they received barley rations.[57] It's not always clear in what form the rations arrived, that is, whether the workers typically received raw, unprocessed barley, as opposed to prepared foods ready for eating. In at least some cases, though, they definitely received bread and/or beer. What's particularly interesting about the tablet that we examined—and a number of similar ones from Garšana—is that it doesn't just record the distribution of beer to workers. It tells us that those workers "drank" (Sumerian ib_2-naĝ) the beer.[58] This wording implies that they consumed their beer on the job, either during or at the end of the workday.

There's nothing particularly odd about them having a beer at work. Many may frown on the practice today, but fueling one's workday with beer is a time-honored tradition with a deep pedigree. It's possible, though, that the day-drinking scene that we witnessed in Garšana, innocuous as it may seem on the surface, is actually a sign of bigger things afoot—or at least a sign that things are not as they once were.

Let's rewind, for a moment, back to the Uruk and Jemdet Nasr periods (4000–2900 BCE). If you recall, beer was, at this point, already being produced in substantial quantities by institutional breweries. People like Kushim (if Kushim was indeed a person) were managing both the brewing and distribution of this beer and recording their activities in some of the world's earliest written documents.

It has been suggested that another key artifact of the Uruk period, the ubiquitous beveled-rim bowl, might also be tied to the distribution of beer.[59] More than that, these distinctly unattractive bowls might tell us something important about the changes underway in Uruk society. What if the beveled-rim bowl was used, not for distributing unprocessed barley rations, as often assumed, but for distributing a prepared food like beer or porridge? You would not want to have to schlep something like beer home in these bowls. It just wouldn't work well. You would want to consume the beer right there on the spot. Yes, well, so what?

The contention is that large-scale, on-the-job consumption of "fast food" rations by workers—evidenced by thousands and thousands of discarded beveled-rim bowls—might indicate a significant shift in the social land-scape. Workers knocking back a quick bowl of beer or porridge during their lunch break would not have been at home eating with their families. So these bowls might signal a breaking down of traditional patterns of household-centered commensality and the emergence of something new: a regime of food/drink consumption that fostered connections among coworkers and, perhaps, new kinds of allegiance to the institutional patrons supplying the foodstuffs.

There's a lot of speculation here, and many specialists would dispute the scenario—not least the suggestion that the beveled-rim bowls might have once held beer.[60] But it's an interesting argument that casts a dif-ferent light on beer and its potential role in the process of state formation. Here we see beer as a political tool, a means of driving a wedge between family members and making space for new relationships, new loyalties, new ways of organizing society. And, whether or not you buy the argument for Uruk-period beer-on-the-job, at least some workers appear to have been drinking beer-rations together at work about a thousand years later. At that point, during the Ur III period, it would be difficult to deny that the process of state formation had indeed transformed the food system and life in general for many inhabitants of the region.

At the tavern

We're strolling down a bustling city street, doing our best to navigate the streams of people and animals making their way quickly in both directions. Most of the passersby are going about their business in shadow, as the midafternoon sun dips behind the buildings to our right. But just ahead and off to our left, the sun's rays have managed to slip through a gap between buildings and illuminate a seemingly insignificant scene. Two men are crouched by a doorway, examining the ground. One reaches down, collects a handful of dirt, and carefully deposits it in a pouch hanging from his belt. Rising back to their feet, they exchange a few words and then continue on down the street, clearly on some kind of a mission.

A peek inside the doorway that they've just vacated reveals it to be a carpenter's workshop. Okay, that's interesting. Let's follow and see what they're up to. The pair weave their way through the city streets for another 15 minutes or so, eventually stopping off at another doorway and crouching down to collect more dirt. As they move on, we glance inside and find a maltster and two assistants hard at work, raking germinating barley grains that have been spread out across the floor of an interior courtyard. I'd love to stay and examine their methods more closely, but let's keep following the two strangers. Their route now takes us downhill toward the river. Indeed, the next stop is the riverbank, where one pulls a small jug out of his knapsack and dips it down into the water. The same man then unties the pouch from his waist and empties the contents—what looks like quite a lot of dirt—into the jug. After stirring the mixture around for thirty seconds or so, he produces a small flask, the kind used for transporting oil, and dribbles something further into the jug. Another quick stir and they're off again. Luckily, the next destination isn't far. We follow the men through a few twists and turns, before they stop in front of another doorway. They chat briefly, and then, with some ceremony, the man holding the jug dips a few fingers inside and spreads some of the contents—what looks now like a sort of paste—across the doorframe. They then enter the doorway together.

A sign hanging above the door indicates that they've entered a tavern. Inside, small clusters of patrons are huddled around tables, sipping from ceramic cups and chatting in what sounds like a pretty late dialect of Akkadian. The man with the jug heads up a set of stairs in the back corner of the room. The other man retires to a back room that must be some sort of office. Five or ten minutes later, the first man comes back down to collect his accomplice. They climb the stairs together to a flat roof that's covered in ritual paraphernalia.

The man who earlier did all of the dirt collecting, mixing, etc., is clearly the one directing the show. He instructs the other man to kneel down and then places some kind of copper statuette beside him. When directed to do so, the kneeling man calls out in a loud voice: "$^{d}i\check{s}$-tar ^{d}na-na-a ^{d}gaz-ba-ba e-li-šu ru-ṣi!" ("Ishtar, Nanay, Gazbaya help me in this matter!").[61] This invocation to the goddess Ishtar, using three of her names, is followed by what can only be described as an incantation, intoned in a sort of rhythmic chant. It's hard to catch all of the details, but near the end a tavern is definitely mentioned.

> Ishtar, stand by me to (further) my affairs! May this tavern trade be your tavern trade! Ishtar, lay your hand on the pot stand and mixing vat [namzītu]. May profit come my way, and never cease! You are the one who has this office.[62]

So that's what this is all about. Profit. The kneeling man must be the owner of the tavern below, and he is asking the goddess to bless his business and make it profitable.

What we've witnessed is a ritual designed to guarantee "brisk trade" and "profit" for a tavern.[63] A detailed set of instructions for this ritual is preserved on three known tablets: one from the city of Assur, one from Nineveh, and one from either Babylon or Borsippa.[64] The first two are written in Assyrian script and date to the seventh century BCE (late Neo-Assyrian period). The third is written in Babylonian script and dates to the Neo-Babylonian period (605–539 BCE). Each tablet actually documents three distinct rituals paired with incantations, all dedicated to ensuring the prosperity of a tavern. As it turns out, we just caught the very tail end of the first of the three rituals. Among other actions, the guidelines for this ritual stipulate the collecting of dust from a wide variety of locations. The instructions begin:

The ritual procedure for it: dust from a god's house, dust from a god's sanctuary, dust from a city gate, dust from a ditch, dust from a cult niche, dust from a bridge whereupon Ištar (as the star Venus) shines, dust from a crossroad of streets, dust from a sandstorm, dust from a door of a prostitute, dust from a door of a lover, dust from a door of a tailor, dust from a door of a palace, dust from a door of a maltster, dust from a door of an innkeeper, dust from a road, dust from a door of a gardener, dust from a door of a carpenter, [dust from (the house) of the m]an of the *naditu*, all these (kinds of) dust you shall crush together and mix in water from a river. You shall pour cypress oil in the middle (of the mixture). You shall smear the door of the man's house from outside (with it).[65]

The next section then details the activities that should be carried out on the roof of the house (i.e., the roof of the tavern). These include purification rites, offerings, and the incantation that we witnessed. Many of these actions were to be undertaken by a ritual specialist, while others were specifically assigned to the tavern owner.

This seems pretty straightforward, right? You're a tavern owner. Your tavern isn't doing so well, so you decide to call in a ritual specialist for help. You perform the ritual, the tables are turned, and business booms once again. Well, not quite. This ritual actually belongs to a broader category of *namburbi* rituals, which translates to "(rituals for) releasing therefrom."[66] In this particular case, what exactly was being released? This is where things get interesting. The ritual was not intended to be performed in order to rescue a failing tavern. It was, rather, an apotropaic measure, designed to preemptively counteract the effects of a negative omen regarding the future of a tavern. The Mesopotamian world was overflowing with signs that could be read by those who possessed the knowledge and know-how.[67] Omens were everywhere: in the flight patterns of birds, in the coloring and folds of a sheep's entrails, in the bark of a dog, in the stars. Omens could be good, or they could be bad, and not necessarily in a generic sense. Many omens were quite specific. And they were listed out in excruciating detail in so-called omen lists for the sake of posterity. The study of omens—and divination, more broadly—constituted one of the major branches of knowledge in ancient Mesopotamia. From the highest levels of government on down, important decisions could not be made without first consulting specialists in the arts of divination. A negative omen was a serious matter and often a cause for great alarm.

So it's not surprising that methods emerged for counteracting such omens. For example, the *namburbi* ritual: a carefully prescribed means of releasing one from the oncoming effects of a specific negative omen. In our imagined scenario, we can assume that the tavern owner had received a negative omen regarding the future success of his tavern. To forestall the predicted outcome, he called on the aid of a ritual specialist to guide him through the appropriate actions and incantations. Yes, I've concocted the details of their journey through the city streets in my mind, but it's entirely possible that some kind of analogous plotline could have actually played out in the cities of Assur, Nineveh, or Babylon sometime in the first millennium BCE. In fact, one of the three tablets documenting this *namburbi* ritual, the one excavated by a German team at Assur in 1904, features a pierced handle protruding from one side.[68] It's possible that this tablet may have actually been designed for hanging. That is, it might have been put on display in a tavern as a means of proclaiming and furthering the protection afforded by the rituals described.

I have spent some time reflecting on this particular *namburbi* ritual because the tavern is a space that appears only sporadically in the written record.[69] In this fascinating set of rituals, we see the tavern depicted, above all, as a commercial space, one whose ultimate purpose was to profit the owner. The tavern was a place of business, where one came to purchase and drink beer but also to engage in other pursuits. One of those was sex.[70] In fact, one segment of this *namburbi* ritual is explicitly dedicated to sex as an element in the success of the tavern. The incantation is full of sexual imagery, innuendo, wordplay, and double entendre. In my imaginative scenario, I have refrained from describing this side of tavern life, but its inclusion could certainly have been justified.

Taverns were also themselves recognized to possess a special kind of ritual potency. In other *namburbi* rituals, for example, the patient seeking to deflect an evil portent was directed to go to a tavern and there touch both the *namzītu* (brewing vessel) and the *kannu* (wooden stand for the brewing vessel)—perhaps as a means of transferring over any remaining ritual impurities. But why touch the tools of the tavern keeper, in particular? Almost certainly because of their connection with the mysterious force of fermentation. In other ritual texts, for example, brewing vessels (gakkul/ kakkullu) were employed in incantations designed to capture demons or render them harmless. Even the doorway of the tavern held ritual significance, especially as a dumping ground for ritually impure materials. In one *namburbi* ritual, for example, a man who has had sexual intercourse with a goat—and wishes to deflect the consequences of this action—is directed to deposit a goat skin at the doorway of a tavern and leave it there for fifteen days.[71]

So taverns had a special ritual significance. It's even possible that, as a result, they were themselves considered in some sense dangerous or impure. According to one reading, that first *namburbi* ritual that we examined might have been less about ensuring profit for a tavern than about purifying a tavern that had been corrupted, in the process rendering it safe for customers and, therefore, profitable for the proprietor. In fact, it might not have been a *namburbi* ritual at all but rather a ritual that had to be performed because of the polluting effects of *namburbi* rituals and their fixation on taverns.[72] Either way, the tavern was not just a business and not just a place where people gathered for relaxation, romantic encounters, celebration, and social interaction. It was also a place with a unique sort of ritual aura.

The effects of beer consumption

Whether you're dining with the king, sending a loved one off to the underworld, imbibing on the job, or keeping your local watering hole afloat, you drink enough beer, and you're going to feel the effects. This might seem obvious, but it's not a trivial point, for at least two reasons. On the one hand, plenty of people have argued (or suggested) that the beers of ancient Mesopotamia would (or might) have been low in alcohol content.[73] As we've seen, these arguments sometimes rest on what I consider shaky assumptions: for example, the notion that the beer must have been low in alcohol content because children drank it.[74] To my mind, the fact that literary descriptions of beer consumption in Mesopotamia regularly describe bodily effects consistent with alcohol consumption is an important indicator of the nature of this beverage. On the other hand—and this is an important caveat—the experience of alcohol consumption can vary significantly from culture to culture. Yes, alcohol does produce certain predictable effects on human bodies and minds, but these effects are filtered through dense layers of cultural framing. What one experiences when consuming alcohol and how that experience is narrated, explained, and made meaningful depends a lot on everything else that one brings to the table, on cultural context in the broadest sense. The description of Enki's inebriated state, following his drinking bout with Inana, is just one of many clues regarding the specifically Mesopotamian experience of beer consumption.

Another comes from a bilingual lexical list known as An = *Anum*. It's basically just a long list of deities, with the Sumerian version of the deity's name in one column and the Akkadian equivalent in the other. Near the end of the first of six tablets, we encounter the goddess of beer, Ninkasi, and here she's directly equated with Siraš, the other beer goddess. But what we're really interested in comes a few lines later: a list of five deities, followed by a line that reads "five children of Ninkasi."

^{d}Me.ḫuš.a	Glowing ME
^{d}Me.ku$_3$ / ^{d}Men.ku$_3$	Beautiful ME/Beautiful crown
^{d}Eme$^{e\text{-}me}$-me-te / Men-me-te	Ornate speech/Ornate crown
^{d}Ki.tuš.ka.zal / ^{d}Ki-tuš-giri$_{17}$-zal	Splendid seat, dwelling
^{d}Nu-šilig-ga	Never-ending, not drying up
5 dumu.meš ^{d}Nin-ka-si-ke$_4$	Five children of Ninkasi[75]

Each of these names appears to reference some aspect of the experience of beer consumption: how beer affects the imbiber, how it transforms spaces, a hope that it will never end. And some take us back into the realm of the ME, those special powers or "arts of civilization" that we met in the tale of Inana and Enki. Perhaps another hint that beer held within it—and could manifest in its drinkers—a spark of the divine. In a similar vein, I particularly like an epithet that was occasionally applied to Siraš herself (actually, the phrasing here suggests "himself"). Siraš is "the one who releases god and man" (*pāšir ili u amēli*) or perhaps who "loosens" or "relaxes" god and man.[76]

Again, this might seem obvious, but I think it bears repeating. In Mesopotamia, beer was not just a generic foodstuff that people consumed for the sake of nourishment or because they liked how it tasted. It was clearly recognized as a special sort of beverage that did things to people.[77] On the individual level, as we've seen, one of the things that it did was make people (and gods) do things that they might regret in the morning. It impaired the judgment. Enki, for example, may have been hoodwinked by Inana while under the influence, but more often than not he was on the other side of the table, cleverly using beer to manipulate others. In a literary text known as "Enki's Journey to Nippur," for example, he plies the other gods with beer and then tricks them into blessing his city of Eridu.[78]

Beer also appears as an agent of confusion in texts drawn from everyday life, for example, letters. In Chapter 5, we discussed the Old Assyrian trading system, an extensive trade network that linked the city of Assur in northern Mesopotamia with cities and towns across central Anatolia. This system was maintained through a near-constant back-and-forth of letters written on cuneiform tablets. In one letter, a trader is chided for selling some cloth to a man named Ikun-pīya while "in your beer," that is, while drunk.[79] Presumably, the trader had not come out so well in this particular trans-action, his judgment clouded by beer. And here's one more example, per-haps the clearest possible statement regarding beer and impaired judgment, drawn from a text known as "The Instructions of Šuruppak." Among a litany of advice offered by the narrator to his son, we read: "You should not pass judgment when you drink beer."[80] I think that sums it up pretty well.

The drinking of beer was also linked to some other negative outcomes: for example, impotence. As far as I know, the only evidence for this un-fortunate side effect comes from a difficult text known as "The Fowler's Wife."[81] It's possible that we don't quite understand what's going on in this brief tale, couched as it is in a dense mixture of humor, metaphor, and innuendo. But, according to one reading, it's all about a man's inability to perform sexually. He comes home drunk on beer and is unable to please his wife in bed. She makes fun of him, at which point he claims that it's up to her to remedy the situation.

We can also turn to the Mesopotamian medical literature, where beer shows up regularly in a medicinal capacity. These two examples come from a body of so-called diagnostic texts, that is, texts that describe symptoms, diagnose causes, and offer solutions.

> [If . . . he has been sick for] three days. If he has a stone in the urethra, if that person drinks beer, [that stone] will [fall] out. If that person does not drink beer but drinks a lot of water, he will certainly die.[82]

> [If ṣētu (dehydration) burns a person] and on the day (you see the patient), he has chills, that person has been sick for three days; [in order that] [his] [ill-ness] not be prolonged, if you repeatedly rub him gently with hot oil and first quality beer, he should recover.[83]

Beer- and wine-based remedies like these are common in the medical lit-erature, but these are not really what interests us here.

In a number of cases, the symptoms described in diagnostic texts (not the remedies) are directly linked with the drinking of beer. And they're pretty much what you might expect: impaired vision, impaired balance, impaired speech.

If a person drinks fine beer and then he is unsteady on his foundations (and) his eye-sight is diminished, to cure him . . .[84]

If a person drinks fine beer and as a result his head continually afflicts him, he continually forgets his words and slurs them when speaking, he is not in full possession of his faculties, and that person's eyes stand still, to cure him . . .[85]

If his words are [unintelligible] and he continually asks for beer at regular intervals (and he has been sick) [for ten days . . .][86]

Okay, that last one sounds pretty serious, and all three probably belong in the domain of problem drinking. They do appear, after all, in a compendium of medical afflictions, deserving of treatment by a specialist (known as an *āšipu*). So we may be dealing here with something more than the predictable outcome of a drink too many one evening down at the tavern.

Indeed, one detailed study of the medical literature interprets these symptoms as signs of serious substance abuse, that is, addiction to alcohol. It also points toward a number of other examples that might—emphasis on *might*, since no mention is made of beer or wine—indicate diseases related to excessive alcohol consumption. For example, the following symptoms might indicate alcoholic withdrawal or delirium tremens.

If (the skin under) his headband stings him, his ears roar, the hair of his body continually seems to stand on end, his whole body crawls as if there were lice but when he brings his hand up, there is nothing to scratch, "hand" of ghost *ṣētu* (dehydration); (if) the person (bends and stretches out) his feet as in the scepter of [the god] Sîn, "hand" of ghost.[87]

Right at the end, this text offers a somewhat mysterious diagnosis: hand of ghost. What is this? Well, without going into great detail, medical practice in Mesopotamia was what one might call holistic in approach. Medical conditions were attributed to a broad range of factors, from environmental conditions (heat, cold, wind, dampness) or a person's behavior (consuming tainted food or water) to the "hand" of various gods, demons, and ghosts. The study in question suggests that conditions related to prolonged or excessive drinking were often attributed to the actions of a ghost, also a common explanation for dehydration and diseases that cause dehydration.[88] And the authors see potential evidence for a broad range of alcohol-related conditions: hypoglycemia, seizures, cirrhosis, Wernicke-Korsakoff syndrome, ethanol poisoning.[89] Maybe? I'm certainly not qualified to judge their diagnoses, but the connection to alcohol consumption seems a bit tenuous to me, or at least speculative.

This potential evidence for alcohol as a public health problem aside, the people of Mesopotamia clearly understood that the drinking of beer could impact individuals in a negative fashion. And yet, drink it they did. As do we. So, why? You will not be surprised by the answer. Drinking beer made people (and deities and other anthropomorphic beings) feel good. It inspired feelings of freedom, elation, lightness, energy, satisfaction, and general well-being.[90] The kind of inebriation described here strikes me as closer to what we might call tipsy or buzzed than properly drunk. We have already seen, for example, the impact of seven goblets of beer on Enkidu in the Epic of Gilgamesh: "His mood became free, he started to sing, his heart grew merry, his face lit up."[91] And we've seen the joys of beer consumption celebrated in a Drinking Song.

> While I turn around the abundance of beer,
> While I feel wonderful, I feel wonderful.
> Drinking beer, in a blissful mood,
> Drinking *liquor*, feeling exhilarated.
> With joy in the heart (and) a happy liver...[92]

The effects described here are recounted in the first person, as an element of individual, embodied experience. But the drinking that produced these effects was clearly taking place in a social context—perhaps a tavern presided over by Ninkasi, the goddess of beer.[93]

Indeed, the drinking of beer in ancient Mesopotamia was a distinctly social activity. I wouldn't want to dismiss out of hand the potential existence of a tradition of solo drinking. Absence of evidence, after all, is not necessarily evidence of absence. Who knows exactly what people were getting up to in the privacy of their own homes, perhaps leaving only the faintest trace in the archaeological record. And the artistic record does include depictions of solo drinkers. But the overwhelming impression from our source material is that people drank beer with other people. It's hardly surprising, then, that the effects of beer consumption were recognized to incorporate a social or collective dimension.

In one sense, this just means that, when people (and other beings) enjoyed their beer, they enjoyed it together. In the *Enūma Eliš* (also known as the "Babylonian Epic of Creation"), for example, it is in the context of a well-lubricated banquet that the divine community comes together and collectively hands over the reins to the ascendant god Marduk.

> They swarmed together and came.
> All the great gods, ordainers of [destinies],
> Came before Anshar and were filled with [joy].
> One kissed the other in the assembly [ ],
> They conversed, sat down at a feast,
> On produce of the field they fed, imbibed of the vine,
> With sweet liquor they made their gullets run,
> They felt good from drinking the beer.
> Most carefree, their spirits rose,
> To Marduk their champion they ordained destiny.[94]

So beer consumed together could lift the spirits of a collectivity. That was, perhaps, predictable enough. If drinking beer was known to make one person feel good, chances are it was also going to be known for making a whole bunch of people feel good. But I think we can go further and specify at least four other collective effects of beer consumption—as articulated in the cuneiform record.[95]

First, drinking beer together didn't just result in similar experiences, like feeling good and carefree. It helped facilitate *shared* experiences.[96] For example, the association between beer and sex—that most intimate of shared experiences—was not occasional or accidental. The two were closely linked. We've seen this already in *coitus a tergo* drinking scenes and in the world of the tavern. Many other illustrations could be provided, but perhaps the most vivid appears in a series of rather explicit Sumerian love poems.[97] Here are two snippets to give you the general flavor.

> The gazing of your eye is pleasant to me, come my beloved sister.
> The greeting of your mouth is pleasant to me, my honey-mouth of her mother.
> Your lips' kissing (my) breast is pleasant to me, come my beloved sister.
> My sister, the beer of your grain is good, my honey-mouth of her mother.
> The sparkling drink of your bappir is good, come my beloved sister.[98]

> My . . . barmaiden, her beer is sweet.
> Like her beer her vulva is sweet, her beer is sweet.
> Like her mouth her vulva is sweet, her beer is sweet.
> Her small beer, her beer is sweet.[99]

Note: In the first snippet, the speaker is not meant to be addressing his actual sister. The term "sister" is being employed as a term of endearment.

And yes, bappir, the enigmatic brewing ingredient from Chapter 3, even makes an appearance. In the second, the speaker, Ur III king Šu-Suen, is not addressing his actual "barmaiden" or tavern keeper but is likening his beloved to a tavern keeper who provides him with sweet beer.

Beer also helped to create the distinctive shared experience of the banquet. Whether a small-scale affair for a select few or a public feast that brought the whole community together, a banquet wasn't really a banquet without beer. And it's not just that attendees would have come expecting to be served beer (although they certainly would have). I would argue that the inebriating effects of beer played an active role in making the banquet what it was: in Mesopotamian literature, a dynamic setting of celebration, camaraderie, lowered inhibitions, conflict, possibility, and transformation.

Mention of conflict leads into a second collective effect of beer consumption. When people were drinking beer together, there was a heightened potential for interpersonal friction.[100] Beer may have made people feel good, but it also stirred up rivalries and antagonisms of one sort or another. Time and time again, in Mesopotamian literature, the joint drinking of beer serves as a catalyst for arguments, debates, and competitions. We have already witnessed a high-stakes, beer-fueled competition between the god Enki and goddess Ninmah and another between Enki and the goddess Inana. In both cases, the link between the drinking of beer and the launching of the competition does not have to be inferred. It's spelled out quite clearly. The two parties sit down to drink beer and wine together, and a competition immediately ensues.

The ubiquity of such competitive displays, often with an audience in attendance, leads one to suspect that people of Mesopotamia appreciated a good argument. Indeed, formalized debates appear to have been staged for the entertainment of the Ur III (2112–2004 BCE) court.[101] These performances have come down to us in the form of a genre of Sumerian debate literature: heated rhetorical contests pitting hoe vs. plow, sheep vs. grain, summer vs. winter, bird vs. fish, etc. Not all of them feature beer as an instigator, but some do. For example, after a lengthy prelude that reaches back deep to a time before the contestants even existed, the "Debate Between Sheep and Grain" kicks off with a shared drink.

> They drank sweet wine, they enjoyed sweet beer. When they had drunk sweet wine and enjoyed sweet beer, they started a quarrel concerning the arable

fields, they began a debate in the dining hall. Grain called out to Sheep:"Sister, I am your better; I take precedence over you."[102]

Sure, we're talking here about beer generating friction between deities or between plants and animals, not human beings. But I suspect that this recurring trope reflects a more general recognition that an amiable beer shared among friends or associates could very well lead to interpersonal conflict and contention.

The third collective effect of beer consumption takes us even deeper into the dark side of beer, into another sort of shared experience. In Mesopotamian literature, beer was sometimes employed as a tool of trickery and deceit.[103] In other words, beer and its inebriating effects were exploited in a cynical fashion to manipulate others. Probably the most egregious case appears in the tale of "Enki and Ninḥursaĝa," a disturbing account of uncontrolled lust, incest, and rape.[104] The tale is set in the city of Dilmun (modern-day Bahrain) in a distant, primeval past. In those early days, "that place was still virginal . . . still pristine."[105] It was empty of life and all the trappings of urban existence. Ninḥursaĝa, patron goddess of the city, begs Enki—yes, him again—for help. He obliges and transforms the city into a thriving metropolis, a trading emporium with goods flowing in from all the distant lands.

Exulting in his triumph, Enki runs through the marshes, "digging his phallus into the dykes, plunging his phallus into the reedbeds,"[106] and he in turn begs Ninḥursaĝa (also known here as Nintur and Ninsikila) to sleep with him. She obliges and in a remarkable nine days gives birth to a daughter Ninnisig. When he sees the young woman by the riverbank, Enki is smitten and, with the aid of his minister Isimud—yes, him again—proceeds to seduce and impregnate his daughter. She then gives birth, and the pattern repeats itself. Three more times. Enki impregnates his granddaughter Ninkura, his great-granddaughter Ninimma, and his great-great-granddaughter Uttu.

The last of these, Uttu, is actually warned by Ninḥursaĝa about Enki's predilections and tries to avoid the fate of her predecessors. But Enki shows up at her door with food and, crucially, with beer to tear down her defenses. In her inebriated state, Uttu gives in, but in the aftermath she cries out, "Woe, my thighs. . . . Woe, my body. Woe, my heart."[107] Presumably in an effort to break the cycle, Ninḥursaĝa removes the semen from Uttu's womb and plants it in the ground, resulting in a series of plants as offspring. Enki

sees what's going on—or at least sees that some unfamiliar plants have made
an appearance—and he proceeds to eat them. They don't sit so well with
him, causing various pains in his body. Eventually, having cursed Enki and
then been persuaded to back down, Ninḫursaĝa extracts this final set of
offspring from his body and assigns a reward to each. In an interesting twist,
one of the offspring of Enki and Uttu is Ninkasi, goddess of beer. Her reward: she "shall be what satisfies the heart."[108]

Overall, beer doesn't get much airtime in this tale. But it is a key player
in the pivotal episode, the seducing and violation of Uttu. Enki uses beer
and its inebriating effects to manipulate Uttu and his relationship with her.
My point here is simple. Occasional examples like this in the literary record suggest a recognition that the shared experience of beer consumption
could open up space for deception and exploitation.

The fourth collective effect that I would like to highlight is a little more
abstract. It's about the crossing of boundaries, exceeding of limits, breaking
of taboos, casting aside of norms. In the world of Mesopotamian literature,
the communal consumption of beer often signals entrance into a slightly
different reality, one where anything can happen, where things not normally possible (or permitted) become possible.[109] Beer has a disruptive and
transformational character. As one scholar argues, " . . . the unnatural manipulation of the world is done under the influence of alcohol. . . . The result
is a structured bracketing for unnatural acts and for unbridled ambition and
desire."[110]

The suggestion here is that the sharing of beer opens up a sort of temporary autonomous zone where the normal rules no longer apply. And,
especially in stories set in the divine realm, it is this "bracketing" or setting
aside of custom and convention that allows room for change: uprisings,
power grabs, momentous decisions. In the world of the gods, transformative
moments often pivot around the joint consumption of alcohol. Perhaps this
is pushing the evidence further than it can go, but beer seems to occupy
an interesting position within Mesopotamian conceptions of history. In a
world understood to be governed by ancient, divinely ordained customs
and traditions, how does one account for change in the human realm? Why
do dynasties rise and fall? Why are flourishing cities suddenly abandoned,
left to the mice and rats? Why do destructive floods or swarms of locusts
burst onto the scene and wreak havoc? The typical answer is divine whim.
The gods giveth, and the gods taketh away. But what about change in the

divine realm? How does one explain that? Interestingly, it often arrives through the disruptive force of alcohol, through the decision to sit down together to enjoy some beer and wine.

So the people of Mesopotamia themselves recognized that beer could change the world. Or at least that it could help set the right mood. This is an important point. But what if we look beyond the immediate effects of beer consumption—its evanescent ability to transform individuals, groups, atmospheres, and events—and think more broadly about what beer was doing in this society? We've covered a lot of ground in this book, addressing a whole series of difficult questions. Who was brewing the beer? How? With what ingredients and equipment? Who had control over distribution of the finished product? And who was drinking the beer? With whom? Where? When? Why? Were some people left out? What benefits did beer provide? And at what cost? All of these questions matter. They matter today, and they did in the past. A careful look at how beer is produced, distributed, and consumed can tell you a lot about a society: for example, about the structure of the economy; about the concentration of wealth and power; about class and labor relations; about the construction of gender; about commensal traditions; about religious practices; about notions of taste, pleasure, morality, excess, and restraint.

But what I'd really like to emphasize here is the active role that beer can and does play in making our social worlds. Beer clearly acts on us, on our bodies, our minds, our emotions. But, whether we notice or not, it is also busy performing all kinds of other feats and functions: building fortunes, maintaining or pushing back against the status quo, perpetuating or helping break down inequities, solidifying or transforming gender roles, creating community, cementing or destroying friendships, establishing conduits to the divine, to the ancestors, to loved ones recently gone. In many ways, we're still in the early days of getting our heads around exactly what beer was doing in ancient Mesopotamia. Having now spent some time getting to know the world's first great beer culture, you should now have a pretty good sense for what we know, how we know it, and how much we have yet to learn. I hope that you'll be inspired to continue the journey. The search for knowledge about the deep history of alcoholic beverages and about the world of ancient Mesopotamia is always on the move. You can be sure that there will be new discoveries, new insights, and more beer right around the bend.

Epilogue: Reviving an ancient art

The pleasure—it is the beer! The discomfort—it is the journey!

Sumerian proverb[1]

We're back at Great Lakes Brewing Co. in Cleveland, for the first of what will turn out to be a series of tasting events. The lights have just been flipped back on. A hundred or so intrepid souls, seated at large, circular tables, are getting up to stretch their legs. Conversation starts to pick up. I've finished delivering my lecture about the evidence for beer and brewing in Mesopotamia. The brewers from Great Lakes have gone through our experimental brewing process. The owner of the brewery, Pat Conway, has waxed poetic and maybe poked a little fun at me, as he likes to do. While we talked, people have been sipping on our experimental brews, Enkibru and Gilgamash, and snacking on hors d'oeuvres inspired by the cuisine of ancient Mesopotamia.

But now is the real moment of truth. Will anyone be willing to try the Enkibru through a straw from the big ceramic vessel at the front of the room? We've put forward the invitation, not really expecting many takers. You know, hygiene and whatnot. But there's no hesitation whatsoever. Pretty much the whole lot seem to be making their way toward the neon yellow and green plastic straws that poke out from the mouth of the jar. Unfortunately, we didn't manage to procure any reed straws for this first event. Many people have to patiently wait their turn to get at the murky, yellowish liquid, bubbles and grain husks floating at the surface. But they seem to be enjoying themselves. There's a lot of laughter, occasional surprised exclamations (for some reason, the alcohol seems to hit you quicker through a straw), many photos.

I certainly hope that the attendees got something out of our lectures. But I suspect that it's the beers themselves and the experience of drinking through straws from a communal vessel that will really stick with them. There's just something special about developing this sort of embodied connection with the past. Our effort to breathe new life into beers gone by—like other projects exploring similar territory—straddles the boundary between experimental and experiential archaeology. Experimental archaeology is now a well-established subdiscipline, recognized by most archaeologists as a legitimate means of engaging with the material that we study.[2] The basic idea is simple. We don't have to be content with speculating about how this or that might have been done in the past, how certain patterns of breakage or wear might have been produced, how archaeological sites might form and evolve over time. We can also put our ideas, our hypotheses, our theories into practice. We can try, in a sense, to re-create past practices and processes. Exactly how one chooses to go about this and how one chooses to interpret the results will depend on many factors: the theoretical and methodological frameworks employed, for example, and the specific questions being asked.

What I would like to highlight here, though, is how such experimental approaches—often conducted in a carefully controlled, scientifically rigorous fashion—intersect with the experiential dimension. What if it's not only the measurable, quantifiable, statistically significant results of an experiment that matter? Could there not also be a value in the doing of the experiment, that is, in the experience itself? We can learn things about the past and make connections with that past through our bodies, through doing, touching, tasting, hearing, smelling. And this applies not just to public outreach efforts, like our beer tasting events, but also to the classroom, the laboratory, and the field site. It's increasingly being recognized that, alongside experimental archaeology, there is also room for—indeed, a need and demand for—experiential archaeology.

Those who attended our tasting event were not, of course, experiencing the brewing of the beer firsthand. But they were certainly experiencing the beer itself firsthand—observing its color and texture, smelling it, tasting it, ingesting it into their bodies, feeling the effects of the alcohol. And many were trying out an alternative method for getting the beer into their bodies. This, to me, is experiential archaeology in action. Our project was not, of course, the first to have had the brilliant idea of bringing ancient beverages back to life and inviting the public to taste them. This kind of thing has been going on for some time now.

In recent decades, the pace has really been set by Dogfish Head Brewing and their numerous collaborations with biomolecular archaeologist Pat McGovern.[3] Their "Ancient Ales" series has included an array of beverages from all over the ancient world: a beer-wine-mead hybrid from Iron Age Anatolia (Midas Touch), a beer-wine-mead hybrid from Neolithic China (Chateau Jiahu), a cacao beer from early Mesoamerica (Theobroma), a corn beer from ancient Peru (Chicha), a barley beer from ancient Egypt (Ta Henket), an Etruscan beer from Iron Age Italy (Birra Etrusca), a hybrid beverage from Bronze Age Denmark (Kvasir). Interestingly, though, nothing from Mesopotamia. At least not yet. What ties all of these diverse re-creations by Dogfish Head together is the availability of organic residues. That's not the only line of evidence employed, but that is McGovern's specialty. And he has traveled all over the world collecting and analyzing the traces of early alcoholic beverages. These traces can be difficult to interpret—and there's lots of debate about the matter—but what they do most effectively is reveal the ingredients employed in ancient beverages.

So, for their experimental brews, McGovern and Dogfish Head Brewing have focused especially on getting the ingredients right—or at least as close to right as possible, with some creative license employed here and there. Though they have sometimes experimented with alternative brewing equipment (e.g., a bronze fermentation vessel for their Birra Etrusca) and brewing methods (e.g., chewing corn for their Chicha), they have generally stuck with their usual modern equipment and methods. And they've been guided, at least in part, by a desire to produce something that will be palatable, if a little challenging, for modern audiences. They have also bottled up all of these Ancient Ales, outfitted them with nicely designed labels, and sent them out for relatively broad distribution.

I think it's safe to say that these beverages do not qualify as exact replicas of any particular ancient beverages. And I don't think they are really intended as such. They're something more like creative revivals, each grounded in solid archaeological evidence but re-imagined for twenty-first century audiences. So what exactly is the aim here? Is this experimental archaeology in the strict sense, that is, experimental brewing conducted with the aim of elucidating specific archaeological conundrums, questions, or hypotheses? No, I'd say probably not. But they have certainly brought a unique experience of the past—a past refracted, as it always must be, through a modern lens—to many interested consumers. It seems to me that the overarching goal has been to bring something different to the beer-drinking public, to stretch their palates in new directions, to bring them into contact with other places and times, and, of course, to produce something that will ultimately be profitable for the company. And those are perfectly reasonable goals.

Let's turn now to several efforts to recreate Mesopotamian beers: two that I had nothing to do with and another that I did. First, "Ninkasi" Sumerian beer, a collaboration between Anchor Brewing Company in San Francisco, Solomon Katz of the University of Pennsylvania, and Miguel Civil of the University of Chicago (Figure E.1).[4] This venture was dreamed up in 1989 as a fitting way to celebrate the ten-year anniversary of Anchor's current (at the time) brewing facility. So the idea appears to have come from the brewing industry side of the partnership. But it was still envisioned as an academic endeavor. In a published account of their brewing experiments, Fritz Maytag, president of Anchor Brewing, and Solomon Katz framed the project as a reopening of what was by then a cold case: the bread vs. beer debate (see Chapter 1).[5] I can certainly see that they may have taken inspiration from this legendary showdown over the ultimate impetus behind crop domestication. But it's not clear exactly how their Sumerian brewing efforts were meant to contribute to the debate. As they acknowledge, the written texts informing their work were produced many thousands of years after the domestication of wheat and barley in the region.[6]

The project was explicitly presented as a meeting up of brewing traditions past and present, "a sincere effort to bring the art of the modern brewer to bear on the mystery of how ancient beer might have been made four millennia ago."[7] Their primary source of evidence was the Hymn to Ninkasi, with its poetic and difficult-to-interpret account of the brewing process. So it makes perfect sense that they turned for help to Miguel Civil, renowned Sumerologist and foremost expert on the topic, having himself produced the definitive analysis and translation of the Hymn. With Civil's guidance, the brewers strove to replicate Ninkasi's brewing process step-by-step. Here's how Katz and Maytag describe the experience.

> Satisfied with our interpretation of the "Hymn to Ninkasi," we decided to give the recipe a try. From this moment on we began to feel a thrilling link with brewers from ages past. After nearly 4,000 years, Sumerian beer terms such as bappir and gestin would be spoken in a brewery once again.[8]

Figure E.1. Ninkasi Sumerian beer, brewed by Anchor Brewing Co. in collaboration with Solomon Katz and Miguel Civil. (Anchor Brewing Co.)

I love this idea of an ancestral connection to brewers past made via the re-suscitation, the putting to use, of a long-forgotten brewing language.

And it wasn't, of course, just a matter of language. The brewers also sought to bring certain ingredients, bappir ("beer bread") and geštin (grapes or wine) among them, back into use in the brewery. As we discussed in Chapter 3, their rendition of bappir was something like Italian *biscotti*, a hard, crunchy, twice-baked bread, one that could theoretically have been stored for later use, as suggested by some cuneiform texts. And they added it directly to the mash, rather than employing it later in the process as a fermentation starter. You know enough about bappir now to realize that these were interpretive choices. When the goal is to move from theorizing about beer to brewing actual beer for drinking, one has to go out on a limb and make some hard calls. They also had to make some accommodations along the way to stay on the right side of the law and obey governmental guidelines. They were not able, for example, to follow their interpretation of the Hymn to Ninkasi and employ grapes (geštin) as a fermentation starter, because of a need "to keep the product within controllable standards of pu-rity" and to avoid infecting their brewing equipment with "foreign" yeast. Instead, they opted for a typical brewer's yeast, a choice that almost certainly had a significant impact on the finished product. They also did not have permission from the Federal Government to employ dates in their bappir, so they substituted honey in place of dates or date syrup.

Equipment-wise, this effort by Anchor Brewing was, like that of Dogfish Head, very much grounded in the modern world. They stuck with their usual brewing equipment, rather than attempting to replicate the actual equipment that would have been used in Mesopotamia. So this project was another ancient-modern hybrid. In the end, the beer clocked in at a mild 3.5% alcohol by volume. It was bottled and served at two tasting events. Pat McGovern himself—before he had yet embarked on his own brewing adventures—was there for the second tasting, at which point the beer had spent seven months aging in the bottle. He remarked that it "had the smoothness and effervescence of champagne and a slight aroma of dates."[9]

Would the beers of ancient Mesopotamia really have had that kind of effervescence, presumably the result of a buildup of carbon dioxide during a secondary fermentation in the bottle? Probably not, but it's a question worth asking. Indeed, we don't really know whether fermentation was typ-ically open or closed, that is, whether fermentation took place in a vessel that was open to the air or in a vessel that had been sealed up. If open, we can probably assume no significant buildup of carbon dioxide. If closed, perhaps the beers would have retained some carbonation at the time of consumption. But the evidence is pretty meager. Some pierced jar-stoppers have been interpreted as potential fermentation locks, allowing for the controlled release of carbon dioxide during a closed fermentation.[10] And there are some suggestions of sealed fermentation vessels in the written record. An Old Babylonian (2004–1595 BCE) spell for constipation, for example, compares the patient's belly to a gakkul vessel.

> The sick belly is closed up like a basket,
> Like the water of a river it does not know where it should go,
> it has no flow like water of a well,
> its orifice is covered like (that of) a fermenting vat [*kakkullu*],
> no food and drink can enter it.[11]

(Sorry, I couldn't resist one more nod to the gakkul's scatalogical connotations.) The point is: This topic definitely needs more work.

And the storage of beer is an even bigger unknown. The general assumption is that the beers would have been consumed right away, on the spot, probably while they were still fermenting. But the written record also documents the delivery of beer, often in specific vessel types: for example, the *pīḫu* in the second millennium BCE or the *dannu* in the first millennium BCE.[12] Delivery implies, I think, at least some degree of storage.

The bigger point—and I'll come back to this in a moment—is that one reason to do experimental archaeology in the first place is that it often raises interesting and unexpected questions. Anchor Brewing creates its ancient-modern hybrid Ninkasi beer and gives McGovern a taste. He mentions effervescence, which makes me think of bottles, which makes me wonder about the evidence for open/closed fermentation in Mesopotamia and beer storage. That's the kind of small spark that could launch one down a productive research rabbit hole. Sure, I might have arrived at those same questions from some other direction, but I think experimental archaeology is a particularly effective generator of questions.

Of course, it can also provide answers. How did the edges of these chipped stone blades come to be all glossy looking? From the harvesting of grain. What kind of tool created the notches in these cow bones? A bronze axe. Actually, let's insert a caveat, a *might*. How *might* the edges of these chipped stone blades have come to be all glossy looking? What kind of tool *might* have created the notches in these cow bones? Seldom are the answers provided by experimental archaeology absolutely definitive. In most cases, an experimental approach is not, on its own, going to tell you that your hypothesized explanation is definitely the correct explanation. But it might very well tell you that it's a viable explanation. Or that it's not. And that's important information.

This brings us to a second effort to re-create Mesopotamian beer, conducted by the excavators of Tell Bazi, Syria, in collaboration with brewing scientists from the Technical University of Munich in Weihenstephan, Germany.[13] In this case, the impetus came from the archaeological side. During their excavations at Tell Bazi, the team had come across a distinctive assemblage of ceramic vessels, found over and over again in houses at the site. And they believed that these vessels might have something to do with the brewing of beer. As a first step toward testing their hypothesis, they invited the brewing scientists to come out and conduct organic residue analysis on these vessels. As you will now be well aware, having reached this point in the book, the analyses showed that beer had once been present in many of the vessels.

The next step was to figure out exactly how the vessels in question might have been used to brew the beer. The team focused their attention on two vessels in particular: a large one, always found half buried in the floor, and a smaller one with a hole pierced in its base. I'm not going to run through the full argument, but, as we've already discussed, they hypothesized that these vessels had been used to brew beer without the aid of added heat. According to their reconstruction, the pierced vessel would have been used for the malting of barley, and the half-buried vessel, for a "cold-mashing" process that took advantage of a natural temperature gradient created in the vessel.

They then set out to test the hypothesis by brewing some actual beer. As far as I am aware, they did not create replica ceramic vessels but, rather, focused on re-creating the brewing process. They malted the barley themselves, milled it by hand using a stone saddle quern, and "mashed in" (i.e., mixed the malt with water) at a deliberately low ratio of malt to water and at a deliberately low temperature of 34 degrees C (93 degrees F). They then pitched the resulting wort with a mixed culture of yeasts and lactic acid bacteria, seeking to mimic the culture that would likely have colonized the wort during a process of spontaneous fermentation (i.e., if it had been left out in the open to collect microbes from the surrounding environment). After thirty-six hours of fermentation, they gave the beer a taste and were pleased with the results: a low-alcohol beer (1.6% ABV) with "a pleasant lively character with enjoyable consumption potential."[14]

So, from a technical perspective, the cold-mashing process appears to be a viable hypothesis. Did the experiments demonstrate that beer was definitely brewed at Tell Bazi using a cold-mashing process? I don't think so. There are other pieces to that argument that cannot be proven or disproven using such experiments. Also, unfortunately, the result that has often caught the attention of outside observers is the low alcohol content of the beers. As we've already discussed, that was simply a choice made by the brewers, based on the fact that children were known to have consumed beer in Mesopotamia. The low malt-to-water ratio ensured that the beer would be low in alcohol content.

Let's move on now to my own brewing experiments. And let me be clear. These were not *my* brewing experiments. This was very much a team effort, the team consisting of a rotating cast of perhaps twenty people, split half-and-half between the University of Chicago's Institute for the Study of Ancient Cultures (ISAC) and Great Lakes Brewing Co. (GLBC).[15] As I mentioned in the Prologue, I signed on as a grad student and, alongside fellow student Mike Fisher, became a sort of go-between, responsible for linking up the Chicago and Cleveland sides of the team.

So how exactly did this experimental brewing effort get started? The ultimate impetus came from Pat Conway, co-owner of Great Lakes Brewing and a University of Chicago graduate. Following one of many visits to the ISAC Museum, he came up with the idea of doing some kind of collaboration. Maybe an Egyptian beer? Maybe Mesopotamian? Maybe Hittite? I don't think the motivation was necessarily commercial in nature. (In fact, I suspect that some on the business side of the GLBC team were not always so thrilled with this particular use of time, energy, and money.) Throughout the process, Pat insisted over and over again to us and to various audiences that this project was not about making a beer that could be bottled and sold. It was all about curiosity and educational value. That's certainly a noble sentiment, but I was also a little sad that there was no plan to bottle any of our beers.

In any case, Pat got in touch with Gil Stein, Director of ISAC, sometime in 2011, and the project took off from there. The first stage was a series of brainstorming sessions in Cleveland and Chicago, always with plenty of GLBC beer on hand. As the game plan took shape, these sessions morphed into a virtual phase, where many details were hashed out in lengthy email chains. Basically, those of us on the ISAC team started by putting together a summary of our best understanding of how brewing might have worked in Mesopotamia. This summary was woefully insufficient. The brewers at Great Lakes responded with a list of perhaps thirty questions—questions that were, from their perspective, absolutely essential and, from ours, very difficult (some definitely unanswerable). But we did our best to cobble together some answers. And things carried on like that, back and forth, back and forth, for some time.

Eventually, the points of uncertainty narrowed, and we reached a consensus that it was time for some actual brewing. From those first brainstorming meetings, we had arrived at one basic principle: As far as possible, we would try to replicate the ingredients, equipment, and brewing process actually employed in ancient Mesopotamia. As you now know—having explored the evidence and seen how many questions remain to be answered—that's a pretty tall order. I think we made a reasonable effort, but there's no way that we could claim to have achieved absolute accuracy in any of those three dimensions.

On the ingredients side, we malted our own barley. If you'll recall, though, it's not entirely clear how malting was carried out in Mesopotamia. We opted for a very simple process: soaking barley in water for a few days, straining out the water, spreading the grains out in a cool spot for germination, and then spreading them out in the sun to stop the germination. For this last step, which took place on the roof of the brewery, we had to employ some chicken wire to prevent the birds from getting to it. Fortunately, we managed to follow in the footsteps of the widow mentioned in the tale of Enki and Ninḫursaĝa: "When a widow has spread malt on the roof, the birds did not yet eat that malt up there."[16] We didn't process the malt any further beyond a coarse grind. But, as we've discussed, it's entirely possible that at least some malt in Mesopotamia was roasted, toasted, or otherwise processed in preparation for brewing. And we could have missed all kinds of other potential complexity in the malting process that just doesn't show up in the available source material. In a society that prized its beer so heavily, it's likely that malt production was a sophisticated and carefully controlled process. And, to tell you the truth, we didn't actually malt our own barley for every batch of beer. Early on, the brewers compared our malt to their commercially produced malt and determined that they were close enough in character that we could comfortably substitute one for the other. So some corners were cut.

The other key ingredient was, of course, bappir (Figure E.2). The team spent a lot of time arguing about this one, before settling on one interpretation to test out. We would treat bappir as a fermentation starter—not a source of fermentable sugars to be added to the mash but a source of yeast and bacteria that would transform our wort into beer. We toyed with the idea of sending someone off to collect a wild yeast culture from the region, to infuse our beer with some authentic Mesopotamian terroir. But we decided instead to rely on a local Cleveland sourdough culture. Our bappir was made with unmalted barley and was "baked" for a long period of time at a very low temperature in order to dry it out without killing off the all-important micro-flora (yeasts and bacteria). This gave us a dry,

Figure E.2. Experimental brewing: the author adding bappir to the fermentation vessel. Collaboration between Great Lakes Brewing Co. and the Institute for the Study of Ancient Cultures, University of Chicago. (Photo: Brian Zimerle)

crumbly barley bread that was full of still viable yeast and could be stored up and added to a batch of beer whenever we needed to get fermentation going. We were very happy with the results. But, again, some corners were eventually cut. We didn't always rely on this same sourdough culture for our beers. At some point, the brewers switched over to the same proprietary mix of yeast and bacteria that they were using for some of their other mixed-culture beers.

We also used emmer wheat for some beers, as well as a range of different aromatics. As you know, the question of aromatics is a difficult one. Our solution was to provide the brewers with a long list of fruits, vegetables, herbs, and spices that we know were available in Mesopotamia—but that may or may not have been used for brewing—and let them choose. The specific mix of aromatics varied from batch to batch but, at one point or another, included coriander, cardamom, fennel, juniper berries, and dates. We also used a lot of date syrup. Actually, what we are able to get our hands on—we didn't attempt to make any ourselves—was really a date paste (Figure E.3). We sometimes added this paste directly to the mash to contribute fermentable sugars and flavors. But we also regularly added date paste directly to the finished beer right before serving. This sweetened option was not a fan favorite.

It's on the equipment side that our project differed most substantially from the others we've examined. Our beers were brewed almost entirely using replica ceramic vessels. At the very beginning, we did some experimenting with a metallic vat for mashing. And our first bappir iterations were baked in metal tins in a modern, industrial oven, before we switched over to a local baker's domed baking oven. But otherwise we relied on an all-ceramic, purpose-built brewing kit (Figure E.4). Our pots were built and fired by ceramist Brian Zimerle, who was employed at the time as a preparator in the ISAC Museum. They were all modeled on specific examples excavated by ISAC's Diyala Expedition in the 1930s at the sites of Khafajeh and Tell Asmar in Iraq.[17]

But—and this is a big but—we don't know that any of those vessels were actually used for the brewing of beer. The Diyala Expedition was, for its time, well ahead of the curve in terms of excavation and recording strategies, but organic residue analysis, for example, would not come into its own for another half century. We can be pretty confident that our fermentation vessels, modeled on the distinctive vessel-with-a-hole-in-its-base,

Figure E.3. Experimental brewing: adding date paste to the mash vessel. Collaboration between Great Lakes Brewing Co. and the Institute for the Study of Ancient Cultures, University of Chicago. (Photo: Tate Paulette)

were once used for brewing, even if not specifically for fermentation. But the ring-based collection vessels that sat beneath, the round-bottomed mashing vessels that we heated atop portable burners, the ladles and sieves that we used for transferring liquids and filtering out solids—these were all the result of educated guesswork. Drawing on many of the same sources

Figure E.4. Experimental brewing: replica brewing assemblage. Collaboration between Great Lakes Brewing Co. and the Institute for the Study of Ancient Cultures, University of Chicago. (Photo: Tate Paulette)

that you've examined in this book, we came up with a best-guess approximation for how brewing might have worked in Mesopotamia. We then pieced together a hypothetical brewing assemblage using vessels illustrated in the Diyala Expedition's published reports. The vessels were all approximately contemporary with one another and, therefore, at least plausible as elements of a functionally related brewing assemblage. Our ceramist then did his best to recreate these vessels, adjusting the scale somewhat to suit our purposes, and we put them to work.

Of course, how exactly the vessels should be put to work is also an open question, or actually a whole series of open questions. Let me just mention a few points in the brewing process that generated significant debate among team members. First, mashing. The evidence offers no clear guidance regarding the application of heat during mashing. Should the mash, for example, be kept at relatively constant temperature through the continuous application of heat? Or should we rely on the addition of water heated elsewhere? Or should we follow the lead of the Tell Bazi team and exclude heat from the equation entirely? The brewers did not find this last option very compelling. In the end, we went with a direct heating of the mash using a portable ceramic burner (usually called a "brazier") stocked with wood or charcoal.[18]

Another topic that inspired endless debate was the question of boiling. These days, the wort is typically boiled prior to fermentation. We do this for a variety of reasons, including sterilization and to facilitate the extraction of alpha acids from hops for bittering. But boiling is not absolutely necessary, and there's no particularly clear evidence one way or the other from Mesopotamia. I generally argued against boiling (though I'm not entirely sure why, at this point . . . perhaps concern about whether our pots could handle it). Pat Conway, on the other hand, definitely thought that we should include a boiling step. Nearly every meeting included at least one, and often more than one, interjection from Pat on the topic: "So are we really not going to boil? Really? Why not?" In the end, we left out the boiling step. I'm not quite sure how I won that battle.

Finally, fermentation. Once we had decided to employ the vessel-with-a-hole-in-its-base as a fermentation vessel, we had to make some further decisions. And just remember that the function of this iconic vessel is not certain. Some have emphasized its filtering potential over any role in fermentation. The Tell Bazi team, for example, used it for the soaking and germination of the barley during malting, relying on the hole as a means of evacuating the liquid, while leaving the grains in place. If you're going to use the vessel for fermentation, though, what exactly is the role of the hole?

We spent a lot of time debating this question. On the one hand, perhaps the filtering function was still paramount. Perhaps, for example, the mash was fermented as is, without filtering out the solid matter (grain husks, etc.) ahead of time. Our typical assumption would be that it's preferable to filter everything out first, leaving you with just the liquid wort to ferment. But that doesn't have to have been the case. If one opted to ferment the entire mash, the hole in the base of the fermentation vessel could serve as a post-fermentation filter, allowing for the spent grain to be removed before drinking. We didn't follow this path, but it would have been an interesting variation to try. We chose, instead, to filter out the solid matter using a ceramic sieve placed in the mouth of the fermentation vessel. So, during the move from mashing vessel to fermentation vessel, the spent grain was removed, leaving just the wort in the fermentation vessel. Well, the wort and whatever stray husks managed to make their way through the holes in the sieve. Of course, we also had to add bappir to the wort in this vessel to start the fermentation, and this introduced another component of grain into the mix. So the hole in the base of our fermentation vessel did still serve a filtering function.

But our biggest point of contention revolved around the plugging up of the hole. Some members argued that hole would have been left open during the fermentation process, perhaps lined with some kind of cloth for additional filtering. As they envisioned the process, the beer would have been drip-drip-dripping—"dubul dabal, dubul dabal"—slowly down into the collection vessel throughout the fermentation process.[19] This option didn't make a lot of sense to the brewers or to me and some other team members. We thought, instead, that the hole should be plugged up during fermentation and then unplugged to allow the finished beer to pour down into the waiting collection vessel like "the onrush of the Tigris and the Euphrates."[20] In the end, this option won out, and it worked well. As with all of these choices that we made, it would have also been instructive to try both options side by side. For one reason or another, though, we never managed to do that.

As far as I'm concerned, this questioning, doubting, debating, comparing, critiquing, rehashing, revising is what experimental archaeology is all about. Or at least, it's what this particular (rather informal) kind of experimental archaeology is all about. There's so much more that we could have done with this project, but I think that it was, without a doubt, a valuable undertaking. As I like to say when I give talks on the topic, did we produce a perfect re-creation of ancient Mesopotamian beer? Definitely not. But I think we achieved a pretty reasonable approximation, and, ultimately, the value of the project didn't lie in the final destination but in the journey. Of course, the destination was beer, and that's not the worst place to end up.

We served our experimental beers to hundreds of tasters at a series of seven events in Cleveland, Chicago, Columbus, and Philadelphia. In each case, we offered at least two beers to try side-by-side (Figure E.5). Enkibru (named after the wild man Enkidu), the "wilder" of the two, was brewed in the replica ceramic vessels, using bappir (i.e., a mixed culture fermentation starter) as a yeast source. Gilgamash (named after the hero Gilgamesh), on the other hand, was brewed using modern brewing equipment and the same basic ingredients, except that a saison yeast was substituted for bappir. The idea was to really showcase the difference that technologies and techniques can make in the character of the finished product.

Enkibru varied pretty significantly from batch to batch, partly due to changes in the recipe but partly, we think, due to seasonal fluctuations in

Figure E.5. Enkibru, served in tasting glasses. Sumerian Beer Dinner, Great Lakes Brewing Co., Cleveland, Ohio. August 14, 2013. (Photo: Kathryn Grossman)

Figure E.6. Sipping Enkibru through straws from a communal vessel. Sumerian Beer Dinner, Great Lakes Brewing Co., Cleveland, Ohio. August 14, 2013. (Photo: Tate Paulette)

temperature, humidity, etc. It ranged from mildly tart to puckeringly sour, from mildly alcoholic (3.5%) to no joke (8%), from milky white to an opaque, yellowish brown, from slightly effervescent to flat as can be. The Gilgamash was stable and steady, a crisp, clear, pale-yellow brew, somewhere in the vicinity of a Belgian-style saison, with an herbal twist, not at all out of place when it appeared a few times on the draft list at the GLBC taproom in Cleveland. Both beers sometimes included date syrup added directly to the mash. And we often offered a taste of Enkibru with date syrup added just before drinking. We always served the beers in tasting glasses, side-by-side, to allow for direct comparison. But then, of course, for the full experience, we also offered the Enkibru through straws from a communal vessel (Figure E.6).

If you'd like to try brewing Gilgamash at home, you'll find a recipe in Box E.1 and a more technical version of the same recipe in Appendix A. If you do, I would strongly advise that you invest in some long straws

Box E.1 **Brew-it-yourself: Gilgamash**

The recipe below is for all-grain brewing. If you would like to approximate this recipe using malt extract, you can skip steps 1–4 and move directly to the boiling stage. Bring the water to a boil, remove from the heat, and add either 6 pounds of liquid malt extract or 4.8 pounds of dry malt extract (either a pure barley malt extract or a mixture of barley and wheat malt extract). Return to a boil and proceed to step 5.

For either all-grain brewing or extract brewing, if you would like to brew a beer that is closer to Enkibru (rather than Gilgamash), you can replace the saison yeast with a mixed culture of yeast and bacteria (e.g., a culture designed for Belgian sours). This option will probably require some experimentation and tweaking of the recipe.

Ingredients

Amount	Type	Timing
6.5 gallons	Water	Pre-boil
6.85 pounds	Pale Ale malt	Mash
1.21 pounds	Wheat	Mash
2.6 ounces	Dates	60 minutes
1.3 ounces	Figs	60 minutes
0.48 quarts	Pomegranate Juice	End of boil
1 packet	French Saison 3711	Fermentation
1 cup	Priming sugar	Bottling
	Bottles and caps	Bottling

Original Gravity: 1.042
Final Gravity: 1.008
ABV: 4.4%
IBU: 0
Volume: 5 gallons

Process

1. In mash tun, heat 6.5 gallons of water to ~155°F.
2. Infuse water with milled Pale Ale malt and wheat according to your preferred method.
3. Hold mash at 150°F for 60 minutes.

4. After conversion is complete, run wort off to kettle and bring to a boil.
5. Add dates and figs in a muslin sack at beginning of boil.
6. After boiling for 60 minutes, remove from heat and add pomegranate juice.
7. Cool wort and rack to a fermenter.
8. Pitch yeast to cooled wort and aerate by shaking fermenter.
9. Ferment at 65–77°F, ideally at 68°F, for roughly 1–2 weeks.
10. Clean and sanitize bottles and caps before bottling.
11. Rack finished beer from fermenter to sterilized bottling bucket.
12. Create priming solution by boiling water with 1 cup of sugar and add to beer.
13. Bottle and cap beer, then set aside in a cool dark space to carbonate.
14. Beer will be ready to drink in roughly two weeks.

and a big clay pot. And why not dedicate that first sip to Ninkasi, goddess of beer, she who is "what satisfies the heart." Might I also suggest a toast, drawn from our ancient Sumerian drinking song: "May Ninkasi live together with you!" Or maybe give it a try in Sumerian: "Ninkasi zada ḫumu'udanti!"[21]

Acknowledgments

I owe so many people a beer—and many, more than just one. This book has been a decade plus in the making, and though I may have been the one who put words on paper, many people have lent a hand along the way. So a huge thank you to all of you. And please forgive me if I've forgotten to mention you here.

My venture into the world of Mesopotamian beer began in a bar. So thanks, first of all, to Mike Fisher for that first, beer-fueled brainstorming session and the years of collaboration that followed—and to our experimental brewing companions at the University of Chicago's Institute for the Study of Ancient Cultures (Gil Stein, Chris Woods, Brian Zimerle, and Steve Camp) and Great Lakes Brewing Co. (Pat Conway, Joel Warger, Luke Purcell, Bridget Gauntner, Nate Gibbon, Michael Williams, Mark Hunger, Steve Forman, Jeff West, and Emmett Conway). Thanks for letting us be part of the team.

My venture into the world of ancient Mesopotamia, though, began long before that experimental brewing effort. I owe a substantial debt of gratitude to a series of mentors who have helped me along the way: in particular, Trevor Watkins, my undergraduate advisor at the University of Edinburgh, Mac Gibson, my graduate advisor at the University of Chicago, and Jesse Casana of Dartmouth College, who has (unofficially) guided me through the post-PhD years. Thank you also to the institutions that have supported me over the years of working on this project. I have been incredibly fortunate to share an academic home with many wonderful colleagues and students at the University of Chicago, Brown University, and North Carolina State University. Thank you, especially, to my colleagues in the History department at NC State, who have generously offered advice, read drafts, and helped me to carve out time and resources during the writing of the book. David Zonderman, Julia Rudolph, and Tracy Brynne Voyles have each gone out of their way as department head to ease my path. Our departmental administrators, Courtney Hamilton and Ingrid Hoffius, have amiably put up with incessant requests for help of all sorts. And two faculty mentors, Tom Parker and David Gilmartin, have offered crucial guidance at multiple junctures. I just wish that Tom were still here so I could say thank you with a pint or three at Sammy's.

A number of colleagues have really gone above and beyond by reading large chunks (or the entirety) of the book in draft form. Thank you to Gojko Barjamovic, Matthew Booker, Rob Dunn, Mike Fisher, Janling Fu, David Gilmartin, Kate Grossman, John Millhauser, and Seth Richardson. Amanda Schupak also read the whole thing cover-to-cover and offered detailed editorial comments on tone, style, audience, and organization. Many other friends and colleagues have also contributed in one way or another over the years. Thank you especially to Khaled Abu Jayyab, Salam Al Kuntar, John Arthur, Darren Ashby, Greg Beckwith, Giacomo Benati, Emily Booker, Daniel Calderbank, John Cherry, Eric Cline, Lindy Crewe, Shannon Lee Dawdy, Michael Dietler, Christian Doll, Asa Eger, Gertrud Farber, Walter Farber, Frederico Freitas, Janling Fu, Claudia Glatz, Jill Goulder, Lisa Graham, Arim Hawsho, Jason Herrmann, Virginia Herrmann, Debra Ireland, Domino Ireland, Alex Joffe, Chuck Jones, Kate Kelley, Morag Kersel, Will Kimler, Mara King, Jeff Kosiorek, Jake Lauinger, Margaret Lejeune, Erik Lindahl, Lucas Livingston, Stephen Lyford, Mac Marston, Andrew McCarthy, Alicia McGill, Dru McGill, Pat McGovern, Levi McLaughlin, Max Miller, Kathleen Mineck, Kate Morgan, Miriam Mueller, Trey Nation, Elsa Perruchini, Monica Phillips, Nicholas Postgate, Max Price, Kevin Qiu, Rune Rattenborg, Clemens Reichel, Matt Reilly, Steve Renette, François Richard, Yorke Rowan, Walther Sallaberger, David Schloen, Ari Schriber, Tim Shea, John Sheppard, Adam Smith, Alexia Smith, Alex Sollee, Tracy Spurrier, Lucas Stephens, Claire Stevens, Cody Stevens, Matthew Stolper, Jason Ur, Peter van Dommelen, Deborah Wakefield, Rachel Webberman, Erica Weiberg, Colin West, Sebastian Wolfrum, Federico Zaina, and Melania Zingarello. Foy Scalf deserves special mention for helping me—over and over again—to track down references on short notice.

A big thanks to NC State students Dmitri Fisher, Jadyn Mann, and Olivia Schladt for putting in long hours to help with figures during the final stages of book production. Thank you also to the students in my "Alcohol in the Ancient World" courses at Brown, Dartmouth, and NC State and to the students and staff on my archaeological field school in Cyprus who enthusiastically embraced a contest to come up with a title for the book. There were some excellent and hilarious entries, but Gwyneth Fletcher's "Unfiltered" stood out as a top contender.

I am grateful for many opportunities to present my work to a variety of audiences, who pushed me to clarify my ideas and explanations in many different directions. Thank you to these audiences and to the colleagues who invited me to participate in the following conference sessions and symposia: Alcohol and the Ancient Near East (ASOR, Michael Homan), Double Visions (TAG USA, Rebecca Graff and Megan Edwards Alvarez), The "Hidden Intelligence" of Kitchens (AAA, Chantel White and Sheena Ketchum), Full of Food and Drink (ASOR, Margaret Cohen, Deirdre Fulton, and Elizabeth Arnold), After the Harvest (ICAANE, Noemi Borrelli and Giulia Scazzosi), Science and Culture of Fermentation (Dartmouth College, Nate Dominy and Olga Zhaxybayeva), Alcohol, Rituals, and Spiritual World in China and Beyond (Stanford Archaeology Center, Li Liu and Jiajing Wang), Zones of Transformation (Freie Universität Berlin, Cale Johnson and Susan Pollock), Drinking Beer in a Blissful Mood (SAA, Marie Hopwood), Beer Cultures in Bronze Age Mesopotamia (ICAANE, Melania Zingarello), Archaeology in the Mediterranean and Ancient Near East (Friends of ASOR, Jennie Ebeling), Food and Feasting in the Ancient Near East (East Carolina University, Megan Perry).

Thanks also to the following individuals and institutions for inviting me to deliver lectures: Jesse Casana (Department of Anthropology, Dartmouth College), Archaeology on Tap (ASOR), Joukowsky Institute Brown Bag Series in Archaeology (Brown University), Dr. Craig's Office Hours (Brown University), Lisa Guzzetta and Shelby Brown (Getty Museum), Fermentology series (NC State), Andrew Gurstelle (Lam Museum of Anthropology, Wake Forest University), and AAMW Colloquium (University of Pennsylvania). I have also thoroughly enjoyed participating in the Archaeological Institute of America's National Lecture Program. Thank you to the following AIA societies for hosting me: Western Illinois, Springfield, Cincinnati, North Carolina (Triangle Area), San Joaquin Valley, North Alabama, Central Pennsylvania, and Jacksonville. Thanks also to the following for inviting me to contribute blog posts, interviews, or other pieces: *First Bite* (Radio National, Australian Broadcasting Corporation), *Indiana Jones: Myth, Reality and 21st Century Archaeology* (VoiceAmerica), *The Ancient Near East Today* (ASOR), *Accolades* (College of Humanities and Social Sciences, NC State), *The Conversation*, and *Peopling the Past*.

Thank you to the following bars, breweries, restaurants, and institutions for hosting lectures and/or beer tasting events: Great Lakes Brewing Company (Cleveland), Fountainhead (Chicago), The Gage (Chicago), Institute for the Study of Ancient Cultures (Chicago), Barley's Smokehouse & Brewpub

(Columbus), Martha (Philadelphia), Cornwall's Pub (Boston), Cool Beanz Coffeehouse (Rock Island), Grad Center Bar (Providence), Mother Stewart's Brewing Co. (Springfield), and Rhinegeist Brewery (Cincinnati). And thanks to these bars, breweries, and restaurants for nurturing my love of beer over the years and providing such wonderful spaces for drinking, conversation, and contemplation: Sandy Bells (Edinburgh), The Royal Oak (Edinburgh), Olde Hickory Taproom (Hickory), The Map Room (Chicago), Hopleaf (Chicago), The Publican (Chicago), Duke of Perth (Chicago), The Pub (Chicago), Jimmy's Woodlawn Tap (Chicago), Half Acre Beer Co. (Chicago), Off Color Brewing (Chicago), Lord Hobo (Cambridge), Bukowski Tavern (Cambridge), Tasty Beverage Co. (Raleigh), (ish) delicatessen (Raleigh), and Poole's Diner (Raleigh). Also, a special mention for Johnny at Tasty Beverage Co. in Raleigh, who hand-delivered beer to my doorstep throughout the dark days of the pandemic while I was hard at work on this book.

Thanks also to my editor Stefan Vranka—who first envisioned this book—and the whole team at Oxford University Press for gently shepherding a first-time book author through the process. And thanks to Andrea Rosenberg for skillfully compiling the index. The book also benefited substantially from the thoughtful comments of a series of peer reviewers.

Final thanks go to my family. Janet, Richard, and Kent Paulette—only one of whom can even stand the thought of beer—have put up with years and years of beer-talk and have generously read and commented on anything that I've sent their way. They even formed a family book club, reading carefully through the entire manuscript, sitting down to discuss it chapter-by-chapter, and offering many thoughtful comments. They have always supported me in everything that I do, and this book is no exception. Finally, Kate Grossman and our short-long, beagle-ish, corgi-ish dog Daisy have been constant companions throughout the process. Thanks to both for always being there and to Kate for the endless hours of listening, reading, and discussing as I tried to figure out how exactly it is that one writes a book.

Cheers, everyone! May Ninkasi live together with you!

Appendix A
Brew-it-yourself: Gilgamash

Thank you to Great Lakes Brewing Co. for providing this full technical breakdown of the recipe for Gilgamash, as brewed for a series of tasting events in collaboration with the University of Chicago's Institute for the Study of Ancient Cultures. See Box E.1 for a more user-friendly version of the same recipe.

Brew Method: All Grain
Style Name: No Profile Selected
Boil Time: 60 min.
Batch Size: 5 gallons (fermentor volume)
Boil Size: 6.5 gallons
Boil Gravity: 1.032
Efficiency: 70% (brewhouse)

Hop Utilization Multiplier: 1

STATS:
Original Gravity: 1.042
Final Gravity: 1.008
ABV (standard): 4.4%
IBU (tinseth): 0
SRM (morey): 4.64
Mash pH: 0

FERMENTABLES:
6.85 lb. – Pale Ale (85%)
1.21 lb. – Wheat (15%)

OTHER INGREDIENTS :

2.6 oz. – Dates, Time: 60 min., Type: Spice, Use: Boil

1.3 oz. – Figs, Time: 60 min., Type: Spice, Use: Boil

0.48 qt. – Pomegranate Juice, Type: Spice, Use: Whirlpool

YEAST:

Yeast – French Saison 3711

Starter: No

Form: Liquid

Attenuation (avg): 80%

Flocculation: Low

Optimum Temp: 65–77 degrees F

Fermentation Temp: 68 degrees F

Pitch Rate: 0.35 (M cells/ml/deg P)

PRIMING:

Method: CO_2

Amount: 30 psi

CO_2 Level: 2.65 Volumes

TARGET WATER PROFILE:

Profile Name: Balanced Profile

Ca_2: 0

Mg_2: 0

Na: 0

Cl: 0

SO_4: 0

HCO_3: 0

MASH GUIDELINES:

1) Infusion, Start Temp: 150 degrees F, Target Temp: -- F, Time: 60 min.,
   Amount: 6.5 gal.

Starting mash thickness: 1.75 qt./lb.

WATER REQUIREMENTS:

Strike water volume at mash thickness of 1.75 qt./lb., 3.53 gal. (14.1 qt.)

Mash volume with grains, 4.17 gal. (16.7 qt.)

Grain absorption losses, -1.01 gal. (-4 qt.)

Remaining sparge water volume, 4.23 gal. (16.9 qt.)

Mash lauter tun losses, -0.25 gal. (-1qt.)

Pre boil volume, 6.5 gal. (26 qt.)

Boil off losses, -1.5 gal. (-6 qt.)

Post boil volume, 5 gal. (20 qt.)

Going into fermentor, 5 gal. (20 qt.)

Total water needed: 7.76 gal. (31 qt.)

Abbreviations

CAD   *The Assyrian Dictionary of the Oriental Institute of the University of Chicago.* The Oriental Institute of the University of Chicago, 1956–2010).

CDLI   *Cuneiform Digital Library Initiative* (online), https://cdli.ucla.edu.

ETCSL Black, J. A., G. Cunningham, J. Ebeling, E. Flückiger-Hawker, E. Robson, J. Taylor, and G. Zólyomi. 1998–2006. *The Electronic Text Corpus of Sumerian Literature* (online), http://etcsl.orinst.ox.ac.uk.

PSD   *The Pennsylvania Sumerian Dictionary* (online), http://psd.museum. upenn.edu.

Notes

EPIGRAPH

1. ETCSL t.6.2.2 (Proverbs: from Susa), MDP 27 215, line 1.

DEDICATION

1. The term šikarologists refers to students of Mesopotamian beer, known as *šikaru* in the Akkadian language. We owe this wonderful neologism to Marvin Powell, who offers the following advice: "The best training for a modern šikarologist is to worship Ninkasi in all her incarnations. . . .[F]uture šikarologists who really want to make progress in the study of this fascinating but still poorly understood aspect of ancient social and alimentary culture will, after having poured sufficient libations to Ninkasi, have to go back and attack the problem of Mesopotamian brewing terminology afresh, keeping in mind both the insights and the mistakes of those of us who have been šikarologists in our time" (1994: 118–119).

PROLOGUE

1. This account of the excavation of a cylinder seal at the site of Hamoukar comes from first-hand experience. I took part in the excavations at Hamoukar as a graduate student between 2005 and 2010, and my wife, Kate Grossman, oversaw the excavation of the cemetery in Area E as part of her dissertation research. Codirected by Clemens Reichel and Salam Al Kuntar, the project was a collaboration between the University of Chicago's Institute for the Study of Ancient Cultures (ISAC) and the Directorate-General of Antiquities and Museums (DGAM) Syria.
2. Where gender is uncertain, I use the gender-neutral form they/them/their.
3. The concept of terroir comes from the world of wine, but it is often assumed that a similar principle might apply to a broader range of fermented foods, specifically with respect to the microbes responsible for fermentation. In other words, it is often assumed that each place will harbor its own local culture of yeast/bacteria, giving the fermented foods produced in that place a distinctly local flavor. This assumption is now, however, being questioned.

4. If we had done our homework at this point, we would have known that there are, in fact, many good analogues in our own world, that is, technologies and techniques that are used today for drying out sourdough cultures. As we'll see in the Epilogue, though, one of the main reasons for engaging in experimental archaeology—e.g., attempting to replicate the brewing of Mesopotamian beer—is that the effort can open up questions, problems, and perspectives that researchers (like us) might not have recognized otherwise. Prior to engaging in these brewing experiments, for example, we had not recognized that it might be valuable to explore how other people in our own world go about drying out their sourdough cultures for later use.

5. For an introduction to the saisons and other farmhouse ales of Belgium, see Markowski 2004.

NOTE ABOUT ANCIENT LANGUAGES

1. For an accessible introduction to the cuneiform script, see Finkel and Taylor 2015.

CHAPTER 1

1. ETCSL t.6.1.26 (Proverbs: collection 26), Segment A, line 12.
2. This imaginative scenario is based on archaeological remains excavated at the site of Göbekli Tepe in southeastern Türkiye. See, e.g., Dietrich and Dietrich 2020, Dietrich et al. 2012, Notroff et al. 2014, Schmidt 2012.
3. So far, the evidence for beer at Göbekli Tepe is inconclusive. See, e.g., Dietrich et al. 2020: 9–13, Dietrich and Dietrich 2020: 103–105, Dietrich et al. 2012: 687–689.
4. The stones appear to derive from the limestone plateau immediately adjacent to the site. They would have to have been dragged approximately 600–700 meters across difficult, sloping terrain. See Dietrich and Dietrich 2020: 97.
5. The excavators have argued that seasonally mobile groups from the broader region came together periodically for feasting events at Göbekli Tepe. See, e.g., Dietrich et al. 2012: 684–692, Dietrich and Dietrich 2020: 100–109.
6. See, e.g., Dietler and Herbich 2001.
7. See, e.g., Dietrich 2023, Dietrich et al. 2012, Dietrich et al. 2017, Dietrich and Dietrich 2020, Dietrich et al. 2020, Notroff et al. 2014.
8. Dietrich and Dietrich 2020: 12, Dietrich et al. 2012: 684.
9. Dietrich and Dietrich 2020: 100–103, Dietrich et al. 2012: 684–687.
10. Dietrich and Dietrich 2020: 103–105, Dietrich et al. 2012: 687–689.
11. Dietrich et al. 2020: 3, 9–13, Dietrich and Dietrich 2020: 105, Dietrich et al. 2012: 687–689.
12. Dietrich and Dietrich 2020, Dietrich et al. 2012.

13. Dietrich et al. 2012; for work feasts in general, see, e.g., Dietler and Herbich 2001.

14. Braidwood et al. 1953; for subsequent efforts to revisit this question, see, e.g., Katz and Maytag 1991, Katz and Voigt 1986, Hayden et al. 2013.

15. Braidwood et al. 1953: 519–520.

16. See, e.g., Dietler 2006, 2020, Fitzpatrick 2018, Goodman et al. 2007, Hockings and Dunbar 2020, Sherratt 1997b, 2007, Stein et al. 2022.

17. See, e.g., Arthur 2022, Guerra-Doce 2015, 2020, Hayden et al. 2013, Liu et al. 2018, Liu et al. 2020, McGovern 2009, 2020, Wang et al. 2016.

18. Jackson 2007: 26.

19. McGovern 2009: 39.

20. Hayden et al. 2013: 104–108, McGee 2004: 740, Steinkraus 1979.

21. Mastication also inoculates the beverage-to-be with oral microbes.

22. Dirar 1993: 224–280, Haggblade and Holzapfel 2004: 271–299, Steinkraus 1996: 407–439.

23. Sherman 2017.

24. McGovern 2009.

25. McGovern 2009: 3–16.

26. I have drawn this scenario from Katz and Voigt 1986: 32–34 but have added a few details of my own.

27. Hayden et al. 2013.

28. For examples of the identification of brewing contexts via the recovery of intact, malted grains, see, e.g., Bouby et al. 2011: 353–356, Moore 1989: 686–688, Müller-Karpe 2005: 175.

29. See, e.g., Liu et al. 2018, Liu et al. 2020, Wang et al. 2016, Wang et al. 2021.

30. Liu et al. 2018, 2019; for a critical response to this argument, see Eitam 2019.

31. Kennedy 2012: 145–146, Kennedy 2019: 283–289.

32. Patrick E. McGovern: Biomolecular Archaeology Project (website), http://www.biomolecular-archaeology.com/.

33. McGovern 2009: 39, 2017: 19–20.

34. McGovern 2017: 66–67.

35. McGovern 2009: 31–46, 57–77, McGovern et al. 2004.

36. Liu et al. 2020.

37. Wang et al. 2016.

38. McGovern et al. 2005.

39. Guerra-Doce 2015: 757–769, 2020: 61–69, McGovern 2009: 129–158, 2017: 147–171, Nelson 2005, 2014, Sherratt 1997a, 1997b.

40. Blasco et al. 2008: 429–431; Guerra-Doce 2015: 760.

41. Moffat 1993: 108–110.

42. Bergerbrant 2019, Frei et al. 2015.

CHAPTER 2

1. ETCSL t.6.1.03 (Proverbs: collection 3), Segment A, lines 17–20.
2. The story is the Epic of Gilgamesh. If you would like to see a full translation of the Epic, many options are available, but I would recommend one of those produced by an Assyriologist: for example, Dalley 1989, Foster 2019, George 1999, Helle 2021. For a recent and engaging account of the reception of the Epic of Gilgamesh by poets and other literary figures, see Schmidt 2019.
3. George 1999: 10 (Epic of Gilgamesh, Standard Version, Tablet I, I 247–250).
4. George 1999: 11 (Epic of Gilgamesh, Standard Version, Tablet I, I 291).
5. George 1999: 13–14. The first stanza quoted here is drawn from the Standard Version of the Epic of Gilgamesh (Epic of Gilgamesh, Standard Version, Tablet II, II 44–45), which then becomes fragmentary. The second and third stanzas, therefore, are drawn from an earlier, Old Babylonian version known as the Pennsylvania Tablet (Epic of Gilgamesh, Pennsylvania Tablet, P 90–105). George has chosen to translate the much-debated term *ḫarimtu* as "harlot." Many other options have been employed in other translations: e.g., prostitute, courtesan, priestess, etc. Also, I have added the clarification "[i.e., Shamhat]."
6. It is important to mention that the Epic of Gilgamesh is definitely not *the* oldest piece of literature in the world. Plenty of other, better candidates could be cited from Mesopotamia. Sophus Helle, for example, has recently suggested that we consider the poems of the priestess Enheduana, who can also be argued to hold the title of first author in world history (Helle 2023).
7. Damerow 2012: 18, Powell 1994: 91–92, 118, Stol 1989: 325, Zarnkow et al. 2006: 5, 21–23, Zarnkow et al. 2011: 53.
8. In the Akkadian language, the term *māt bīrītim* can mean something like "the land between (the rivers)" or "the land in the midst of (the river)." And this term was used as a geographical designation as early as the second millennium BCE, though its precise meaning, in a geographical sense, appears to have shifted over time. See Matthews 2003: 5–6.
9. See, e.g., Bahrani 1998, Matthews 2003: 5–6.
10. Mallowan 1946: 163.
11. See, e.g., Potts 1997: 100–103.
12. Bahrani 2017: 144.
13. Bahrani 2017: 54.
14. See, e.g., Craig et al. 2020, Evershed 2008, Liu et al. 2018, Liu et al. 2020, McGovern 2009, 2017, McGovern and Hall 2016, Perruchini et al. 2018.
15. See, e.g., Cooper 2004, Glassner 2003, Nissen et al. 1993, Schmandt-Besserat 1992, Woods 2010.
16. See, e.g., Finkel and Taylor 2015, Postgate 1992: 51–70, Van De Mieroop 1999.
17. See, e.g., Bahrani 2017, Matthews 2003, Van De Mieroop 1999.
18. If you find yourself needing or wanting a more detailed introduction to the history and archaeology of Mesopotamia, a number of excellent overviews are available in print and online. See, e.g., Akkermans and Schwartz 2003,

Bahrani 2017, Foster and Foster 2011, Kuhrt 1992, Matthews 2003, Nissen 1990, Nissen and Heine 2009, Podany 2022, Pollock 1999, Postgate 1992, Potts 1997, Radner et al. 2020–2023, Roaf 1990, Van De Mieroop 2015.

19. For an introduction to debates about the early state in Mesopotamia, see, e.g., Adams 2001, Barjamovic 2004, Bernbeck 2009, Cooper 2010, Fleming 2004, Garfinkle 2008, 2013, Grossman and Paulette 2020, Matthews 2003: 93–126, Michalowski 2004, 2013, Paulette 2012, 2016, 2021, Pollock 2012, Richardson 2012, 2014, 2017, Sallaberger 2007, Seri 2005, Smith 2003, 2011, Stein 2001a, 2001b, Steinkeller 2017, Ur 2014, Westenholz 2002, Yoffee 1995, 2005, 2016, Yoffee and Seri 2019.

20. Graeber and Wengrow 2021: 297–313.

21. See, e.g., Bernbeck 2009, Richardson 2014: 70–75, Smith 2011, Ur 2014.

22. For a discussion of the connection between beer and the state in Mesopotamia, see, e.g., Joffee 1998, Kennedy 2022, Paulette 2021, Pollock 2003, Renette 2014.

23. For an introduction to debates about cities and urbanization in Mesopotamia, see, e.g., Adams 1981, 2008, 2012, Algaze 2005, 2013, 2018, Al Quntar et al. 2012, Baker 2011, 2014, Childe 1950, Emberling 2015, Lawrence and Wilkinson 2015, Leick 2001, Matthews and Richardson 2020, McMahon 2013, 2020, McMahon et al. 2023, Nissen 2015, Otto 2015, Pournelle and Algaze 2014, Richardson 2007, Smith 2003, Stein 2004, Steinkeller 2007, Stone 2005, 2007, Ur 2010, 2012, 2014, Van De Mieroop 1997, Wilkinson 1994, 2000, Wilkinson et al. 2014.

24. For an introduction to debates about the nature of the Mesopotamian economy, see, e.g., Baines and Yoffee 1998, Barjamovic and Yoffee 2020, Bongenaar 2000, Deimel 1931, Diakonoff 1982, Garfinkle 2005, Gelb 1971, Hudson and Levine 1996, 1999, Hudson and Van De Mieroop 2002, Jursa 2010, Larsen 2015, Mynářová and Alivernini 2020, Paulette 2015, 2016, Powell 1996a, 1999, Prentice 2010, Renger 1994, 1995, Robertson 1995, Sharlach 2004, Stein 2001b, Steinkeller 1999, Steinkeller and Hudson 2015, Van De Mieroop 2004.

25. For an introduction to debates about inequality in Mesopotamia, see, e.g., Annunziata 2018, Baines and Yoffee 1998, Bartash 2018, 2020, 2022, Bernbeck 2009, Bolger and Wright 2013, Foster 1995, Garcia-Ventura 2018, Gelb 1972, 1973, Hudson and Van De Mieroop 2002, Lion and Michel 2016, Paulette 2012, 2015, Pollock 2012, 2017, Pollock and Bernbeck 2000, Powell 1987, Reid 2015, 2017, Richardson 2016, 2023, Robertson 2005, Selz 2010, Snell 2001, 2011, Stol 2016, Tenney 2011, Wright 1996, Wunsch 2014.

26. E.g., Childe 1951: 118, 124.

CHAPTER 3

1. ETCSL t.6.1.21 (Proverbs: collection 21), line 7.

2. Algaze 2013: 74, Note 4, citing Nissen 2003. Nissen 2016: 37 estimates a population of 25,000–50,000. For an introduction to the city of Uruk and the

Uruk period more broadly, see, e.g., Algaze 2008, 2013, Crüseman et al. 2019, Englund 1998, Nissen 2015.

3. For a discussion of Kushim (written KU ŠIM), see, e.g., Damerow 1996: 157–159, Englund 1998: 181–203, Nissen et al. 1993: 36–46.

4. Damerow 1996: 157, Nissen et al. 1993: 36; elsewhere, however, another member of the team (Englund 1998: 31, 188) suggests that Kushim was responsible for a brewery.

5. Nissen et al. 1993: 36.

6. Nissen et al. 1993: 36.

7. Englund 1998: 31.

8. See, e.g., Steinkeller 2004.

9. See Englund 1998: 31–32, 181–204, Nissen et al. 1993: ix–xi, 36–46.

10. In this context, the term "archaic" refers to the earliest phases of the cuneiform writing system, c. 3200–2700 BCE (the later part of the Late Uruk period and the early part of the Early Dynastic period). See, e.g., Englund 1998: 16.

11. Englund 1998: 15–41, 65.

12. Englund 1998: 32–41.

13. See, e.g., Crüseman et al. 2019.

14. See, e.g., Englund 1998: 32–41, Nissen 2002, Nissen 2016: 36–37, Nissen et al. 1993: 4–7.

15. See, e.g., Englund 1998: 71–72, Fig. 22, Nissen 2016: 36–37, Nissen et al. 1993: 4–7, 19–24.

16. Englund 1998: 42.

17. Englund 2004: 28–30.

18. Damerow 2012: 4, Englund 1998: 203, Englund 2001: 29, 34–35.

19. Again, it's possible that Kushim was not responsible for brewing the beer but, rather, for storing and distributing the ingredients.

20. There's no evidence that supervisors were held responsible in this way during this period, but there is during the Ur III period. See, e.g., Damerow 1996: 153.

21. Nissen et al. 1993: 43–46 (MSVO 3, 6).

22. Damerow and Englund 1987, Englund 1998: 118–122, Englund 2001: 3–5, Englund 2004: 31–32, Nissen et al. 1993: 25–27.

23. Nissen et al. 1993: 44–46 (MSVO 3, 11).

24. Nissen et al. (1993: 43–46) argue that two of these four beer types are actually large and small jars of the same type of beer. That would mean that this tablet only documents three different types of beer.

25. Nissen et al. 1993: 46.

26. As already mentioned, it's also possible that these tablets were not produced on-the-job by a brewery supervisor tracking the movement of ingredients and beer through his brewery but, instead, by an administrator working elsewhere and/or after the fact. If so, my account of "covering one's butt" and "cooking the books" would probably need to be adjusted.

27. Müller-Karpe 2005: 175.
28. McGuirk 1993: 141 ("To Daunton Me").
29. Mallett 2014: 219.
30. ETCSL t.1.1.1 (Enki and Ninḫursaĝa), lines 17–19. I have left the term munu$_4$ untranslated. The ETCSL translates munu$_4$ as "malt."
31. Civil 2005: 236 (MMA 86.11.368, Urra = ḫubullu, Tablet 23, lines 3–13). I have left the term munu$_4$ untranslated. Civil translates munu$_4$ as "green malt."
32. ETCSL t. 2.2.3 (The lament for Sumer and Urim), lines 304–309. I have left the term munu$_4$ untranslated. The ETCSL translates munu$_4$ as "malt."
33. Van De Mieroop 1994: 312 (L91-400); here, Van De Mieroop renders the sign for malt as munu$_3$ rather than munu$_4$. I have left the term munu$_3$ untranslated. Van De Mieroop translates munu$_3$ as "malt."
34. Translation after ETCSL t.4.32.e (A šir-namšub to Utu, Utu E), lines 68–71. I have left the term munu$_4$ untranslated. The ETCSL translates munu$_4$ as "malt."
35. PSD s.v. munu [MALT], CAD B s.v. buqlu; see also Brunke 2011b: 47–49, Civil 1964: 76, 78–79, Damerow 2012, Oppenheim 1950: 13–15, Powell 1994: 94–96, Sallaberger 2012a: 316–317, Stol 1989.
36. See, e.g., Hayden et al. 2013: 118–125.
37. Potts 1997: 57–60, Widell et al. 2013: 85.
38. Rattenborg 2016: 112–136, Van De Mieroop 1994.
39. Pulhan 2000: 18–64, Tell Leilan Project website (Qarni-Lim Palace), https://leilan.yale.edu/about-project/excavations/qarni-lim-palace.
40. Van De Mieroop 1994: 316.
41. Archaeobotanical evidence for malted barley has been reported from Kenan Tepe (Terminal Ubaid period; Kennedy 2012: 145–146, Kennedy 2019: 283–289) and Tell Bazi (Late Bronze Age; Zarnkow et al. 2006: 9; Zarnkow et al. 2011: 50).
42. Bouby et al. 2011: 353–356.
43. Liu et al. 2018, Liu et al. 2020, Wang et al. 2016, Wang et al. 2021.
44. PSD s.v. aman [MALTSTER], munumud [MALTSTER], munumudgal [MALTSTER], CAD B s.v. bāqilu; see also Boivin 2018: 158–160, Civil 1964: 78, Sallaberger 2012a: 316, Stol 1989: 327.
45. 1,200 liters = 1.2 m^3 = 0.02 (7.75m^2).
46. As discussed in Chapter 5, the "beer archive" from Tell Leilan was excavated within just such a nonresidential building, centered on a courtyard that measured approximately 10 x 10.4 meters (see Pulhan 2000: 8–66, Van De Mieroop 1994).
47. Crewe and Hill 2012.
48. Gates 1988: 67–68, Gibson 1972: 248–253, Grossman 2014, Ławecka 2008.
49. PSD s.v. bappir [~BEER].
50. CAD B s.v. bappiru.
51. See, e.g., Bottéro 1995: 40, 2004: 62–63, Brunke 2011b: 47–51, Civil 1964: 76–78, Damerow 2012: 6–15, Hrozný 1914: 140–177, Huber 1938, Oppenheim 1950: 10–11, 14, Powell 1994: 97–99, Röllig 1970: 39, Sallaberger 2012a: 308–316, Stol 1971: 168–169, 1989: 325–326, Zarnkow et al. 2020.

52. Civil 1964: 72, lines 15–18.
53. Translation after Sallaberger 2012a: 308. I have translated Sallaberger's rend-
    ering from German into English, and I have left the term babir$_2$ untranslated.
    Sallaberger translates babir$_2$ as "Sauerteig" (i.e., sourdough). His translation
    reads: "Ninkasi, dein *aufgehender* Teig, wurde der mit der stattlichen Spatel
    geformt / ein Aroma von weichem Honig, der durchmischte Sauerteig /
    deine Sauerteig(klumpen), wurden sie im stattlichen Ofen gebacken, sind sie
    sauber angeordnete Garben von *gunida*-Emmer."
54. Civil 1964: 76–78, 2005: 234–240.
55. Katz and Maytag 1991: 30, 32.
56. Sallaberger 2012a: 308–316.
57. See, e.g., Stol 1971: 169.
58. See, e.g., Powell 1994: 98–99.
59. For dough see, e.g., Brunke 2011b 47–51, Civil 1964: 77, Sallaberger 2012a:
    308–316. For a contrasting opinion, see Powell 1994: 97–99. For the oven/
    stove see, e.g., Civil 1964: 78, Sallaberger 2012a: 312–314, Powell 1994: 98.
60. CUSAS 3, 197 (bappir diri sila$_{11}$-[ga$_2$-de$_3$] gub-ba), CUSAS 3, 190 (bappir
    du$_8$-de$_3$ gub-[ba]). Translation after Heimpel 2009: 329. Heimpel renders
    the sign that appears in these constructions as bappir, but Kleinerman and
    Owen (2009: 28) render the sign that appears in the same constructions in the
    Garšana texts as bappir$_2$.
61. Translation after ETCSL t.5.3.2 (The debate between Grain and Sheep),
    lines 116–119. I have left the terms bappir and titab untranslated. The ETCSL
    translates bappir as "beer dough" and titab as "mash."
62. Translation after Civil 2005: 236 (Urra = *ḫubullu*, Tablet 23, column iii, lines
    8'–14'). I have left the term bappir untranslated. Civil translates bappir as
    "barley bread." For an alternative translation (in German), see Sallaberger
    2012a: 311.
63. See, e.g., Brunke 2011b: 47–51, Damerow 2012: 10, 13–14, Powell 1994: 96–97.
64. Brunke 2011b: 48, CDLI P324702 (CUSAS 03, 0975). I have left the term
    babir$_2$ untranslated. Brunke translates babir$_2$ as "beer bread."
65. For the measurement of bappir by weight at Garšana, see Brunke 2011b: 32,
    Note 3. For the measurement of bappir by volume, see Brunke 2011b: 50,
    Note 29, Powell 1994: 97. For the measurement of bappir by count, jar, or
    sack, see CAD s.v. bappiru, Civil 1964: 76, Damerow 2012, Michel 2009: 205,
    Oppenheim 1950: 11, Sallaberger 2012a: 313, 315–316.
66. Translation after Michel 2020: 216–217, Text 129 (CCT 3, 25), lines 8–16. I
    have left the term *ba-pi$_2$-ra-am* untranslated. Michel translates *ba-pi$_2$-ra-am* as
    "beer bread." See also Michel 2009: 206.
67. See, e.g., Barjamovic et al. 2019: 123, Bottéro 1995: 40, 2004: 62–63, 68.
68. Translation after Barjamovic et al. 2019: 123. I have left the term *ba-pi-ra* un-
    translated. Barjamovic et al. translate *ba-pi-ra* as "dried sourdough."
69. Sallaberger 2012a: 309.

70. PSD s.v. lungak [BREWER], CAD S s.v. sirāšû, Powell 1994: 99, Sallaberger 2012a: 309.
71. See, e.g., Powell 1994: 97, Damerow 2012: 6–7.
72. Here, I'm recounting an argument made by Assyriologist Hagan Brunke (Brunke 2011b: 49–51).
73. Brunke 2011b: 50, Note 30.
74. Modernist Cuisine 2018.
75. Brunke 2011b: 51; Damerow 2012: 14.
76. These calculations could equally indicate a denser product stored in lumps with space between them.
77. See, e.g., Brunke 2011b: 49–51, Sallaberger 2012a: 308–316, Zarnkow et al. 2020.
78. See, e.g., Barghini 2020, Dirar 1993: 224–302, Huang 2000: 257–282, Lee et al. 2017, Sha et al. 2019, Steinkraus 1996: 363–508.
79. See, e.g., Grossman 2014.
80. See, e.g., Lee et al. 2017, McKay et al. 2011: 212–222.
81. See, e.g., Samuel 1996, Samuel 2000.
82. Written kaš₂ KAL. Although other readings and interpretations have been offered, Powell (1994: 104) renders this kaš₂ sig or "golden beer."
83. See, e.g., Powell 1994: 104–115.
84. PSD s.v. še [BARLEY], CAD Š s.v. še'u.
85. PSD s.v. ziz [EMMER], CAD K s.v. kiššatu B.
86. PSD s.v. imĝaĝa [EMMER], CAD D s.v. dišiptuḫḫu, Powell 1984: 52.
87. PSD s.v. niĝara [GROATS], CAD M s.v. mundu; see, e.g., Brunke 2011b: 40–41, 43, Kleinerman and Owen 2009: 130, Milano 1993: 25, Powell 1984: 52.
88. Brunke 2011b: 47–49, Damerow 2012: 10, Milano 1993: 25.
89. PSD s.v. niĝ [THING], PSD s.v. ara [GRIND].
90. PSD s.v. titab [~BEER], CAD T s.v. titāpū.
91. PSD s.v. gug [CAKE], PSD s.v. munu [MALT].
92. Civil 1964: 76–77, Damerow 2012: 8, Sallaberger 2012a: 319, Stol 1989: 325.
93. Civil 1964: 79–80; Sallaberger 2012a: 318–319, Note 27.
94. Translation after Kleinerman and Owen 2009: 193 (CUSAS 3 1381).
95. Sallaberger 2012a: 318–319.
96. Translation after Kleinerman and Owen 2009: 193 (CUSAS 3 1381); see also Heimpel 2009: 83, 175–176. I have left the term titab untranslated.
97. Translation after Civil 1964: 80 (Contest Between the Reed and the Tree, lines 89–90). I have left the term titab untranslated. Here Civil translates titab as "mash."
98. Translation after Civil 2005: 236 (Urra = ḫubullu, Tablet 23, column iii, line 28'–column iv, line 1). For an alternative translation of some terms, see Sallaberger 2012a: 319. Civil indicates that titab is written titab in this passage, while Sallaberger indicates that it is written titab₂. I have left the term titab untranslated. Here Civil translates titab as "dried malt," except in the case of "watered malt."
99. Civil 1964: 73 (Hymn to Ninkasi, lines 29, 31).

100. Civil 1964: 73 (Hymn to Ninkasi, line 31).

101. Civil 2005: 240; PSD s.v. sumun [VESSEL].

102. CAD T s.v. titāpū.

103. See, e.g., Damerow 2012: 8, Powell 1994: 101, Stol 1989: 325.

104. Sallaberger 2012a: 318–320.

105. See, e.g., Powell 1994: 100–101, Röllig 1970: 39.

106. PSD kum [HOT].

107. Powell 1994: 100–101; for further discussion, see Damerow 2012: 6, 8, Stol 1989: 325.

108. PSD s.v. lal [SYRUP], CAD D s.v. dišpu; see, e.g., Ellison 1984: 94, Potts 1997: 150, Powell 1994: 99, Stol 1994: 157.

109. Stol 1994: 156–157; see, e.g., ETCSL c.1.1.4 (Enki's Journey to Nibru), line 102.

110. For a detailed discussion of the evidence for date beer (i.e., date wine) in Mesopotamia, see Stol 1994. As Stol (1994: 157) argues, a few pieces of evidence might indicate the presence of date beer during earlier periods.

111. This use of the word šikaru to refer to both barley beer and date wine is almost certainly due to the underlying meaning of the term. It is derived from the verbal root škr, which simply means "to become inebriated or drunk" (CAD Š s.v. šakāru). So, although šikaru was often used to refer specifically to barley beer, its basic meaning was more like "an inebriating [i.e., alcoholic] beverage." See, e.g., CAD Š s.v. šikaru, Stol 1994: 160–161.

112. Stol 1994: 161.

113. Stol 1994: 157.

114. PSD zulum [DATE], CAD S s.v. suluppū.

115. After ETCSL t.1.1.4 (Enki's Journey to Nibru), lines 98–103. The ETCSL has chosen to render the Sumerian word kurun (a type of beer) as "liquor," presumably to distinguish this beverage from the kaš (beer) mentioned in the same sentence. This is an unfortunate choice, since the term "liquor," as used today, generally implies a distilled beverage. Here, the term "liquor" should just be taken as another reference to beer, not a distilled beverage.

116. After Stol 1994: 156–157.

117. In this text, date syrup (lal$_3$ zu$_2$-lum-ma) is explicitly indicated, as opposed to honey/syrup (lal$_3$) more generally.

118. PSD s.v. duh [BRAN].

119. Dirar 1993: 284–285.

120. Stol 1994: 156.

121. Hojlund 1990: 77–78.

122. Hojlund 1990: 78–79.

123. Hojlund 1990: 79–84.

124. In the United States, for example, Scratch Brewing in Ava, Illinois, and (closer to home for me) Fonta Flora Brewery in Morganton, North Carolina, have each been experimenting with all sorts of locally foraged and/or cultivated flora. For Scratch Brewing, see Josephson et al. 2016.

125. Damerow 2012: 8, Powell 1994: 98, Röllig 1970: 22, 80, note 34, Stol 1994: 176.
126. Stol 1994: 175–179.
127. CAD K s.v. kasû, PSD s.v. gazi [CONDIMENT]; see, e.g., Brunke 2011b: 393, note 32, Civil 1964: 77, note 14, Englund 1995: 417–418, note 70, Geller 1982, Landsberger and Gurney 1957–58: 337–338, Powell 2003: 20, Röllig 1970: 80, notes 33–34, Sallaberger 2012a: 312–313, Steinkeller 1987: 92, Stol 1994: 175–179.
128. Stol 1994: 175–179.
129. Brunke 2011b: 177–178.
130. See, e.g., Sallaberger 2012a: 294, 313.
131. See, e.g., Peyronel et al. 2014, Vacca et al. 2017, Wachter-Sarkady 2013.
132. Urra = ḫubullu, col. iii, lines 1–7, Civil 2005: 235, Oppenheim 1950: 24–25, Sallaberger 2012a: 311.
133. The Pennsylvania Sumerian Dictionary defines the terms sahin and sahindu as "yeast" (PSD s.v. sahin [YEAST], PSD s.v. sahindu [YEAST]). The Chicago Assyrian Dictionary defines sikkatu as "an ingredient of beer" and the related term saḫindu as "yeast (?)" (CAD S s.v. sikkatu C, CAD S s.v. saḫindu).
134. Civil 2005: 235, Oppenheim 1950: 24–25, 47, Note 61, Sallaberger 2012a: 309–312.
135. PSD s.v. si [HORN]; interestingly, in other contexts, the term si can also refer to "the brewing of beer," PSD s.v. si [FILL].
136. Stol 1989: 324.
137. Oppenheim 1950: 24–25.
138. Civil 2005: 235.
139. Sallaberger 2012a: 310–311.
140. Civil 1964: 69, 72, line 15, 77.
141. Sallaberger 2012a: 308, "(Ninkasi,) dein *aufgehender* Teig, wurde der mit der stattlichen Spatel geformt" (my translation into English).
142. CAD A s.v. agarinnu, PSD agarin [MATRIX].
143. Oppenheim 1950: 24–25, col III, lines 5–6, Civil 2005: 235, col iii, lines 5'–6', Sallaberger 2012a: 311, lines 5'–6'.
144. PSD s.v. ama [MOTHER].
145. PSD s.v. šim [AROMATICS].
146. Oppenheim 1950: 25, line 5, Civil 2005: 235, lines 5'–6'.
147. Sallaberger 2012a: 311–312.
148. Sallaberger 2012a: 308–316.
149. In the lexical list Urra = ḫubullu, the word si also appears in the construction si buru₃ bu-ru-da. Civil takes this phrase to mean "of the holes," a possible reference to what is left behind in the holes of the filtering vat during the brewing of beer. Following this train of logic, he suggests that what is left behind might be "pulverized yeast(?)," his tentative translation for si buru₃ bu-ru-da (Civil 2005: 236, column iii, line 7', 239). Sallaberger, on the other hand, argues that the "holes" in question are actually bubbles, more specifically the bubbles

produced by a fermenting sourdough. So, he tentatively translates the phrase si buru$_3$ bu-ru-da as "rising, throwing bubbles" (Sallaberger 2012a: 311, line 7').

150. See, e.g., Damerow 2012: 17, Oppenheim 1950: 16.

151. Zarnkow et al. 2006: 12, Zarnkow et al. 2011: 49.

152. See, e.g., Bendixsen et al. 2021, Gallone et al. 2016.

153. The term "animalcule" was once used to refer to microscopic animals but has now fallen out of use.

154. See, e.g., Damerow 2012: 5–8, Powell 1994.

155. In converting these measures to the metric system, I have followed Powell 1994: 101–103.

156. DP 166: obverse, column 1, lines 1–4 (CDLI P220816), Powell 1994: 108–109.

157. See, e.g., Damerow 2012: 5–8, Powell 1994, Röllig 1970: 28–43, Stol 1989: 326.

158. Here I'm drawing on Marvin Powell's detailed analysis of the Girsu texts (Powell 1994).

159. Damerow 2012: 4, Englund 1998: 203, Englund 2001: 29, 34–35.

160. Foster 1982: 14.

161. See, e.g., Dornbusch 2012.

162. See, e.g., Brunke 2011b: 47–52, Damerow 2012: 8–15.

163. CUSAS 3 975 (CDLI P324702), Brunke 2011b: 47–49. The tablet also documents the production of another 20 liters of good beer and 40 liters of ordinary beer, but Brunke argues that these were not intended for the main festivity (Brunke 2011b: 47–49).

164. Lacambre 2008, Lacambre 2009.

165. Rattenborg 2016: 116–118.

166. CAD K s.v. kurunnu, PSD s.v. kurun [BEER], Stol 1994: 165.

167. After ETCSL 2.5.3.1 (A šir-namursaĝa to Ninsiana for Iddin-Dagan, Iddin-Dagan A); see also Black et al. 2004: 262–269. I have left the word kurun untranslated. The ETCSL translates kurun here as "beer." I have also adjusted the translation slightly in order to render it line-by-line, rather than in paragraph form.

168. PSD s.v. ulušin [BEER], CAD U s.v. ulušinnu.

169. CAD D s.v. dišiptuḫḫu, CAD A s.v. alappānu, Powell 1984: 52, Sasson 2004: 191–192.

170. Boivin 2018: 164–166, Calderbank 2021: 54.

171. For a detailed discussion, see Stol 1994.

172. Stol 1994: 161–167.

173. Stol 1994: 164–165.

174. Stol 1994: 165, CAD B s.v. billatu, PSD s.v. dida [WORT].

175. Urra = ḫubullu, col. ii, lines 2'–37', Civil 2005: 234–235.

CHAPTER 4

1. Hymn to Ninkasi, lines 43–44, Civil 1964: 73.

2. Ni 4569 = ISET 1, 118–119, CDLI P343146, Kramer et al. 1969 (ISET 1): 118–119, Sallaberger 2012a: 296–300.

3. Alster 1985, Assante 2002, Jacobsen 1987, 85–98, Sallaberger 2012a: 306–307, 322–324, Sefati 1998.

4. For translations of the first, third, and fourth of these songs, see ETCSL t.4.08.07 (Dumuzid-Inana G: A balbale to Inana), t.4.08.15 (Dumuzid-Inana O: A balbale to Inana), and t.4.08.32 (Dumuzid-Inana F1: A song of Inana and Dumuzid). The second song is not as well understood but begins in a similar vein to another song (ETCSL t.2.4.4.1, Šu-Suen A: A balbale to Bau for Šu-Suen).

5. See, e.g., Kramer 1946, Kramer 1947, Kramer et al. 1969, Westenholz 1992, Zettler 1997.

6. Peters 1905. See also, e.g., Hilprecht 1908.

7. Peters 1905: 164.

8. Peters 1905: 163.

9. Peters 1905: 163, citing Hilprecht 1904: 500.

10. Black et al. 2004: xli–xliv, Delnero 2019: 174–179, McCown and Haines 1967: 64–66, Paulus 2023, Robson 2001, Stone 1987: 56–59.

11. AO 5385 = TCL 15, 20, CDLI P345364, Sallaberger 2012a: 296–300.

12. For a translation, see ETCSL t.4.08.05 (The song of the lettuce: a *balbale* to Inana, Dumuzid-Inana E).

13. Sallaberger 2012a: 296.

14. VAT 6705 = VS 10, 156, CDLI P342964, Sallaberger 2012a: 296–300.

15. Sallaberger 2012a: 296.

16. Civil 1964: 68, Sallaberger 2012a: 296.

17. Sallaberger 2012a: 297.

18. Sallaberger 2012a: 303, 305.

19. There are two major "editions" (i.e., detailed scholarly presentations and discussions) of the Hymn to Ninkasi and the Drinking Song. The classic edition, published by Miguel Civil in 1964, includes a composite text and an English translation, backed up by extensive footnotes. Civil's discussion of brewing ingredients and the brewing process is buried within these footnotes, where it intermingles with complicated philological commentary. If you've ever seen an English translation of either text, it was almost certainly based on Civil's work and, ultimately, on his understanding of how beer was brewed in Mesopotamia. For a slightly updated translation by Civil, see Katz and Maytag 1991: 19. In Box 4.1, I have reproduced Civil's original translation of the Hymn to Ninkasi with one small adjustment. I have included an additional title, in parentheses, based on the first line of the text (a-zal-le u-tu-da).

20. Walther Sallaberger (2012a) has published a new edition of the Hymn to Ninkasi and the Drinking Song that draws on nearly fifty years' worth of further work in the discipline and that lays out his own understanding of the brewing process. His publication includes a collation of the three versions of the Hymn to Ninkasi, a composite text and translation for the Hymn, a translation for the Drinking Song, detailed philological commentary, and a much more detailed explication of brewing ingredients and the brewing process.

21. For an online transliteration and translation, based on Civil 1964, see ETCSL 4.23.1.

22. In Box 4.2, I have reproduced Civil's translation of the drinking song with a few small adjustments. When specific vessels are referenced (e.g., gakkul, lam-sa$_2$-re, am-am), Civil included some qualifications regarding the nature of these vessels (e.g., the gakkul vat, the lam-sa$_2$-re vat, the am-am jar). I have included just the original Sumerian terms without qualification. I have also included an additional title, in parentheses, based on the first line of the text (gakkul-e gakkul-e).

23. Civil 1964: 68.

24. Sallaberger 2012a: 322–324.

25. Foster 1993: 404 (The Descent of Ishtar to the Netherworld, lines 7–8); for a general discussion of death and the afterlife in Mesopotamia, see, e.g., Scurlock 1995.

26. George 1999: 124 (Epic of Gilgamesh, a tablet reportedly from Sippar, lines Si iii 2 – Si iii 9).

27. Wilcke 1988. The translation in Box 4.3 follows Alster 2005: 312–317 (The Ballade of Early Rulers, the "Syro-Mesopotamian" Version).

28. For an introduction to the different versions of the text and the interpretations that have been offered, see Alster 2005: 288–322.

29. Alster 2005: 291.

30. Alster 2005: 290–292, Wilcke 1988.

31. Civil 1964: 71, 74, lines 71–74. Civil has chosen to translate gurun$_x$ (DIN) as "liquor." Given uncertainty about how to translate the term, his intention here was to indicate an alcoholic beverage in general but certainly not a distilled beverage, as often implied by the term liquor today.

32. Sallaberger 2012a: 296.

33. The Clancy Brothers, 1969, *Flowers in the Valley*, "Beer, Beer, Beer."

34. McGuirk 1993: 6–8, 195.

35. ETCSL 5.3.2 (The Debate Between Grain and Sheep).

36. Civil 1964: 72, lines 17–28.

37. For an overview of what we know about Ninkasi and Siraš, see Frayne and Stuckey 2021: 259–260, 311, Krebernik 1998–2001.

38. Krebernik 1998–2001: 442–443.

39. Krebernik 1998–2001: 444.

40. George 1993: 158 (1214), 168 (1391).

41. George 1992: 106–107, rev. iii, line 7' (K 2107 + 6086).

42. Assante 1998: 69.

43. CAD S II s.v. siraš, Krebernik 1998–2001: 442.

44. Civil 1964: 72–73.

45. See, e.g., Stol 1994: 173–175, CAD B s.v. balālu, PSD s.v. lu [MIX], CAD M I s.v. mazû, CAD E s.v. epēšu, CAD N s.v. nadû I.

46. I've compiled the summary in Box 4.6 based on information provided in Civil 1964. See this publication for further detail. Civil (1964: 76) acknowledges

that the bappir would at some point have been mixed with the malt, but he demurs on the specifics. In a later publication (Civil 2005: 238, 240), he offers a brief, modified account in which the malt (munu₄) is transformed into a dried malt product (titab), which is then mixed with bappir during the mashing phase to produce a wort for fermentation. In this account he also suggests that the mash was subjected to repeated spargings (i.e., repeated additions of water and extractions of wort) to produce beers of increasingly low alcohol content.

47. Belliard 2011.

48. I have compiled the summary in Box 4.7 based on Belliard 2011. See this publication for further details.

49. See, e.g., Otto 2006, Otto 2012, Zarnkow et al. 2006, Zarnkow et al. 2011.

50. Zarnkow et al. 2006, Zarnkow et al. 2011.

51. I've compiled this summary based on information provided in Zarnkow et al. 2006 and Zarnkow et al. 2011. See these publications for further detail.

52. Zarnkow et al. 2006: 22, Zarnkow et al. 2011: 53.

53. Olsen et al. 2012.

54. See, e.g., Bennett 2010, DeLanda 2006, Latour 2005, Tsing 2015.

55. See, e.g., Hamilakis and Jones 2017.

56. Civil 1964: 73 (lines 41, 43, 53–54).

57. Osirisnet: Tombs of Ancient Egypt (The mastaba of Ty, The Storeroom, West Wall, Registers 5 and 6), https://osirisnet.net/mastabas/ty/e_ty_04.htm.

58. The translations in Box 4.10 derive from the following sources: ᵈᵘᵍam-am (Sallaberger 1996: 98, PSD s.v. amam [JAR]), ᵍⁱba-an-du₈ (Attinger 2021: 186–187), ᵍᵉˢbuniĝ (PSD s.v. buniĝ [TROUGH]), dag-dug (PSD s.v. dagdug [POTSTANDS]), dug titab (Sallaberger 1996: 108), ᵈᵘᵍdur₂-bur₃ (Sallaberger 1996: 99, 104, PSD s.v. niĝdurburu [VAT]), ᵈᵘᵍdur₂-PU₂ (Sallaberger 1996: 100), ᵈᵘᵍellaĝ-si-sa₂ (Sallaberger 1996: 100, PSD s.v. lamdre [VAT]), ᵍᵉˢgan-nu-um kaš (PSD s.v. ganum [STAND] ~ kaš[beer]), ᵍⁱkid-titab (PSD s.v. kid [MAT] ~ titab[~beer]), ᵈᵘᵍkir₂ (Sallaberger 1996: 102), ᵈᵘᵍgakkul (Sallaberger 1996: 100, PSD s.v. gakkul [MASH-TUB]), ᵈᵘᵍlaḫtan (Sallaberger 1996: 103, PSD s.v. lahtan [VAT]), ᵈᵘᵍma-an-ḫara₄ (Sallaberger 1996: 104), ᵍⁱˢmar niĝ₂-sur-ra (PSD s.v. mar [SHOVEL] ~ niĝsur[beer]), ᵈᵘᵍnig₂-dur₂-bur₃-tur-ra (Sallaberger 1996: 104), ᵈᵘᵍša₃-gub (Sallaberger 1996: 107, PSD s.v. šaggub [CONTAINER]), udun-bappir (PSD s.v. udun [KILN] ~ bappir[~beer]), udun-titab (PSD s.v. udun [KILN] ~ titab[~beer]), ᵈᵘᵍu-gur-bala (Sallaberger 1996: 108, PSD s.v. ugurbal [JAR]), ammammu (CAD A I s.v. ammammu A), dannu (Sallaberger 1996: 111, CAD D s.v. dannu), gangannu (CAD G s.v. gangannu 1, Stol 1994: 172), ḫubūru (Sallaberger 1996: 112, CAD Ḫ s.v. ḫubūru), kakkullu (Sallaberger 1996: 112, CAD K kakkullu), kannu (Sallaberger 1996: 112, CAD K s.v. kannu A 1b, Stol 1994: 171), kirru (CAD K s.v. kirru A 2), kītu titāpu (CAD K s.v. kītu), laḫtānu (Sallaberger 1996: 112, CAD L s.v. laḫtānu), marru (CAD M I s.v. marru b 4'), muraṭṭibu (Sallaberger 1996: 114, CAD M2 s.v. muraṭṭibu), nablalu (CAD N I s.v. nablalu), namḫāru (Sallaberger 1996: 115, CAD N I s.v. namḫaru 1d), namzītu

(Sallaberger 1996: 115, CAD N I s.v. namzītu, Stol 1994: 173–174), *naprahtu* (Sallaberger 1996: 115, CAD N I s.v. naprahtu), *nartabu* (Sallaberger 1996: 115, CAD N I s.v. nartabu B), *naspû* (Sallaberger 1996: 115), *pīhu* (CAD P s.v. pīhu), *šagubbu* (CAD Š I s.v. šagubbu), *šiddatu* (Stol 1994: 172, CAD Š II s.v. šiddatu A), *tēbibtu* (CAD T I s.v. tēbibtu), *terhu* (CAD T I s.v. terhu). See also, e.g., Calderbank 2021, Civil 1964, Oppenheim 1950, Salonen 1965, 1966, Stol 1994.

59. PSD s.v. gakkul [MASH-TUB], CAD K s.v. kakkullu. For discussion, see, e.g., Civil 1964: 83–84, Sallaberger 1996: 72–75, 85–87, 100, 112, Salonen 1966: 183–194.

60. ETCSL 1.8.2.2 (Lugalbanda and the Anzud Bird).

61. After ETCSL 1.8.2.2 (Lugalbanda and the Anzud Bird), lines 16–23, but with vessel names left untranslated.

62. Civil 1964: 82–84; see also Salonen 1966: 183–194.

63. CAD H s.v. *huhāru* (KAR 94: 26); Civil 1964: 83.

64. See Calderbank 2021: 45, Note 99 and Hojlund 1990: 80, both citing Eidem 1987: 179.

65. See, e.g., Civil 1964: 83–85, Röllig 1970: 26–27, Sallaberger 1996: 72–75, 83, Salonen 1966: 183–194, Sollee 2012.

66. PSD s.v. niĝdurburu [VAT]. For discussion, see, e.g., Sallaberger 1996: 72–75, 85–87, 104, Salonen 1966: 183–194.

67. Landsberger and Balkan 1950: 246, Note 58 ("Das Idgr. bedeutet wörtlich 'mit Afterloch' . . . "), Civil 1964: 82, Gates 1988: 66–68, Sallaberger 1996: 72, PSD s.v. dug, PSD s.v. niĝ, PSD s.v. dur, PSD s.v. burud.

68. CAD M s.v. mazû, CAD N s.v. namzītu. For discussion, see, e.g., Gates 1988: 66–68, Sallaberger 1996: 83, Salonen 1966: 183–194, Stol 1994: 170–174, Waetzoldt 1971: 14–15.

69. See, e.g., Civil 1996: 144.

70. See, e.g., Civil 1964: 82, Faivre 2013: 383, Gates 1988: 66–68, Paulette 2020: 69–70, Pulhan 2000: 153–154, Sallaberger 1996: 83, Sollee 2012.

71. Perruchini et al. 2018, Zarnkow et al. 2006, Zarnkow et al. 2011.

72. Sollee 2012.

73. More specifically, Sollee (2012: 628–633) calls the open version (Type B) "Babylonian" and the closed version (Type A) "North Syrian."

74. Sollee 2012: 628–633.

75. See, e.g., Appadurai 1986.

76. Civil 1964: 82, Sallaberger 1996: 72–74, Sallaberger 2012a: 321–322, Salonen 1966: 183–194, Stol 1994: 170–174, Paulette 2020: 69–70.

77. After Civil (1964: 73). I have left the terms $^{dug}nig_2$-dur_2-bur_3 and lahtan untranslated. Civil translates $^{dug}nig_2$-dur_2-bur_3 as "fermenting vat" and lahtan as "collector vat."

78. Sallaberger 2012a: 321–322.

79. ETCSL 2.5.3.1, lines 154–156. I have included the Sumerian terms for beer types in brackets. In our earlier discussion of this text (Chapter 3), I left these

terms untranslated to highlight our uncertainty about the character of these beer types.

80. Black et al. 2010: 266, ETCSL t.2.5.3.1, line 156, Rendu Loisel 2017: 40, Sallaberger 1996: 73.

81. Rendu Loisel 2017: 40.

82. Sallaberger 1996: 73–74.

83. See, e.g., Sallaberger 1996: 57–59, 72–75, 83.

84. Civil 1964: 73 (Drinking Song, lines 49–57). Italics indicate an uncertain translation (see Civil 1964: 87, Note 57). I have reproduced Civil's translation with some small modifications. When specific vessels are referenced (e.g., gakkul, lam-sa$_2$-re, am-am), Civil included some qualifications regarding the nature of these vessels (e.g., the gakkul vat, the lam-sa$_2$-re vat, the am-am jar). I have included just the original Sumerian terms without qualification.

85. Sallaberger 1996: 57–59.

86. Nik 1 264. Sallaberger 1996: 57, Sallaberger 2013: 106, Selz 1989: 487–488, Selz 1994: 224.

87. *Nik* 1 264. After Sallaberger 2013: 106, which offers an update to his earlier and partial translation of the same text (Sallaberger 1996: 57). I have translated this new version from German into English. In the new version, Sallaberger renders lines ii, 5–6 as ge-num / ka-saman$_4$-da and offers the translation "bei Kēnum, dem vom Ölgefäßlager." In the earlier version, he does not offer a full rendering of these lines, but does indicate that the text lists the vessels that were present "bei Gi-nim, dem 'an der Öffnung des Gefäßlagers' (ka-šakan)." This shift in the Sumerian reading and translation calls into question his earlier claim that this text is a household inventory. In the discussion here, I have assumed that this interpretation still holds, but Sallaberger (pers. comm.) now thinks it more likely that the inventory is related to Kēnum's work in the jar warehouse.

88. VAS 6 182 (lines 23–25). Graziani 1986: 43–45 (Text 34), Salonen 1970: 204, Stol 1994: 172.

89. After Graziani 1986: 43–45 (Text 34, lines 23–25).

90. Stol 1994: 172.

91. BRM 1 92, lines 1–2, 6–8. Salonen 1970: 197–198, 203, Salonen 1976: 36–37 (Text 86), Stol 1994: 171–172.

92. Stolper 2005: 326.

93. Stol 1994: 173.

94. BE 9 43, CDLI P261598. Translation after Stol 1994: 173 and Tolini 2015.

95. Joannès 1992a (*Camb* 330, *Camb* 331); for another tavern inventory, see Joannès 1992b (OECT 10, 229). For a recent summary of what we know about Ishunnatu and her tavern/inn, see Podany 2022: 523–526.

96. *Camb* 330, lines 3–7. After Joannès 1992a: 48–49.

97. *Camb* 331, lines 1–5. After Joannès 1992a: 49–50. Joannès translates gazi^{sar} as celery salt (sel de céleri), but I have left the term untranslated and indicated a connection to the *kasû* plant (see Chapter 3).

98. Joannès 1992a: 50. But see Podany 2022: 525 for a cautionary note about jumping to any conclusions.
99. Joannès 1992a: 50.
100. Baker 2014.
101. HE 145, YOS 6: 62, YOS 6: 192, YOS 6: 189, YOS 7: 185. Joannès 1981.
102. In the lists, these vessels (except the *adaru*) appear in their plural forms: *dannûtu, kankannâtu, namharâtu, šiddâtu, namzâtu*. Here, I have used their singular forms.
103. Joannès 1981: 143–148; CAD B s.v. *birītu*.
104. Sillar 1996.
105. Fuller and Rowlands 2011, Haaland 2007, Wengrow 2010: 46–49.
106. See, e.g., Landsberger and Balkan 1950: 245, Oppenheim 1950: Plate 15–6, Röllig 1970: 25, https://collections.louvre.fr/en/ark:/53355/cl010170804.
107. AOD 21, CCO D 21, https://collections.louvre.fr/en/ark:/53355/cl010170804
108. See, e.g., Calderbank 2021, Perruchini et al. 2018.
109. Zarnkow et al. 2006: 9–13; Zarnkow et al. 2011: 47–49.
110. See, e.g., Gibson et al. 1981: 73–75, Pl. 45–46, 97, Martin et al. 1985: 19–37, 101–104, 178–180, Moon 1987: 182, Postgate and Moorey 1976: 151, 163–164, Zingarello 2020.
111. Zingarello 2020; see also Gibson et al. 1981: 73–75.
112. Postgate 2020.

CHAPTER 5

1. The building of Ninĝirsu's temple (Gudea Cylinders A and B), ETCSL t.2.1.7, lines 766–769; the translation "its wine-cellar" (Sumerian ne-saĝ-bi) is uncertain.
2. This fictional vignette is based on remains uncovered by archaeologists at the site of Tello, Iraq (ancient Girsu), but also includes a heavy dose of imaginative reconstruction. For a general introduction to the excavations at Tello, see, e.g., Matthews 1997, Rey 2016. For a more detailed account, see de Sarzec and Heuzey 1884–1912, Huh 2008.
3. Louvre, AO 2353, https://collections.louvre.fr/ark:/53355/cl010120705
4. Frayne 2008: 213–215 (E1.9.5.12).
5. Frayne 2008: 215–216 (E1.9.5.13).
6. PSD s.v. nin [LADY].
7. PSD s.v. e [HOUSE], ninnu [FIFTY].
8. Ashby 2017: 201–203, de Sarzec and Heuzy 1884–1912: 420–422, Frayne 2008: 213–216.
9. Ashby 2017: 201–202.
10. de Sarzec and Heuzy 1884–1912: 420–422; see also Ashby 2017: 201–2013.
11. Ashby 2017: 143–166, 198–205, Hansen 1978: 82–85, Hansen 1983: 430, Hansen 1992: 209.
12. Hansen 1970, 1973, 1978.

13. The final reports on the excavations at Tell al-Hiba are being produced as part of the Al-Hiba Publication Project (https://al-hiba.net/).

14. Ashby 2017.

15. Ashby 2017: 83–110, Hansen 1978: 72–74, Hansen 1983: 424–425, Hansen 1992: 207–208, PSD s.v. ebgal [OVAL].

16. Ashby 2017: 110–209, Hansen 1978: 79–83, Hansen 1983: 428–430, Hansen 1992: 208–210. Note that the excavators originally dated the Bagara complex to the Early Dynastic IIIb period. Ashby (2017: 211) has now reassigned several building levels, resulting in a date range of ED IIIb (2450–2350 BCE) to early Ur III (2100–2000 BCE) for the complex.

17. Ashby 2017: 203–204.

18. AO 4162; Frayne 2008: 276–279 (E1.9.9.5).

19. All of the features and artifacts described in this hypothetical, time-traveling tour were actually recovered by archaeologists. Multiple "floors" (i.e., multiple surfaces, indicating distinct episodes of activity and rebuilding) were uncovered in many of the rooms described. In some cases, these floors can be correlated with one another, from room to room. In other cases, it is more difficult. I have not attempted to draw solely from features and objects that were found on floors demonstrated to be contemporary with one another. Instead, my account draws more generally from features and objects found within the 3HB III and 4HB IVB buildings as a whole.

20. For the 3HB III building, see Ashby 2017: 115–126. For a broader discussion of the 3HB building, see Ashby 2017: 173–198.

21. Such votive objects were not recovered in association with this particular platform, but excavations at Girsu and elsewhere have uncovered caches of votive objects that had been taken out of use for one reason or another. And numerous maceheads, stone vessels, metal weapons, and inlaid objects were recovered elsewhere in the 3HB building (Ashby 2017: 185–186). So we can reasonably imagine that such objects might have been deposited on the platform described here (Ashby 2017: 295–196).

22. Ashby 2017: 187–197.

23. For the 4HB IVB building, see Ashby 2017: 145–151. For a broader discussion of the 4HB building, see Ashby 2017: 198–205.

24. Room 30 (Ashby 2017: 147).

25. Room 31 (Ashby 2017: 147–148).

26. Room 29 (Ashby 2017: 148).

27. Room 33 (Ashby 2017: 148–149).

28. Room 32 (Ashby 2017: 149).

29. This fragmentary tablet (max. height 10.87 cm, max. width 10.56 cm, max. thickness 3 cm) was excavated in Locus 32 (4HB IVB 32 in Ashby 2017) during the 1975–1976 season. It was assigned find numbers 4H-T38 and 4H

9o. See Ashby 2017: 149, 199, Plate 66, CDLI P285667, Crawford 1977: 198–200, 219–222 (4H-T38, 4H90), Hansen 1978: 83.

30. Room 35 (Ashby 2017: 150).

31. As I was finishing up this book, a tavern/restaurant was, in fact, brought to light at Tell al-Hiba (ancient Lagash) by excavators from the University of Pennsylvania, but few details have been published so far. See, e.g., Kuta 2023.

32. North Carolina Craft Brewers Guild, https://ncbeer.org/consumer/.

33. As of December 2021, https://www.homebrewersassociation.org/members hip/american-homebrewers-association/.

34. Crawford 1977: 198–199.

35. Sallaberger 2018: 172.

36. See, e.g., Beld 2002, Maekawa 1973–1974, Prentice 2010, Sallaberger 2018.

37. I'm relying here on a detailed analysis of these mašdaria deliveries by Walther Sallaberger (2018).

38. Sallaberger 2018: 178.

39. Sallaberger 2018: 195–198.

40. Pulhan 2000: 60–64, Rattenborg 2016: 112–136, Van De Mieroop 1994, Tell Leilan Project, Qarni-Lim Palace, https://leilan.yale.edu/about-project/exca vations/qarni-lim-palace.

41. Van De Mieroop 1994: 317–338.

42. Van De Mieroop 1994: 320–321 (L91–247).

43. Van De Mieroop 1994: 311–317.

44. See, e.g., Lacambre 2008, Lacambre 2009, Rattenborg 2016: 112–136.

45. See, e.g., Dalley et al. 1976, Rattenborg 2016: 112–136.

46. See, e.g., Rattenborg 2016: 118–123.

47. Pulhan 2000: 8–66, 150–167, Tell Leilan Project, Qarni-Lim Palace, https://lei lan.yale.edu/about-project/excavations/qarni-lim-palace.

48. Boivin 2018: 10, 12–14, 156–166, Dalley 2009.

49. Boivin 2018: 12–14, 158–162.

50. Boivin 2018: 158–160, CAD S s.v. *sirāšû*, CAD B s.v. *bāqilu*, Neumann 1994: 324–325, PSD s.v. lungak [BREWER], munumud [MALTSTER], Röllig 1970: 44–48, Stol 1989: 327.

51. Boivin 2018: 158–160. In a few cases, brewers also received barley (Boivin 2018: 158). In many cases, the actual title "brewer" was either omitted (but can be assumed based on other contextual clues) or replaced by a term that Boivin considers equivalent to brewer, *bēlū pīḫati ana Egipar*, *bēlū pīḫati LU$_2$ Egipar*, or *bēlū pīḫati ša Egipar* (Boivin 2018: 158).

52. For female brewers (*sirāšītu*), see CAD S s.v. sirāšītu, Salonen 1970: 192, sirašītu.

53. See, e.g., Bennett 1999, Oppenheim 1950: 12.

54. McCorriston 1997.

55. Neumann 1994: 324.

56. Neumann 1994: 325.

57. Powell 1994: 98, Stol 1989: 93. Some earlier treatments interpreted this person as a sort of flavor specialist, responsible for providing the brewer with herbs and other flavoring ingredients (Deimel 1928: 59, Röllig 1970: 48).

58. Heimpel 2009: 329.

59. Heimpel 2009.

60. Heimpel 2009: 150–156.

61. See, e.g., Arraf 2021, Felch 2013.

62. Ashby 2017: 201–203, Plate 5, de Sarzec and Heuzy 1884–1912: 420–422.

63. See, e.g., Frayne 2008: 213–216.

64. Ashby 2017: 143–166, 198–205, Hansen 1978: 82–85, Hansen 1983: 430, Hansen 1992: 209.

65. Ashby 2017: 149, 199, Plate 66, CDLI P285667, Crawford 1977: 198–200, 219–222 (4H-T38, 4H90), Hansen 1978: 83.

66. Ashby 2017: 203.

67. Here I'm relying on Ashby's recent analysis of the 4 HB Building (Ashby 2017: 143–166).

68. Pulhan 2000: 60–64, Rattenborg 2016: 112–136, Van De Mieroop 1994, Tell Leilan Project, Qarni-Lim Palace, https://leilan.yale.edu/about-project/excavations/qarni-lim-palace

69. Van De Mieroop 1994: 307–314.

70. Pulhan 2000: 18–64.

71. Pulhan 2000: 60–64.

72. Pulhan 2000: 60–64, 159.

73. Here I'm relying on Gül Pulhan's detailed analysis of the building (Pulhan 2000: 18–64, 158–159).

74. Tell Leilan Project, Qarni-Lim Palace, https://leilan.yale.edu/about-project/excavations/qarni-lim-palace

75. Pulhan 2000: 159.

76. Pulhan 2000: 159.

77. Pulhan 2000: 164, 170–173, 489–492, 507–508.

78. Dorneman 1979: 143–145, Dorneman 1981: 29–41, Gates 1988: 66–68.

79. Gates 1988: 66–68.

80. For this argument about potential distinctions in vessel function, see Gates 1988: 66–68.

81. The chart in Box 5.1 is based on Dornemann 1981: Table 1.

82. van Loon 1979: 108.

83. Grossman 2014: 50–52.

84. Calderbank 2021: 44–46, 53–59.

85. See, e.g., Faivre 2013: 386–389, Trümpelmann 1981.

86. Trümpelmann 1981.

87. Faivre 2013: 383–386, Otto 2006: 151–153, 158–160, 212–213.

88. Faivre 2013: 384–385, Otto 2006: 212–213.

89. Faivre 2013: 385–386, Otto 2006: 158–160.

90. George 1999: 78–79 (Epic Gilgamesh, standard version, Tablet X, X79–X91).

91. George 1999: 124–125 (Epic of Gilgamesh, a tablet reportedly from Sippar, Si ii 1'–Si iii 27).

92. George 1999: 78–79 (Epic Gilgamesh, standard version, Tablet X, X79–X91).

93. George 1999: 122–126 (Epic Gilgamesh, a tablet reportedly from Sippar).

94. For the discussion of these tablets, I'm relying heavily on De Graef 2018a.

95. De Graef 2018a: 91.

96. See, e.g., De Graef 2018a, DeGraef 2018b, Harris 1964, Harris 1989, Podany 2022: 291–303, Richardson 2010, Roth 1999, Stol 2016, Yoffee 2005: 113–130.

97. See, e.g., Assante 1998: 67–68, De Graef 2018a, Lafont 1999, Maul 1992, Roth 1999, van Wyk 2015.

98. De Graef 2018a: 79. For consistency, I have removed the final "m" from *nadītum* and *ugbabtum*.

99. See, e.g., Lafont 1999.

100. See, e.g., Maul 1992, Assante 1998.

101. See, e.g., Roth 1999.

102. De Graef 2018a: 94–95.

103. CAD S s.v. sābû, PSD s.v. munus [WOMAN] ~lukurunak [BREWER].

104. After Roth 1997: 101 (CH 108–109). I have replaced Roth's "woman innkeeper" with "female tavern keeper."

105. See, e.g., CAD A II s.v. astammu, CAD S I s.v. sābû, CAD S I s.v. sābû in bīt sābî, CAD S II s.v. sībi in bīt sībi, De Graef 2018a, Langlois 2016, Lion 2013, PSD s.v. ešdam [TAVERN], lukurunak [BREWER], Steinkeller 2022.

106. Langlois 2016: 115–116, Lion 2013: 394–395.

107. After Langlois 2016: 116–117; see also Charpin 1988: 21–22 and Note 40 (HG 148); for duh/*tuhhū*, see CAD T s.v. tuḫḫū, PSD s.v. duḫ [BRAN].

108. Langlois 2016: 115; see also Kraus 1977: 155 (CT 52 / AbB 7, 183; BM 81099), Lion 2013: 396.

109. Lion 2013: 396, Langlois 2016: 115.

110. Zarnkow et al. 2006, Zarnkow et al. 2011.

111. For an introduction to the site of Kültepe (ancient Kanesh) and the cuneiform archives uncovered there, see Barjamovic 2018, Larsen 2015, Michel 2017.

112. Larsen 2015: 17–26.

113. Van De Mieroop 1999: 94, after Michel 1991: vol. 2, 13–5, no. 3.

114. CCT 3 25, 15–16; LAPO 19 345, after Michel 2009: 206, my translation from French to English. In another publication (Michel 1991: 104), Michel translates "too old" (*trop vieux*), rather than "rancid" (*rance*).

115. CCT 3 20, 36–37; LAPO 19 307, Michel 2009: 206–207.

116. TC 3, 181. Michel 1997: 104.

117. VS 26 19 (LAPO 19 359; OAA 1 54, 20-26). Michel 2009: 207.

118. Michel 1997: 103–104, Michel 2009: 206–207.

119. Kt 88/k 71, Dercksen 2008: 96–99, Michel 2009: 206, Note 70. Thank you to Gojko Barjamovic for providing an updated translation of this text.

120. For the Old Assyrian period in particular, however, see Michel 1997, 2009.

121. Zarnkow et al. 2006, Zarnkow et al. 2011.

122. For a house-by-house description of the excavation results, see Otto 2006.

123. Faivre 2013: 380–381.

124. Otto 2006: 151–152.

CHAPTER 6

1. ETCSL t.6.1.01 (Proverbs: collection 1), Segment B, line 30.

2. *New York Times*, February 26, 1928.

3. For a brief introduction to Woolley's excavations at Tell al-Muqayyar, see, e.g., Zettler 1998c.

4. For a general introduction to the city of Babylon at the time of Nebuchadnezzar, see, e.g., Finkel and Seymour 2008, Dalley 2021.

5. Zettler 1998c.

6. Zettler 1998b. For an introduction to the Royal Cemetery of Ur, see, e.g., Baadsgaard et al. 2012, Baadsgaard and Zettler 2014, Dickson 2006, Hafford 2019b, Moorey 1977, Pollock 1991, 2007, Woolley 1934, Zettler and Horne 1998. If we want to precise about things, the appellation "Royal Cemetery" really only applies to the sixteen graves that Woolley dubbed "royal" in character, but in practice the term is often used to refer to the cemetery as a whole. I've opted for the less precise option here. Just bear in mind that the majority of the graves in the cemetery were not in any sense royal.

7. Zettler 1998b.

8. Woolley 1934: 73–91, Zettler 1998a, Zettler 1998b.

9. Woolley 1934: 83–90, Zettler 1998a: 35–36.

10. B16728, Pittman 1998: 77–78, Figs. 17A, 17B, Zettler 1998a: 35.

11. WA 121544 (U.10939), Pittman 1998: 78, Fig. 46b, Zettler 1998a: 35.

12. WA 121545 (U.10871), Pittman 1998: 78, Fig. 46a, Zettler 1998a: 35.

13. Weber and Zettler 1998, Woolley 1934: 83–90, Zettler 1998a: 35–36.

14. Zettler 1998a: 34–35.

15. Baadsgaard et al. 2012, Baadsgaard and Zettler 2014.

16. Hafford 2019b: 210–218, Zimmerman 1998.

17. Zettler 1998b: 23–24, Fig. 24.

18. These gender attributions are based largely on the artifactual assemblages associated with each individual (clothing, jewelry, weapons, etc.), a tricky proposition to say the least. So just bear in mind that caution is warranted here.

19. See, e.g., Vidale 2011.

20. Hafford 2019a.

21. Pittman 1998: 83.

22. 30-12-3 (U.12380), Pittman 1998: 83, Fig. 27A.

23. 30-12-2 (U.12374), Pittman 1998: 79, Fig. 19A. See also Hafford 2019b: 215–218.

24. Stein 2021: 449–50.
25. Selz 1983.
26. Romano 2015: 291.
27. Gudrun Selz has compiled a wonderful series of charts illustrating the different types of vessels depicted in banquet scenes (Selz 1983: Abb. 3, 6, 9, 12, 15, 18). Figure 6.5 shows a selection of these. For discussions of the vessel types represented, see the sections devoted to "Bankettsspezifische Antiquaria" for each time period in the main text of Selz 1983.
28. Selz offers many potential matches between illustrated and excavated examples in the footnotes within the sections devoted to "Bankettsspezifische Antiquaria" for each time period (Selz 1983). See also Barjamovic and Fairbairn (2018: 261–266) for an effort to distinguish vessels used for beer consumption vs. wine consumption in both the glyptic record (i.e., depictions on cylinder seals) and the archaeological record (i.e., excavated vessels) from the Middle Bronze Age site of Kültepe (ancient Kanesh) in Türkiye.
29. Smith et al. 2014: 242–243.
30. See, e.g., Breniquet 2009.
31. Otto 2006: 114–116, Abb. 57, 5, Otto 2012: 188–190.
32. See, e.g., Maier and Garfinkle 1992, Sparks 2014.
33. Mallowan 1937: 99–100, 151, Plate XIVc; perhaps also Mallowan 1936: 28, no. 18, Fig. 8, no. 18. One grave (G 2) published in Mallowan 1936 appears to have included a wine strainer, though it is called a copper nail (Mallowan 1936: 28, no. 18, 55, Fig. 8, no. 18). Eight graves (G 108, 122, 124, 128, 131, 141, 148, 183) published in Mallowan 1937 are said to have included a "copper wine strainer" (Mallowan 1937: 99, 118–123, Plate XIVc). McMahon 2009: 212 indicates that another one was recovered from G 3 and highlights the fact that those from G 2 and G 3 were found in vessels with pierced (rather than flat-bottomed) bases.
34. For an example of the type of vessel in which the filters were recovered, see Mallowan 1937: Fig. 21, no. 10.
35. McMahon 2009: 113, 118, 122–123, 126–127, 198, 212–213, 412–413.
36. McMahon 2009: 118, 244–245.
37. McMahon 2009: 244–245 (CB 989 and CB 990).
38. As published, there seems to be some confusion regarding the pot in which the filter tip was found. In one case, the "bronze beer strainer" (CB 985) is said to have been found in vessel CB 990 (McMahon 2009: 412, Plate 85). In another, however, it is said to have been found in CB 989, the vessel that also contained a fine ware beaker (McMahon 2009: 118).
39. McMahon 2006: 51–52, 126, Plates 65–68, 152, 157.
40. McMahon 2006: 51–52, Plate 157.
41. McMahon 2006: 124–125.
42. Kt 88/k 71, Dercksen 2008: 96–99, Michel 2009: 206, Note 70. For the term *qanû* (meaning reed, tube, pipe, etc.), see CAD Q s.v. qanû.
43. Sallaberger 2013.
44. Weber and Zettler 1998, Zettler 1998a: 35–36.

45. In addition to the examples discussed here, a bronze/copper drinking straw was recovered at Tell Leilan, in a burial, lying across the chest of the individual. See Pulhan 2000: 170–173, 493, Appendix 5, Figure 7. A Khabur ware vessel was also recovered in the burial, as well as some "beer jars," in one of which was found a copper/bronze filter tip (Pulhan 2000: 487–502, 507–508). Straw tip filters were also uncovered in a series of Middle Bronze Age burials at the site of Baghouz in Syria (du Mesnil du Buisson 1948: 51–52, Plate LVII). A copper drinking straw— 58 cm long, 7 cm in diameter, and pierced with a series of holes near one end— was recovered from Middle Bronze Age remains at the site of Kültepe, ancient Kanesh (Barjamovic and Fairbairn 2018: Fig. 5, Kulakoglu and Kangal 2010: 292, Catalog entry 300). See also Trifonov et al. 2022 for discussion of a set of (possible) metal drinking straws from the Maikop kurgan in the southern Caucasus and for an interesting argument suggesting that the filters on these straws may have been intended to mimic reeds whose ends had been cut and woven to create filters.

46. Delougaz 1967: 117 (Grave 126); for the dating of this grave, which belongs to the level Khajafeh, Houses 2 or 3, see Gibson 1982.

47. Lloyd 1967: 184–185, Plate 74, Frankfort 1934: 35–39.

48. Lloyd 1967: 183–185, Plate 36, Frankfort 1934: 23–39; for dating of the Early Northern Palace, see Gibson 1982.

49. Lloyd 1967: 184–185, Plate 74, Frankfort 1934: 35–39.

50. Jacobsen 1942: 298, no. 12.

51. Frankfort 1934: 39.

52. Frankfort 1934: 35–39; Lloyd 1967: 184–185, Plate 74.

53. Assante 2000: e.g., 2–3, 76–83, 172–173, Assante 2002: 27–36, Cooper 1972–1975

54. Assante 2000: 2–3, 76–83, Assante 2002: 27–36.

55. Assante 2000: 172–173.

56. See, e.g., Cooper 1972–1975.

57. Assante 2002: 30–36.

58. See, e.g., Pinnock 1994, Reade 1995, Renette 2014, Romano 2015, Selz 1983.

59. Pollock 2003: 27–32.

60. See, e.g., Weber and Zettler 1998.

61. Lloyd 1967: 184–185, Plate 74, Frankfort 1934: 35–39, McMahon 2006: 51–52, 124–125.

62. Müller-Karpe 1993.

63. See, e.g., Zingarello 2020. For an alternative interpretation, see Postgate 2020.

64. Glatz et al. 2019: 450–454, 461–462, Perruchini et al. 2018.

65. Calderbank 2021.

66. See, e.g., Powell 1996b.

67. ETCSL 1.1.2 (Enki and Ninmah), Michalowski 1994: 41–44.

68. One other goddess, ŠAR.ŠAR.GABA, appears between Ninmug and Ninguna, but the reading of her name is uncertain (ETCSL 1.1.2, line 35).

69. Selz 1983.

70. Pollock 2003: 21–24.

71. Stein 2021: 448–451.

72. See, e.g., Neumann 1994 for the Ur III period.

73. Van De Mieroop 1994: 317–338.

74. The reading "female carriers" is uncertain (Van De Mieroop 1994: 331).

75. Heimpel 2009.

76. Heimpel 2009: 116–121, Text 379.

77. Alster 1985, Jacobsen 1987, Sefati 1998.

78. ETCSL 1.1.1 (Enki and Ninḫursanĝa), Michalowski 1994: 42–44.

79. Assante 2000, Assante 2002.

80. CAD Ḫ s.v. ḫarīmtu. For the debate over how to translate this term and the broader role of the ḫarīmtu, see, e.g., Assante 1998, 2002, Cohen 2015, Cooper 2006, DeGrado 2018. For a discussion of the evidence from the third millennium BCE and a connection with the profession of tavern-keeper, see Steinkeller 2022.

81. See, e.g., De Graef 2018a, Lafont 1999, Maul 1992, Roth 1999, van Wyk 2015.

82. See, e.g., Neumann 1994, Heimpel 2009, Van De Mieroop 1994.

83. Pollock 2003: 21–25.

84. See, e.g., Lissarrague 1990, Lynch 2012.

85. For the term "gastro-politics," see Appadurai 1981; see also, e.g., Dietler 2006, 2020.

86. See, e.g., Michalowski 1978, Michalowski 1994: 30–31, Neumann 1994: 327.

87. Benati 2019.

88. Otto 2012: 190–191, Sallaberger 2018: 195–198.

89. Neumann 1994: 328.

90. Nik 2, 329, CDLI P122012, Gelb 1973: 74–75, Neumann 1994: 328.

91. Anawalt 1993: 17. But note that, despite this famous injunction against *pulque* consumption, there is also plenty of evidence to the contrary, including the serving of *pulque* to children (Anawalt 1993: 33–35).

CHAPTER 7

1. ETCSL t.5.6.1 (The instructions of Šuruppag), line 67.

2. ETCSL 1.3.1 (Inana and Enki).

3. ETSCL t.1.3.1 (Inana and Enki), Segment A, lines 2–7, 23–25.

4. ETSCL t.1.3.1 (Inana and Enki), Segment B, lines 12–15, Segment C, lines 7–12.

5. ETSCL t.1.3.1 (Inana and Enki), Segment C, lines 27–30.

6. ETSCL t.1.3.1 (Inana and Enki), Segment D, lines 2–5, 10–11, 14–15.

7. ETSCL t.1.3.1 (Inana and Enki), Segment F, lines 9–13.

8. ETSCL t.1.3.1 (Inana and Enki), Segment F, lines 14–20.

9. Michalowski 1994: 30–31.

10. Though it translates literally as "my king", the term "lugal mu" is now recognized to refer to "his majesty" (Michalowski 1978: 12–13, Michalowski 1994: 30, Note 14, Neumann 1994: 327, Note 65, Sallaberger 1999: 249). Michalowski 1978 (5–6, 12–13) translates the second part of this line "on the

way to the E-bappir-Šulgira." Here I have followed Neumann (1994: 327 and Note 64), who instead translates "in" the e$_2$-ŠIM (brewery) of Šulgi.

11. AUAM 73.0836. Michalowski 1978: 12–13.
12. 1 shekel = 8⅓ grams (Widell 2005: 390, Note 1).
13. Neumann 1994: 327.
14. Neumann 1994: 327.
15. Grossman and Paulette 2020, Michalowski 2006, Michalowski 2013, Sallaberger 2004, Sharlach 2005.
16. Zarnkow et al. 2006, Zarnkow et al. 2011.
17. Otto 2012: 182–184, 189–190.
18. Otto 2012: 182–185, 190.
19. Benati 2019.
20. Benati 2019: 62.
21. Calderbank 2021.
22. Calderbank 2021: 59.
23. Glatz et al. 2019, Perruchini et al. 2018.
24. Perruchini et al. 2018: 179–181, 183–188.
25. Einwag and Otto 2019, Otto 2012.
26. Otto 2012: 187–191.
27. Otto 2012: 189 (Emar VI/3, 369: 11).
28. See, e.g., Sallaberger 2012b.
29. Michalowski 1994: 29–30.
30. Brunke 2011a, Brunke 2011b, CDLI P325171, Owen and Mayr 2008: no. 981 (CUSAS 3, 981).
31. For Šu-Kabta, see, e.g., Heimpel 2009: 2–3, Owen 2013: 100.
32. Brunke 2011a: 177–179, Brunke 2011b: 43–52.
33. Brunke 2011a: 177; Brunke opts to avoid a direct translation of the terms for different types of flour (some of which are subject to heated debate) and instead offers an approximate description of each.
34. Brunke 2011a: 177; Brunke opts to avoid a direct translation of the type of flour and instead offers an approximate description of the flour.
35. nig$_2$-ar$_3$-ra saga$_{10}$; See Brunke 2011b: 40–41.
36. See Brunke 2011b: 40–41, 43.
37. Brunke 2011a: 177.
38. 83 minas (approx.) = 41.5 kg, if 1 mina = 0.5 kg (Brunke 2011b: 50, Note 30).
39. The tablet is broken here.
40. nig$_2$-ar$_3$-ra saga$_{10}$; see Brunke 2011b: 40–41, 43.
41. Brunke does not provide a translation for the section devoted to brewing ingredients. The translation provided here is based on his discussion of the text in question (Brunke 2011b: 47–49), his notational system for capacity measures (Brunke 2011b: 31–32, Note ★), and his conversion factors for expressing Mesopotamian measurements in the metric system (Brunke 2011b: 50, Note 30).
42. Brunke 2011b: 46–49.

43. See, e.g., CAD K s.v. *kispu*, Tsukimoto 1985, 2010, van der Toorn 2014. Nation (2024) argues that the *nasbītum* rite—which was etymologically linked with the brewing or drawing of beer (*sabā'um*) and involved the offering of libations—performed a similar role during the Old Assyrian period.
44. Bonatz 2014, Herrmann 2014, Pardee 2014.
45. Pardee 2014: 45.
46. It's important to mention a few qualifications here. First, there's some debate over whether or not the inscription is actually referring to wine, as interpreted by Pardee (2014). It's possible that this line actually refers to a sheep instead (Lemaire 2012). Based on some other contemporary evidence and the depiction of a cup in Katumuwa's hand, though, it's probably still reasonable to assume that wine would have been consumed. Second, it's also possible that the stele distinguishes between the presentation of six animals at the inaugural feast and the annual presentation of a single sheep.
47. Herrmann 2014: 54–56.
48. Zettler 1998b: 22.
49. Martin et al. 1985, Pollock 2015: 282–284.
50. I have followed the excavators here in dating these graves to the Early Dynastic II period, but note that there is a long-running debate over whether the Early Dynastic II period exists at all.
51. Black et al. 2004: 59 (The Death of Ur-Namma); see also ETCSL t.2.4.1.1 (The death of Ur-Namma, Ur-Namma A).
52. George 1999: 206 (The Death of Bilgames).
53. Pollock 2003: 26–27.
54. After Kleinerman and Owen 2009: 690 (s.v. e_2-lunga u_3 e_2-kikken$_2$, 3. Provisions During Construction, 428: 1–4), CDLI P324754 (CUSAS 03, 0428). As discussed in Chapter 3, it's possible that such tablets were not actually produced on-the-spot, as in my imagined scenario.
55. Heimpel 2009: 150–156.
56. For a detailed discussion of the workforce at Garšana, see Heimpel 2009: 45–156.
57. Heimpel 2009: 90–122.
58. Heimpel 2009: 105–107.
59. Bernbeck 2009: 52–55, Pollock 2003: 29–32, Pollock 2012: 160–163.
60. One recent study (Sanjurjo-Sánchez et al. 2018), for example, drawing on organic residue analysis of beveled-rim bowls from a collection of sites in the Middle Euphrates region, has suggested (as have a number of others, e.g., Goulder 2010) that beveled-rim bowls might have been used to bake and distribute bread.
61. Ebeling 1955: 178–179, Text 26, line 10, Caplice 1974: 23; see also Panayotov 2013: 291–296, line 10. I have used Caplice's English translation. He renders the full line: "He recites as follows: Ishtar, Nanay, Gazbaya help me in this matter!" Ebeling renders the same line: "also soll er sprechen: Ištar, Nanâ,

Gazbaba, hilf ihm!" Panayotov renders the line: "Thus he/she shall say: O, Ištar, Nanāya and Gazbaba, rush to aid him!"

62. After Caplice 1974: 23, lines 20–22. I have provided the term *namzītu* (written here as *nam-zi-ti*) in brackets to emphasize our uncertainty regarding the precise translation of this term (see Chapter 4), which Caplice renders as "mixing vat." See also Ebeling 1955: 181, Text 26, lines 20–22, Panayotov 2013: 295, lines 20–22.

63. See, e.g., Assante 1998: 77–82, Caplice 1974: 23–24, Ebeling 1955, Farber 1986: 448–449; Foster 1993: 898, Maul 1992: 395–396, Panayotov 2013.

64. VAT 9728, K 3464 + N 3554, BM 53655. Panayotov 2013: 285–289.

65. Here I have relied on Panayotov's translation (Panayotov 2013: 295–296).

66. Maul 1999, Veldhuis 1995/1996.

67. See, e.g., Annus 2010, Bahrani 2008, Bottéro 1992, Farber 1995, Maul 2018, Rochberg 2016.

68. VAT 9728, Maul 1992: 395–396, Panayotov 2013: 286, 288, 302–304.

69. For taverns in Mesopotamia, see, e.g., Assante 1998: 65–82, 2002, CAD A s.v. aštammu, Faivre 2013, Langlois 2016, Lion 2013, Maul 1992, PSD s.v. ešdam [tavern].

70. For the connection between taverns and sex, see, e.g., Assante 1998: 65–82, 2002.

71. I have drawn these examples from Maul 1992.

72. For this argument, see Maul 1992.

73. See, e.g., Damerow 2012: 18, Powell 1994: 91–92, 118 Stol 1989: 325, Zarnkow et al. 2006: 22, Zarnkow et al. 2011: 53.

74. See, e.g., Zarnkow et al. 2006: 22, Zarnkow et al. 2011: 53.

75. Litke 1998: 61–62, AN = ᵈA-nu-um, lines 336–345; Krebernik translates the five children as "glühende Me," "schöne Me/Krone," "schmuckvolle Rede/Krone," "Prachtsitz," and "Nicht-versiegend" (Krebernik 1998–2001: 444).

76. The CAD translates *pāšir ili u amēli* as "releaser of god and man" (CAD P s.v. paṭāru 10a). Krebernik translates the phrase as "der den Gott und den Menschen löst" (Krebernik 1998–2001: 443). To give a sense for the semantic range covered by the verb pašāru, I have included several possible readings (CAD P s.v. pašāru).

77. The discussion that follows relies heavily on several excellent treatments of the topic of inebriation in the Assyriological literature (Michalowski 1994, Rendu Loisel 2017, von Soden 1976), as well as my own recent article on the topic (Paulette 2021).

78. ETCSL 1.1.4 (Enki's Journey to Nibru), Michalowski 1994: 34–35.

79. TC 3 61, 3-6; Michel 2009: 204, Notes 48–49, Rendu Loisel 2017: 38, von Soden 1976: 318.

80. ETCSL t.5.6.1, line 126.

81. Alster 2005: 371–372, Michalowski 1981, Michalowski 1994: 39–40.

82. DPS 18, lines 40'–41'. Scurlock 2014: 176.

83. DPS 31, lines 1–2. Scurlock 2014: 227.
84. BAM 575 iii, lines 49–50. Scurlock 2014: 637, Scurlock and Andersen 2005: 361. The text then provides a remedy for the condition described: " . . . you grind together these five plants: *sikillu* seed, "lone plant" seed, *bīnu*-tamarisk seed, *amḫara* seed, (and) *maaštakal* seed. You whisk (it) into wine. If you have him drink (it) on an empty stomach, he should recover."
85. BAM 575 iii, lines 51–54. Scurlock 2014: 637, Scurlock and Andersen 2005: 363. The text then provides a remedy for the condition described: " . . . you grind together these eleven plants: *imḫur-lim*, *imḫur-ešra*, *tarmuš*, *ḫašû*-thyme, *sikillu*, "lone plant," *imbû tamtim*, *nuḫurtu*, *egemgirû* seed, *kamkādu*, (and) *elikulla*. You leave (it) out overnight in oil and beer under Gula's star. If you have him drink (it) in the morning before the sun rises (and) before anybody kisses him, he should recover."
86. DPS 7 B rev, line 13. Scurlock 2014: 62, Scurlock and Andersen 2005: 361.
87. Scurlock and Andersen 2005: 362 (15.18).
88. Scurlock and Andersen 2005: 361.
89. Scurlock and Andersen 2005: 360–363.
90. Michalowski 1994, Rendu Loisel 2017, von Soden 1976.
91. George 1999: 13–14 (Epic of Gilgamesh, Standard Version, Tablet II, P 104–105).
92. Civil 1964: 74 (Drinking song, lines 71–75). In line 74, Civil has chosen to translate gurun$_x$ (DIN) as "liquor." Given uncertainty about how to translate the term, his intention here was to indicate an alcoholic beverage in general but certainly not a distilled beverage, as often implied by the term "liquor" today.
93. Civil 1964: 68.
94. Foster 1993: 371 (Epic of Creation, lines 129–138). The term "liquor" in this translation is intended to indicate an alcoholic beverage in general but not a distilled beverage, as often implied by the term "liquor" today.
95. Paulette 2021: 7–9; see also Michalowski 1994, Rendu Loisel 2017, von Soden 1976.
96. Paulette 2021: 8.
97. Alster 1985, Jacobsen 1987, Sefati 1998.
98. After Alster 1985: 144 (SRT 31, lines 4–8). I have left the term bappir untranslated. Alster translates bappir as "beer bread" (with quotation marks to indicate uncertainty).
99. Alster 1985: 141–142 (SRT 23, lines 19–22).
100. Paulette 2021: 8–9.
101. Black et al. 2004: 225–240, ETCSL 5.3.1–5.3.7, Vanstiphout 1990, 1992.
102. Black et al. 2004: 227 (The Debate Between Sheep and Grain, lines 65–72); see also ETCSL t.5.3.2 ("The Debate Between Sheep and Grain"), lines 65–72.
103. Paulette 2021: 9.

104. ETCSL 1.1.1 (Enki and Ninhursaga), Michalowski 1994: 42–43.
105. ETCSL t.1.1.1 (Enki and Ninhursaga), line 10.
106. ETCSL t.1.1.1 (Enki and Ninhursaga), lines 65–66.
107. ETCSL t.1.1.1 (Enki and Ninhursaga), line 186.
108. ETCSL t.1.1.1 (Enki and Ninhursaga), line 276.
109. Paulette 2021: 9.
110. Michalowski 1994: 43.

EPILOGUE: REVIVING AN ANCIENT ART

1. ETCSL t.6.1.07 (Proverbs: collection 7), Segment C, lines 57–58.
2. See, e.g., Outram 2008, Shimada 2005, Skibo 2000.
3. See, e.g., McGovern 2009, McGovern 2017.
4. Civil 1991, Katz and Maytag 1991.
5. Katz and Maytag 1991: 24–27.
6. Katz and Maytag (1991: 27) argue that later Sumerian practices can serve as a "time platform" from which to ask questions about earlier periods, but they do not develop this approach in a systematic fashion.
7. Katz and Maytag 1991: 33.
8. Katz and Maytag 1991: 32.
9. Katz and Maytag 1991: 33.
10. See, e.g., Homan 2004.
11. After Steinert 2019: 133. I have provided the term *kakkullu* (written here as ka-ak-ku-li-[im]) in brackets to emphasize our uncertainty regarding the precise translation of this term (see Chapter 4), which Steinert renders as "fermenting vat." See also Foster 1993: 121 (II.19 Against constipation), Salonen 1966: 188.
12. For the *piḫu*, see, e.g., Boivin 2018: 163, note 150, Calderbank 2021: 54–55, Sallaberger 1996: 116, Van De Mieroop 1994: 338. For the *dannu*, see, e.g., Stol 1994: 167–170.
13. Zarnkow et al. 2006, Zarnkow et al. 2011, Zarnkow et al. 2020.
14. Zarnkow et al. 2011: 53.
15. Key participants included Gil Stein, Christopher Woods, Brian Zimerle, Michael Fisher, and myself on the ISAC side and Pat Conway, Joel Warger, Luke Purcell, Bridget Gauntner-Johnson, Nate Gibbon, Mark Hunger, Steve Forman, and Mike Williams on the Great Lakes Brewing Co. side.
16. ETCSL t.1.1.1: lines 17–18.
17. Delougaz 1952: e.g., Plate 190 (D.201.201a, D.201.201b), Plate 194 (D.555.340, D.555.510b), Plate 195 (D.565.310).
18. Although the "braziers" worked well as portable burners in our experiments, a recent visit to the ISAC museum has made me question our interpretation.

On display was one of these braziers from Tell Asmar (dating to the Akkadian period) and, beside it, a small clay model (dating to the third millennium BCE) showing a group of rams feeding from what appears to be a brazier. The display interprets these artifacts not as braziers but as compartmented troughs for feeding livestock. These "braziers" demonstrate a key point about experimental archaeology: the fact that an artifact functioned well in a particular experiment cannot generally be taken, on its own, as proof that the artifact was actually used in that particular fashion in the past.

19. ETCSL 2.5.3.1 (A *šir-namursaĝa* to Ninsiana for Iddin-Dagan, Iddin-Dagan A), lines 154–156.

20. Civil 1964: 73 (Hymn to Ninkasi), lines 46, 48.

21. Civil 1964: 71, 74 (Drinking Song), line 66. I've normalized the Sumerian here to make it easier to read. The original text reads ᵈnin-ka-si za-da ḫu-mu-u₈-da-an-ti.

References

Adams, R. McC. 1981. *Heartland of cities: Surveys of ancient settlement and land use on the central floodplain of the Euphrates.* University of Chicago Press, Chicago.

Adams, R. McC. 2001. Complexity in archaic states. *Journal of Anthropological Archaeology* 20: 345–360.

Adams, R. McC. 2008. An interdisciplinary overview of a Mesopotamian city and its hinterlands. *Cuneiform Digital Library Journal* 2008, 1: 1–23.

Adams, R. McC. 2012. Ancient Mesopotamian urbanism and blurred disciplinary boundaries. *Annual Review of Anthropology* 41: 1–20.

Akkermans, Peter M. M. G., and Glenn M. Schwartz. 2003. *The archaeology of Syria: From complex hunter-gatherers to early urban societies (c. 16,000–300 BC).* Cambridge University Press, Cambridge.

Algaze, G. 2005. The Sumerian takeoff. *Structure and Dynamics* 1, 1: 1–43.

Algaze, G. 2008. *Ancient Mesopotamia at the dawn of civilization: The evolution of an urban landscape.* University of Chicago Press, Chicago.

Algaze, G. 2013. The end of prehistory and the Uruk period. In *The Sumerian world,* ed. H. Crawford, 68–94. Routledge, London.

Algaze, G. 2018. Entropic cities: The paradox of urbanism in ancient Mesopotamia. *Current Anthropology* 59, 1: 23–54.

Al Quntar, S., L. Khaidi, and J. Ur. 2012. Proto-urbanism in the late fifth millennium BC: Survey and excavations at Khirbet al-Fakhar (Hamoukar), northeast Syria. *Paléorient* 37, 2: 151–175.

Alster, B. 1985. Sumerian love songs. *Revue d'Assyriologie et d'archéologie orientale* 79, 2: 127–159.

Alster, B. 2005. *Wisdom of ancient Sumer.* CDL Press, Bethesda.

Anawalt, P. R. 1993. Rabbits, *pulque,* and drunkenness: A study of ambivalence in Aztec society. In *Current topics in Aztec studies: Essays in honor of Dr. H. B. Nicholson,* eds. A. Cordy-Collins and D. Sharon, 17–38. San Diego Museum Papers 30. San Diego Museum of Man, San Diego.

Annunziata, R. 2018. From freedom to slavery: Work and words at the House of Prisoners of War in the Old Babylonian Period. *Journal of Global Slavery* 3: 41–67.

Annus, A. (ed.). 2010. *Divination and interpretation of signs in the ancient world.* Oriental Institute Seminars 6. The Oriental Institute of the University of Chicago, Chicago.

Appadurai, A. 1981. Gastro-politics in Hindu South Asia. *American Ethnologist* 8, 3: 494–511.

Appadurai, A. 1986. *The social life of things: Commodities in cultural perspective.* Cambridge University Press, Cambridge.

Arraf, J. 2021. Iraq reclaims 17,000 looted artifacts, its biggest-ever repatriation. *New York Times,* August 3, 2021 (updated August 16, 2021). https://www.nytimes.com/2021/08/03/world/middleeast/iraq-looted-artifacts-return.html (accessed March 7, 2023).

Arthur, J. W. 2022. *Beer: A global journey through the past and present.* Oxford University Press, Oxford.

Ashby, D. P. 2017. *Late third millennium BCE religious architecture at Tell Al-Hiba, ancient Lagash.* PhD dissertation, University of Pennsylvania.

Assante, J. 1998. The kar.kid/ḫarimtu, prostitute or single woman? A reconsideration of the evidence. *Ugarit Forschungen* 30: 5–96.

Assante, J. 2000. *The erotic reliefs of ancient Mesopotamia.* PhD dissertation, Columbia University.

Assante, J. 2002. Sex, magic, and the liminal body in the erotic art and texts of the Old Babylonian period. In *Sex and gender in the ancient Near East: Proceedings of the 47th Rencontre Assyriologique Internationale, Helsinki, July 2–6, 2001,* eds. S. Parpola and R. M. Whiting, 27–52. Compte rendu de la Rencontre Assyriologique Internationale 47. Helsinki.

Baadsgaard, A., J. Monge, and R. L. Zettler. 2012. Bludgeoned, burned, and beautified: Reevaluating mortuary practices in the Royal Cemetery of Ur. In *Sacred killing: The archaeology of sacrifice in the ancient Near East,* eds. A. M. Porter and G. M. Schwartz, 125–158. Eisenbrauns, Winona Lake.

Baadsgaard, A., and R. L. Zettler. 2014. Royal funerals and ruling elites at Early Dynastic Ur. In *Contextualizing grave inventories in the ancient Near East,* eds. P. Pfälzner, H. Niehr, E. Pernicka, S. Lange, and T. Köster, 105–121. Qatna Studien Supplementa 3. Harrassowitz Verlag, Wiesbaden.

Bahrani, Z. 1998. Conjuring Mesopotamia: Imaginative geography and a world past. In *Archaeology under fire: Nationalism, politics, and heritage in the eastern Mediterranean and Middle East,* ed. L. Meskell, 159–174. Routledge, London.

Bahrani, Z. 2008. *Rituals of war: The body and violence in Mesopotamia.* Zone Books, New York.

Bahrani, Z. 2017. *Art of Mesopotamia.* Thames & Hudson, New York.

Baines, J., and N. Yoffee. 1998. Order, legitimacy, and wealth in ancient Egypt and Mesopotamia. In *Archaic states,* eds. G. M. Feinman and J. Marcus, 199–260. School of American Research Press, Santa Fe.

Baker, H. D. 2011. From street altar to palace: Reading the built environment of urban Babylonia. In *The Oxford Handbook of Cuneiform Culture,* ed K. Radner and E. Robson, 533–552. Oxford University Press, Oxford.

Baker, H. D. 2014. Temple and city in Hellenistic Uruk: Sacred space and the transformation of Late Babylonian society. In *Redefining the Sacred: Religious Architecture and Text in the Near East and Egypt 1000 BC–AD 300,* eds. E. Frood and R. Raja, 183–208. Brepols, Turnhout.

Barghini, A. 2020. Ethnohistoric review of amylolytic fermentation in Amazonia. *Boletim do Museu Paraense Emílio Goeldi. Ciências Humanas* 15, 2: 1–23.

Barjamovic, G. 2004. Civic institutions and self-government in southern Mesopotamia in the mid-first millennium BC. In *Assyria and Beyond: Studies Presented to Mogens Trolle Larsen*, ed. J. G. Dercksen, 47–98. PIHANS 100. Nederlands Instituut voor het Nabije Oosten, Leiden.

Barjamovic, G. 2018. Traders and travelers: Assyrians in Anatolia (2000–1600 BC). In *The Assyrians: Kingdom of the god Aššur from Tigris to Taurus*, eds. K. Köroğlu and S. Adalı, 26–53. Yapı Kredi, Istanbul.

Barjamovic, G., and A. Fairbairn. 2018. Anatolian wine in the Middle Bronze Age. *Die Welt des Orients* 48: 249–284.

Barjamovic, G., P. J. Gonzalez, C. Graham, A. W. Lassen, N. Nasrallah, and P. M. Sörensen. 2019. Food in ancient Mesopotamia: Cooking the Yale Babylonian culinary recipes. In *Ancient Mesopotamia speaks: Highlights of the Yale Babylonian Collection*, eds. A. W. Lassen, E. Frahm, and K. Wagensonner, 109–125. Peabody Museum of Natural History, Yale University, New Haven.

Barjamovic, G., and N. Yoffee. 2020. Working at home, traveling abroad: Old Assyrian trade and archaeological theory. In *Working at home in the ancient Near East*, eds. J. Mas and P. Notizia, 107–116. Archaeopress, Oxford.

Bartash, V. 2018. Sumerian "child." *Journal of Cuneiform Studies* 70: 3–25.

Bartash, V. 2020. Coerced human mobility and elite social networks in Early Dynastic Iraq and Iran. *Journal of Ancient Near Eastern History* 7, 1: 25–57.

Bartash, V. 2022. Gudea's Iranian slaves: An anatomy of transregional forced mobility. *Iraq* 84: 25–42.

Beld, S. G. 2002. *The queen of Lagash: Ritual economy in a Sumerian state.* PhD dissertation, University of Michigan.

Belliard, F. 2011. Brewing sorghum beer in Burkina Faso: A study in food technology from the perspective of anthropological linguistics. In *Liquid bread: Beer and brewing in cross-cultural perspective*, eds. W. Schiefenhövel and H. Macbeth (eds), 171–181. Berghahn Books, New York.

Benati, G. 2019. Shaping social dynamics in early 3rd millennium BC Mesopotamia: Solid-footed goblets and the politics of drinking. In *Pearls of the past: Studies on Near Eastern art and archaeology in honour of Frances Pinnock*, eds. M. D'Andrea, M. G. Micale, D. Nadali, S. Pizzimenti, and A. Vacca, 53–76. Zaphon, Münster.

Bendixsen, D. P., N. Gettle, C. Gilchrist, Z. Zhang, R. Stelkens. 2021. Genomic evidence of an ancient East Asian divergence event in wild Saccharomyces cerevisiae. *Genome Biology and Evolution* 13, 2: 1–12.

Bennett, J. 2010. *Vibrant matter: A political ecology of things.* Duke University Press, Durham.

Bennett, J. M. 1999. *Ale, beer, and brewsters in England: Women's work in a changing world, 1300–1600.* Oxford University Press, Oxford.

Bergerbrant, S. 2019. Revisiting the "Egtved girl." In *Arkeologi og kulturhistorie fra norskekysten til Østersjøen: Festskrift til professor Birgitta Berglund*, eds. R. Berge and M. M. Henriksen, 19–39. NTNU Vitenskapsmuseet, Institutt for arkeologi og kulturhistorie og Museumsforlaget, Trondheim.

Bernbeck, R. 2009. Class conflict in ancient Mesopotamia: Between knowledge of history and historicizing knowledge. *Anthropology of the Middle East* 4, 1: 33–64.

Black, J., G. Cunningham, E. Robson, and G. Zólyomi. 2004. *The literature of ancient Sumer.* Oxford University Press, Oxford.

Blasco, A., M. Edo, and M. J. Villalba. 2008. Evidencias de procesado y consumo de cerveza en la cueva de Can Sadurní (Begues, Barcelona) durante la prehistoria. In *IV Congreso del Neolítico Peninsular*,Volume 1, eds. M. S. Hernández Pérez, J. A. Soler Díaz, and J. A. López Padilla, 428–431. Museo Arqueológico de Alicante, Alicante.

Boivin, O. 2018. *The First Dynasty of the Sealand in Mesopotamia.* Studies in Ancient Near Eastern Records 20. De Gruyter, Berlin.

Bolger, D., and R. P. Wright. 2013. Gender in Southwest Asian prehistory. In *A companion to gender prehistory*, ed. D. Bolger, 372–394. Wiley-Blackwell, Oxford.

Bonatz, D. 2014. Katumuwa's banquet scene. In *In remembrance of me: Feasting with the dead in the ancient Middle East*, eds. V. R. Herrmann and D. Schloen, 39–44. Oriental Institute Museum Publications 37. The Oriental Institute of the University of Chicago, Chicago.

Bongenaar, A. C. V. M. (ed.). 2000. *Interdependency of institutions and private entrepreneurs.* MOS Studies 2. Nederlands Historisch-Archaeologisch Instituut te Istanbul, Istanbul. Nederlands Instituut voor het Nabije Oosten, Leiden.

Bottéro, J. 1992. *Writing, reasoning, and the gods.* University of Chicago Press, Chicago.

Bottéro, J. 1995. *Textes culinaires Mésopotamiens: Mesopotamian culinary texts.* Eisenbrauns, Winona Lake.

Bottéro, J. 2004. *The oldest cuisine in the world: Cooking in Mesopotamia.* Trans. T. L. Fagan. The University of Chicago Press, Chicago.

Bouby, L., P. Boissinot, and P. Marinval. 2011. Never mind the bottle: Archaeobotanical evidence of beer-brewing in Mediterranean France and the consumption of alcoholic beverages during the 5th century BC. *Human Ecology* 39: 351–360.

Braidwood, R. J., J. D. Sauer, H. Helbaek, P. C. Mangelsdorf, H. C. Cutler, C. S. Coon, R. Linton, J, Steward, and A. L. Oppenheim. 1953. Did man once live by beer alone? *American Anthropologist*, New Series 55, 4: 515–526.

Breniquet, C. 2009. Buvait-on de la bière au chalumeau en Mésopotamie à l'époque protodynastique? *Cahier des thèmes transversaux ArScAn* 9: 359–365.

Brunke, H. 2011a. Feasts for the living, the dead, and the gods. In *The Oxford Handbook of Cuneiform Culture*, eds. K. Radner and E. Robson, 167–183. Oxford University Press, Oxford.

Brunke, H. 2011b. Food in the Garšana texts. In *Garšana studies*, ed. D. I. Owen, 31–65. Cornell University Studies in Assyriology and Sumerology 6. CDL Press, Bethesda.

Calderbank, D. 2021. What's in a vessel's name? A relational text-object approach to the uses of Mesopotamian pottery. *American Journal of Archaeology* 125, 1: 29–64.

Caplice, R. 1974. *The Akkadian namburbu texts: An introduction.* Sources from the ancient Near East 1, 1. Undena Publications, Malibu.

Charpin, D. 1988. Sippar: Deux villes jumelles. *Revue d'Assyriologie et d'archéologie orientale* 82, 1: 13–32.

Childe, V. G. 1950. The urban revolution. *The Town Planning Review* 21, 1: 3–17.

Childe, V. G. 1951. *Man makes himself.* Revised edition. New American Library, New York.

Civil, M. 1964. A hymn to the beer goddess and a drinking song. In *Studies Presented to A. Leo Oppenheim, June 7, 1964*, 67–89. Oriental Institute of the University of Chicago, Chicago.

Civil, M. 1991. Modern brewers recreate ancient beer. *The Oriental Institute, News & Notes* 132: 1–2.

Civil, M. 1996. HAR-ra = *hubullu: Tablet X* = *karpatu*. Mesopotamian History and Environment, Memoirs 3. University of Ghent, Ghent.

Civil, M. 2005. Nos 55–60: Texts from the series Urra = *ḫubullu*. In *Literary and scholastic texts of the first millennium B.C.*, eds. I. Spar and W. G. Lambert, 230–244. Cuneiform Texts in the Metropolitan Museum of Art II. Metropolitan Museum of Art, New York.

Cohen, Y. 2015. The wages of a prostitute: Two instructions from the wisdom composition "Hear the Advice" and an excursus on Ezekiel 16, 33. *Semitica* 57: 43–55.

Cooper, J. S. 1972–1975. Heilige Hochzeit. In *Reallexikon der Assyriologie und Vorderasiatischen Archäologie* 7 (Ḫa-a-a – Hystaspes), ed. D. O. Edzard, 259–269. Walter de Gruyter, Berlin.

Cooper, J. S. 2004. Babylonian beginnings: The origin of the cuneiform writing system in comparative perspective. In *The first writing: Script invention as history and process*, ed. S. D. Houston, 71–99. Cambridge University Press, Cambridge.

Cooper, J. S. 2006. Prostitution. In *Reallexikon der Assyriologie und Vorderasiatischen Archäologie* 11 (Prinz, Prinzessin–Qaṭṭara), ed. E. Ebeling and B. Meissner, 12–21. Walter de Gruyter, Berlin.

Cooper, L. 2010. States of hegemony: Early forms of political control in Syria during the third millennium BC. In *Development of pre-state communities in the ancient Near East*, eds. D. Bolger and L. C. Maguire, 87–94. Oxbow Books, Oxford.

Craig, O. E., H. Saul, and C. Spiteri. 2020. Residue analysis. In *Archaeological Science: An Introduction*, eds. M. Richards and K. Britton, 70–98. Cambridge University Press, Cambridge.

Crawford, V. E. 1977. Inscriptions from Lagash, season four, 1975–76. *Journal of Cuneiform Studies* 29, 4: 189–222.

Crewe, L. and I. Hill. 2012. Finding beer in the archaeological record: A case study from Kissonerga-*Skalia* on Bronze Age Cyprus. *Levant* 44, 2: 205–237.

Crüseman, N., M. van Ess, M. Hilgert, and B. Salje (eds.). 2019. *Uruk: First city of the ancient world*, ed. and trans. T. Potts. The J. Paul Getty Museum, Los Angeles.

Dalley, S. 1989. *Myths from Mesopotamia: Creation, the Flood, Gilgamesh, and others.* Oxford University Press, Oxford.

Dalley, S. 2009. *Babylonian tablets from the First Sealand Dynasty in the Schøyen collection.* Cornell University Studies in Assyriology and Sumerology 9. CDL Press, Bethesda.

Dalley, S. 2021. *The city of Babylon: A history, c. 2000 BC–AD 116.* Cambridge University Press, Cambridge.

Dalley, S., C. B. F. Walker, and J. D. Hawkins. 1976. *The Old Babylonian Texts from Tell Al-Rimah.* British School of Archaeology in Iraq, London.

Damerow, P. 1996. Food production and social status as documented in proto-cuneiform texts. In *Food and the status quest: An interdisciplinary perspective*, eds. P. Wiessner and W. Schiefenhövel, 149–169. Berghahn Books, Providence.

Damerow, P. 2012. Sumerian beer: The origins of brewing technology in ancient Mesopotamia. *Cuneiform Digital Library Journal* 2012, 2: 1–20.

Damerow, P., and R. K. Englund. 1987. *Die Zahlzeichensysteme der archaischen Texte aus Uruk.* Archaische Texte aus Uruk 2. Mann Verlag, Berlin.

De Graef, K. 2018a. *In taberna quando sumus:* On taverns, *nadītum* women, and the *gagûm* in Old Babylonian Sippar. In *Gender and methodology in the ancient Near East: Approaches from Assyriology and beyond*, eds. S. L. Budin, M. Cifarelli, A. Garcia-Ventura, and A. Millet, 77–115. Barcino Monographica Orientalia 10. Edicions de la Universitat Barcelona, Barcelona.

De Graef, K. 2018b. Puppets on a string? On female agency in Old Babylonian economy. In *Studying gender in the ancient Near East*, eds. S. Svärd and A. Garcia-Ventura, 133–156. Eisenbrauns, University Park.

DeGrado, J. 2018. The *qdesha* in Hosea 4:14: Putting the (myth of the) sacred prostitute to bed. *Vetus Testamentum* 68: 1–33.

Deimel, A. 1928. Getreidelieferungs(gar)-Listen aus der Zeit Urukaginas und seiner beiden Vorgänger. *Orientalia* 32: 1–83.

Deimel, A. 1931. *Sumerische Tempelwirtschaft zur Zeit Urukaginas und seiner Vorgänger.* Analecta Orientalia 2. Pontificio Istituto Biblico, Rome.

DeLanda, M. 2006. *A new philosophy of society: Assemblage theory and social complexity.* Continuum, London.

Delnero, P. 2019. Archives and libraries in the Old Babylonian period, c. 1900–1600 BCE. In *Libraries before Alexandria: Ancient Near Eastern traditions*, eds. K. Ryholt and G. Barjamovic, 168–191. Oxford University Press, Oxford.

Delougaz, P. 1952. *Pottery from the Diyala region.* Oriental Institute Publications 63. The University of Chicago Press, Chicago.

Delougaz, P. 1967. Khafajah. In *Private houses and graves in the Diyala region*, eds. P. Delougaz, H. D. Hill, and S. Lloyd, 1–142. Oriental Institute Publications 88. The University of Chicago Press, Chicago.

Dercksen, J. G. 2008. Subsistence, surplus, and the market for grain and meat at ancient Kanesh. *Altorientalische Forschungen* 35: 86–102.

de Sarzec, E., and L. Heuzey. 1884–191.2 *Découverte en Chaldée.* Ernest Leroux, Paris.

Diakonoff, I. 1982. The structure of Near Eastern society before the middle of the 2nd millennium B.C. *Oikumene* 3: 7–100.

Dickson, B. 2006. Public transcripts expressed in theatres of cruelty: The Royal Graves at Ur in Mesopotamia. *Cambridge Archaeological Journal* 16, 2: 123–144.

Dietler, M. 2006. Alcohol: Anthropological/archaeological perspectives. *Annual Review of Anthropology* 35: 229–249.

Dietler, M. 2020. Alcohol as embodied material culture: Anthropological reflections on the deep entanglement of humans and alcohol. In *Alcohol and humans: A long and social affair*, eds. K. J. Hockings and R. Dunbar, 115–129. Oxford University Press, Oxford.

Dietler, M., and I. Herbich. 2001. Feasts and labor mobilization: Dissecting a fundamental economic practice. In *Feasts: Archaeological and ethnographic perspectives on food, politics, and power*, eds. M. Dietler and B. Hayden, 240–264. Smithsonian Institution Press, Washington.

Dietrich, O. 2023. Shamanism at Early Neolithic Göbekli Tepe, southeastern Turkey: Methodological contributions to an archaeology of belief. *Praehistorische Zeitschrift* 2023: 1–48.

Dietrich, L., E. Götting-Martin, J. Hertzog, P. Schmitt-Kopplin, P. E. McGovern, G. R. Hall, W. C. Petersen, M. Zarnkow, M. Hutzler, F. Jacob, C. Ullman, J. Notroff, M. Ulbrich, E. Flöter, J. Heeb, J. Meister, and O. Dietrich. 2020. Investigating the function of Pre-Pottery Neolithic stone troughs from Göbekli Tepe—an integrated approach. *Journal of Archaeological Science: Reports* 34: 1–20.

Dietrich, O., and L. Dietrich. 2020. Rituals and feasting as incentives for cooperative action at Early Neolithic Göbekli Tepe. In *Alcohol and humans: A long and social affair*, eds. K. J. Hockings and R. Dunbar, 93–114. Oxford University Press, Oxford.

Dietrich, O., M. Heun, J. Notroff, K. Schmidt, and M. Zarnkow. 2012. The role of cult and feasting in the emergence of Neolithic communities: New evidence from Göbekli Tepe, southeastern Turkey. *Antiquity* 86: 674–695.

Dietrich, O., J. Notroff, and K. Schmidt. 2017. Feasting, social complexity and the emergence of the Early Neolithic of Upper Mesopotamia: A view from Göbekli Tepe. In *Feast, famine, or fighting? Multiple pathways to social complexity*, eds. R. J. Chacon and R. G. Mendoza, 91–132. Springer, New York.

Dirar, H. 1993. *The indigenous fermented foods of the Sudan: A study in African food and nutrition*. CAB International, Wallingford.

Dornbusch, H. 2012. Shilling system. In *The Oxford companion to beer*, ed. G. Oliver, 730. Oxford University Press, Oxford.

Dorneman, R. H. 1979. Tell Hadidi: A millennium of Bronze Age city occupation. In *Excavation reports from the Tabqa Dam Project—Euphrates valley, Syria*, ed. D. N. Freedman, 113–151. Annual of the American Schools of Oriental Research 44. American Schools of Oriental Research, Cambridge.

Dorneman, R. H. 1981. The Late Bronze Age pottery tradition at Tell Hadidi, Syria. *Bulletin of the American Schools of Oriental Research* 241: 29–47.

du Mesnil du Buisson, le Comte. 1948. *Baghouz, l'ancienne Corsôtê: le tell archaïque et la nécropole de l'âge du bronze*. Brill, Leiden.

Ebeling, E. 1955. Beiträge zur Kenntnis der Beschwörungsserie Namburbi. *Revue d'Assyriologie et d'archéologie orientale* 49, 4: 178–192.

Eidem, J. 1987. The inscribed pottery. In *Failaka/Dilmun: The second millennium settlements, Vol. 2: The Bronze Age pottery*, ed. F. Højlund, 179–80. Jutland Archaeology Society Publications 17, 2. Jutland Archaeological Society, Aarhus.

Einwag, B., and A. Otto 2019. The inventory of the temple at Tall Bazi. In *Ancient Near Eastern temple inventories in the third and second millennia BCE: Integrating archaeological, textual, and visual sources*, eds. J. M. Evans and E. Roßberger, 159–174. Münchener Abhandlungen zum Alten Orient, PeWe-Verlag, Gladbeck.

Eitam, D. 2019. " . . . Yo-ho-ho, and a bottle of [beer]!" (R.L. Stevenson) no beer but rather cereal-Food. Commentary: Liu et al. 2018. *Journal of Archaeological Science: Reports* 28: 1–5.

Ellison, R. 1984. Methods of Food preparation in Mesopotamia (c. 3000–600 BC). *Journal of the Economic and Social History of the Orient* 27: 89–98.

Emberling, G. 2015 Mesopotamian cities and urban process, 3500–1600 BCE. In *The Cambridge world history, Vol. III: Early cities in comparative perspective, 4000 BCE–1200 CE*, ed. N. Yoffee, 253–278. Cambridge University Press, Cambridge.

Englund, R. K. 1995. Regulating dairy productivity in the Ur III period. *Orientalia, Nova Series* 64, 4: 377–429.

Englund, R. K. 1998. Texts from the Late Uruk period. In *Mesopotamien: Späturuk-Zeit und Frühdynastische Zeit*, eds. J. Bauer, R. K. Englund, and M. Krebernik, 15–233. Orbis Biblicus et Orientalis 160/1. Universitätsverlag Freiburg Schweiz, Freiburg. Vandenhoeck and Ruprecht, Göttingen.

Englund, R. K. 2001. Grain accounting practices in archaic Mesopotamia. In *Changing views on ancient Near Eastern mathematics*, eds. J. Høyrup and P. Damerow, 1–35. Berliner Beiträge zum vorderen Orient 19. Dietrich Reimer Verlag, Berlin.

Englund, R. K. 2004. Proto-cuneiform account-books and journals. In *Creating economic order: Record-keeping, standardization, and the development of accounting in the ancient Near East*, eds. M. Hudson and C. Wunsch, 23-46. CDL Press: Bethesda, Maryland.

Evershed, R. P. 2008. Organic residue analysis in archaeology: The archaeological biomarker revolution. *Archaeometry* 50, 6: 895–924.

Faivre, L. 2013. La bière de la brasserie au cabaret: Approche archéologique. In *L'alimentation dans l'Orient ancien: Cuisines et dependences*, ed. C. Michel, 375–392. Cahier des thèmes transversaux ArScAn 11. ArScAn, Nanterre.

Farber, W. 1986. Associative magic: Some rituals, word plays, and philology. *Journal of the American Oriental Society* 106, 3: 447–449.

Farber, W. 1995. Witchcraft, magic, and divination in ancient Mesopotamia. In *Civilizations of the Ancient Near East*, vol. 3, ed. J. M. Sasson, 1895–1909. Charles Scriber's Sons, New York.

Felch, J. 2013. Cornell to return 10,000 ancient tablets to Iraq. *Los Angeles Times*, November 3, 2013. https://www.latimes.com/entertainment/arts/culture/la-et-cm-iraq-tablets-cornell-university-20131103-story.html (accessed March 7, 2023).

Finkel, I. and J. Taylor. 2015. *Cuneiform*. The British Museum, London.

Finkel, I. L. and M. J. Seymour. 2008. *Babylon*. Oxford University Press, Oxford.

Fitzpatrick, S. M. (ed.). 2018. *Ancient psychoactive substances*. University Press of Florida, Gainesville.

Fleming, D. 2004. *Democracy's ancient ancestors: Mari and early collective governance.* Cambridge University Press, Cambridge.

Foster, B. R. 1982. *Umma in the Sargonic period.* Memoirs of the Connecticut Academy of Arts and Sciences 20. Archon Books, Hamden.

Foster, B. R. 1993. *Before the muses: An anthology of Akkadian literature.* CDL Press, Bethesda.

Foster, B. R. 1995. Social reform in ancient Mesopotamia. In *Social justice in the ancient world,* eds. K. D. Irani and M. Silver, 165–177. Greenwood Press, Westport.

Foster, B. R. 2019. *The Epic of Gilgamesh.* Second edition. W. W. Norton, New York.

Foster, B. R., and K. P. Foster. 2011. *Civilizations of ancient Iraq.* Princeton University Press, Princeton.

Frankfort, H. 1934. *Iraq excavations of the Oriental Institute 1932/33: Third preliminary report of the Iraq Expedition.* Oriental Institute Communications 17. The University of Chicago Press, Chicago.

Frayne, D. R. 2008. *Presargonic (2700–2350 BC).* Royal Inscriptions of Mesopotamia Early Periods 1. University of Toronto Press, Toronto.

Frayne, D., and J. H. Stuckey. 2021. *A handbook of gods and goddesses in the ancient Near East: Three thousand deities of Anatolia, Syria, Israel, Sumer, Babylonia, and Elam.* Pennsylvania State University Press, University Park.

Frei, K. M., U. Mannering, K. Kristiansen, M. E. Allentoft, A. S. Wilson, I. Skals, S. Tridico, M. L. Nosch, E. Willerslev, L. Clarke, and R. Frei. 2015. Tracing the dynamic life story of a Bronze Age female. *Scientific Reports* 5, 10431: 1–7.

Fuller, D. Q., and M. Rowlands. 2011. Ingestion and food technologies: Maintaining differences over the long-term in West, South, and East Asia. In *Interweaving worlds: Systemic interactions in Eurasia, 7th to 1st millennia BC,* eds. T. C. Wilkinson, S. Sherratt, and J. Bennet, 37–60. Oxbow Books, Oxford.

Gallone, B., J. Steensels, T. Prahl, L. Soriaga, V. Saels, B. Herrera-Malaver, A. Merlevede, M. Roncoroni, K. Voordeckers, L. Miraglia, and C. Teiling. 2016. Domestication and divergence of *Saccharomyces cerevisiae* beer yeasts. *Cell* 166, 6: 1397–1410.

Garcia-Ventura, A. (ed.). 2018. *What's in a name? Terminology related to the work force and job categories in the ancient Near East.* Alter Orient und Altes Testament 440. Ugarit-Verlag, Münster.

Garfinkle, S. J. 2005. Public versus private in the ancient Near East. In *A Companion to the ancient Near East,* ed. D. C. Snell, 384–396. Blackwell, Oxford.

Garfinkle, S. J. 2008. Was the Ur III state bureaucratic? Patrimonialism and bureaucracy in the Ur III period. In *The growth of an early state in Mesopotamia: Studies in Ur III administration,* eds. S. J. Garfinkle and J. C. Johnson, 55–61. Biblioteca Próximo Oriente Antiguo 5. Consejo Superior de Investigaciones Cientificas, Madrid.

Garfinkle, S. J. 2013. The Third Dynasty of Ur and the limits of state power in early Mesopotamia. In *From the 21st century B.C. to the 21st century A.D.: Proceedings of the International Conference on Sumerian Studies held in Madrid 22–24 July 2010,* eds. S. Garfinkle and M. Molina, 153–167. Eisenbrauns, Winona Lake, IN.

Gates, M.-H. 1988. Dialogues between ancient Near Eastern texts and the archaeological record: Test cases from Bronze Age Syria. *Bulletin of the American Schools of Oriental Research* 270: 63–91.

Gelb, I. J. 1971. On the alleged temple and state economies in ancient Mesopotamia. In *Studi in Onore di Edoardo Volterra*, Vol. 6, ed. D. O. Edzard, 137–154. Giuffrè, Milan.

Gelb, I. J. 1972. From freedom to slavery. In *Gesellschaftsklassen im Alten Zweistromland und in den angrenzenden Gebieten*, ed. D. O. Edzard, 81–92. Rencontre Assyriologique Internationale 18. Verlag der Bayerischen Akademie der Wissenschaften, München.

Gelb, I. J. 1973. Prisoners of war in early Mesopotamia. *Journal of Near Eastern Studies* 32, 1/2: 70–98

Geller, M. J. 1982. A recipe against ŠU-GIDIM. *Archiv für Orientforschung* 19: 192–197.

George, A. R. 1992. *Babylonian topographical texts*. Orientalia Lovaniensia Analecta 40. Departement Oriëntalistiek, Leuven. Uitgeverij Peeters, Leuven.

George, A. R. 1993. *House most high: The temples of ancient Mesopotamia*. Eisenbrauns, Winona Lake.

George, A. R. 2003. *The Babylonian Gilgamesh Epic: Introduction, critical edition, and cuneiform texts*. Oxford University Press, Oxford.

George, A. (trans.). 1999. *The Epic of Gilgamesh*. Penguin Books, London.

Gibson, McG. 1972. Umm el-Jīr, a town in Akkad. *Journal of Near Eastern Studies* 31, 4: 237–294.

Gibson, McG. 1982. A Re-evaluation of the Akkad period in the Diyala region on the basis of recent excavations at Nippur and in the Hamrin. *American Journal of Archaeology* 86, 4: 531–538.

Gibson, McG., J. C. Sanders, and B. Mortensen. 1981. Tell Razuk: Stratigraphy, architecture, finds. In *Uch Tepe I: Tell Razuk, Tell Ahmed al-Mughir, Tell Ajamat*, ed. McGuire Gibson, 28–87. Hamrin Report 10. The Chicago-Copenhagen Expedition to the Hamrin. Oriental Institute of the University of Chicago, Chicago. Institute of Assyriology and Institute of Classical and Near Eastern Archaeology, University of Copenhagen, Copenhagen.

Glassner, J.-J. 2003. *The invention of cuneiform: Writing in Sumer*, trans. and ed. Z. Bahrani and M. Van De Mieroop. The Johns Hopkins University Press, Baltimore.

Glatz, C., J. Casana, R. Bendrey, E. Baysal, D. Calderbank, F. Chelazzi, F. Del Bravo, N. Erskine, M. M. Hald, E. Jakoby Laugier, E. Jensen, and E. Perruchini. 2019. Babylonian encounters in the Upper Diyala River Valley: Contextualizing the results of regional survey and the 2016–2017 excavations at Khani Masi. *American Journal of Archaeology* 123, 3: 439–471.

Goodman, J., P. E. Lovejoy, and A. Sherratt (eds.). 2007. *Consuming habits: Global and historical perspectives on how cultures define drugs*. Second edition. Routledge, London.

Goulder, J. 2010. Administrators' bread: An experiment-based re-assessment of the functional and cultural role of the Uruk bevel-rim bowl. *Antiquity* 84: 351–362.

Graeber, D., and D. Wengrow. 2021. *The dawn of everything: A new history of humanity*. Farrar, Straus and Giroux, New York.

Graziani, S. 1986. *I testi Mesopotamici datati al regno di Serse (485–465 a.C.)*. Istituto Universitario Orientale, Napoli. Supplement 47, *Annali* 46, 2. Herder, Roma.

Grossman, K. 2014. Fire installations in a Late Ninevite 5 Complex at Hamoukar, Syria. In *Proceedings of the 8th International Congress on the Archaeology of the Ancient Near East*, eds. P. Bieliński, M. Gawlikowski, R. Koliński, D. Ławecka, A. Sołtysiak, and Z. Wygnańska, 47–59. Harrassowitz Verlag, Wiesbaden.

Grossman, K., and T. Paulette. 2020. Wealth-on-the-hoof and the low-power state: Caprines as capital in early Mesopotamia. *Journal of Anthropological Archaeology* 60: 1–20.

Guerra-Doce, E. 2015. The origins of inebriation: Archaeological evidence of the consumption of fermented beverages and drugs in prehistoric Europe. *Journal of Archaeological Method and Theory* 22: 751–782.

Guerra-Doce, E. 2020. The earliest toasts: Archaeological evidence of the social and cultural construction of alcohol in prehistoric Europe. In *Alcohol and humans: A long and social affair*, eds. K. J. Hockings and R. Dunbar, 60–80. Oxford University Press, Oxford.

Haaland, R. 2007. Porridge and pot, bread and oven: Food ways and symbolism in Africa and the Near East from the Neolithic to the present. *Cambridge Archaeological Journal* 17, 2: 165–182.

Hafford, W. B. 2019a. The Great Death Pit: Reconstructing a funeral feast. In *Journey to the city: A companion to the Middle East galleries at the Penn Museum*, eds. S. Tinneyn and K. Sonik, 219–221. University of Pennsylvania Museum of Archaeology and Anthropology, Philadelphia.

Hafford, W. B. 2019b. The Royal Cemetery of Ur. In *Journey to the city: A companion to the Middle East galleries at the Penn Museum*, eds. S. Tinneyn and K. Sonik, 195–233. University of Pennsylvania Museum of Archaeology and Anthropology, Philadelphia.

Haggblade, S., and W. H. Holzapfel. 2004. Industrialization of Africa's indigenous beer brewing. In *Industrialization of indigenous fermented foods*, ed. K. H. Steinkraus, 271–361. Second edition. Marcel Dekker, Inc., New York.

Hamilakis, Y., and A. M. Jones. 2017. Archaeology and assemblage. *Cambridge Archaeological Journal* 27, 1: 77–84

Hansen, D. P. 1970. Al-Hiba, 1968–1969: A preliminary report. *Artibus Asiae* 32, 4: 243–258.

Hansen, D. P. 1973. Al-Hiba, 1970–1971: A preliminary report. *Artibus Asiae* 35, 1/2: 62–70.

Hansen, D. P. 1978. Al-Hiba: A summary of four seasons of excavation, 1968–1976. *Sumer* 34, 1/2: 72–85.

Hansen, D. P. 1983. Lagaš: B. Archäologisch. In *Reallexikon der Assyriologie und Vorderasiatischen Archäologie 6 (Klagegesang–Libanon)*, ed. D. O. Edzard, D.O., 422–430. Walter de Gruyter, Berlin.

Hansen, D. P. 1992. Royal building activity at Sumerian Lagash in the Early Dynastic period. *Biblical Archaeologist* 55, 4: 206–211.

Harris, R. 1964. The *nadītu* women. In *Studies presented to A. Leo Oppenheim, June 7, 1964*, eds. R. D. Biggs and J. A. Brinkman, 106–135. University of Chicago Press, Chicago.

Harris, R. 1989. Independent women in ancient Mesopotamia? In *Women's earliest records from ancient Egypt and Western Asia*, ed. B. S. Leski, 145–165. Scholars Press, Atlanta.

Hayden, B., N. Canuel, and J. Shanse. 2013. What was brewing in the Natufian? An archaeological assessment of brewing technology in the Epipaleolithic. *Journal of Archaeological Method and Theory* 20: 102–150.

Heimpel, W. 2009. *Workers and construction work at Garšana*. Cornell University Studies in Assyriology and Sumerology 5. CDL Press, Bethesda.

Helle, S. 2021. *Gilgamesh: A new translation of the ancient epic.* Yale University Press, New Haven.

Helle, S. 2023. *Enheduana: The complete poems of the world's first author.* Yale University Press, New Haven.

Herrmann, V. R. 2014. The Katumuwa stele in archaeological context. In *In remembrance of me: Feasting with the dead in the ancient Middle East*, eds. V. R. Herrmann and D. Schloen, 49–56. Oriental Institute Museum Publications 37. The Oriental Institute of the University of Chicago, Chicago.

Hilprecht, H. V. 1904. *The excavations in Assyria and Babylonia.* The Babylonian Expedition of the University of Pennsylvania, Series D: Researches and Treatises. Department of Archaeology of the University of Pennsylvania, Philadelphia.

Hilprecht, H. V. 1908. The so-called Peters-Hilprecht Controversy. A. J. Holman & Company, Philadelphia.

Hockings, K.J., and R. Dunbar, R. (eds.). 2020. *Alcohol and humans: A long and social affair.* Oxford University Press, Oxford.

Hojlund, F. 1990. Date honey production in Dilmun in the mid 2nd millennium B.C.: Steps in the technological evolution of the *madbasa. Paléorient* 16, 1: 77–86.

Homan, M. M. 2004. Beer and its drinkers: An ancient Near Eastern love story. *Near Eastern Archaeology* 67, 2: 84–95.

Hrozný, F. 1914. *Das Getreide im alten Babylonien: Ein Beitrag zur Kultur- und Wirtschaftsgeschichte des alten Orients.* Sitzungsberichte der Kaiserlichen Akademie der Wissenschaften, Philosophisch-Historische Klasse 173, 1. k. u. k. Hof- und Universitäts-Buchhändler, Buchhändler der kaiserlichen Akademie der Wissenschaften, Wien.

Huang, H. T. 2000. *Science and civilization in China, Vol. 6: Biology and biological technology, Part V: Fermentations and food science.* Cambridge University Press, Cambridge.

Huber, E. 1938. Bier und Bierbereitung in Babylonien. *Reallexikon der Assyriologie und Vorderasiatischen Archäologie* 2 (Ber–Ezur), eds. E. Ebeling and B. Meissner, 25–28. Walter de Gruyter, Berlin.

Hudson, M., and B. A. Levine (eds.). 1996. *Privatization in the ancient Near East and Classical world.* Peabody Museum Bulletin 5. Peabody Museum of Archaeology and Ethnology, Harvard University, Cambridge.

Hudson, M., and B. A. Levine (eds.). 1999. *Urbanization and land ownership in the ancient Near East.* Peabody Museum Bulletin 7. Peabody Museum of Archaeology and Ethnology, Harvard University, Cambridge.

Hudson, M., and M. Van De Mieroop (eds.). 2002. *Debt and economic renewal in the ancient Near East.* International Scholars Conference on Ancient Near Eastern Economics 3. CDL Press, Bethesda.

Huehnergard, J. 2000. *A grammar of Akkadian.* Harvard Semitic Museum PEisenbrauns, Winona Lake.

Huh, S. K. 2008. Studien zur Region Lagaš von der Ubaid-bis zur altbabylonian Zeit. Alter Orient und Altes Testament 345. Ugarit-Verlag, Münster.

Jackson, M. (ed.). 2007. *Beer.* Eyewitness Companions. DK Publishing, New York.

Jacobsen, T. 1942. The inscriptions. In *Pre-Sargonid temples in the Diyala region,* eds. P. Delougaz and S. Lloyd, 289–298. Oriental Institute Publications 58. The University of Chicago Press, Chicago.

Jacobsen, T. 1987. *The harps that once. . . : Sumerian poetry in translation.* Yale University Press, New Haven.

Joannès, F. 1981. Un inventaire de mobilier sacré d'époque néo-babylonienne. *Revue d'Assyriologie et d'Archéologie Orientale* 75: 143–150.

Joannès, F. 1992a. Inventaire d'un cabaret. *Nouvelles Assyriologiques Brèves et Utilitaires (N.A.B.U.)* 1992, 2: 48–50.

Joannès, F. 1992b. Inventaire d'un cabaret (suite). *Nouvelles Assyriologiques Brèves et Utilitaires (N.A.B.U.)* 1992, 3: 69.

Joffe, A. 1998. Alcohol and social complexity in ancient Western Asia. *Current Anthropology* 39, 3: 297–310.

Josephson, M., A. Kleidon, and R. Tockstein. 2016. *The homebrewer's almanac: A seasonal guide to making your own beer from scratch.* The Countryman Press, New York.

Jursa, M. 2010. *Aspects of the economic history of Babylonia in the first millennium BC: Economic geography, economic mentalities, agriculture, the use of money, and the problem of economic growth.* Veröffentlichungen zur Wirtschaftsgeschichte Babyloniens im 1. Jahrtausend v. Chr. 4. Ugarit Verlag, Münster.

Katz, S. H., and F. Maytag. 1991. Brewing an Ancient Beer. *Archaeology* 44, 4: 24–33.

Katz, S. H., and M. M. Voigt. 1986. Bread and beer: The early use of cereals in the human diet. *Expedition* 28, 2: 23–34.

Kennedy, J. R. 2012. Commensality and labor in Terminal Ubaid Northern Mesopotamia. *eTopoi,* Special volume 2: 125–156.

Kennedy, J. R. 2019. Commensality and labor at Kenan Tepe: A use-alteration analysis of Terminal Ubaid ceramics. Unpublished PhD dissertation, Binghamton University, State University of New York.

Kennedy, J. R. 2022. Work is the curse of the drinking class: Beer, labor and class in ancient Mesopotamia and Egypt. *Archaeology of Food and Foodways* 1, 2: 103–122.

Kleinerman, A., and D. I. Owen, D. I. 2009. *Analytical concordance to the Garšana archives.* Cornell University Studies in Assyriology and Sumerology 4. CDL Press, Bethesda.

Kramer, S. N. 1946. Interim report of work in the museum at Istanbul (to October 16, 1946). *Bulletin of the American Schools of Oriental Research* 104: 8–12.

Kramer, S. N. 1947. Second interim report on work in the museum at Istanbul. *Bulletin of the American Schools of Oriental Research* 105: 7–11.

Kramer, S. N. 1963. Cuneiform studies and the history of literature: The Sumerian sacred marriage texts. *Proceedings of the American Philosophical Society* 107, 6: 485–527.

Kramer, S. N., M. Çiğ, and H. Kızılyay. 1969. Sumer edebî tablet ve parçaları - I (Sumerian literary tablets and fragments in the Archaeological Museum of Istanbul - I). İstanbul Arkeoloji Müzelerinde Bulunan. Türk Tarih Kurumu Yayınlarından - VI. Seri, Sa. 13. Türk Tarih Kurumu Basımevi, Ankara.

Kraus, F. R. 1977. *Briefe aus dem British Museum (CT 52).* Altbabylonische Briefe in Umschrift und Übersetzung 7. Brill, Leiden.

Krebernik, M. 1998–2001. Nin-kasi und Siraš/Siris. In *Reallexikon der Assyriologie und Vorderasiatischen Archäologie*, ed. D. O. Edzard, 442–444. Walter de Gruyter, Berlin.

Kuhrt, A. 1992. *The Ancient Near East*, Vol. I and II. Routledge History of the Ancient World. Routledge, London.

Kulakoğlu, F., and S. Kangal (eds.). 2010. *Anatolia's prologue, Kültepe Kanesh Karum, Assyrians in Istanbul*. Kayseri Metropolitan Municipality Cultural Publication 78. Directorate of Kültepe-Kanesh Excavations, Istanbul.

Kuta, S. 2023. 5,000-year-old tavern with food still inside discovered in Iraq. *Smithsonian Magazine*, February 2, 2023. https://www.smithsonianmag.com/smart-news/5000-year-old-tavern-discovered-in-iraq-180981564/ (accessed March 7, 2023).

Labat, R. 1976. *Manuel d'épigraphie Akkadienne.* 5th edition. Librairie Orientaliste Paul Geuthner, Paris.

Lacambre, D. 2008. Le bureau de la bière. In *Chagar Bazar (Syrie) III: Les trouvailles épigraphiques et sigillographiques du chantier I (2000–2002)*, eds. Ö. Tunca and A. M. Baghdo, 179–207. Peeters, Louvain.

Lacambre, D. 2009. Le bureau de la bière de Chagar Bazar (Syrie). *Cahier des thèmes transversaux ArScAn* 9: 385–391.

Lafont, S. 1999. *Femmes, droit et justice dans l'antiquité orientale: Contribution à l'étude du droit pénal au Proche-Orient ancien*. Orbis Biblicus et Orientalist 165. Universitätsverlag, Freiburg. Vandenhoeck & Ruprecht, Göttingen.

Landsberger, B., and K. Balkan. 1950. Die Inschrift des Assyrischen Königs Irişum, gefunden in Kültepe 1948. *Türk Tarih Kurumu, Belleten* 14, 54: 219–268.

Landsberger, B., and O. R. Gurney. 1957–58. Practical Vocabulary of Assur. In *Archiv für Orientforschung* 18: 328–341.

Langlois, A.-I. 2016. The female tavern-keeper in Mesopotamia: Some aspects of daily life. In *Women in antiquity: Real women across the ancient world*, eds. S. L. Budin and J. M. Turfa, 113–125. Routledge, New York.

Larsen, M. T. 2015. *Ancient Kanesh: A merchant colony in Bronze Age Anatolia.* Cambridge University Press, Cambridge.

Latour, B. 2005. *Reassembling the social: An introduction to Actor-Network Theory.* Oxford University Press, Oxford.

Ławecka, D. 2008. Heating places and ovens of the 3rd millennium BC in sector SD on Tell Arbid. *Polish Archaeology in the Medterranean* 18: 562–569.

Lawrence, D., and T. J. Wilkinson. 2015. Hubs and upstarts: Pathways to urbanism in the northern Fertile Crescent. *Antiquity* 89, 344: 328–344.

Lee, J.-E., A. R. Lee, H. Kim, E. Lee, T. W. Kim, W. C. Shin, and J. H. Kim. 2017. Restoration of traditional Korean nuruk and analysis of the brewing characteristics. *Journal of Microbiology and Biotechnology* 27, 5: 896–908.

Leick, G. 2001. *Mesopotamia: The invention of the city.* Penguin Books, London.

Lemaire, A. 2012. Rites des vivants pour les morts dans le royaume de Sam'al (viiie siècle av.n.è.). In *Les vivants et leurs morts. Actes du colloque organisé par le Collège de France, Paris, les 14-15 avril 2010,* ed. by J.-M. Durand, Th. Romer, and J. Hutzli, 129–37. Orbis Biblicus et Orientalis 257. Academic Press, Freiburg. Vandenhoeck & Ruprecht, Göttingen.

Lion, B. 2013. Les cabarets à l'époque paléo-babylonienne. In *L'alimentation dans l'Orient ancien: Cuisines et dependences,* ed. C. Michel, 393–400. Cahier des thèmes transversaux ArScAn 11.

Lion, B., and C. Michel (eds.). 2016. *The role of women in work and society in the ancient Near East.* Studies in Ancient Near Eastern Records 13. De Gruyter, Berlin.

Lissarrague, F. 1990. *The aesthetics of the Greek banquet: Images of wine and ritual.* Princeton University Press, Princeton.

Litke, R. L. 1998. *A reconstruction of the Assyro-Babylonian god-lists,* AN: ^{d}*A-nu-um* and AN: *Anu šá amēli.* Texts from the Babylonian Collection 3. Yale Babylonian Collection, New Haven.

Liu, L., J. Wang, D. Rosenberg, H. Zhao, G. Lengyel, and D. Nadel. 2018. Fermented beverage and food storage in 13,000-y-old stone mortars at Raqefet Cave, Israel: Investigating Natufian ritual feasting. *Journal of Archaeological Science: Reports* 21: 783–793.

Liu, L., J. Wang, D. Rosenberg, H. Zhao, G. Lengyel, and D. Nadel. 2019. Response to comments on archaeological reconstruction of 13,000-y-old Natufian beer making at Raqefet Cave, Israel. *Journal of Archaeological Science: Reports* 28: 1–6.

Liu, L., L. Yongqiang, and J. Jianxing. 2020. Making beer with malted cereals and qu starter in the Neolithic Yangshao culture, China. *Journal of Archaeological Science: Reports* 29: 1–9.

Lloyd, S. 1967. The Northern Palace area. In *Private houses and graves in the Diyala region,* eds. P. Delougaz, H. D. Hill, and S. Lloyd, 181–196. Oriental Institute Publications 88. The University of Chicago Press, Chicago.

Lynch, K. M. 2012. Drinking and dining. In *A companion to Greek art,* eds. T. J. Smith and D. Plantzos, 525–542. Blackwell, Oxford.

Maekawa, K. 1973–1974. The development of the É-MÍ in Lagash during the Early Dynastic III. *Mesopotamia* 8–9: 77–144.

Maier, A. M., and Y. Garfinkle. 1992. Bone and metal straw-tip beer-strainers from the ancient Near East. *Levant* 24: 218–223.

Mallett, J. 2014. *Malt: A practical guide from field to brewhouse.* Brewers Publications, Boulder.

Mallowan, A. C. 1946. *Come, tell me how you live.* William Morrow.

Mallowan, M. E. L. 1936. The excavations at Tall Chagar Bazar, and an archaeological survey of the Habur region, 1934–5. *Iraq* 3, 1: 1–59, 61–85.

Mallowan, M. E. L. 1937. The excavations at Tall Chagar Bazar and an archaeological survey of the Habur region. Second campaign, 1936. *Iraq* 4, 2: 91–177.

Markowski, P. 2004. *Farmhouse ales: Culture and craftsmanship in the Belgian tradition.* Brewers Publications, Boulder.

Martin, H. P., J. Moon, and J. N. Postgate. 1985. *Graves 1 to 99.* Abu Salabikh Excavations 2. British School of Archaeology in Iraq, London.

Matthews, R. 1997. Girsu and Lagash. In *The Oxford encyclopedia of archaeology in the Near East*, ed. E. M. Meyers, 406–409. Oxford University Press, Oxford.

Matthews, R. 2003. *The archaeology of Mesopotamia: Theories and approaches.* Routledge, London.

Matthews, R., and A. Richardson. 2020. Cultic resilience and inter-city engagement at the dawn of urban history: Protohistoric Mesopotamia and the "city seals," 3200–2750 BCE. *World Archaeology* 50, 5: 723–747.

Maul, S. M. 1992. Der Kneipenbesuch als Heilsverfahren. In *La circulation des biens, des personnes et des idées dans le Proche-Orient aleot*, eds. D. Charpin and F. Joannès, 389–396. ERC, Paris.

Maul, S. M. 1999. How the Babylonians protected themselves against calamities announced by omens. In *Mesopotamian magic. Textual, historical, and interpretative perspectives*, eds. T. Abusch and K. van der Toorn, 123–129. Ancient Magic and Divination I. STYX Publications, Groningen.

Maul, S. M. 2018. *The art of divination in the ancient Near East: Reading the signs of heaven and earth.* Baylor University Press, Waco.

McCorriston, J. 1997. The Fiber Revolution: Textile extensification, alienation, and social stratification in ancient Mesopotamia. *Current Anthropology* 38, 4: 517–535.

McCown, D. E., and R. C. Haines. 1967. *Nippur I: Temple of Enlil, scribal quarter, and soundings.* Oriental Institute Publications 78. The University of Chicago Press, Chicago.

McGee, H. 2004. *On food and cooking: The science and lore of the kitchen.* Scribner, New York.

McGovern, P. E. 2009. *Uncorking the past: The quest for wine, beer, and other alcoholic beverages.* University of California Press, Berkeley.

McGovern, P. E. 2017. *Ancient brews: Rediscovered and re-created.* W. W. Norton & Company, New York.

McGovern, P. E. 2020. Uncorking the past: Alcoholic fermentation as humankind's first biotechnology. In *Alcohol and humans: A long and social affair*, eds. K. J. Hockings and R. Dunbar, 81–92. Oxford University Press, Oxford.

McGovern, P. E., and G. R. Hall. 2016. Charting a future course for organic residue analysis in archaeology. *Journal of Archaeological Method and Theory* 23, 2: 592–622.

McGovern, P. E., A. P. Underhill, H. Fang, F. Luan, G. R. Hall, H. Yu, C. Wang, F. Cai, Z. Zhao, and G. M. Feinman. 2005. Chemical identification and cultural implications of a mixed fermented beverage from late prehistoric China. *Asian Perspectives* 44, 2: 249–275.

McGovern, P. E., J. Zhang, J. Tang, Z. Zhang, G. R. Hall, R. A. Moreau, A. Nuñez, E. D. Butrym, M. P. Richards, C. Wang, G. Cheng, Z. Zhao, and C. Wang. 2004. Fermented beverages of pre- and proto-historic China. *Proceedings of the National Academy of Sciences* 101, 51: 17593–17598.

McGuirk, C. 1993. *Robert Burns: Selected poems*. Penguin Books, London.

McKay, M., A. J. Buglass, and C. G. Lee. 2011. Fermented beverages: Beers, ciders, wines, and related drinks. In *Handbook of alcoholic beverages: Technical, analytical, and nutritional aspects*, Volume 1, ed. A. J. Buglass, 63–454. Wiley, Chichester.

McMahon, A. 2006. *The Early Dynastic to Akkadian transition: The Area WF sounding at Nippur*. Excavations at Nippur. Oriental Institute Publications 129. The Oriental Institute of the University of Chicago, Chicago.

McMahon, A. 2009. *Once there was a place: Settlement archaeology at Chagar Bazar, 1999–2002*. British Institute for the Study of Iraq.

McMahon, A. 2013. Mesopotamia. In *The Oxford handbook of cities in world history*, ed. P. Clark, 32–48. Oxford University Press, Oxford.

McMahon, A. 2020. Early urbanism in northern Mesopotamia. *Journal of Archaeological Research* 28, 3: 289–337.

McMahon, A., H. Pittman, Z. al-Rawi, D. Ashby, K. Burge, R. Goodman, E. Hammer, and S. Pizzimenti. 2023. Dense urbanism and economic multi-centrism at third-millennium BC Lagash. *Antiquity* 97, 393: 596–615.

Michalowski, P. 1978. *The Neo-Sumerian silver ring texts*. Syro-Mesopotamian Studies 2/3. Undena Publications, Malibu.

Michalowski, P. 1981. On "The Fowler and His Wife." *Revue d'Assyriologie et d'archéologie orientale* 75, 2: 170.

Michalowski, P. 1994. The drinking gods: Alcohol in Mesopotamian ritual and mythology. In *Drinking in ancient societies: History and culture of drinks in the ancient Near East*, ed. L. Milano, 27–44. History of the Ancient Near East / Studies 6. Sargon srl, Padova.

Michalowski, P. 2004. The ideological foundations of the Ur III state. In *2000 v. Chr.: Politische, Wirtschaftliche une Kulturelle Entwicklung im Zeichen einer Jahrtausendwende*, eds. J.-W. Meyer and W. Sommerfeld, 219–235. Saarbrücker Druckerei und Verlag, Saarbrücken.

Michalowski, P. 2006. Love or death? Observations on the role of the gala in Ur III ceremonial life. *Journal of Cuneiform Studies* 58: 49–61.

Michalowski, P. 2013. Networks of authority and power in Ur III Times. In *From the 21st Century B.C. to the 21st Century A.D.* Proceedings of the International Conference on Sumerian Studies Held in Madrid 22–24 July 2010, eds. S. Garfinkle and M. Molina, 169–206. Eisenbrauns, Winona Lake.

Michel, C. 1991. *Innāya dans les tablettes paléo-assyriennes*. Éditions Recherche sur les Civilisations, Paris.

Michel, C. 1997. À table avec les marchands paleo-assyriens. In *Assyrien im Wandel der Zeiten*, eds. H. Waetzoldt and H. Hauptmann, 95–113. Compte rendu de la Rencontre Assyriologique lnternationale 39. Heidelberger Studien zum alten Orient 6. Heidelberger Orientverlag, Heidelberg.

Michel, C. 2009. "Dis-moi ce que tu bois...": Boissons et buveurs en haute Mésopotamie et Anatolie au début du Iie millénaire av. J.-C. In *Et il y eut un esprit dans l'Homme: Jean Bottéro et la Mésopotamie*, eds. X. Faivre, B. Lion, and C. Michel, 197–220. Travaux de la Maison René-Ginouvès 6. De Boccard, Paris.

Michel, C. 2017. Economy, society, and daily life in the Old Assyrian period. In *A companion to Assyria*, ed. E. Frahm, 80–107. Wiley Blackwell, Chichester.

Michel, C. 2020. *Women of Assur and Kanesh: Texts from the archives of Assyrian merchants*. Writings from the Ancient World 42. SBL Press, Atlanta.

Milano, L. 1993. Mehl. In *Reallexikon der Assyriologie und Vorderasiatischen Archäologie* 8, 1/2 (Meek – Miete), ed. D. O. Edzard, 457–517. Walter de Gruyter, Berlin.

Modernist Cuisine. 2018. Bread is lighter than whipped cream. *Modernist Cuisine*, June 22, 2018. https://modernistcuisine.com/mc/bread-is-lighter-than-whipped-cream/.

Moffat, B. 1993. An assessment of the residues on the Grooved Ware. In *Excavations in the ceremonial complex of the fourth to second millennium BC at Balfarg/Balbirnie, Glenrothes, Fife*, eds. G. J. Barclay and C. J. Russell-White, 108–110. *Proceedings of the Society of Antiquaries of Scotland* 123: 43–210.

Moon, J. 1987. *Catalogue of Early Dynastic Pottery*. Abu Salabikh Excavations 3. British School of Archaeology in Iraq, London.

Moore, J. D. 1989. Pre-Hispanic beer in coastal Peru: Technology and social context of prehistoric production. *American Anthropologist*, New Series 91, 3: 682–695.

Moorey, P. R. S. 1977. What do we know about the people buried in the Royal Cemetery? *Expedition* 20, 1: 24–40.

Müller-Karpe, M. 1993. *Metallgefäße im Iraq I: Von den Anfängen bis zur Akkad-Zeit*. Prähistorische Bronzefunde, Abteilung 2, Band 14. Franz Steiner Verlag, Stuttgart.

Müller-Karpe, V. 2005. Bier und Bierproduktion in Anatolien zur Bronzezeit. In *Das Schiff von Uluburun: Welthandel vor 3000 Jahren*, eds. Ü. Yalçin, C. Pulak, R. Slotta, 171–184. Deutschen-Bergbau Museum, Bochum.

Mynářová, J., and S. Alivernini (eds.). 2020. *Economic complexity in the ancient Near East: Management of resources and taxation (third–second millennium BC)*. Charles University, Prague.

Nation, T. 2024. Rites for the dead, amity for the Living: The Old Assyrian *nasbītum* rite and its relation to the Old Babylonian *kispum*. *Journal of Ancient Near Eastern Religions* 24, 1.

Nelson, M. 2005. *The barbarian's beverage: A history of beer in ancient Europe*. Routledge, London.

Nelson, M. 2014. The geography of beer in Europe from 1000 BC to AD 1000. In *The geography of beer*, eds. M. Patterson and N. Hoalst-Pullen, 9–21. Springer, Dordrecht.

Neumann, H. 1994. Beer as a means of compensation for work in Mesopotamia during the Ur III period. In *Drinking in ancient societies: History and culture of drinks in the ancient Near East*, ed. L. Milano, 321–331. History of the Ancient Near East/ Studies 6. Sargon srl, Padova.

Nissen, H. J. 1990. *The early history of the ancient Near East, 9000–2000 B.C.*, trans. E. Lutzeier. University of Chicago Press, Chicago.

Nissen, H. J. 2002. Uruk: Key site of the period and key site of the problem. In *Artefacts of complexity: Tracking the Uruk in the Near East*, ed. J. N. Postgate, 1–16. Iraq Archaeological Reports 5. British School of Archaeology in Iraq, Baghdad.

Nissen, H. J. 2003. Uruk and the formation of the city. In *Art of the first cities: The third millennium B.C. from the Mediterranean to the Indus*, ed. J. Aruz, 11–20. Metropolitan Museum of Art, New York.

Nissen, H. J. 2015. Urbanization and the techniques of communication: The Mesopotamian city of Uruk during the fourth millennium BCE. In *The Cambridge World History, Vol. III: Early cities in comparative perspective, 4000 BCE– 1200 CE*, ed. N. Yoffee, 113–130. Cambridge University Press, Cambridge.

Nissen, H. J. 2016. Uruk: Early administration practices and the development of proto-cuneiform writing. *Archéo-Nil* 26: 33–48.

Nissen, H. J., P. Damerow, and R. K. Englund. 1993. *Archaic bookkeeping: Early writing and techniques of economic administration in the ancient Near East*. University of Chicago Press, Chicago.

Nissen, H. J., and P. Heine. 2009. *From Mesopotamia to Iraq: A concise history*, trans. H. J. Nissen. University of Chicago Press, Chicago.

Notroff, J., O. Dietrich, and K. Schmidt. 2014. Creating communities: Early monumental architecture at Pre-Pottery Neolithic Göbekli Tepe. In *Approaching monumentality in archaeology*, ed. J. F. Osborne, 83–105. IMEA Proceedings Volume 3. SUNY Press, Albany.

Olsen, B., M. Shanks, T. Webmoor, and C. Witmore. 2012. *Archaeology: The discipline of things*. University of California Press, Berkeley.

Oppenheim, A. L. 1950. The XXIIIrd tablet of the series Ḫar.ra=ḫubullu. In *On beer and brewing techniques in ancient Mesopotamia according to the XXXIIIrd tablet of the series Ḫar.ra = ḫubullu*, L. F. Hartman and A. L. Oppenheim, 5–54. Supplement to the Journal of the American Oriental Society 10. The American Oriental Society, Baltimore.

Otto, A. 2006. *Alltag und Gesellschaft zur Spätbronzezeit: Eine Fallstudie aus Tall Bazi (Syrien)*. Subartu 19. Brepols, Turnhout.

Otto, A. 2012. Defining and transgressing the boundaries between ritual commensality and daily commensal practices: The case of Late Bronze Age Tall Bazi. In *Between feasts and daily meals: Toward an archaeology of commensal spaces*, ed. S. Pollock, 179–195. *Journal for Ancient Studies*, Special Volume 2.

Otto, A. 2015. Neo-Assyrian capital cities: From imperial headquarters to cosmopolitan cities. In *Early cities in comparative perspective, 4000 BCE–1200 CE*, ed. Norman Yoffee, 469–490. The Cambridge World History, Vol. 3. Cambridge University Press, Cambridge.

Outram, A. K. 2008. Introduction to experimental archaeology. *World Archaeology* 40, 1: 1–6.

Owen, D. I. 2013. A tale of two cities: New Ur III archives and their implication for early Old Babylonian history and culture. In *Diversity and standardization: Perspectives on ancient Near Eastern cultural history*, eds. E. Cancik-Kirschbaum, J. Klinger, and G. G. W. Müller, 99–111. Akademie Verlag, München.

Owen, D. I., and R. Mayr. 2008. *The Garšana archives.* Cornell University Studies in Assyriology and Sumerology 3. CDL Press, Bethesda.

Panayotov, S. V. 2013. A ritual for a flourishing bordello. *Bibliotheca Orientalis* 70, 3–4: 285–309.

Pardee, D. 2014. The Katumuwa inscription. In *In remembrance of me: Feasting with the dead in the ancient Middle East*, eds. V. R. Herrmann and D. Schloen, 45–48. Oriental Institute Museum Publications 37. The Oriental Institute of the University of Chicago, Chicago.

Paulette, T. 2012. Domination and resilience in Bronze Age Mesopotamia. In *Surviving sudden environmental change*, eds. J. Cooper and P. Sheets, 167–195. University Press of Colorado, Boulder.

Paulette, T. 2015. *Grain storage and the moral economy in Mesopotamia (3000–2000 BC).* PhD dissertation. University of Chicago.

Paulette, T. 2016. Grain, storage, and state making in Mesopotamia (3200–2000 BC). In *Storage in ancient complex societies: Administration, organization, and control*, eds. L. Manzanilla and M. Rothman, 85–109. Routledge, New York.

Paulette, T. 2020. Archaeological perspectives on beer in Mesopotamia: Brewing ingredients. In *After the harvest: Storage practices and food processing in Bronze Age Mesopotamia*, eds. N. Borrelli and G. Scazzosi, 65–89. Subartu 43. Brepols, Turnhout.

Paulette, T. 2021. Inebriation and the early state: Beer and the politics of affect in Mesopotamia. *Journal of Anthropological Archaeology* 63: 1–19.

Paulus, S. (ed.). 2023. *Back to school in Babylonia.* ISAC Museum Publications 1. Institute for the Study of Ancient Cultures of the University of Chicago, Chicago.

Perruchini, E., C. Glatz, M. M. Hald, J. Casana, and J. L. Toney. 2018. Revealing invisible brews: A new approach to the chemical identification of ancient beer. *Journal of Archaeological Science* 100: 176–190.

Peters, J. P. 1905. The Nippur Library. *Journal of the American Oriental Society* 26: 145–164.

Peyronel, L., A. Vacca, and C. Wachter-Sarkady. 2014. Food and drink preparation at Ebla, Syria: New data from the Royal Palace G (c. 2450–2300 BC). *Food & History* 12, 3: 3–38.

Pinnock, F. 1994. Considerations of the "banquet theme" in the figurative art of Mesopotamia and Syria. In *Drinking in ancient societies: History and culture of drinks in the ancient Near East*, ed. L. Milano, 15–26. History of the Ancient Near East / Studies 6. Sargon srl, Padova.

Pittman, H. 1998. Cylinder seals. In *Treasures from the Royal Tombs of Ur*, eds. R. L. Zettler and L. Horne, 75–84. University of Pennsylvania Museum of Archaeology and Anthropology, Philadelphia.

Podany, A. H. 2022. *Weavers, scribes, and kings: A new history of the ancient Near East.* Oxford University Press, Oxford.

Pollock, S. 1991. Of priestesses, princes, and poor relations: The dead in the Royal Cemetery of Ur. *Cambridge Archaeological Journal* 1, 2: 171–189.

Pollock, S. 1999. *Ancient Mesopotamia: The Eden that never was.* Cambridge University Press, Cambridge.

Pollock, S. 2003. Feasts, funerals, and fast food in early Mesopotamian states. In *The archaeology and politics of food and feasting in early states and empires*, ed. T. L. Bray, 17–38. Kluwer Academic/Plenum Publishers, New York.

Pollock, S. 2007. The Royal Cemetery of Ur: Ritual, tradition, and the creation of subjects. In *Representations of political power: Case histories from times of change and dissolving order in the ancient Near East*, eds. M. Heinz and M. H. Feldman, 89–110. Eisenbrauns, Winona Lake.

Pollock, S. 2012. Politics of food in early Mesopotamian centralized societies. *Origini* 34: 153–168.

Pollock, S. 2015. Abu Salabikh: History of a southern Mesopotamian town. In *It's a long way to a historiography of the Early Dynastic period(s)*, eds. R. Dittman and G. J. Selz, 267–287. Altertumskunde des Vorderen Orients 15. Ugarit-Verlag, Münster.

Pollock, S. 2017. Working lives in an age of mechanical reproduction: Uruk-period Mesopotamia. In *The interplay of people and technologies: Archaeological case studies on innovations*, eds. S. Burmeister and R. Bernbeck, 205–224. Berlin Studies of the Ancient World 43. Edition Topoi, Berlin.

Pollock, S., and R. Bernbeck. 2000. And they said, let us make gods in our image: Gendered ideologies in ancient Mesopotamia. In *Reading the body: Representations and remains in the archaeological record*, ed. A. E. Rautman, 150–164. University of Pennsylvania Press, Philadelphia.

Postgate, J. N. 1992. *Early Mesopotamia: Society and economy at the dawn of history.* Routledge, London.

Postgate, J. N. 2020. Soap for Zabala? In *The third millennium: Studies in early Mesopotamia and Syria in honor of Walter Sommerfeld and Manfred Krebernik*, eds. I. Arkhipov, L. Kogan, and N. Koslova, 617–629. Brill, Leiden.

Postgate, J. N., and P. R. S. Moorey. 1976. Excavations at Abu Salabikh, 1975. *Iraq* 38, 2: 133–169.

Potts, D. T. 1997. *Mesopotamian civilization: The material foundations.* Cornell University Press, Ithaca.

Pournelle, R., and G. Algaze. 2014. Travels in Edin: Deltaic resilience and early urbanism in Greater Mesopotamia. In *Preludes to urbanism: The Late Chalcolithic of Mesopotamia*, eds. A. McMahon and H. Crawford, 7–34. McDonald Institute Monographs. McDonald Institute for Archaeological Research, Cambridge.

Powell, M. A. 1984. Sumerian cereal crops. *Bulletin on Sumerian Agriculture* 1: 48–72.

Powell, M. A. 1989. Masse und Gewichte. In *Reallexikon der Assyriologie und Vorderasiatischen Archäologie* 7 (Libanukšabaš–Medizin), ed. D. O. Edzard, 457–517. Walter de Gruyter, Berlin.

Powell, M. A. 1994. Metron ariston: Measure as a tool for studying beer in ancient Mesopotamia. In *Drinking in ancient societies: History and culture of drinks in the ancient Near East*, ed. L. Milano, 91–119. History of the Ancient Near East, Studies 6. Sargon srl, Padova.

Powell, M. A. 1996a. Money in Mesopotamia. *Journal of the Economic and Social History of the Orient* 39, 3: 224–242.

Powell, M. A. 1996b. Wine and the vine in ancient Mesopotamia: The cuneiform evidence. In *The origins and ancient history of wine*, eds. P. E. McGovern, S. J. Fleming, and S. H. Katz, 97–122. The University of Pennsylvania Museum of Archaeology and Anthropology, Philadelphia. Gordon and Breach Publishers, Amsterdam.

Powell, M. A. 1999. Wir müssen alle unsere Nische nutzen: Monies, motives, and methods in Babylonian economics. In *Trade and finance in ancient Mesopotamia*, ed. J. G. Dercksen, 5–23. MOS Studies 1. Nederlands Historisch-Archaeologisch Instituut te Istanbul, Istanbul. Nederlands Instituut voor het Nabije Oosten, Leiden.

Powell, M. A. 2003. Obst und Gemüse. In *Reallexikon der Assyriologie und Vorderasiatischen Archäologie* 10 (Oannes–Priesterverkleidung), eds. E. Ebeling, E. F. Weidner, and M. P. Streck, 13–22. Walter de Gruyter, Berlin.

Powell, M. A. (ed.). 1987. *Labor in the ancient Near East.* American Oriental Series 68. American Oriental Society, New Haven.

Prentice, R. 2010. *The exchange of goods and services in Pre-Sargonic Lagash.* Alter Orient und Altes Testament 368. Ugarit-Verlag, Münster.

Pulhan, G. 2000. *On the eve of the Dark Age: Qarni-Lim's Palace at Tell Leilan.* Unpublished doctoral dissertation, Yale University.

Radner, K., N. Moeller, and D. T. Potts. 2020–2023. *The Oxford History of the Ancient Near East,* Vol. I–V. Oxford University Press, Oxford.

Rattenborg, R. 2016. *The scale and extent of political economies of the Middle Bronze Age Jazīrah and the Bilād al-Šām (c. 1800–1600 BCE).* PhD dissertation, Durham University.

Reade, J. E. 1995. The *symposion* in ancient Mesopotamia: Archaeological evidence. In *In vino veritas*, eds. O. Murray and M. Tecuşan, 35–56. British School at Rome, London.

Reid, N. 2015. Runaways and fugitive-catchers during the Third Dynasty of Ur. *Journal of the Economic and Social History of the Orient* 58: 576–605.

Reid, N. 2017. The children of slaves in early Mesopotamian laws and edicts. *Revue d'Assyriologie* 111: 9–23.

Rendu Loisel, A.–C. 2017. L'ivresse en Mésopotamie: de la plénitude des sens à la déraison. *Mythos* 11 (n.s.): 37–47.

Renger, J. 1994. On economic structures in ancient Mesopotamia. *Orientalia Nova Series* 63, no. 3: 157–208.

Renger, J. 1995. Institutional, communal, and individual ownership or possession of arable land in ancient Mesopotamia from the end of the fourth to the end of the first millennium B.C. *Chicago-Kent Law Review* 71, 1: 269–319.

Renette, S. 2014. Feasts on many occasions: Diversity in Mesopotamian banquet scenes during the Early Dynastic period. In *Feasting in the archaeology and texts of the Bible and the ancient Near East*, eds. P. Altmann and J. Fu, 61–86. Eisenbrauns, Winona Lake.

Rey, S. 2016. *For the gods of Girsu: City-state formation in ancient Sumer.* Archaeopress, Oxford.

Richardson, S. 2007. The world of Babylonian countrysides. In *The Babylonian world*, ed. G. Leick, 13–38. Routledge, London.

Richardson, S. 2010. A light in the *gagûm* window: The Sippar cloister in the late Old Babylonian period. In *Near Eastern Studies in Honor of Benjamin R. Foster*, eds. S. Melville and A. Slotsky, 329–346. Culture and History of the Ancient Near East 42. Brill, Leiden: Brill.

Richardson, S. 2012. Early Mesopotamia: The presumptive state. *Past & Present* 215, 1: 3–49.

Richardson, S. 2014. Mesopotamian political history: The perversities. *Journal of Ancient Near Eastern History* 1, 1: 61–93.

Richardson, S. 2016. Obedient bellies: Hunger and food security in ancient Mesopotamia. *Journal of the Economic and Social History of the Orient* 59: 750–792.

Richardson, S. 2017. Before things worked: A "low-power" model of early Mesopotamia. In *Ancient states and infrastructural power: Europe, Asia, and America*, eds. S. Richardson and C. Ando, 17–62. University of Pennsylvania Press, Philadelphia.

Richardson, S. 2023. Mesopotamian slavery. In *The Palgrave handbook of global slavery throughout History*, eds. D. A. Pargas and J. Schiel, 17–39. Palgrave Macmillan, London.

Roaf, M. 1990. *Cultural atlas of Mesopotamia and the ancient Near East.* Facts on File, New York.

Robson, E. 2001. The Tablet House: A scribal school in Old Babylonian Nippur. *Revue d'Assyriologie et d'archéologie orientale* 95, 1: 39–66.

Robertson, J. F. 1995. The social and economic organization of ancient Mesopotamian temples. In *Civilizations of the ancient Near East*, ed. J. M. Sasson, 443–454. Hendrickson Publishers, Peabody.

Robertson, J. F. 2005. Social tensions in the ancient Near East. In *A companion to the ancient Near East*, ed. D. C. Snell, 196–201. Blackwell, Malden.

Rochberg, F. 2016. *Before nature: Cuneiform knowledge and the history of science.* University of Chicago Press, Chicago.

Röllig, W. 1970. *Das Bier in alten Mesopotamien.* Gesellschaft für die Geschichte und Bibliographie des Brauwesens EV, Berlin.

Romano, L. 2015. Holding the cup: Evolution of symposium and banquet scenes in the Early Dynastic period. In *It's a long way to a historiography of the Early Dynastic period(s)*, eds. R. Dittman and G. J. Selz, 289–302. Altertumskunde des Vorderen Orients 15. Ugarit-Verlag, Münster.

Roth, M. T. 1997. *Law collections from Mesopotamia and Asia Minor.* Second edition. Writings from the Ancient World 6. Society of Biblical Literature. Scholars Press, Atlanta.

Roth, M.T. 1999.The priestess and the tavern: LH §110. In *Munuscula Mesopotamica: Festschrift für Johannes Renger,* eds. B. Böck, E. Cancik-Kirschbaum, and T. Richter, 445–464. Alter Orient und Altes Testament 267. Ugarit Verlag, Münster.

Sallaberger, W. 1996. *Der Babylonische Töpfer und seine Gefässe.* Mesopotamian History and Environment, Memoirs 3. University of Ghent, Ghent.

Sallaberger, W. 1999. Ur III-Zeit. In *Mesopotamien: Akkade-Zeit und Ur III-Zeit,* W. Sallberger and A. Westenholz, 121–390. Orbis Biblicus et Orientalis 160/ 3. Universitätsverlag Freiburg Schweiz, Freiburg. Vandenhoeck & Ruprecht, Göttingen.

Sallaberger, W. 2004. Schlachtvieh aus Puzriš-Dagān. *Annuaire de la Société Orientale Ex Oriente Lux* 38: 45–62.

Sallaberger, W. 2007. The palace and the temple in Babylonia. In *The Babylonian world,* ed. G. Leick, 265–275. Routledge, London.

Sallaberger, W. 2012a. Bierbrauen in Versen: Eine neue Edition und Interpretation der Ninkasi-Hymne. In *Altorientalische Studien zu Ehren von Pascal Attinger,* eds. C. Mittermayer and S. Ecklin, 291–328. Orbis Biblicus et Orientalis 256. Academic Press, Fribourg. Vandenhoeck & Ruprecht, Göttingen.

Sallaberger, W. 2012b. Homemade bread, municipal mutton, royal wine: Establishing social relations during the preparation and consumption of food in religious festivals at Late Bronze Age Emar. In *Between feasts and daily meals: Toward an archaeology of commensal spaces,* ed. S. Pollock, 157–177. *Journal for Ancient Studies,* Special Volume 2.

Sallaberger, W. 2013. Der Trinkhalm für Bier: Ein präsargonischer Textbeleg. *Revue d'Assyriologie et d'archéologie orientale* 107: 105–110.

Sallaberger, W. 2018. Festival provisions in Early Bronze Age Mesopotamia. *KASKAL* 15: 171–200.

Salonen, E. 1965. *Die Hausgeräte der alten Mesopotamier nach sumerisch-akkadischen Quellen: Eine lexikalische und kulturgeschichtliche Untersuchung, Teil I.* Suomalainen Tiedeakatemia, Helsinki.

Salonen, E. 1966. *Die Hausgeräte der alten Mesopotamier nach sumerisch-akkadischen Quellen: Eine lexikalische und kulturgeschichtliche Untersuchung, Teil II: Gefässe.* Suomalainen Tiedeakatemia, Helsinki.

Salonen, E. 1970 . *Über das Erwerbsleben im alten Mesopotamien: Untersuchungen zu den Akkadischen Berufsnamen* 1. Studia Orientalia 41. Helsinki.

Salonen, E. 1976. *Neubabylonische Urkunden verschiedenen Inhalts.* Suomalainen Tiedeakatemia, Helsinki.

Samuel, D. 1996. Archaeology of ancient Egyptian beer. *Journal of the American Society of Brewing Chemists* 54: 3–12.

Samuel, D. 2000. Brewing and baking. In *Ancient Egyptian materials and technology*, eds. P. T. Nicholson and I. Shaw, 537–576. Cambridge University Press, Cambridge.

Sanjurjo-Sánchez, J., J. Kaal, and J. L. Montero Fenollós. 2018. Organic matter from bevelled rim bowls of the Middle Euphrates: Results from molecular characterization using pyrolysis-GC–MS. *Microchemical Journal* 141: 1–6.

Sasson, J. M. 2004. The king's table: Food and fealty in Old Babylonian Mari. In *Food and identity in the ancient world*, eds. C. Grottanelli and L. Milano, 179–215. History of the Ancient Near East/Studies 9. S.A.R.G.O.N. Editrice e Libreria, Padova.

Schmandt-Besserat, D. 1992. *Before writing: Volume 1, From counting to cuneiform*. University of Texas Press, Austin.

Schmidt, K. 2012. Anatolia. In *A companion to the archaeology of the ancient Near East*, ed. D. T. Potts, 144–160. Wiley-Blackwell, Chichester.

Schmidt, M. 2019. *Gilgamesh: The life of a poem*. Princeton University Press, Princeton.

Scurlock, J. A. 1995. Death and the afterlife in ancient Mesopotamian thought. In *Civilizations of the ancient Near East*, ed. J. M. Sasson, 1883–1893. Charles Scribner's Sons, New York.

Scurlock, J. A. 2014. *Sourcebook for ancient Mesopotamian medicine*. SBL Press, Atlanta.

Scurlock, J., and B. Andersen. 2005. *Diagnoses in Assyrian and Babylonian medicine: Ancient sources, translations, and modern medical analyses*. University of Illinois Press, Champaign.

Sefati, Y. 1998. *Love songs in Sumerian literature: Critical edition of the Dumuzi-Inanna songs*. Bar-Ilan University Press, Ramat Gan.

Selz, G. 1983. *Die Bankettszene: Entwicklung eines "überzeitlichen" Bildmotifs in Mesopotamien von der Frühdynastichen bis zur Akkad-Zeit*. Freiburger altorientalische Studien 11. Franz Steiner Verlag, Wiesbaden.

Selz, G. J. 1989. *Die Altsumerischen Wirtschaftsurkunden der Eremitage zu Leningrad*. Altsumerische Verwaltungstexte aus Lagaš 1. Freiburger Altorientalische Studien 15, 1. Franz Steiner Verlag Wiesbaden GMBH, Stuttgart.

Selz, G. J. 1994. Verwaltungsurkunden in der Eremitage in St. Petersburg. *Acta Sumerologica* 16: 207–229.

Selz, G. J. 2010. "The poor are the silent ones in the country": On the loss of legitimacy; challenging power in early Mesopotamia. In *Who was king? Who was not king? The rulers and the ruled in the ancient Near East*, eds. P. Charvát and P. Vlčková, 1–15. Institute of Archaeology of the Academy of Sciences of the Czech Republic, v.v.i., Prague.

Seri, A. 2005. *Local power in Old Babylonian Mesopotamia*. Equinox, London.

Sha, S. P., M. V. Suryavanshi, and J. P. Tamang. 2019. Mycobiome diversity in traditionally prepared starters for alcoholic beverages in India by high-throughput sequencing method. *Frontiers in Microbiology* 10, 348: 1–11.

Sharlach, T. M. 2004. *Provincial taxation and the Ur III State*. Cuneiform Monographs 26. Brill-Styx, Leiden-Boston.

Sharlach, T. M. 2005. Diplomacy and the rituals of politics in the Ur III court. *Journal Cuneiform Studies* 57, 1: 17–29.

Sherman, E. 2017. "Snake Venom" beer might be the strongest in the world. *Food & Wine*. Updated August 9, 2017.

Sherratt, A. 1997a [1987]. Cups that cheered: The introduction of alcohol to prehistoric Europe. In *Economy and society in prehistoric Europe: Changing perspectives*, A. Sherratt, 376–402. Princeton University Press, Princeton.

Sherratt, A. 1997b [1991]. Sacred and profane substances: The ritual use of narcotics in later Neolithic Europe. In *Economy and society in prehistoric Europe: Changing perspectives*, A. Sherratt, 403–430. Princeton University Press, Princeton.

Sherratt, A. 2007. Alcohol and its alternatives: Symbol and substance in pre-industrial cultures. In *Consuming habits: Global and historical perspectives on how cultures define drugs*, eds. J. Goodman, P. E. Lovejoy, and A. Sherratt, 11–45. 2nd edition. Routledge, London.

Shimada, I. 2005. Experimental archaeology. In *Handbook of archaeological methods*, Vol. 1, eds. H. D. G. Maschner and C. Chippindale, 603–642. Altamira Press, Lanham.

Sillar, B. 1996. The dead and the drying: Techniques for transforming people and things in the Andes. *Journal of Material Culture* 1, 3: 259–289.

Skibo, J. M. 2000. Experimental archaeology. In *Archaeological method and theory: An encyclopedia*, ed. L. Ellis, 199–204. Garland Publishing, New York.

Smith, A., T. Bagoyan, I. Gabrielyan, R. Pinhasi, and B. Gasparyan. 2014. Late Chalcolithic and Medieval archaeobotanical remains from Areni-1 (Birds' Cave), Armenia. In *Stone Age of Armenia: A guide-book to the Stone Age archaeology in the Republic of Armenia*, eds. B. Gasparyan and M. Arimura, 233–260. Monograph of the JSPS-Bilateral Joint Research Project. Center for Cultural Resource Studies, Kanazawa University, Kanazawa.

Smith, A. T. 2003. *The political landscape: Constellations of authority in early complex polities*. University of California Press, Berkeley.

Smith, A. T. 2011. Archaeologies of sovereignty. *Annual Review of Anthropology* 40: 415–432.

Snell, D. C. 2001. *Flight and freedom in the ancient Near East*. Brill, Leiden.

Snell, D. C. 2011. Slavery in the Ancient Near East. In *The Cambridge world history of slavery, Vol. 1, The ancient Mediterranean World*, eds. K. Bradley and P. Cartledge, 4–21. Cambridge University Press, Cambridge.

Sollee, A. 2012. Zur Verteilung und Verbreitung der Lochbodengefäße im syro-mesopotamischen Kulturraum. In *Stories of Long Ago: Festschrift für Michael D. Roaf*, eds. H. Baker, K. Kaniuth, and A. Otto, 625–47. Alter Orient und Altes Testament 397. Ugarit-Verlag, Münster.

Sparks, R. 2014. Canaan in Egypt: Archaeological evidence for a social phenomenon. In *Invention and innovation: The social context of technological change 2, Egypt, the Aegean and the Near East, 1650–1150 B.C.*, eds. J. Bourriau and J. Phillips, 25–54. Oxbow Books, Oxford.

Stein, D. L. 2021. The third millennium banquet scene at Ur and its archaeological correlates. In *Ur in the twenty-first century CE: Proceedings of the 62nd Rencontre Assyriologique Internationale at Philadelphia, July 11–15, 2016*, eds. G. Frame, J. Jeffers, and H. Pittman, 441–474. Eisenbrauns, University Park.

Stein, D. L., S. K. Costello, and K. P. Foster (eds.). 2022. *The Routledge companion to ecstatic experience in the ancient world*. Routledge, London.

Stein, G. J. 2001a. Understanding ancient state societies in the Old World. In *Archaeology at the Millennium*, eds. G. Feinman and T. Price, 353–379. Springer, Boston.

Stein, G. J. 2001b. "Who was king? Who was not king?": Social group composition and competition in early Mesopotamian state societies. In *From leaders to rulers*, ed. J. Haas, 205–231. Kluwer Academic/Plenum Publishers, New York.

Stein, G. J. 2004. Structural parameters and sociocultural factors in the economic organization of North Mesopotamian urbanism in the third millennium B.C. In *Archaeological perspectives on political economies*, eds. G. M. Feinman and L. M. Nicholas, 61–78. University of Utah Press, Salt Lake City.

Steinert, U. 2019. Mesopotamian medicine and the body. In *Ancient Mesopotamia speaks: Highlights of the Yale Babylonian Collection*, eds. A. W. Lassen, E. Frahm, and K. Wagensonner, 127–137. Peabody Museum of Natural History, Yale University, New Haven.

Steinkeller, P. 1987. The foresters of Umma: Toward a definition of Ur III labor. In *Labor in the ancient Near East*, ed. M. A. Powell, 73–115. American Oriental Series 68. American Oriental Society, New Haven.

Steinkeller, P. 1999. Land-tenure conditions in third-millennium Babylonia: The problem of regional variation. In *Urbanization and land ownership in the ancient Near East*, eds. M. Hudson and B. A. Levine, 289–330. Peabody Museum of Archaeology and Ethnology, Harvard University, Cambridge.

Steinkeller, P. 2004. The function of written documentation in the administrative praxis of early Babylonia. In *Creating economic order: Record-keeping, standardization, and the development of accounting in the ancient Near East*, eds. Michael Hudson and Cornelia Wunsch, 65–88. International Scholars Conference on Ancient Near Eastern Economies 4. CDL, Bethesda, Maryland.

Steinkeller, P. 2007. City and countryside in third-millennium southern Babylonia. In *Settlement and society: Essays dedicated to Robert McCormick Adams*, ed. E. C. Stone, 185–211. Cotsen Institute of Archaeology, University of California, Los Angeles. The Oriental Institute of the University of Chicago, Chicago.

Steinkeller, P. 2017. *History, texts, and art in early Babylonia: Three essays*. Walter de Gruyter, Berlin.

Steinkeller, P. 2022. On prostitutes, midwives, and tavern-keepers in third millennium BC Babylonia. *KASKAL* 19: 1–38.

Steinkeller, P., and M. Hudson (eds.). 2015. *Labor in the ancient world*. International Scholars Conference on Ancient Near Eastern Economies 5. ISLET, Dresden.

Steinkraus, K. H. 1979. Nutritionally significant indigenous foods involving an alcoholic fermentation. In *Fermented food beverages in nutrition*, eds. C. F. Gastineau, W. J. Darby, and T. B. Turner, 35–59. Academic Press, New York.

Steinkraus, K. H. (ed.). 1996. *Handbook of indigenous fermented foods.* Second edition. Marcel Dekker, Inc., New York.

Stol, M. 1971. Zur altmesopotamischen Bierbereitung. *Bibliotheca Orientalis* 28, 3/ 4: 167–171.

Stol, M. 1989. Malz. In *Reallexikon der Assyriologie und Vorderasiatischen Archäologie* 7 (Libanukšabaš–Medizin), ed. D. O. Edzard, 422–430. Walter de Gruyter, Berlin.

Stol, M. 1994. Beer in Neo-Babylonian times. In *Drinking in ancient societies: History and culture of drinks in the ancient Near East,* ed. L. Milano, 155–183. History of the Ancient Near East/Studies 6. Sargon srl, Padova.

Stol, M. 2016. *Women in the ancient Near East,* trans. H. and M. Richardson. De Gruyter, Boston/Berlin.

Stolper, M. W. 2005. Farming with the Murašûs and others: Costs and returns of cereal agriculture in fifth-century Babylonian texts. In *Approaching the Babylonian economy,* eds. H. D. Baker and M. Jursa, 323–342. Veröffentlichen zur Wirtschaftsgeschichte Babyloniens im 1. Jahrtausent v. Chr. 2. Alter Orient und Altes Testament 330. Ugarit-Verlag, Münster.

Stone, E. C. 1987. *Nippur neighborhoods.* Studies in Ancient Oriental Civilization 44. The Oriental Institute of the University of Chicago, Chicago.

Stone, E. C. 2005. Mesopotamian cities and countryside. In *A companion to the ancient Near East,* ed. D. C. Snell, 141–154. Blackwell, Oxford.

Stone, E. C. 2007. The Mesopotamian urban experience. In *Settlement and society: Essays dedicated to Robert McCormick Adams,* ed. E. C. Stone, 213–234. Cotsen Institute of Archaeology, University of California, Los Angeles. The Oriental Institute of the University of Chicago, Chicago.

Tenney, J. S. 2011. *Life at the bottom of Babylonian society: Servile laborers at Nippur in the 14th and 13th centuries B.C.* Brill, Leiden.

Tolini, G. 2015. Murašu BE 9, 43. *Achemenet.* Posted November 2, 2015. http:// www.achemenet.com/en/item/?/2043570.

Trifonov, V., D. Petrov, and L. Savelieva. 2022. Party like a Sumerian: Reinterpreting the "sceptres" from the Maikop kurgan. *Antiquity* 96, 385: 67–84.

Tsing, A. L. 2015. *The mushroom at the end of the world: On the possibility of life in capitalist ruins.* Princeton University Press, Princeton.

Tsukimoto, A. 1985. *Untersuchungen zur Totenpflege (kispum) im alten Mesopotamien.* Alter Orient und Altest Testament 216. Butzon & Bercker, Kevelaer. Neukirchener Verlag, Neukirchen-Vluyn.

Tsukimoto, A. 2010. Peace for the dead, or *kispu(m)* again. *Orient* 45: 101–9.

Trümpelmann, L. 1981. Eine Kneipe in Susa. *Iranica Antiqua* 16: 35–44.

Ur, J. 2010. Cycles of civilization in Northern Mesopotamia, 4400–2000 BC. *Journal of Archaeological Research* 18: 387–431.

Ur, J. 2012. Southern Mesopotamia. In *A companion to the archaeology of the ancient Near East,* ed. D. T. Potts, 533–555. Wiley-Blackwell, Chichester.

Ur, J. 2014. Households and the emergence of cities in ancient Mesopotamia. *Cambridge Archaeological Journal* 24: 249–268.

Vacca, A., L. Peyronel, and C. Wachter-Sarkady. 2017. An affair of herbal medicine? The "special" kitchen in the Royal Palace of Ebla. *The Ancient Near East Today* 5, 11, November 2017.

Van De Mieroop, M. 1994. The Tell Leilan tablets 1991: A preliminary report. *Orientalia, Nova Series* 63, 4: 305–344.

Van De Mieroop, M. 1997. *The ancient Mesopotamian city*. Oxford University Press, Oxford.

Van De Mieroop, M. 1999. *Cuneiform texts and the writing of history*. Routledge, London.

Van De Mieroop, M. 2004. Economic theories and the ancient Near East. In *Commerce and monetary systems in the ancient world: Means of transmission and cultural interaction*, eds. R. Rollinger and C. Ulf, 54–64. Franz Steiner Verlap, Stuttgart.

Van De Mieroop, M. 2015. *A history of the ancient Near East, ca. 3000–323 BC*. 3rd edition. Wiley-Blackwell, Chichester.

van der Toorn, K. 2014 . Dead that are slow to depart: Evidence for ancestor rituals in Mesopotamia. In *In remembrance of me: Feasting with the dead in the ancient Middle East*, eds. V. R. Herrmann and D. Schloen, 81–84. Oriental Institute Museum Publications 37. The Oriental Institute of the University of Chicago, Chicago.

van Loon, M. 1979. 1974 and 1975 preliminary results of the excavations at Selenkahiye near Meskene, Syria. In *Excavation reports from the Tabqa Dam Project– Euphrates valley, Syria*, ed. D. N. Freedman, 97–112. Annual of the American Schools of Oriental Research 44. American Schools of Oriental Research, Cambridge.

Vanstiphout, H. L. J. 1990. The Mesopotamian debate poems: A general presentation (Part I). *Acta Sumerologica* 12: 271–318.

Vanstiphout, H. L. J. 1992. The banquet scene in the Mesopotamian debate poems. In *Banquets d'Orient*, ed. R. Gyselen, 9–21. Res Orientales 4. Groupe pour l'E ́tude de la Civilisation du Moyen-Orient, Bures-sur-Yvette.

van Wyk, S. J. 2015. The concealed crime of the *nadītu* priestess in §110 of the Laws of Hammurabi. *Journal for Semitics* 24, 1: 109–145.

Vidale, M. 2011. PG 1237, Royal Cemetery of Ur: Patterns in death. *Cambridge Archaeological Journal* 21, 3: 427–451.

von Soden, W. 1976. Trunkenheit im Babylonisch-Assyrischen Schrifttum. In *Festschrift Joseph Henninger zum 70. Geburtstag am 12. Mai 1976*, 317–324. Studia Instituti Anthropos 28. Anthropos-Institut, St. Augustin bei Bonn.

Veldhuis, N. 1995/1996. On interpreting Mesopotamian namburbi rituals. *Archiv für Orientforschung* 42–43: 145–154.

Wachter-Sarkady, C. 2013. Consuming plants: Archaeobotanical samples from Royal Palace G and Building P4. In *Ebla and its landscape: Early state formation in the Ancient Near East*, eds. P. Matthiae and N. Marchetti, 376–402. Left Coast Press, Walnut Creek.

Waetzoldt, H. 1971. Zwei unveröffentlichte Ur-III-Texte über die Herstellung von Tongefässen. *Die Welt des Orients* 6, 1: 7–41.

Wang, J., R. Friedman, and M. Baba. 2021. Predynastic beer production, distribution, and consumption at Hierakonpolis, Egypt. *Journal of Anthropological Archaeology* 64: 1–16.

Wang, J., L. Liu, T. Ball, L. Yu, Y. Li, and F. Xing. 2016. Revealing a 5,000-y-old beer recipe in China. *Proceedings of the National Academy of Sciences* 113, 23: 6444–6448.

Weber, J. A. and R. L. Zettler. 1998. Metal vessels. In *Treasures from the Royal Tombs of Ur*, eds. R. L. Zettler and L. Horne, 125–140. University of Pennsylvania Museum of Archaeology and Anthropology, Philadelphia.

Wengrow, D. 2010. *What makes civilization? The ancient Near East and the future of the West*. Oxford University Press, Oxford.

Westenholz, A. 2002. The Sumerian city-state. In *A comparative study of six city-state cultures*, ed. M. H. Hansen, 23–42. Historisk-filosofiske Skrufter 27. C. A. Reitzels Forlag, Copenhagen.

Widell, M. 2005. Some reflections on Babylonian exchange during the end of the third millennium BC. *Journal of the Economic and Social History of the Orient* 48, 3: 388–400.

Widell, M., B. Studevent-Hickman, J. Tenney, J. Lauinger, D. Mahoney, and T. Paulette. 2013. Staple production, cultivation, and sedentary life: Model input data. In *Models of Mesopotamian landscapes: How small-scale processes contributed to the growth of early civilizations*, eds. T. J. Wilkinson, McG. Gibson, and M. Widell, 81–101. BAR International Series 2552. Archaeopress, Oxford.

Wilcke, C. 1988. Die Sumerische Königsliste und erzählte Vergangenheit. In *Vergangenheit in mündlicher Überlieferung*, eds. J. von Ungern-Sternberg and H. Reinau, 3–40. Colloquium Rauricum Band 1. B. G. Teubner, Stuttgart.

Wilkinson, T. J. 1994. The structure and dynamics of dry-farming states in Upper Mesopotamia. *Current Anthropology* 35, 5: 483–520.

Wilkinson, T. J. 2000. Regional approaches to Mesopotamian archaeology: The contribution of archaeological surveys. *Journal of Archaeological Research* 8, 3: 219–267.

Wilkinson, T.J., G. Philip, J. Bradbury, R. Dunford, D. Donoghue, N. Galiatsatos, D. Lawrence, A. Ricci, S. L. Smith. 2014. Contextualizing early urbanization: Settlement cores, early states, and agro-pastoral strategies in the Fertile Crescent during the fourth and third millennia BC. *Journal of World Prehistory* 27: 43–109.

Woods, C. 2010. The earliest Mesopotamian writing. In *Visible language: Inventions of writing in the ancient Middle East and beyond*, ed. C. Woods, 33–84. Oriental Institute Museum Publications 32. The Oriental Institute of the University of Chicago, Chicago.

Woolley, C. L. 1934. *The Royal Cemetery*. Ur Excavations 2. Trustees of the British Museum and the Museum of the University of Pennsylvania, London.

Wright, R. P. 1996. Technology, gender, and class: Worlds of difference in Ur III Mesopotamia. In *Gender and archaeology*, ed. R. P. Wright, University of Pennsylvania Press, Philadelphia, 79–110.

Wunsch, C. 2014. Freedom and dependency: Neo-Babylonian manumission documents with oblation and service obligation. In *Extraction and control: Studies in honor of Matthew W. Stolper*, ed. M. Kozuh, 337–346. Studies in Ancient Oriental Civilizations 68. Oriental Institute of the University of Chicago, Chicago.

Yoffee, N. 1995. Political economy in early Mesopotamian states. *Annual Review of Anthropology* 24, 1: 281–311.

Yoffee, N. 2005. *Myths of the archaic state: Evolution of the earliest cities, states, and civilizations*. Cambridge University Press, Cambridge.

Yoffee, N. 2016. The power of infrastructures: A counternarrative and a speculation. *Journal of Archaeological Method and Theory* 23: 1053–1065.

Yoffee, N., and A. Seri. 2019. Negotiating fragility in ancient Mesopotamia: Arenas of contestation and institutions of resistance. In *The evolution of fragility: Setting the terms*, ed. N. Yoffee, 183–196. McDonald Institute Conversations. McDonald Institute for Archaeological Research, Cambridge.

Zarnkow, M., W. Sallaberger, and F. Jacob. 2020. Bappir: Sauerteigbrot für die sumerische Bierbereitung. *Journal Culinaire* 31: 11–19.

Zarnkow, M., E. Spieleder, W. Back, B. Sacher, A. Otto, and B. Einwag. 2006. Interdisziplinäre Untersuchungen zum altorientalischen Bierbrauen in der Siedlung von Tell Bazi/Nordsyrien vor rund 3200 Jahren. *Technikgeschichte* 73: 3–25.

Zarnkow, M., A. Otto, and B. Einwag. 2011. Interdisciplinary investigations into the brewing technology of the ancient Near East and the potential of the cold mashing process. In *Liquid bread: Beer and brewing in cross-cultural perspective*, eds. W. Schiefenhövel and H. Macbeth, 47–54. Berghahn Books, New York.

Zettler, R. L. 1997. Nippur. In *The Oxford encyclopedia of the archaeology of the ancient Near East*, Vol. 4, ed. E. M. Meyers, 148–152. Oxford University Press, Oxford.

Zettler, R. L. 1998a. The burials of a king and queen. In *Treasures from the Royal Tombs of Ur*, eds. R. L. Zettler and L. Horne, 33–38. University of Pennsylvania Museum of Archaeology and Anthropology, Philadelphia.

Zettler, R. L. 1998b. The Royal Cemetery of Ur. In *Treasures from the Royal Tombs of Ur*, eds. R. L. Zettler and L. Horne, 21–31. University of Pennsylvania Museum of Archaeology and Anthropology, Philadelphia.

Zettler, R. L. 1998c. Ur of the Chaldees. In *Treasures from the Royal Tombs of Ur*, eds. R. L. Zettler and L. Horne, 8–19. University of Pennsylvania Museum of Archaeology and Anthropology, Philadelphia.

Zettler, R. L., and L. Horne (eds.). 1998. *Treasures from the Royal Tombs of Ur*. University of Pennsylvania Museum of Archaeology and Anthropology, Philadelphia.

Zimmerman, P. 1998. Two tombs or three? In *Treasures from the Royal Tombs of Ur*, eds. R. L. Zettler and L. Horne, 39. University of Pennsylvania Museum of Archaeology and Anthropology, Philadelphia.

Zingarello, M. 2020. Beer-making and drinking between life and death: A fresh look at the "four-part sets." In *After the harvest: Storage practices and food processing in Bronze Age Mesopotamia*, eds. N. Borrelli and G. Scazzosi, 91–112. Subartu 43. Brepols, Turnhout.

Index

For the benefit of digital users, indexed terms that span two pages (e.g., 52–53) may, on occasion, appear on only one of those pages.

Notes are indicated by "n" following the page number.

Tables are indicated by an italic *t* following the page number; figures are indicated by an italic *f* following the page number; and boxes are indicated by an italic *b* following the page number.